Photoshop 5
The Cram Sheet

This Cram Sheet contains the distilled, key facts about Photoshop 5. Review this information just before you enter the test room, paying special attention to those areas where you feel you need the most review. You can transfer any of these facts from your head onto a blank sheet of paper when you enter the test room.

PHOTOSHOP BASICS

1. Photoshop is a bitmap-image editing and painting program that you use to edit the pixel data that comprises a bitmap image. When you edit a bitmap image in Photoshop, you alter the stored data about each affected pixel.

2. Don't confuse *bitmap images* with *bitmap mode*. The term *bitmap images* defines a type of computer graphic, whereas *bitmap mode* is a Photoshop color mode.

3. The number of bits stored for each pixel determines a file's *bit depth* (also called either *pixel depth* or *color depth*) and directly affects the quality of the representation of color in the image.

4. Although Photoshop supports files with up to 16 bits per channel (16-bit grayscale, 48-bit RGB, and 64-bit CMYK images), not all Photoshop tools and commands work with 16-bit images.

5. Scratch Disks are virtual memory stored on hard disks. The virtual memory used by the operating system and by Photoshop takes up space on your hard disk. If your hard disk is too full, you might find that you cannot save to the disk.

6. You can select any folder to designate as the plug-ins folder. If you do so, however, you must either put all plug-ins that you use in that other folder or go back and tell Photoshop (in Preferences) the plug-ins folder to use, and quit and restart Photoshop every time you want to change folders.

7. The Purge command allows you to dump data from RAM to make more memory available for an operation.

8. The Reselect command reselects the most recent selection.

9. Hide/Show the Toolbox and palettes with Tab. Pressing Shift+Tab hides or shows only the palettes.

10. The History palette saves 20 states by default, and up to 100 states. The History Paintbrush icon in the History palette indicates which state will be used for painting and erasing.

11. The numerical values defined by the Measure tool appear in the Info palette.

12. Toggle the S key to change between the display modes and the Q key to toggle between the Standard mode and the Quick Mask mode.

13. You can drag and drop between Adobe Illustrator and Photoshop.

61. The 3D Transform filter enables you to transform images in ways that make them appear 3D and is accessed under Filter| Render.

LAYERS

62. The Photoshop (PSD) file format is the only file format in which you can save layers.
63. Depending on how much memory you have in your system, you can create up to 100 layers in an image.
64. You can move the Background layer up in the stacking order of layers only after you convert it to a layer by double-clicking on its name in the Layers palette and giving it a new name.
65. Any two-dimensional transformations that you apply to a layer are also applied to all layers linked to that layer.
66. Adjustment layers are used to apply color and tonal adjustments on a "trial" basis for previewing and/or removal before being rendered permanently to an image.
67. A transparency mask is a selection based on the opaque areas of a layer. You load a transparency mask by pressing Cmd/Ctrl as you click the thumbnail of a layer.
68. Clipping groups allow you to use the contents of a layer as a mask and apply that mask to the content of other layers. You can create clipping groups only from layers that are adjacent in the stacking order.
69. The Type Layer allows you to edit type even after you've saved, closed, and reopened an image file—but only in the Photoshop (PSD) format.
70. You must render the type layer before you can apply filters.

CHANNELS

71. The fully selected pixels of a mask are full rubylith or full black, and they are protected from whatever you do to the clear areas in the rubylith display or the white and gray areas in the grayscale display.

72. When converting a mask or alpha channel to a selection border, the clear or white areas become the selection.
73. Channels are supported in every color mode except Bitmap.
74. Photoshop supports up to 24 channels per image—including all color channels, alpha channels, and spot color channels.
75. If you want to show or hide more than one channel at a time, just slide (drag) your cursor up or down the column of eyeball icons.
76. Using Photoshop's Channel Mixer, you can combine the brightness values of two or more channels.
77. The Quick Mask mode creates a temporary, quick mask that you can paint and edit like any other layer or channel.
78. If you hide all the other channels in the image, the Quick Mask overlay turns to black and white, black represents the opaque or unselected areas and white represents the transparent or selected areas.

ACTIONS AND AUTOMATION

79. You can duplicate individual commands, complete actions, and complete sets using one of the following: dragging Commands or Actions to the New Action button, dragging Sets to the New Set button, choosing the Duplicate command in the Actions palette menu (after selecting any command, action, or set), or pressing Option/Alt and dragging a Command or Action to an new spot in the Action palette list.
80. Batch Processing is available with File|Automate|Batch.
81. The Multi-Page PDF To PSD assistant/wizard automatically opens an individual Photoshop (PSD) file for each page of a PDF-format file with multiple pages.

PRINTING

82. The four process colors are Cyan (C), Magenta (M), Yellow (Y), and Black (K).
83. Spot color channels are generated as separate plates when converting from RGB to CMYK for printing.

Certification
Insider™ Press

36. When opening an Adobe Illustrator, PDF, or EPS file as a new Photoshop file, adjust the file's resolution and size in the Rasterize Generic EPS dialog box.
37. Use the Exclude Non-Image Data, Exclude Alpha Channels, and Flatten Image options in the Save A Copy dialog box to minimize file sizes.
38. Only GIF89a files support background transparency.

ADJUSTING IMAGES

39. Turn off color table animation with the Video LUT Animation checkbox in File|Preferences|Display & Cursor.
40. Histograms appear in the Histogram, Levels, and Threshold dialog boxes.
41. The Image cache saves image previews in memory, and the Cache Levels option can be set to save from 1 to 8 previews, with 4 as a default.
42. Levels is an adjustment option that allows you to view a histogram of an image's colors and make adjustments to the image's highlights, midtones, and/or shadows.
43. In the Curves dialog box, add points to only the composite channel by pressing Cmd/Ctrl, and clicking on the curve, add points to the component channels and not the composite channel by pressing Shift+Cmd/Shift+Ctrl and clicking on the curve.
44. The Replace Color command allows you to adjust the hue, saturation, and lightness of the specifically selected colors across an image.
45. The Variations dialog box presents thumbnails of various color and tonal adjustments, allowing you to select adjustments visually.
46. Resampling is the increasing or decreasing of the number of pixels in an image that occurs when an image's pixel dimensions are altered, which can result in a uncorrectable loss of image quality when Resampling up.
47. Interpolation is the guessing—or approximating—that Photoshop does when adding pixels to an image. Of the three interpolation options, Bicubic best preserves image quality.
48. After resampling an image, apply Unsharp Mask.

SELECTING IMAGE AREAS

49. While selecting with the Magnetic Lasso tool, you can temporarily use the Freehand Lasso tool by pressing Option/Alt and dragging, and you can temporarily use the Polygon Lasso tool by pressing Option/Alt and clicking the next point.
50. The Magic Wand tool selects adjacent areas of similar color.
51. The Color Range command selects areas of similar color throughout the image.
52. Modify selections with the Inverse, Border, Smooth, Expand, Contract, Grow, Similar, and Feather commands.
53. Use the Pen tools to draw paths. The Pen tool provides much greater precision and control over the drawing of paths than the Freeform Pen tool or the Magnetic Pen tool.
54. Use the Direct Selection tool (A) to adjust anchor points and direction points.
55. Clipping paths allow you to mask areas of an image to create background transparency when printing an image from another application.
56. Export Photoshop paths to Adobe Illustrator with File|Export|Paths To Illustrator.

PAINTING AND EDITING

57. You can now paint with a previous state of the image with the History Paintbrush tool.
58. The Paint Bucket tool allows you to change areas of adjacent color.
59. You can now use Edit|Transform to transform images, selections and selection borders, layers, and paths.
60. Filters are not supported in Bitmap, Indexed Color, or 16-bit-per-channel images, and at least a few of them support only RGB images. Review the Filter categories and Filters.

PHOTOSHOP COLOR

14. A color model is a method of describing color objectively so that it can be generally reproduced on a monitor or on paper. A Photoshop color mode is a numeric system used by the application for reproducing a specific color model.

15. The default mode for images created in Photoshop is RGB. Because computer monitors always use the RGB color model and mode to display images, editing in RGB mode is preferable.

16. The First and Second Color Readout options allow you to set the color model that the Info palette will display in the two color info boxes in the top row of the palette. You could use these options to define a color's values if you changed the image from one image mode to another.

17. Colors that can't be printed by the CMYK process are called out-of-gamut colors.

18. If you convert an image from RGB to CMYK, Photoshop converts the image to Lab mode before converting it to CMYK.

19. Bitmap mode images don't support layers, channels, or filters.

20. Indexed color images are single-channel images that can have up to 8-bits-per-pixel, for a maximum of 256 colors. Indexed color also offers limited editing capability.

21. An ICC profile is data that describes the color space of a particular device, such as a monitor or output device.

22. Dithering is a technique of applying an approximate gradation from one color to another when a file contains more bits-per-pixel than a monitor can display.

23. The Adobe Gamma utility sets up monitors for use with Photoshop.

24. Calibration of monitors is the most important step in reproducing the colors you have worked on in your computer system and expect to see in the final output.

25. Transfer functions are a last-resort option for dot gain problems, such as those produced by a miscalibrated imagesetter, that have no other apparent solution.

26. The separation options: GCR adds black to areas of equal CMY density, regardless of color, UCR adds black only to neutral areas of equal CMY density. Remembering that UCA adds black to the neutral areas and is available only in GCR separations can help you remember the difference between GCR and UCR.

27. The Eyedropper tools sampling options (as well as those of the Color Samplers) are Point Sample, 3 by 3 Average, and 5 by 5 Average.

28. You can set up to four Color Samplers, and can sample another area with the Eyedropper tool. Delete Color Samplers by dragging them out of the image window or by pressing Option/Alt and clicking the sampler.

FILES AND FILE FORMATS

29. Photoshop (PSD) is the default file format for images created in Photoshop and is the only file format from which you can work with every one of Photoshop's features. These files save all Photoshop non-image data.

30. To export color separations to another application, you must save CMYK and Multichannel files in Photoshop DCS 2.0, which saves the color channels, spot color channels, and a single alpha channel.

31. The following are the common halftone screen frequencies used for various publications:
    - 65 lpi: Low-quality jobs on porous paper
    - 85 lpi: Newspapers
    - 133 lpi: Four-color magazines
    - 177 lpi: High-quality jobs on coated paper

32. When determining optimum scanning resolution, use a ratio of 1.5:1 or 2:1.

33. Digimarc watermarks protect copyrighted images.

34. There are lossy and lossless compression methods. JPEG is lossy, the others, such as LZW, RLE, and ZIP, are lossless.

35. The Place command is used to import Adobe Illustrator, PDF, or EPS files into an open Photoshop file.

Photoshop 5

**Adobe
Certified
Expert**

Mike Cuenca

ACE Photoshop 5 Exam Cram
Copyright © The Coriolis Group, 1999

All rights reserved. This book may not be duplicated in any way without the express written consent of the publisher, except in the form of brief excerpts or quotations for the purposes of review. The information contained herein is for the personal use of the reader and may not be incorporated in any commercial programs, other books, databases, or any kind of software without written consent of the publisher. Making copies of this book or any portion for any purpose other than your own is a violation of United States copyright laws.

Limits of Liability and Disclaimer of Warranty

The author and publisher of this book have used their best efforts in preparing the book and the programs contained in it. These efforts include the development, research, and testing of the theories and programs to determine their effectiveness. The author and publisher make no warranty of any kind, expressed or implied, with regard to these programs or the documentation contained in this book.

The author and publisher shall not be liable in the event of incidental or consequential damages in connection with, or arising out of, the furnishing, performance, or use of the programs, associated instructions, and/or claims of productivity gains.

Trademarks

Trademarked names appear throughout this book. Rather than list the names and entities that own the trademarks or insert a trademark symbol with each mention of the trademarked name, the publisher states that it is using the names for editorial purposes only and to the benefit of the trademark owner, with no intention of infringing upon that trademark.

The Coriolis Group, Inc.
An International Thomson Publishing Company
14455 N. Hayden Road, Suite 220
Scottsdale, Arizona 85260

602/483-0192
FAX 602/483-0193
http://www.coriolis.com

Library of Congress Cataloging-in-Publication Data
Cuenca, Mike
    ACE Photoshop 5 exam cram / by Mike Cuenca.
        p. cm.
    Includes index.
    ISBN 1-57610-374-9
    1. Computer graphics--Examinations--Study guides.   2. Adobe
Photoshop.   3. Electronic data processing personnel--
Certification.   I. Title.
T385.C85   1999
006.6'869--dc21   98-40659
                                                        CIP

Printed in the United States of America-
10 9 8 7 6 5 4 3 2 1

Publisher
Keith Weiskamp

Acquisitions Editor
Shari Jo Hehr

Marketing Specialist
Cynthia Caldwell

Project Editor
Don Eamon

Technical Reviewer
David Xenakis

Production Coordinator
Jon Gabriel

Cover Design
Anthony Stock

Layout Design
April Nielsen

an International Thomson Publishing company

Albany, NY • Belmont, CA • Bonn • Boston • Cincinnati • Detroit • Johannesburg • London • Madrid
Melbourne • Mexico City • New York • Paris • Singapore • Tokyo • Toronto • Washington

14455 North Hayden, Suite 220 • Scottsdale, Arizona 85260

The Smartest Way To Get Certified™

Thank you for purchasing one of our innovative certification study guides, just one of the many members of the Coriolis family of certification products.

Certification Insider Press™ was created in late 1997 by The Coriolis Group to help professionals like you obtain certification and advance your career. Achieving certification involves a major commitment and a great deal of hard work. To help you reach your goals, we've listened to others like you, and have designed our entire product line around you and the way you like to study, learn, and master challenging subjects. Our approach is the *Smartest Way to Get Certified*.

In less than a year, Coriolis has published over one million copies of our highly popular *Exam Cram*, *Exam Prep*, and *On Site* guides. Our *Exam Cram* series, specifically written to help you pass an exam, are the number one certification self-study guides in the industry. They are the perfect complement to any study plan you have, as well as to the rest of the Certification Insider Press series: *Exam Prep* comprehensive study guides designed to help you thoroughly learn and master certification topics, and *On Site* guides that really show you how to apply your skills and knowledge on the job.

Our commitment to you is to ensure that all of the certification study guides we develop help you save time and frustration. Each one provides unique study tips and techniques, memory joggers, custom quizzes, insight about test taking, practical problems to solve, real-world examples, and much more.

We'd like to hear from you. Help us continue to provide the very best certification study materials possible. Write us or email us at **craminfo@coriolis.com** and let us know how our books have helped you study, or tell us about new features that you'd like us to add. If you send us a story about how an *Exam Cram*, *Exam Prep*, or *On Site* guide has helped you, and we use it in one of our books, we'll send you an official Coriolis shirt for your efforts.

Good luck with your certification exam and your career. Thank you for allowing us to help you achieve your goals.

Keith Weiskamp
Publisher, Certification Insider Press

This is my first commercially published book, and I dedicate it with loving affection to my son, Austin. During these weeks of me working unusually long hours writing while also teaching full-time and being a half-time single parent to him, he has shown extraordinary understanding and patience.

About The Author

Mike Cuenca first sat at a computer terminal in 1969 at the age of 12 and a year later memorized a California job case. He has been in love with computers and graphic arts technology ever since. Mike has covered all the mass communications bases, working as a news reporter and disk jockey in commercial and public radio; a TV news reporter; a newspaper and magazine reporter, photographer, and editor; a book designer; a Web publisher and designer; an advertising and public relations executive and designer; a corporate television writer, producer, and videographer; a film director; a magazine production manager, photo editor, and art director; a typesetter; an audio/visual technician; a motion picture grip/electrician; and a city bus driver.

He is currently paying his dues as a tenure-track university journalism professor.

Acknowledgments

To my mentor, Bill B., thanks for teaching me how much I love to mass communicate and for inspiring me with your great love of all things journalistic.

To Renee, thanks for believing and for helping me believe.

Many thanks to acquisitions editor Shari Jo Hehr for bringing me into the family at Certification Insider Press. Working with Don Eamon, my editor, Chuck Hutchinson, copyeditor, Tony Stock, cover design, Jon Gabriel, production coordinator, and April Nielsen, layout design, has been a tremendously positive experience. I am particularly grateful to David Xenakis for his guidance and support as one of the best tech editors any author of a Photoshop book could possibly have.

Thanks are due, of course, to the programmers at Adobe, for producing such a wonderful application.

Contents At A Glance

Chapter 1	Adobe Certification Exams
Chapter 2	Introduction To Photoshop 5
Chapter 3	Photoshop Basics
Chapter 4	Working With And Understanding Photoshop's Color
Chapter 5	Managing Image Files In Photoshop
Chapter 6	Adjusting Images
Chapter 7	Selecting Image Areas
Chapter 8	Painting And Editing
Chapter 9	Working With Layers
Chapter 10	Working With Channels And Masks
Chapter 11	Working With Actions And Automation
Chapter 12	Printing From Photoshop
Chapter 13	Sample Test
Chapter 14	Answer Key To The Sample Test

Table Of Contents

Introduction xvii

Chapter 1
Adobe Certification Exams 1
    The Exam Situation   2
    Exam Layout And Design   3
    Using Adobe's Exam Software Effectively   5
    Exam-Taking Basics   6
    Question-Handling Strategies   7
    Mastering The Inner Game   7
    Additional Resources   8

Chapter 2
Introduction To Photoshop 5 11
    Overview Of Photoshop 5   12
    What's New In Photoshop?   13
    Digital Imaging Basics   14
    Installation and Configuration   19
    Preferences   21
    Practice Questions   24
    Need To Know More?   27

Chapter 3
Photoshop Basics 29
    Photoshop's Menus, Palettes, And Status Bar   30
    The Toolbox   48
    Contextual Menus   53
    The Canvas   53
    Rulers And Measuring   56
    Basics Of Guides And The Grid   58
    Creating, Opening, And Placing Files   59
    Duplicating And Copying Image Files   60

Working With Selections   61
Correcting Mistakes   65
Saving Files   69
Getting The Help You Need From The Program And From Adobe   69
Practice Questions   73
Need To Know More?   78

Chapter 4
Working With And Understanding Photoshop's Color 79
Understanding The Different Color Modes And Models   80
Selecting And Monitoring Colors   95
Accurately Reproducing Colors From The Monitor Display To Output   104
Practice Questions   116
Need To Know More?   123

Chapter 5
Managing Image Files In Photoshop 125
The File Formats   126
Determining The Appropriate Scanning Resolution   132
Creating, Opening, And Importing Images   136
Copyright And File Information   142
Saving And Exporting Images   143
Practice Questions   151
Need To Know More?   157

Chapter 6
Adjusting Images 159
Adjusting Colors And Tones   160
Fixing Color Casts   177
Adjusting Sharpness   177
Adjusting Image Size And Resolution   178
Adjusting The Canvas Size   181
Optimizing The Color And Tone Of Scans   181
Practice Questions   183
Need To Know More?   189

Chapter 7
Selecting Image Areas 191
    Using Photoshop's Selection Tools   192
    Adjusting Selections   198
    Using And Understanding Paths   200
    Practice Questions   213
    Need To Know More?   220

Chapter 8
Painting And Editing 221
    "Painting" And Retouching Images   222
    Specifying Blending Modes   226
    Editing Color Across Large Image Areas   230
    Selecting And Using Brushes   236
    "Stamping" Color, Patterns, And Image Selections   236
    Transforming Images, Selections And Selection
       Borders, Layers, And Paths   238
    Using Filters   243
    Practice Questions   252
    Need To Know More?   259

Chapter 9
Working With Layers 261
    Understanding Photoshop's Layers   262
    Managing Layers In The Layers Palette   262
    Working With Layers   266
    Editing A Layer's Contents   273
    Masking Image Areas With Layers   279
    Applying Special Effects To Layers   284
    Working With Photoshop's New Type Layer   288
    Practice Questions   294
    Need To Know More?   304

Chapter 10
Working With Channels And Masks 305
    Learning Mask Basics   306
    Understanding Channels   306
    Navigating The Channels Palette   309

Working With Channels 310
Working With Spot Color Channels 316
Working In The Quick Mask Mode 320
Practice Questions 322
Need To Know More? 326

Chapter 11
Working With Actions And Automation 327

Learning Action Basics 328
Recording Actions 333
Editing Actions 335
Playing Actions 336
Using Automation Assistants And Wizards 339
Practice Questions 342
Need To Know More? 346

Chapter 12
Printing From Photoshop 347

Converting Images To CMYK For Printing 348
Printing From Photoshop 349
Trapping Colors 353
Printing Color Separations From Other Applications 353
Creating And Printing Duotones 354
Practice Questions 358
Need To Know More? 362

Chapter 13
Sample Test 363

Picking The Right Answer 364
Confusing Questions 364
The Exam Framework 365
Begin The Exam 365

Chapter 14
Answer Key To The Sample Test 389

Appendix
Photoshop 5's New Features 403
    Brand-New Features, Options, Tools, And Commands   403
    Features, Options, Tools, Commands, And Palettes
      That Have Changed   407

Glossary 411

Index 425

Introduction

Welcome to the *ACE Photoshop 5 Exam Cram*! This book aims to help you get ready to take—and pass—the Adobe Certification Exam, numbered "Exam 9A0-006," titled "Adobe Photoshop 5 Product Proficiency Examination." This Introduction explains Adobe's certification programs in general and talks about how the EXAM CRAM series can help you prepare for Adobe's certification exams.

EXAM CRAM books help you understand and appreciate the subjects and materials you need to pass Adobe certification exams. EXAM CRAM books are aimed strictly at test preparation and review. They do not teach you everything you need to know about a topic (such as the ins and outs of digital imaging). Instead, I (the author) present and dissect the questions and problems I've found that you're likely to encounter on a test. We've worked from Adobe's own training materials, preparation guides, and tests. Our aim is to bring together as much information as possible about Adobe Certification Exams.

However, to completely prepare yourself for this Adobe test, I recommend that you begin your studies with some classroom training, or that you pick up and read one of the training and/or study guides that may become available from Adobe or other third-party vendors. I also strongly recommend that you install, configure, and fool around with the software or environment that you'll be tested on, because nothing beats hands-on experience and familiarity when it comes to understanding the questions you're likely to encounter on a certification test. Book learning is essential, but hands-on experience is the best teacher of all!

A word of warning to experienced users of Photoshop: don't rely solely on your working familiarity with previous versions of Photoshop as preparation for this exam. You will be shocked to find in this test many topics and questions that you've never encountered nor even dreamed of. Just try to imagine having to name various keyboard shortcuts and menu options without having the software open right in front of you. You must know the program better than you've ever had to. Moreover, Photoshop 5 has some features that are completely new, and you'll need to know these features very well.

The Adobe Certified Exam (ACE) Program

The ACE Program is currently part of a certification program that includes programs for the Adobe Certified Expert (ACE) and the Adobe Certified Training Provider (ACTP):

➤ The ACE program provides recognition of product expertise for those who may wish to enhance their professional credibility by documenting their product proficiency. This includes designers and others who use the program to create documents and publications, developers who write software to complement Adobe products, resellers, and other professionals who may seek career advancement. You obtain ACE Certification by passing one of the proficiency exams for individual Adobe products. You can be certified in as few or as many products as you may need.

➤ The ACTP program is an extension of the ACE program, for individuals, institutions, and businesses that seek certification of their training programs by Adobe. Certification is obtained by applying to Adobe for ACTP status, using only ACEs as trainers and a one-time verification of instructor proficiency. (See the Adobe Web site listed later in this Introduction for details.)

Adobe Certified Experts are allowed to promote themselves to prospective employers, clients, students and others using the ACE program logo. Adobe offers certification through the ACE program for several other programs (see Table A).

Currently, the Photoshop 5 Exam is available around the world in English, French, German, Japanese and Spanish. Adobe plans to offer exams for their other products in each of these languages in the near future.

Certification is an ongoing activity. If Adobe releases what they call a "major upgrade" (from 4 to 5, for example, but not 5 to 5.1), certification remains valid until 90 days after Adobe releases an exam for the new version. (If individuals do not recertify within the specified time span, their certification becomes invalid.) Because technology keeps changing and new products continually supplant old ones, this should come as no surprise.

The best place to keep tabs on the ACE Program and its various exams is on the Adobe Web site, where you can find answers to FAQs about the program, the terms and conditions of participating in the program, testimonials from ACEs who have seen the benefits of certification, download the official Adobe exam bulletins and take the Adobe Product Proficiency Practice Exams. The

Table 1   ACE Requirements.
In order to become an Adobe Certified Expert (ACE), you need to pass the Adobe Product Proficiency Exam for the product(s) of your choice.

The products include:	
Adobe Photoshop 5	Exam 9A0-006
Adobe PageMaker 6.5	Exam 9A0-008
Adobe After Effects 3.1	Exam 9A0-010
Adobe Acrobat 3	Exam 9A0-007
Adobe Illustrator 7	Exam 9A0-005
Adobe FrameMaker 5.5	Exam 9A0-004
Adobe FrameMaker 5.5 + SGML*	
Adobe PageMill 2	Exam 9A0-009
Adobe Premiere 5	Exam 9A0-014

* The Adobe FrameMaker 5.5 + SGML certification has both an authoring certification level and a developer certification level.

The authoring certification includes the FrameMaker 5.5 exam (Exam 9A0-004) and the FrameMaker + SGML 5.5 Authoring exam (Exam 9A0-012). The developer certification includes the FrameMaker 5.5 (Exam 9A0-004), the FrameMaker + SGML 5.5 Authoring exam (Exam 9A0-012), and the FrameMaker + SGML 5.5 Developer exam (Exam 9A0-013).

current root URL for the ACE program is Adobe Certified Expert Program at www.adobe.com/supportservice/training/aceprogram.html. If, however, the Web site has changed and this URL doesn't work, try using the Search tool on Adobe's site with either "ACE" or the quoted phrase "Adobe Certified Expert Program" as the search string. This will help you find the latest and most accurate information about the company's various exams.

Taking A Certification Exam

Alas, testing is not free. You'll be charged $150 for the first time you take each test, whether you pass or fail. In the U.S. and Canada, tests are administered by Sylvan Prometric. Sylvan Prometric can be reached at 1 (800) 755-3926 or 1 (800) 755-EXAM, any time from 7:00 A.M. to 6:00 P.M., Central Time, Monday through Friday. If this number doesn't work, please try (612) 896-7000 or (612) 820-5707.

To schedule an exam, call at least one day in advance. To cancel or reschedule an exam, you must call at least 12 hours before the scheduled test time (or you may be charged regardless). When calling Sylvan Prometric, please have the following information ready for the telesales staffer who handles your call:

- Your name, organization, and mailing address.

- An ID number. (For most U.S. citizens, this will be your social security number. Citizens of other nations can use their taxpayer IDs or make other arrangements with the order taker.)

- The name and number of the exam you want to take. (For this book, the exam number is 9A0-006, and the exam name is "Adobe Photoshop 5 Product Proficiency Examination.")

- A method of payment must be arranged. (The most convenient approach is to supply a valid credit card number with sufficient available credit. Otherwise, payments by check, money order, or purchase order must be received before a test can be scheduled. If the latter methods are required, ask your order taker for more details.)

When you show up to take a test, try to arrive at least 15 minutes before the scheduled time slot. You must bring and supply two forms of identification, one of which must be a photo ID.

When you complete an Adobe certification exam, the software will tell you whether you've passed or failed. All tests are scored on a basis of 100%, and results are broken into several topic areas. Even if you fail, I suggest you ask for—and keep—the detailed report that the test administrator should print for you. You can use this report to help you prepare for another go-round, if needed.

If you need to retake an exam, you need to call Sylvan Prometric, schedule a new test date, and pay another $100 to take it again. Adobe places no restrictions on how many times or how often you may repeat tests.

Sylvan notifies Adobe of the results and, if you pass, Adobe places you in their ACE database. You can expect your ACE Welcome Kit within 4 to 6 weeks, as well as directions for accessing the ACE logo.

How To Prepare For An Exam

Preparing for any Adobe product proficiency test requires that you obtain and study materials designed to provide comprehensive information about the specific exam for which you are preparing. The following list of materials will help you study and prepare:

- The Adobe product manuals (and/or online documentation and help files, which ship on the CD-ROM with the product).

- The Product Proficiency Exam Bulletin and practice test on the ACE Program Web site (**www.adobe.com/supportservice/training/aceprogram.html**). Find the materials, download them, and use them!

In addition, you'll probably find any or all of the following materials useful in your quest for Photoshop 5 expertise:

➤ **Classroom Training** See the list of training providers at www.adobe.com/supportservice/training/aceprogram.html.

➤ **Other Publications** You'll find direct references to other publications and resources in this text, but there's no shortage of materials available on Photoshop. To help you sift through some of the publications out there, each chapter ends with a "Need To Know More?" section that provides pointers to more complete and exhaustive resources covering the chapter's information. This should give you an idea of where I think you should look for further discussion.

By far, this set of required and recommended materials represents an unequaled collection of sources and resources on Adobe products. I anticipate that you'll find that this book belongs in this company. The section that follows explains how this book works and gives you some good reasons why this book counts as a member of the required and recommended materials list.

About This Book

Each topical *Exam Cram* chapter follows a regular structure, along with graphical cues about important or useful information. Here's the structure of a typical chapter:

➤ **Opening Hotlists** Each chapter begins with a list of the terms, tools, and techniques or tasks that you must learn and understand before you can be fully conversant with that chapter's subject matter. We follow the hotlists with one or two introductory paragraphs to set the stage for the rest of the chapter.

➤ **Topical Coverage** After the opening hotlists, each chapter covers a series of at least four topics related to the chapter's subject title. Throughout this section, we highlight topics or concepts likely to appear on a test using a special Study Alert layout, like this:

This is what a Study Alert looks like. Normally, a Study Alert stresses concepts, terms, software, or activities that are likely to relate to one or more certification test questions. For this reason, we think any information found offset in Study Alert format is worthy of unusual attentiveness on your part. Indeed, most of the information that appears on the Cram Sheet appears as Study Alerts within the text.

Occasionally, you may see tables called "Vital Statistics." The contents of Vital Statistics tables are worthy of an extra once-over. These tables usually contain informational tidbits that might show up in a test question, but they're not quite as important as Study Alerts.

Pay close attention to material flagged as a Study Alert; although all the information in this book pertains to what you need to know to pass the exam, we flag certain items that are really important. You'll find what appears in the meat of each chapter to be worth knowing, too, when preparing for the test. Because this book's material is very condensed, we recommend that you use this book along with other resources to achieve the maximum benefit.

In addition to the Study Alerts and Vital Statistics tables, we have provided tips that will help build a better foundation for Photoshop knowledge. Although the information may not be on the exam, it is certainly exam-related and will help you become a better test taker.

This is how tips are formatted. Keep your eyes open for these, and you'll become a Photoshop guru in no time!

▶ **Practice Questions** Although we talk about test questions and topics throughout each chapter, this section presents a series of mock test questions and explanations of both correct and incorrect answers. We also try to point out especially tricky questions by using a special icon, like this:

Ordinarily, this icon flags the presence of a particularly devious inquiry, if not an outright trick question. Trick questions are calculated to be answered incorrectly if not read more than once, and carefully, at that. Although they're not ubiquitous, such questions may appear in the Adobe exams. That's why we say exam questions are as much about reading comprehension as they are about knowing your material inside out and backwards.

▶ **Details And Resources** Every chapter ends with a section titled "Need To Know More?", which provides direct pointers to Adobe and third-party resources offering more details on the chapter's subject. In addition, this section tries to rank or at least rate the quality and thoroughness of the topic's coverage by each resource. If you find a resource you like in this collection, use it, but don't feel compelled to use all the resources. Alternatively, I recommend resources that I use only on a regular basis; so no recommendation will waste your time or money (but purchasing them all at once probably represents an expense that many would-be ACEs might find hard to justify).

The bulk of the book follows this chapter structure slavishly, but there are a few other elements that I'd like to point out. Chapter 13 is a sample test that provides a good review of the material presented throughout the book to ensure that you're ready for the exam. Chapter 14 is an answer key to the sample test that appears in Chapter 13. Additionally, you'll find a glossary that explains terms and an index that you can use to track down terms as they appear in the text.

If you are an experienced Photoshop user (perhaps even a Photoshop 4 ACE), you may find the Appendix (a summary of the many new and revised features of Photoshop 5 and where they appear throughout the book) helpful. This may prove useful if you feel comfortable with previous versions of Photoshop and just want to learn the new features.

Finally, the tear-out Cram Sheet attached next to the inside front cover of this Exam Cram book represents a condensed and compiled collection of facts, figures, and tips that I think you should memorize before taking the test. Because you can dump this information out of your and head onto a piece of paper before answering any exam questions, you can master this information by brute force. You only need to remember it long enough to write it down when you walk into the test room. You might even want to look at it in the car or in the lobby of the testing center just before you walk in to take the test.

> *Note: If you want to recreate any of the Photoshop-supplied sample images included as figures in this book, you will find all of the images used in this book in the installed Adobe Photoshop 5 application folder, in the Goodies/Samples folder.*

How To Use This Book

If you're prepping for a first-time test, we've structured the topics in this book to build on one another. Therefore, some topics in later chapters make more sense after you've read earlier chapters. That's why we suggest you read this book from front to back for your initial test preparation. If you need to brush up on a topic or you have to bone up for a second try, use the index or table of contents to go straight to the topics and questions that you need to study. Beyond the tests, we think you'll find this book useful as a tightly focused reference to some of the most important aspects of Photoshop.

Given all the book's elements and its specialized focus, we've tried to create a tool that will help you prepare for—and pass—Adobe Exam 9A0-006 titled "Adobe Photoshop 5 Product Proficiency Examination." Please share your feedback on the book with us, especially if you have ideas about how we can improve it for future test-takers. We'll consider everything you say carefully, and we'll respond to all suggestions.

You can send us your questions or comments via the Certification Insider Press Web site, located at www.certificationinsider.com. Scroll down the home page's index on the left side of the page to "Feedback" and then choose a feedback option. Please remember to include the title of the book in your message; otherwise, we'll be forced to guess which book you're writing about. And we don't like to guess—we want to KNOW! Also, be sure to check out the Web pages at www.examcram.com, where you'll find information updates, commentary, and clarifications on documents for each book that you can either read online or download for use later on.

Thanks, and enjoy the book!

Adobe Certification Exams

Terms and concepts you'll need to understand:

- √ Radio button
- √ Checkbox
- √ Exhibit
- √ Multiple-choice question formats
- √ Careful reading
- √ Process of elimination

Techniques you'll need to master:

- √ Preparing to take a certification exam
- √ Practicing (to make perfect)
- √ Making the best use of the testing software
- √ Budgeting your time
- √ Saving the hardest questions until last
- √ Guessing (as a last resort)

Exam taking is not something that most people anticipate eagerly, no matter how well prepared they may be. In most cases, familiarity helps diminish test anxiety. In plain English, this means you probably won't be as nervous if you know you've prepared yourself properly by becoming as familiar with Photoshop as you can.

Understanding the details of exam taking (how long to spend on questions, the environment you'll be in, and so on) and the use of the exam software will help you concentrate on the material rather than on the setting. Likewise, mastering a few basic exam-taking skills should help you recognize—and perhaps even outfox—some of the tricks and gotchas you're bound to find in some of the exam questions.

This chapter, besides explaining the exam environment and software, describes some proven exam-taking strategies that you can use to your advantage.

The Exam Situation

When you arrive at the testing center where you scheduled your exam, you'll need to sign in with an exam coordinator. He or she will ask for two forms of identification; one of these forms must be a photo ID. After you sign in and your time slot arrives, you will be asked to deposit any books, bags, or other items you brought with you. Then, you are escorted into a closed room. Typically, the room will be furnished with anywhere from one to half a dozen computers, and each workstation will be separated from the others by dividers designed to keep you from seeing what's happening on someone else's computer.

You will be furnished with a pen or pencil and a blank sheet of paper or, in some cases, an erasable plastic sheet and an erasable felt-tip pen. You're allowed to write down any information you want on both sides of this sheet. Before the exam, memorize as much as you can of the material that appears on the Cram Sheet (inside the front cover of this book), so that you can write that information on the blank sheet as soon as you are seated in front of the computer. You can refer to your rendition of the Cram Sheet any time you like during the test, but you'll have to surrender the sheet when you leave the room.

Most test rooms feature a wall with a large picture window. It permits the exam coordinator standing behind it to monitor the room, to prevent exam takers from talking to one another, and to observe anything out of the ordinary that might go on. The exam coordinator will have preloaded the appropriate Adobe certification exam—for this book, that's Exam 9A0-006—and you'll be permitted to start as soon as you're seated in front of the computer.

All Adobe certification exams allow a certain maximum amount of time in which to complete your work (this time is indicated on the exam by an on-screen counter/clock, so you can check the time remaining whenever you like). Exam 9A0-006 consists of 81 items, 14 of which are survey (nongraded) questions, such as your name, email address, and so on. The remaining 67 questions make up the test. (Some of these questions have multiple answers, so the actual number of answers is a bit higher.) You can take up to 90 minutes to complete the exam.

All Adobe certification exams are computer generated and use a multiple-choice format. Although this approach may sound quite simple, the questions are constructed not only to check your mastery of basic facts and figures about Photoshop but they also require you to evaluate one or more sets of circumstances or requirements. Often, you'll be asked to give more than one answer to a question. Likewise, you might be asked to select the best or most effective solution to a problem from a range of choices, all of which technically are correct. Taking the exam is quite an adventure, and it involves real thinking. This book shows you what to expect and how to deal with the potential problems, puzzles, and predicaments.

Exam Layout And Design

Some exam questions require you to select a single answer, whereas others ask you to select multiple correct answers. Watch your screen carefully. At the bottom left, the test will indicate whether it expects a single answer or will specify how many answers to select.

The following multiple-choice question requires you to select a single correct answer. Following the question is a brief summary of each potential answer and why it is either right or wrong.

Question 1

Which of the following files is both a Photoshop color mode and one of the two types of computer graphics?

○ a. Bitmap

○ b. RGB

○ c. TIFF

○ d. Vector

The correct answer is a. Bitmap images are one of the two computer graphics types—along with vector graphics—and it is a Photoshop color mode, usually reserved for black-and-white line drawings. TIFF is a file format. Vector is not a Photoshop color mode. So answers c and d are definitely incorrect. You are left with choices a and b. Guessing could be tough because you might be thinking that RGB is a color mode and it's what monitors use to show color, so maybe that answer is the correct one.

This sample question format corresponds closely to the Adobe certification exam format; the only difference on the exam is that questions are not followed by answer keys. To select an answer, position the cursor over the radio button next to the answer. Then, click the mouse button to select the answer. This question gives you an idea of how the questions are sometimes formulated in a way that helps you dig out the answer—or at least narrow down your choices. (They don't all shake down this way, so don't count on having a 50/50 chance when guessing.)

Let's examine a question that requires choosing multiple answers. This type of question provides checkboxes rather than radio buttons for marking all appropriate selections.

Question 2

Which of the following are Photoshop pull-down menus?
- ❏ a. File
- ❏ b. Tools
- ❏ c. Image
- ❏ d. Select

The correct answers to this question are a, c, and d. Tools—actually the Toolbox—is accessed by pressing the Tab key on the keyboard, so b is incorrect. However, you might be fooled by this question if you aren't careful.

For this type of question, more than one answer is required. Based on information provided for the sample test at **www.adobe.com/supportservice/training/leadform.html**, you are given partial credit for partially correct answers, so do your best to get at least some of the right answers. For Question 2, you have to check the boxes next to items a, c, and d to obtain full credit. Notice that picking the right answers also means knowing why other answers are wrong.

Although these two basic types of questions can appear in many forms, they constitute the foundation on which all the Adobe certification exam questions rest. More complex questions include so-called exhibits, which are screenshots of Photoshop. You'll be expected to use the information displayed therein to guide your answer to the question. Familiarity with the underlying utility is your key to choosing the correct answer(s).

Using Adobe's Exam Software Effectively

A well-known principle when taking exams is to first read over the entire exam from start to finish while answering only those questions you feel absolutely sure of. On subsequent passes, you can dive into the complex questions more deeply, knowing how many such questions you have left.

Reading over the exam completely before answering the trickier questions provides at least one potential benefit: Sometimes, you can find information in later questions that sheds more light on earlier questions. Other times, information you read in later questions might jog your memory about Photoshop facts, figures, or behavior that also will help with earlier questions. Either way, you'll come out ahead if you defer those questions about which you're not absolutely sure.

Fortunately, Adobe exam software makes this approach easy to implement. At the top-left corner of each question is a checkbox that permits you to mark that question for a later visit. (**Note:** Marking questions makes review easier, but you can return to any question if you are willing to click the Forward or Back button repeatedly.) As you read each question, if you answer only those you're sure of and mark for review those that you're not sure of, you can keep working through a decreasing list of questions as you answer the trickier ones in order.

Another strategy for measuring your progress through the test is to keep a tally on your scratch sheet of the answers you're absolutely sure you've answered correctly. Because you know you have to score at least 67 percent to pass, and the test has approximately 75 correct answers, you know you'll need at least 50 correct answers. Following this strategy can help you determine how much more work you might need to put into the answers you're not sure of.

When you reach the end of the exam, the software presents you with a list of the questions and shows which ones you've marked for review and which ones you've left unanswered. You can use this "item review" to move around through the test to complete your answers. You can also return to the first question and step through the entire test, or go backward, if you prefer. Don't click on the Done button until you're really finished.

Watch that clock in the upper-right corner. Keep working on the questions until you're certain of all your answers or until you know you'll run out of time.

If questions remain unanswered, you should zip through them and guess. Not answering a question guarantees you won't receive credit for it, and a guess has at least a chance of being correct.

 At the very end of your exam period, you're better off guessing than leaving questions unanswered.

When you finish and click on the Done button, the software will prompt you if you have left any answers unanswered. This reminder provides a good chance to go back and guess, if you have time. (You'll get this warning even if it's one of the survey questions that you've left unanswered, so you might want to make sure you answer all of them.)

Exam-Taking Basics

The most important advice about taking any exam is this: Read each question carefully. Some questions are deliberately ambiguous, some use double negatives, and others use terminology in incredibly precise ways. The author has taken numerous exams—both practice and live—and in nearly every one has missed at least one question because he didn't read it closely or carefully enough.

The following are some suggestions on how to deal with the tendency to jump to an answer too quickly:

- Make sure that you read every word in the question. If you find yourself jumping ahead impatiently, go back and start over.

- As you read, try to restate the question in your own terms. If you can reword the question, you should be able to pick the correct answer(s) far more easily.

- When you return to a question after your initial read-through, read every word again; otherwise, your mind can fall quickly into a rut. Sometimes, revisiting a question after turning your attention elsewhere lets you see something you missed, but the strong tendency is to see what you've seen before. Try to avoid this tendency.

- If you return to a question more than twice, try to articulate to yourself what you don't understand about the question, why the answers don't appear to make sense, or what appears to be missing. If you chew on the subject for a while, your subconscious might provide the details that are lacking, or you might notice a "trick" that will point to the right answer.

Above all, try to deal with each question by thinking through what you know about Photoshop—the characteristics, behaviors, facts, and figures involved. By reviewing what you know (and what you've written down on your information sheet), you'll often recall or understand things sufficiently to determine the answer to the question.

Question-Handling Strategies

Based on exams the author has taken, some interesting trends have become apparent. For questions that take only a single answer, usually two or three of the answers will be obviously incorrect, and two of the answers will be plausible. Of course, only one answer can be correct. Unless the answer leaps out (if so, reread the question to look for a trick; sometimes, these questions are the ones you're likely to get wrong), begin the process of answering by eliminating those answers that are most obviously wrong.

Points to look for in obviously wrong answers include spurious menu choices or utility names, nonexistent software options, and terminology you've never seen. If you've done your homework for an exam, no valid information should be completely new to you. In that case, unfamiliar or bizarre terminology probably indicates a totally bogus answer.

Numerous questions assume that the default behavior of a particular utility is in effect. If you know the defaults and understand what they mean, this knowledge will help you cut through many Gordian knots.

As you work your way through the exam, another counter that Adobe thankfully provides will come in handy: the number of questions completed and questions outstanding. Budget your time by making sure that you've completed one-third of the questions one-third of the way through the exam period (or the first 27 or 28 questions in the first 30 minutes) and two-thirds of them two-thirds of the way through (54 or 55 questions in the first 60 minutes).

If you're not finished after 85 minutes, use the last 5 minutes to guess your way through the remaining questions. Remember, guessing is potentially more valuable than not answering because blank answers are always wrong, but a guess may turn out to be right. If you don't have a clue about any of the remaining questions, pick answers at random, or choose all a's, b's, and so on. The important thing is to submit an exam for scoring that has an answer for every question.

Mastering The Inner Game

In the final analysis, knowledge breeds confidence, and confidence breeds success. If you study the materials in this book carefully and review all the exam prep questions at the end of each chapter, you should become aware of those areas in which additional learning and study are required.

Next, follow up by reading some or all of the materials recommended in the "Need To Know More?" section at the end of each chapter. The idea is to become familiar enough with the concepts and situations you find in the sample questions that you can reason your way through similar situations on a real exam. If you know the material, you have every right to be confident that you can pass the exam.

After you've worked your way through the book, take the practice exam in Chapter 13. It will provide a reality check and help you identify areas you need to study further. Make sure you follow up and review materials related to the questions you miss on the practice exam before scheduling a real exam. Only after you cover all the ground and feel comfortable with the whole scope of the practice exam should you take a real one.

Armed with the information in this book and with the determination to augment your knowledge, you should be able to pass the certification exam. However, you need to work at it, or you'll spend the exam fee more than once before you finally pass. If you prepare seriously, you should do well. Good luck!

Additional Resources

A good source of information about Adobe certification exams comes from Adobe itself. Because its products and technologies—and the exams that go with them—change frequently, the best place to go for exam-related information is online.

If you haven't already visited the Adobe Certified Expert Program site, do so right now. The ACE home page resides at **www.adobe.com/supportservice/ training/aceprogram.html** (see Figure 1.1).

> *Note: The Adobe page might not be at this location by the time you read this book, or it might have been replaced by something new and different because things change regularly on the Adobe site. Should this happen, please read the sidebar titled "Coping With Change On The Web."*

The menu options in the left column of the home page point to the most important sources of information in the ACE pages. Be sure to check out these sources:

➤ **How to become an ACE** This page gives you the basic information about the certification process, as well as Adobe's own guidelines for

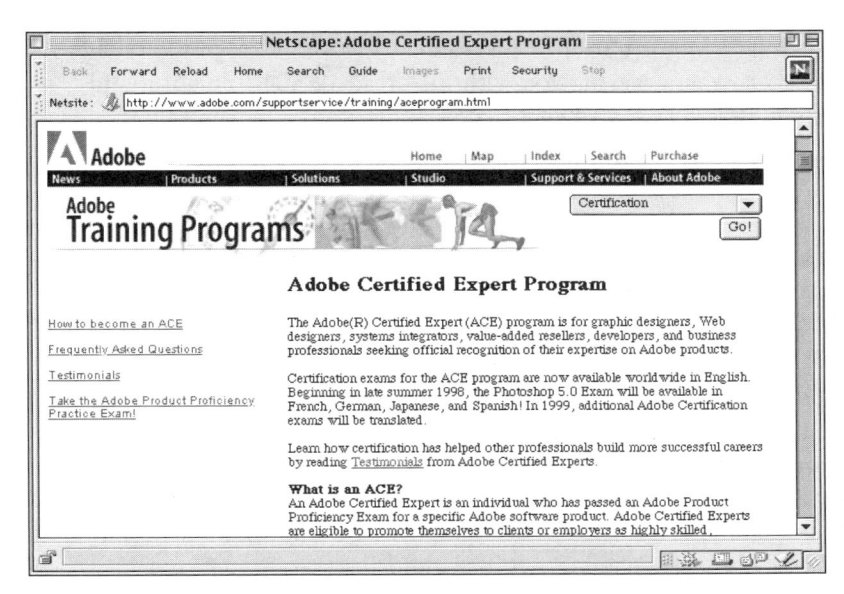

Figure 1.1 The Adobe Certified Expert Program home page.

preparing for the exam and a list of available Adobe study materials and training providers.

➤ **Frequently Asked Questions** This page presents a nice group of FAQs about ACE certification.

➤ **Testimonials** Here, you'll find a few comments from ACEs who feel they've benefited from becoming certified.

➤ **Take the Adobe Product Proficiency Practice Exam!** Become familiar with this page. Take the test; then retake it until you get all the answers correct.

The preceding sources are just the high points of what's available in the Adobe Certified Expert Program pages. As you browse through them—and we strongly recommend that you do—you'll probably find other informational tidbits mentioned that are every bit as interesting and compelling.

Coping With Change On The Web

Sooner or later, all the information we've shared with you about the Adobe Certified Expert Program pages and the other Web-based resources mentioned throughout the rest of this book will go stale or be replaced by newer information. In some cases, the URLs you find here might lead you to their replacements; in other cases, the URLs will go nowhere, leaving you with the dreaded "404 File not found" error message. When you get that message, don't give up.

You can always find a way to locate what you want on the Web if you're willing to invest some time and energy. Most large or complex Web sites—and Adobe's qualifies on both counts—offer a search engine. Looking back at Figure 1.1, you can see that a Search button appears along the top edge of the page. As long as you can get to Adobe's site (it should stay at **www.adobe.com** for a long while yet), you can use this tool to help you find what you need.

The more focused you can make a search request, the more likely the results will include information you can use. For example, you can search for the string "training and certification" to produce a lot of data about the subject in general, but if you're looking for the preparation guide for Exam 9A0-006, titled "Adobe Photoshop 5 Product Proficiency Examination," you'll be more likely to get there quickly if you use a search string similar to the following:

```
"Exam 9A0-006" AND "preparation "
```

Likewise, if you want to find the Training and Certification downloads, try a search string such as this:

```
"training and certification" AND "download page"
```

Finally, feel free to use general search tools—such as **www.search.com**, **www.altavista.com**, and **www.excite.com**—to search for related information. Although Adobe offers the best information about its certification exams online, you'll find plenty of third-party sources of information, training, and assistance in this area that need not follow Adobe's party line. The bottom line is this: If you can't find something where the book says it lives, start looking around. If worse comes to worst, you can always email us. We just might have a clue.

Introduction To Photoshop 5

Terms and concepts you'll need to understand:

- √ Vector Graphics
- √ Bitmap Images
- √ Raster
- √ Pixel
- √ Color Space
- √ Bit Depth (or Color Depth)
- √ Resolution
- √ Scratch Disk
- √ Virtual Memory

Techniques you'll need to master:

- √ Installing Photoshop
- √ Allocating RAM to Photoshop
- √ Setting the Scratch Disks
- √ Installing Plug-Ins
- √ Designating the Plug-Ins Folder

Adobe Photoshop is the world's premier software application for digital imaging. Adobe, the second-largest PC software publishing company in the world, claims that 2 million people worldwide use Photoshop. Photoshop is a painting program that enables users to manipulate scanned digital images and to create new digital images. In this chapter, I introduce you to Photoshop and its capabilities and lead you through installation.

Overview Of Photoshop 5

Photoshop's popularity rests in both its capabilities and its relative ease of use. Some people make adequate use of Photoshop while utilizing only a few of its capabilities, whereas others regularly use every available feature. Consequently, professional computer artists who rely on Photoshop for their income have been joined by thousands of others who merely want to play with their family snapshots. In between, you will find as many levels of Photoshop expertise as there are users.

Photoshop is essentially a painting program that enables you to do the following:

➤ **Retouch photos** Import scanned photos, digital photos, or photo files and clean them up by improving their exposure and color and by eliminating dust spots, scratches, and other imperfections.

➤ **Paint** Photoshop is a full-featured painting program, allowing you to create original digital art from scratch or alter other scanned or imported images.

➤ **Manipulate images** Put Uncle Roger's head on the dog. Change the color of someone's hair. Remove a power line from your favorite scenic photo.

➤ **Convert digital files** Change a file that has been optimized for printing in a magazine to one that is optimized for display on the Web, for example.

➤ **Combine images** Use Photoshop to create complex collages made up of as few as two images or as many as thousands of images.

➤ **Create color separations** Prepare images for printing on four-color printing presses.

➤ **Import and convert vector graphics** Import vector-based graphics files from programs such as Adobe Illustrator and Macromedia Freehand and then convert, or *rasterize*, them for use in Photoshop.

- **Import and export vector-based paths** Import vector-based paths from programs such as Adobe Illustrator and Macromedia Freehand to use as selections or masks in Photoshop. You can also create vector-based paths in Photoshop and export them to those vector-based drawing programs.
- **Support** Photoshop supports up to 24 channels and 100 layers per file.
- **Automate** Photoshop's actions and automation provide a way to speed your work.

What's New In Photoshop?

At this point, you might be asking yourself, "What is new in Photoshop?" What isn't? This new version of Photoshop boasts many welcome and long-awaited new features. Consequently, you have a lot more to learn about how to maximize your effective use of all of Photoshop's many capabilities.

The following is a list of Photoshop's new features:

- History palette
- Reselect command
- Path and selection transformation
- Layer effects
- Type layers with re-editable text
- Alignable layers
- Improved color management
- Expanded support for 16-bit color
- Color samplers
- Enhanced Hue/Separation command
- Channel Mixer
- Spot color
- Measure tool
- Magnetic lasso tool
- Magnetic pen tool
- Freeform pen tool
- Action palette enhancements
- Wizards and Assistants
- 3D transformation
- Expanded scratch space support
- Interface improvements
- More live previews
- PDF import
- New Save As options
- DCS 2.0 support
- PostScript Level 3 support

This book's Appendix describes these new features in more detail and refers to the chapters in this book where they are presented.

Digital Imaging Basics

Understanding digital imaging is essential both for using Photoshop effectively and for succeeding with the ACE exam. Here is a primer on some important digital imaging principles.

Bitmap Images Vs. Vector Graphics

When working in Photoshop, you are working primarily with *bitmap images*. Also known as *raster images*, bitmap images are made up of a grid of small squares called *pixels*. Pixels shine or project or illuminate (however you want to think of them) in various color values or shades—such as a light green, dark blue, or dark red—the variety of which depends on how many bits of information your file provides for each pixel. This display technique is similar to the printing process known as *halftone screening*, which enables the printing on paper of photographs and other continuous line images.

This description may be terribly confusing, so look at the visual examples shown in Figures 2.1 and 2.2.

Notice how the full-view image (Figure 2.1) appears normal, just like a regular photograph. When that same image is blown up (Figure 2.2), however, you can see how the illusion of a photographic image has been created with the grid of different colored squares. In this case, the colors are all various shades

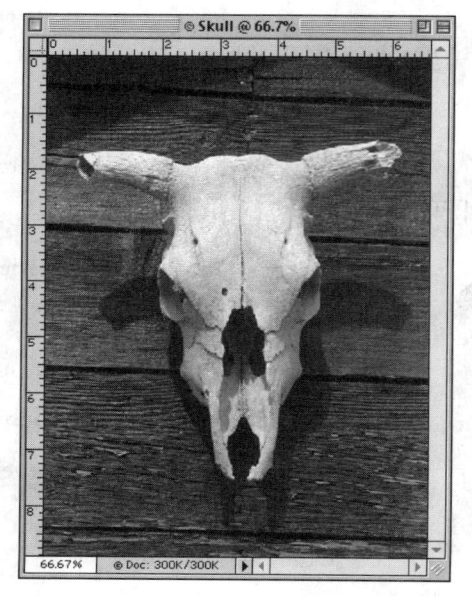

Figure 2.1   A full-view image.

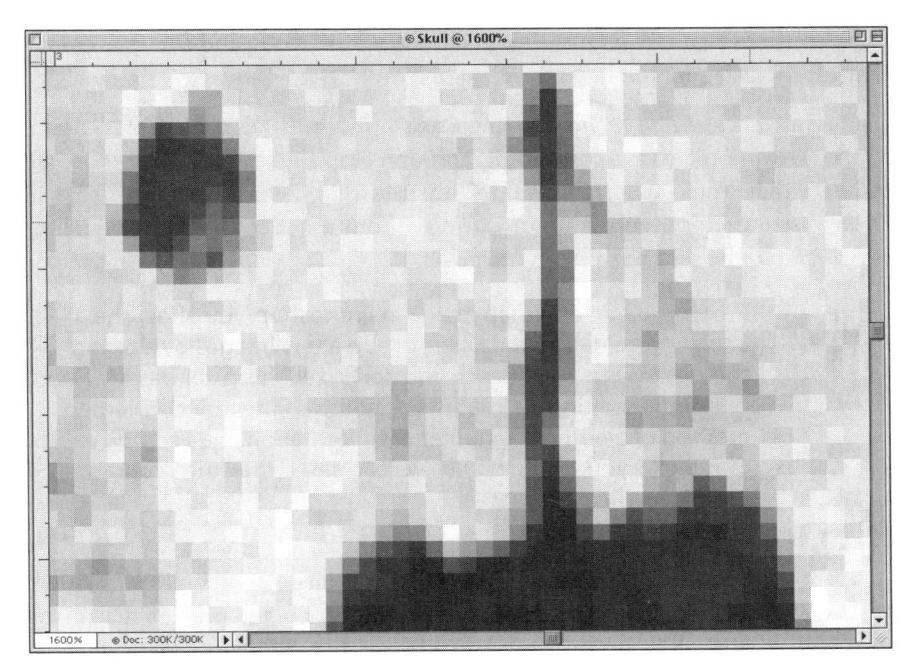

Figure 2.2   A detail of the same image magnified to 1600%.

of gray, but they also can be various shades of many other colors (they would be, if this image were in full color).

> **STUDY ALERT** Do not confuse *bitmap images* with *bitmap mode.* The term *bitmap images* defines a type of computer graphic, whereas *bitmap mode* is one of Photoshop's color modes.

Bitmap images must store all the data for each pixel that represents the image. So, if you have a large image, you have many more pixels and much more pixel data, which results in a larger file. If you want the file to be smaller while the image remains the same size, you must discard some of the pixel data, which results in a loss of image quality.

On the other hand, you have what are called *vector graphics*. Drawing programs such as Adobe Illustrator and Macromedia Freehand create these types of files. Vector graphics are different from bitmap images in that vector graphics define images by assigning numbers—or vectors—to the various elements that make up a *vector image*. Suppose that you open a drawing program and draw a stop sign. The drawing program stores the data that defines the image as numerical information about the placement, size, and shape of the octagon you draw, the lines that make up the letters in the word *STOP*, and even the colors that fill the octagon, the letters, and so on.

As a result, this *vector graphic* drawing of a stop sign makes a smaller file than a *bitmap image* file of a color photograph of a stop sign, which must store all the data that would tell each pixel in the grid what color to be. You also can freely resize vector graphics up or down without a noticeable loss of quality, which cannot be said for bitmap images.

> When you edit a bitmap image in Photoshop, you affect the image's pixel-based data. Photoshop alters images by altering the stored data about each affected pixel. This pixel-based method of editing an image is opposed to the object-oriented method of altering the numerical information of a vector graphic, as you would do in a vector-based drawing program.

Bit Depth

Now, go back to those bitmap images. A bitmap image's pixel information—what color each pixel should be—and the location on the grid of that pixel constitute the stored data of the bitmap image file. This pixel data directly affects the size of the image file, according to how many bits of information are stored for each pixel. In Photoshop, each pixel can have as many as 64 bits of color information stored for it.

A *bit* is the individual digit of binary code, either a zero or a one—which, in the case of computer graphics, could refer to on or off. If a pixel has a bit depth of one, the pixel will be either fully illuminated (on) or not illuminated (off). Thus, one bit has two values (on or off) or in the case of computer graphics, two colors. If you can follow that description, then you know that an 8-bit image has 256 colors. If you can't follow that thinking, here's the math:

```
1-bit = 2 values = 2 colors
8-bit = 2 values x 2 values x 2 values x 2 values x 2 values x
        2 values x
        2 values x 2 values
      = 256 values = 256 colors
```

The number of bits stored for each pixel determines a file's *bit depth* (sometimes also called either *pixel depth* or *color depth*) and directly affects the quality of the representation of color in the image.

> A file with a higher bit depth can more accurately represent color than a file with a lower bit depth.

Introduction To Photoshop 5   17

Now, depending on the color mode (see Chapter 4 for more details about color and color modes), you have what are called color *channels*. Think of channels as individual files for each color of the mode. For example, if you are working with an RGB file, which represents its range of color by using mixtures of red, green, and blue, you have three files—or channels—each one storing the pixel information for one of those colors. These three files are synchronized so that they display their individual pixels in the appropriate place on the grid for that file. As a result, they combine their colors to display the image accurately.

Each channel stores the level of its particular color—the shade of that color—to illuminate for each pixel on the grid. That shade is determined by the pixel's bit depth.

Consider these examples:

➤ Bitmap mode images are black-and-white images with no shades of gray. They have a bit depth of one, and they are known as 1-bit files because they have only one channel, or color, and they store only one bit of information about each pixel. That one bit is on or off—white or black. This type of file usually is reserved for black-and-white line drawings, sketches, and other high-contrast images that have no shades of gray.

➤ The 8-bit grayscale images are black and white with 256 shades of gray. Remember the bit depth math? Because a grayscale image shades only one color, a grayscale image needs only one channel. Therefore, it is an 8-bit file.

➤ All 24-bit RGB images are full-color images that mix three colors to represent 16.7 million colors. Think of it—16.7 million colors! The 24 in 24-bit comes from the three 8-bit channels (one 8-bit channel for red, one 8-bit channel for green, one 8-bit channel for blue, or $3 \times 8 = 24$). Each of those three 8-bit channels has 256 shades of its specific color. Those three channels, then, combine for the 16.7 million possible colors ($256 \times 256 \times 256 = 16,777,216$).

Although Photoshop supports files with up to 16 bits per channel (16-bit grayscale, 48-bit RGB, and 64-bit CMYK images), not all Photoshop tools and commands work with 16-bit images. The tools and commands that do work on 16-bit-per-channel images include the following:

➤ Marquee   ➤ Lasso

➤ Crop   ➤ Measure

➤ Zoom   ➤ Hand

Chapter 2

- Pen
- Color sampler
- Duplicate
- Modify
- Auto Levels
- Histogram
- Brightness/Contrast
- Equalize
- Channel Mixer
- Transform Selection
- Eyedropper
- Rubber stamp
- Feather
- Levels
- Curves
- Hue/Saturation
- Color Balance
- Invert
- Image Size
- Rotate Canvas

If you need to use any of the other Photoshop tools and commands, you must convert the image to an 8-bit-per-channel image.

Resolution

Simply put, *resolution* is the display quality of the image, regardless of the medium. That display quality of an image is determined by the amount of pixel data that it has. More pixel data means higher quality. So, higher quality images have more pixel data, and image files with more pixel data are larger. Get it?

The sharpness and clarity of on-screen and printed images and the size of image files are both related to resolution. Resolution can be originally specified by the amount of information that is either gathered during the original scan or set by the user during creation of a new file. After that, you can alter an image's resolution by changing it, using Photoshop's Image Size command.

Resolution, which is measured in *dpi* (dots per inch) or sometimes *ppi* (pixels per inch), determines how large or small an image can be displayed or printed while maintaining image quality. "Dots per inch" means just that. It's the number of dots—pixels—that a digital image has in every inch, to represent the colors and lines and details of an image.

STUDY ALERT: Do not confuse dpi with lpi. The term *dots per inch* refers to scanning resolution or image resolution, whereas the term *lpi* (*lines per inch*) refers to the halftone screen density specified for printing an image on a press or printer. (For more information on printing specifications, see Chapter 12.)

Remember the description of bitmap images earlier in this chapter, where I said that if you reduce an image's file size while maintaining its screen or printed size, you lose image quality? That's resolution. To reduce that file's size, you have to throw away a bunch of pixel data. If you do so, you don't have as many pixels representing the same colors and shades of colors, so the resolution—the image quality—goes down.

On the other hand, suppose that you have an image with a low resolution—say, 72 dpi. If you want to increase the dpi to 266, while leaving the image the same size, you can use the Image Size command. However, if you use this command, Photoshop has to fill in all those extra, new pixels by guessing—interpolating—what color they should be. Consequently, you lose image quality.

Imagine, on the other hand, that you want to change that image's file size, and you intend to reduce its reproduction size at the same time. You can do so without losing image quality because you use the same number of pixels to represent the image.

What this description boils down to is that, to retain optimum resolution, you should reduce an image's pixel data only if you are also reducing its size. If possible, scan at the highest possible resolution, and then reduce images down to whatever size you need.

(For more details on resolution, see Chapter 5.)

Installation and Configuration

Installation

You can install Photoshop by placing the Photoshop CD-ROM in your computer's drive and following the instructions for installation. You need to consider the issues shown in Tables 2.1 and 2.2.

Table 2.1   Minimum installation requirements.

	Windows	Macintosh
Processor	Intel Pentium class	Power Mac
Operating system	Windows 95, NT/4	Mac OS 7.5
RAM	32MB	32MB
Disk space	60MB	60MB
Video display	8-bit	8-bit
Sound	card required	built-in

Table 2.2 Installation requirements for optimum performance.

	Windows	**Macintosh**
RAM	64MB	64MB
Video display	24-bit	24-bit
Printer	PostScript	PostScript

The two Adobe Photoshop CD-ROMs contain the application and readme files, plug-ins, filters, tutorials, multimedia tours of Photoshop, technical notes, sample image files, Adobe Acrobat Reader, demos of Adobe products, and other third-party software. The Typical (Windows) and Easy Install (Mac) options install the configuration that Adobe has determined will be most beneficial to most users. If, for whatever reason, you don't want to use those options, you can choose Compact and Custom (Windows) or Custom Install (Mac). These options install either a minimum configuration (Compact) or whatever configuration you prefer (Custom).

Allocating RAM To Photoshop

Follow these steps to allocate RAM (random access memory) to Photoshop:

➤ **Mac** While Photoshop is not open, locate the Photoshop application file, highlight it, and pull down the Finder's File menu and choose Get Info (or press Cmd+I). In the Info dialog box (see Figure 2.3), you'll see the Memory Requirements in the lower right. Suggested Size is the minimum that Adobe hopes you'll use. You can enter amounts for either

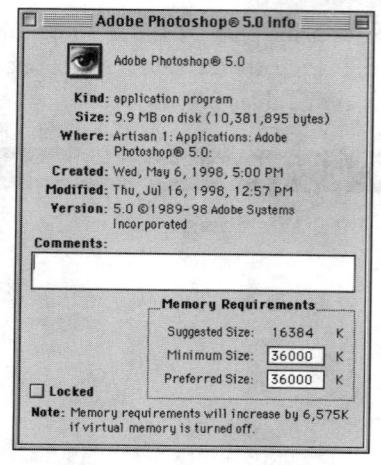

Figure 2.3   The Mac Photoshop Info dialog box.

the Minimum or Preferred Sizes. (You cannot enter a larger Minimum Size amount than the amount already set in Preferred Size. Set Preferred Size first if you need to.) If you want Photoshop to use a specific amount of RAM, just make both numbers the same.

➤ **Windows** Open the Memory & Image Cache Preferences dialog box by choosing File|Preferences|Memory & Image Cache (see Figure 2.4). Alternatively, you can press Ctrl+8 if you're in another preferences box. In this dialog box, you can specify a percentage of available RAM to use for Photoshop.

Preferences

In many computer applications, you can install, start up, and use the application without ever giving a thought to the default preferences. Photoshop, however, includes a couple of important preferences that you should not only learn how to set but also learn what they actually are and do. These settings are important even before you begin using Photoshop.

Configuring Virtual Memory And Scratch Disks

Virtual memory is hard disk space that is used as sort of pretend RAM. This memory allows you to use applications that may need more physical RAM than you have installed in your computer or allocate more memory to the program for better performance.

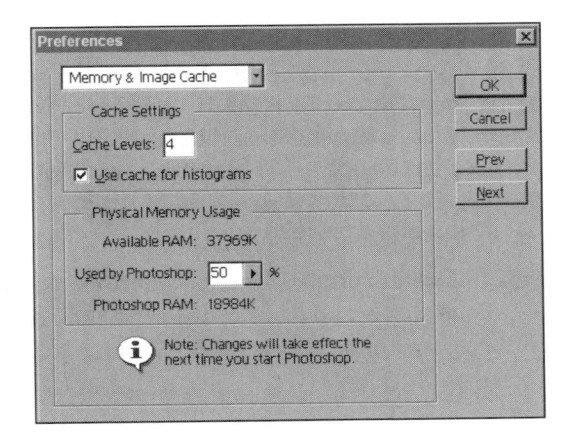

Figure 2.4 The Windows Memory & Image Cache Preferences dialog box.

Photoshop needs a lot of RAM to calculate all the different digital information that is necessary when you change pixel data. In fact, Photoshop probably needs about three times the size of the file you're working on to perform many tasks. You need this much RAM because when you open an image file and change its Image Size, Photoshop needs a place to store a copy of the data—in case you perform an Undo, perhaps. When you work with large image files, you'll probably eat up the entire available RAM pretty fast (unless you have several hundred megabytes of it). All unsaved work must be stored somewhere, right? So, Photoshop uses a *scratch disk*, which is actually virtual memory being used on your hard disk.

If you have only one hard disk, you don't need to worry about what disk Photoshop uses for a scratch disk. However, if you have more than one hard disk—or even a removable disk—and it has a lot of room on it, you can tell Photoshop to use that disk for a scratch disk.

Say you have a 1.2GB hard disk with 1GB of data on it. You're working on several large files, and you try to perform a Photoshop task. Suddenly, Photoshop tells you that it can't perform the action because the scratch disks are full. This message means that the hard drive that you've assigned (or has been chosen by default) is full and has no more room for Photoshop to write to. You need to either save and close some documents or save and close all the documents, reassign the scratch disk in the Preferences, and then restart Photoshop.

> Virtual memory and scratch disks are wonderful, but they do have some important limitations. Remember that the access speed of this "memory" is only as fast as the access speed of the assigned hard disk—and this speed is much slower than real RAM. Also, if you rely on virtual memory and don't have enough hard disk space, you may see frequent error messages informing you that your scratch disk is full. Then, you must consider the problem of using up your hard disk space. The virtual memory being used by the operating system and by Photoshop takes up space on your hard disk. If your hard disk is too full, you might find that you cannot save to the disk.

Ironically, although Photoshop utilizes disk space for scratch disks—just like virtual memory—Adobe suggests that you turn off virtual memory on your computer for better Photoshop performance. (Doing so does not affect Photoshop's scratch disks.)

Using And Locating Plug-Ins

Photoshop uses plug-in architecture, which means that it is open to the running of small, external applications from within Photoshop. These plug-ins perform various tasks such as help import files, help export files, filter images, provide automation, and so on. You have to put the plug-ins in a specific place—usually the default Plug-Ins folder—and Photoshop needs to know at all times where they are.

> You don't have to keep your plug-ins in the Plug-Ins folder in the Adobe Photoshop application folder. You can select, through the Preferences, any folder to designate as the plug-ins folder. However, if you do, you must either put all the plug-ins that you use in that other folder, or go back and tell Photoshop, in the Preferences, which plug-ins folder to use, and quit and restart Photoshop. You must do so every time you want to change folders.

Installing plug-ins can be as simple as activating a plug-in's dedicated installer, which then walks you through the process. Other times, though, you need to open the assigned plug-ins folder and place the plug-in in the appropriate subfolder.

To designate a different plug-ins folder, simply open the Plug-ins & Scratch Disks preference box and click Choose. Then, browse to the folder you want.

Editing The Preferences

To edit the Preferences, choose File|Preferences and select the specific preference window you need. Alternatively, press Cmd+K/Ctrl+K to bring up the General dialog box. Then, select the specific dialog boxes by pressing Cmd+1 through Cmd+8 or Ctrl+1 through Ctrl+8.

The following are the specific preferences dialog boxes and their keyboard shortcuts:

- **General** Cmd+K/Ctrl+K or Cmd+1/Ctrl+1 if in another preference
- **Saving Files** Cmd+2/Ctrl+2
- **Display & Cursors** Cmd+3/Ctrl+3
- **Transparency & Gamut** Cmd+4/Ctrl+4
- **Units & Rulers** Cmd+5/Ctrl+5
- **Guides & Grid** Cmd+6/Ctrl+6
- **Plug-ins & Scratch Disks** Cmd+7/Ctrl+7
- **Memory & Image Cache** (Windows) or **Image Cache** (Mac) Cmd+8/Ctrl+8

Other preferences, affecting different settings, will be discussed in later chapters, with their associated tools and commands.

Practice Questions

Question 1

> Photoshop is a
> - a. small photo-processing store
> - b. drawing program
> - c. vector-based program
> - d. painting program

Answer d is correct. Adobe Photoshop is a bitmap-image painting program.

Question 2

> What level of RAM does Adobe recommend for optimum performance of Photoshop?
> - a. 32MB
> - b. 16MB
> - c. 64MB
> - d. 8-bit

Answer c is correct. The minimum amount of RAM necessary for Photoshop is 32MB. Adobe recommends 64MB for optimum performance.

Question 3

> How many plug-in folders can you have open at one time in Photoshop?
> - a. Unlimited
> - b. 1
> - c. 6
> - d. 32

Answer b is correct. You can designate any folder as your plug-ins folder, but you can designate only one at a time.

Question 4

What is likely to happen to your image's resolution if you reduce its file size but don't reduce its display or print size?

- ○ a. Because Photoshop will be using the same pixels and just changing the image size, nothing will happen.
- ○ b. Because Photoshop will be able to select the best pixels and throw away the bad ones, the resolution will improve.
- ○ c. Because Photoshop will have to throw away pixels, fewer pixels will represent the image, so resolution will degrade.
- ○ d. Because Photoshop will have to interpolate new pixels in the image, resolution will degrade.

Answer c is correct. Remember, don't throw away pixels without reducing the image's size. If you do, the image's resolution will degrade. Answer a would be correct if you were reducing both the file's size and its image size at the same time. Answers b and d could be appropriate answers if the question was about enlarging an image's size, so be careful.

Question 5

What is the maximum bit depth per channel that Photoshop will accept?

- ○ a. Unlimited
- ○ b. 8
- ○ c. 16
- ○ d. 64

Answer c is correct. Photoshop will accept 64-bit files but only 16 bits per channel.

Question 6

How many layers will Photoshop support for each file?

- ○ a. unlimited
- ○ b. 10
- ○ c. 64
- ○ d. 100

Answer d is correct. In Photoshop, you can work on up to 100 layers.

Question 7

If you want to edit the General preferences, which menu or command could you choose? (Select all correct answers.)

- ○ a. Edit|Preferences|General
- ○ b. Cmd+K/Ctrl+K
- ○ c. File|Edit|Preferences|General
- ○ d. Cmd+P/Ctrl+P

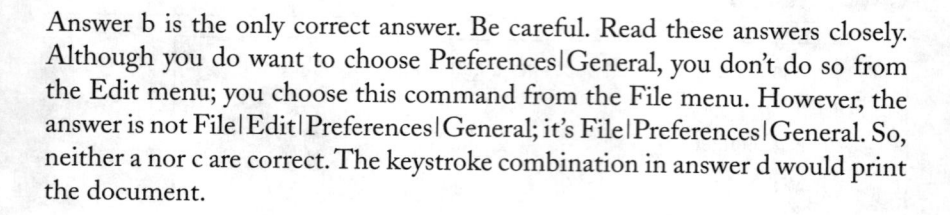

Trick! question

Answer b is the only correct answer. Be careful. Read these answers closely. Although you do want to choose Preferences|General, you don't do so from the Edit menu; you choose this command from the File menu. However, the answer is not File|Edit|Preferences|General; it's File|Preferences|General. So, neither a nor c are correct. The keystroke combination in answer d would print the document.

Need To Know More?

Davis, Jack & Dayton, Linnea: *The Photoshop 4 WOW! Book*. Peachpit Press. ISBN 0-201-68856-5. Read the resolution descriptions starting on page 41.

Farace, Joe: *The Photographer's Digital Studio*. Peachpit Press. ISBN 0-201-88400-3. Has a good section on bit-depth on page 13.

Photoshop Basics

Terms and concepts you'll need to understand:

- √ Menu
- √ Palette
- √ Palette menu
- √ Command
- √ Options
- √ Contextual menu
- √ Toolbox
- √ Canvas

Techniques you'll need to master:

- √ Selecting tools
- √ Using keyboard shortcuts to select tools
- √ Locating hidden tools
- √ Opening palettes
- √ Opening palette menus
- √ Using the History palette
- √ Using the new Measure tool
- √ Changing screen modes

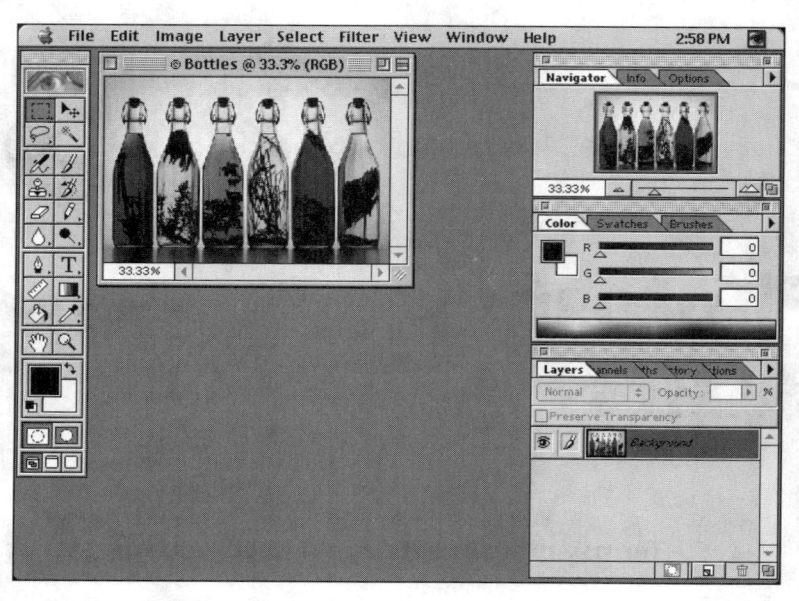

Figure 3.1 The Mac work area.

Photoshop's desktop or work area is similar to most Mac and Windows applications in many respects, particularly the pull-down menus. As you can see in Figures 3.1 and 3.2, the two platforms have minimal differences in the appearance of their work areas. In Windows, the work area is in a window (surprise!), but on the Mac, it stands alone on the desktop. With a few exceptions, using Photoshop on the two platforms is the same. For the most part, only the basic keystrokes of Cmd/Ctrl and Option/Alt differ. One nice feature of the Windows work area is the more elaborate status bar at the bottom of the window, where you see additional information about what Photoshop is doing and pointers or tips to keystrokes and so on.

Photoshop's Menus, Palettes, And Status Bar

To use Photoshop effectively, you must know how to properly access Photoshop's commands and options. This section describes the various features of the Photoshop interface.

The Pull-Down Menus

The Photoshop pull-down menus respond as usual: You hold down your mouse key, drag down to the command you want, and then let go. Available keyboard shortcuts are listed with their commands. An arrow after a command signifies

Photoshop Basics   **31**

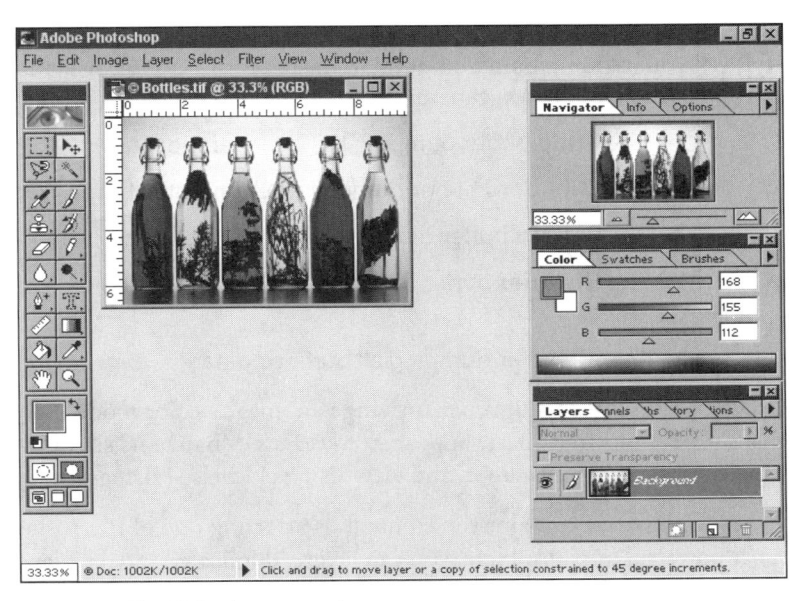

Figure 3.2   The Windows work area.

that a submenu is available. An ellipsis (...) after a command signifies that a dialog box will open. Get to know these menus and their contents.

As you can see in Figures 3.1 and 3.2, the menu bar includes these menus:

➤ **File** As in most applications, this menu contains the commands for opening, creating, saving, and printing files, and quitting the application. In Photoshop, you also see additional commands, such as Save A Copy, Revert, Place, Import and Export, Automate, Preferences and Color Settings, and Adobe Online. In Windows, you can rename a file as you open it (Open As), and you also have a short list of previously opened files you can quickly reopen.

➤ **Edit** This menu also contains familiar commands that are generally universal: Cut, Copy, and Paste. However, Photoshop adds some important and unique commands used specifically for editing images, such as Copy Merged, Paste Into, Fill, Stroke, Free Transform, Transform, Define Pattern, and Purge.

> If you are familiar with Photoshop 4, note that the Transform command has been moved to the Edit menu. It is now context-sensitive. In other words, if you are working with a path, the command and its options change to the Transform Path command, and if you have at least one point on a path selected, the command and its options change to the Transform Points command. Options for transforming selections are in the Select menu.

The Purge command has been expanded. This command allows you to dump data from RAM to make more memory available for an operation. You can now purge the following:

- The **Undo** buffer, dumping the last operation
- The **Clipboard** buffer, dumping the contents of the clipboard
- The **Pattern** buffer, dumping your saved pattern
- The **Histories** buffer, dumping all saved steps in the History palette
- The **All** buffer, dumping all buffered data

➤ **Image** Using this menu, you can change an image's color mode (Mode), make alterations to its basic appearance (Adjust), change its size and its canvas's size, crop it, rotate it, and view its pixel levels (Histogram).

➤ **Layer** This menu contains the commands affecting one of Photoshop's most powerful features. Here, you can create, duplicate, or delete layers; adjust layers (Layer Options, Adjustment Options); access the new Layer Effects and Type layer commands; add and enable Masks; group and ungroup layers; use the new alignment commands (Arrange, Align Linked, Distribute Linked); merge layers; and flatten the image.

➤ **Select** If you are selecting an entire image, you can do so in this menu, with All. Deselect whatever may be selected, and then reselect it by using the Reselect command. Select everything other than what is already selected with Inverse. Select areas of an image based on color (Color Range), and alter selections (Feather, Modify, Grow, Similar, Transform Selection). You also can save selections and load a previously saved selection.

Reselect is a new command to Photoshop 5. It simply reselects the most recent selection. (This action was possible in the previous versions with the Undo command, but only if done before you performed any other operation.)

The Inverse command can be a source of confusion because of the similarly named Invert command (which you access by choosing Image|Adjust) and Invert option (which you access by choosing Image|Apply Image). Remember that Inverse reverses your selection, selecting everything that is not selected and unselecting everything that is selected.

➤ **Filter** This menu lists the available special effects filters supplied by Adobe with Photoshop or any third-party filters you may have installed.

Photoshop Basics 33

They are grouped by type (or by vendor or package if you have others installed), and you can choose to reapply the last filter you used or fade the effects of the last filter. You'll also find the copyright/watermark filter here (Digimarc).

➤ **View** In this menu, you can choose the magnification amounts (Zoom In, Zoom Out, Fit on Screen, Actual Pixels, Print Size); hide the marquee or a path (Hide Edges, Hide Path); and show, control, or hide the guides and grid. Quickly open a new window with the same image in it by using the New View command. You can also look at how much image density you have in each color channel by using the Preview command and check to see whether you are using any out-of-gamut colors with the Gamut Warning command.

➤ **Window** Because of the differences in how the two operating systems present Photoshop, you'll find some differences in this menu from one platform to the other. Basically, you can open and close the Toolbox and the palettes from here, and you can switch between open image files by selecting one or the other from the list at the bottom. In Windows, you can arrange open windows or icons (Cascade, Tile, Arrange Icons); close all open windows at once; and hide or show the status bar. This menu is context-sensitive, so the commands change from Hide to Show, depending on whether or not a palette is open.

> If you ever lose the Toolbox and all the palettes from the screen, you can press Tab to get them all back. Of course, you can use the Tab key to hide them all, too. Pressing Shift+Tab hides or shows only the palettes.

➤ **Help** This menu accesses the different help options—obviously—but also has two automation wizards (Windows) or assistants (Mac) at the bottom (Export Transparent Image and Resize Image). In Windows, you access About Photoshop and About Plug-in from here (both of these selections are found under the Apple menu on the Mac) and have a shortcut to searching the Help file. On the Mac, you can toggle the balloon help on or off.

Photoshop's Palettes

Palettes, of course, are the little windows full of information scattered around the Photoshop work area. Even though they will clutter up smaller screens, these windows are actually helpful and save you a lot of time that might otherwise be needed to pull down menus or use keyboard shortcuts. You also have a good deal of control over them. Open and close them as you prefer; change which palettes contain which options and information; where they are on the screen; whether they are completely open or minimized; and how large or small they are.

> If you have changed and rearranged the palettes, you can easily return all of them to their default appearances and arrangements by selecting File|Preferences|General.
>
> If you want the palettes to return to their default locations every time you open Photoshop, no matter what you've done with them in your previous session, choose File|Preferences|General, and then deselect the Save Palette Locations checkbox.

Actually, each of the little windows you see is a palette group. You can find several individual palettes within each of them. The palette groups have some features that look and act similarly. Each palette in a group is labeled and can be accessed by a little tab at the top (see Figure 3.3). Clicking on this tab brings that palette to the front of the group. The little triangle at the top right opens the palette menu for the palette that is in front.

> In the Info palette options arrows and pointers appear next to the Eyedropper icons. These arrows mean the same thing as if that symbol were next to a tool in the Toolbox: A menu of options is available. If you hold on this icon, the menu appears, and you can change the measurement units or the color model used.

At the bottom of the palette in Figure 3.3, the little triangle beneath a horizontal line is a slider. This one happens to be there in the open; in some cases, however, it is under an options arrow or pointer. If you click on that options arrow pointer, the slider pops up and stays until you click away from it. You can also use the up or down arrow keys to move the slider 1 percent at a time and the Shift+Up arrow or Shift+Down arrow keys to move the slider in 10-percent increments.

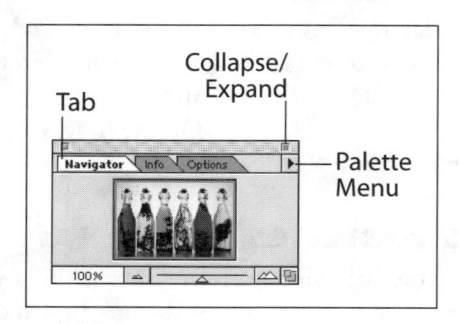

Figure 3.3 Palette anatomy.

If you don't want a palette to appear in a palette group, click the palette's close box or select the option from the Window pull-down menu to "hide" it. Conversely, use the "show" command to bring it back.

To collapse or expand a palette group, double-click a palette's tab or click on the "big box/little box" button on the Mac, and the Minimize/Maximize button in Windows (see Figure 3.4). To resize a palette, drag the big box/little box icon (Mac) or the diagonal lines icon (Windows) in the lower-right corner. (Only palettes that allow resizing have these icons.)

The Function Keys

You also can use the Function keys (see Table 3.1) at the top of your keyboard as shortcuts to hide or show some of the palettes and to complete several other operations.

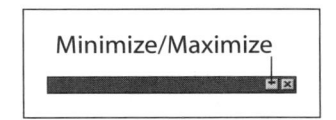

Figure 3.4 Minimize/maximize button in Windows.

Table 3.1 The Photoshop Function key shortcuts.

Key Or Key Combo	Performs This Function
F1	Undo
F2	Cut
F3	Copy
F4	Paste
F5	Hide/Show Brushes palette
F6	Hide/Show Colors palette
F7	Hide/Show Layers palette
F8	Hide/Show Info palette
F9	Hide/Show Actions palette
F12	Revert
Shift+F5	Fill
Shift+F6	Feather
Shift+F7	Select|Inverse

Placement

To move a palette group, just grab its title bar and drag to position it where you want it. Notice that it may "snap" to a position that Photoshop finds preferable.

To add or remove a palette from a palette group, just drag its tab to or from a palette group. If you drag a palette outside any group, you create a new group.

The Individual Palettes

The individual palettes are as follows:

➤ **Navigator** This valuable palette (refer to Figure 3.3) can help you quickly move around in an image that you may have enlarged to work on details. It shows you a thumbnail of the image you are working on, with a border around the area you can see in the window. If you can see the entire image in the window, the border in the Navigator palette is around the entire thumbnail. If you have an image magnified to a size that shows only a portion of the full image, however, the Navigator palette's border reduces to show you where you are in the image (see Figure 3.5).

You can drag the border around in the palette, which moves the image around in the window accordingly. You also can use the slider at the

Figure 3.5 The smaller border in the Navigator palette.

bottom of the Navigator palette (the upper-left box in Figure 3.5) to change the magnification of the image in the window, or you can click on the "close mountains/far mountains" buttons to zoom in and out.

The only palette option you have for this palette is to change the color of the preview border.

> You also can use the keyboard to scroll up and down and left and right in your image window. Use the Page Up/Page Down keys to scroll by one full screen at a time (if another full screen is available), or Shift+Page Up/Shift+Page Down to scroll by only 10 pixels at a time (or to move to the next frame in a Filmstrip file). Use Cmd/Ctrl+Page Up or Page Down to scroll left or right by one screen at a time. Shift+Cmd/Ctrl+Page Up or Page Down scrolls left or right by only 10 pixels at a time. The Home key and the End key will move the view to the upper left or lower right of the image, respectively.

▶ **Info** This palette (see Figure 3.6) tells you not only where the cursor is positioned, but what color values are beneath the cursor. This information can be important if you are sampling colors or trying to make a selection based on color range. Out-of-gamut colors are also noted here with exclamation points.

The Info palette, which is context-sensitive, changes according to the tool you are using. For example, if you use the Measure tool, you will see information regarding the position of the measuring line you've drawn, whereas if you use the Eyedropper tool, you will see the color information.

In Figure 3.6, notice that the color sampler icon and the crosshair icon both have options arrows to the right of the icons. On the color sampler, you can change the color model used for the sample. On the crosshair icon, you can change the measurement units.

Figure 3.6 The Info palette.

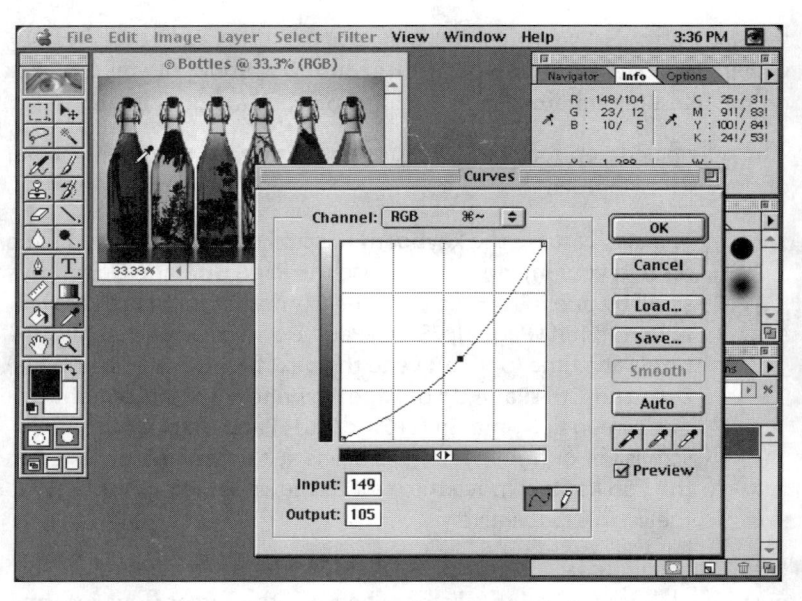

Figure 3.7 Before and after color values in the Info palette.

> Figure 3.7 shows the work area when you are adjusting an image with Curves. Notice that the Info palette shows two different color values in each readout, separated by a slash. They are the *before* colors—the existing colors—and the *after* colors—the ones that you will have if you accept changes to the operation. After you adjust the curve, these before and after values appear for any color samplers you have created, or you can place the cursor—which turns into the eyedropper—over an area of the image.

The Info palette includes the following options:

- **First Color Readout**
- **Second Color Readout**
- **Ruler Units**

> The First and Second Color Readout options allow you to set the color model that the Info palette will display in the two color info boxes in the top row of the palette. You could use these options, for example, to define what a color's values would be if you changed the image from one image mode to another.

> Also included in the Info palette options is the Hide Color Samplers command. It is handy when you want to see your image without obstructions but don't want to remove all the color samplers.

Photoshop Basics **39**

➤ **Options** The options currently selected for the active tool are displayed in the Options palette. (Figure 3.8 shows the Options palette for the Paint Bucket tool.) Here, you can change those options. To access the Options palette for a tool, click on the Option palette tab, double-click on the tool's icon in the Toolbox, press Return (Mac) or Enter (Windows), or choose Window|Show Options.

> You can reset a tool's default options by opening the palette options for that tool. You can reset just that tool's options or reset all the tools' options.

➤ **Color** You can use several methods in the Color palette (see Figure 3.9) to change the foreground and background colors. For each, you should first select the color model you want to use from the palette menu and make sure that either the foreground color or background color is active (denoted by the border around its color box). In this palette, as in the Info palette, a color value followed by an exclamation point signals an out-of-gamut color.

To change the foreground or background color from the Color palette, do the following:

➤ Drag the color sliders one way or the other.

➤ Enter a color value in the box next to the sliders.

➤ Click on the foreground or background color to activate the Color Picker.

➤ Click on the color bar at the bottom of the palette to select a color.

To change the available selection of colors in the Color palette's color bar, select Color Bar from the palette menu, and select one of the listed options. (Current Colors displays the range of colors represented by the

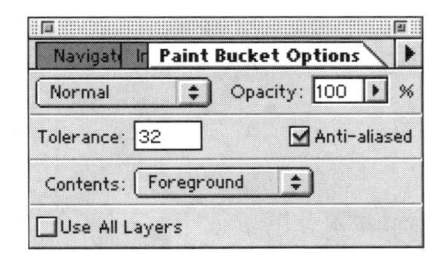

Figure 3.8 The Paint Bucket Options palette.

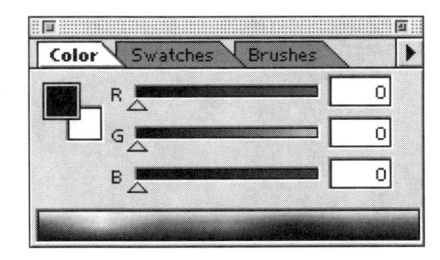

Figure 3.9 The Color palette.

current foreground and background color selections.) Cycle through these options by Shift+clicking on the color bar.

- **Swatches** This palette (see Figure 3.10) shows a selection of colors (little swatches) you can quickly choose as the foreground or background color. You can replace the default set of colors completely or just replace a few colors. You also can create a completely new set of colors, load a swatch from another image file, and/or save a swatch to load into another image file.

  To choose a foreground color from a swatch, simply click on a color. To select a background color, Alt+click/Option+click on a color.

  Add colors to the Swatches palette by clicking on an empty swatch at the bottom of the palette. To insert a swatch next to an existing one, click on a swatch while holding Shift+Alt/Shift+Option. If no empty swatches appear at the bottom of the palette, insert a new swatch, and you'll add a whole new row of empties.

  Replace the color in an existing swatch by holding the Shift key while you click on that color.

- **Brushes** On the Brushes palette (see Figure 3.11), the various brushes are stored. Here, you can choose, create, or delete brushes and custom brushes, and you can set the options for the brushes. You also can save sets of brushes and load saved sets of brushes.

  Notice how the brushes in the bottom row in Figure 3.11 have numbers under them. These numbers tell you that a brush is too large to display in the palette's little square and that it will have a pixel diameter of that number.

  To create a new brush, you can either select New Brush from the palette menu or just click in the open area next to the bottom row of brushes. In the resulting dialog box, you can set the options for a new brush.

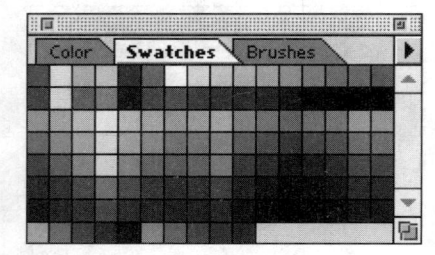

Figure 3.10 The Swatches palette.

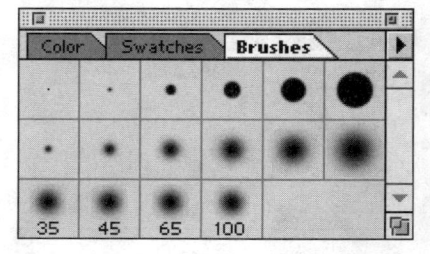

Figure 3.11 The Brushes palette.

To delete a brush, select Delete Brush from the palette menu or press Ctrl/Cmd and click on the brush.

For interesting effects, you also can select a shape from an existing image file to use as a brush. You'll achieve the best results if you use a shape from a high-contrast image. You can create a custom brush by selecting Define Brush from the palette menu.

The options for brushes include the following:

- **Diameter** Specifies the size of the brush in pixels
- **Hardness** Controls whether the edges of the brush are hard or soft (sharp or fuzzy)
- **Spacing** Specifies how close or far apart the brush's strokes will appear as you paint
- **Angle** Controls the apparent angle of an elliptical brush's tip as you paint
- **Roundness** Defines whether a brush is linear (0%), round (100%), or elliptical (1 through 99%)

- **Layers** This palette (see Figure 3.12) controls Photoshop's Layers features. (Using layers is presented in detail in Chapter 9.) In this palette, you see all the separate layers used in an image, listed from top to bottom. From here, you can hide/display, create, duplicate, delete, or merge layers.

The square box next to the layer name is a thumbnail of that layer's contents. The black-and-white thumbnail next to that is a Layer Mask. The chain icon between them shows that they are linked.

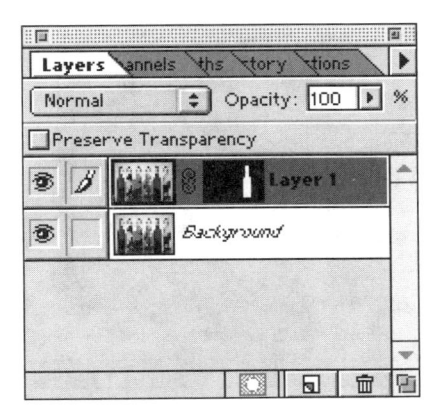

Figure 3.12   The Layers palette.

Select a Blending mode from the box in the upper left, and set the opacity of the layer in the box—which has a pop-up slider—next to that.

> **STUDY ALERT:** If you want to edit a layer that has areas of transparency without changing the transparent areas, click on the Preserve Transparency checkbox. Toggle this option with the / (slash) key.

The little eyeball icon tells you whether a layer is visible. The little paintbrush tells you which layer is active for editing.

> **STUDY ALERT:** If you want to show or hide more than one layer at a time, just slide (drag) your cursor up or down the column of eyeball icons.

The buttons at the bottom of the palette (New Layer Mask, New Layer, Trash) have multiple uses, depending on key/click combinations. They are primarily used to create new layers and layer masks, to load selections as layer masks, and to delete layers and layer masks.

Change the size of the thumbnail in the palette by selecting the Palette Options command from the palette menu.

➤ **Channels** From the Channels palette (see Figure 3.13), you can create, select, hide/show, edit, and delete. You also can convert selections to channels; and mix, split, and merge channels, spot color channels, and alpha channels. (The use of channels is covered in detail in Chapter 10.)

The top of the list of channels in the Channels palette is the composite channel, which shows all the color channels mixed—as the image would

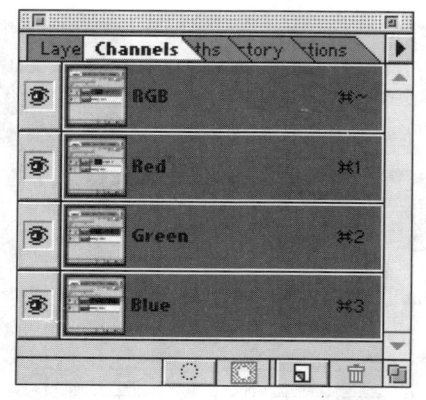

Figure 3.13 The Channels palette.

"normally" appear. Next, depending on the color model you are using, the Channels palette displays the color channels in order of their model's name. For example, in an RGB image, the first channel would be the composite channel of all the colors, followed by the red, green, and blue channels. A CMYK image's channels would be listed as composite, cyan, magenta, yellow, black. Spot color channels and alpha channels are listed after the main color channels.

The little eyeball icon controls a channel's visibility. Click it on or off to hide or show the channel.

> If you want to show or hide more than one channel at a time, just slide (drag) your cursor up or down the column of eyeball icons.

To edit a channel, click on its name in the palette. The active channel is displayed red in the palette.

The thumbnails represent each channel and change as you edit an image. By default, the individual color channels and the alpha and spot color channels—which are essentially masks—are displayed as grayscale thumbnails.

> The selected pixels of an alpha channel are displayed as white, the unselected pixels as black, and partially selected pixels as gray.

You cannot alter the order of the primary color channels, nor can you place a spot color or alpha channel before the primary channels. However, you can alter the order of the alpha and spot color channels by dragging a channel above or below others.

Change the size of the thumbnail in the palette by selecting the Palette Options command from the palette menu.

When you activate the composite channel or individual color channels and then show an alpha channel, you see a colored mask over the color channel. To change the color or transparency of this mask's display, either select Channel Options from the palette menu or double-click on the alpha channel's name.

The buttons at the bottom of the palette (Load Selection, Save Selection, New Channel, Trash) have multiple uses, depending on key/click combinations. They are primarily used to load selections as masks, load masks as selections, create new alpha and spot color channels, and to delete channels.

- **Paths** Simply put, paths are straight and curved vector-based lines that can be combined to create complex shapes and used as very precise selections. From the Paths palette (see Figure 3.14), you can save paths, fill paths with color, give a path a border, load paths, create new paths, convert paths to selections, convert selections to paths, and create clipping paths. (Using paths is presented in detail in Chapter 7.)

The Paths palette is similar to the Layers and Channels palettes. A thumbnail shows the path, and the path's name is next to that. The active path is red in the palette.

You can change the size of the thumbnail by selecting Palette Options from the palette menu.

- **History** The History palette (see Figure 3.15) is one of Photoshop's new—and most welcome—features. You now can undo multiple operations back through a document. For more details on the History palette, see the section on correcting mistakes with Undo and the History palette, later in this chapter.

- **Actions** The Actions palette (see Figure 3.16) controls the powerful scripting/automation tools called actions in Photoshop. (Actions and automation are covered in detail in Chapter 11.) The Actions palette displays all available actions as individual actions, as sets, and as com-

Figure 3.14 The Paths palette.

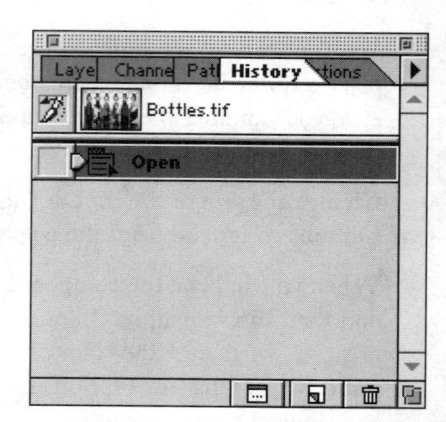

Figure 3.15 The History palette.

mands—or as buttons. From the Actions palette, you create, record, edit, run, save, load, and delete actions and action sets.

Action sets are displayed with a folder icon. Within the actions sets are the individual actions and their commands.

To display the actions in a set, click on the options arrow or pointer next to a folder icon. To display an action's commands, click on the action's options arrow or pointer. To display the individual attributes or values of a command, click on the command's options arrow or pointer.

The checkmarks on the left of the palette indicate which actions or commands will run if you run the action. Clicking a checkmark on or off includes or excludes a command or action.

The little icon of a window with an ellipsis in it is the Modal Control icon. It tells you that an action has a command in it requiring you to respond to a dialog box and then tells you which individual commands have those modal controls in them.

You also can set the palette to display the actions as buttons (see Figure 3.17) by selecting Button Mode from the palette menu. In Button mode, you don't see the checkboxes, the modal control icons, or the list of individual commands in an action.

To set the color of an action's button, select Action Options from the palette menu.

The buttons on the bottom of the palette are Stop, Record, Play, New Set, New Action, and Trash, from left to right.

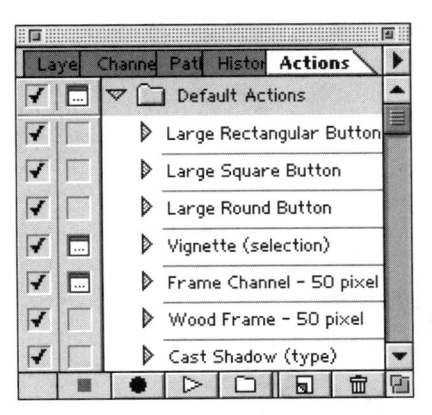

Figure 3.16 The Actions palette.

Figure 3.17 The Actions palette in Button mode.

The Status Bar

The status bar is located along the bottom of the application window in Windows (see Figure 3.18) and the image window on the Mac (see Figure 3.19). On both, you see the magnification percentage of the image and have a selection of other information you can choose to display next to that.

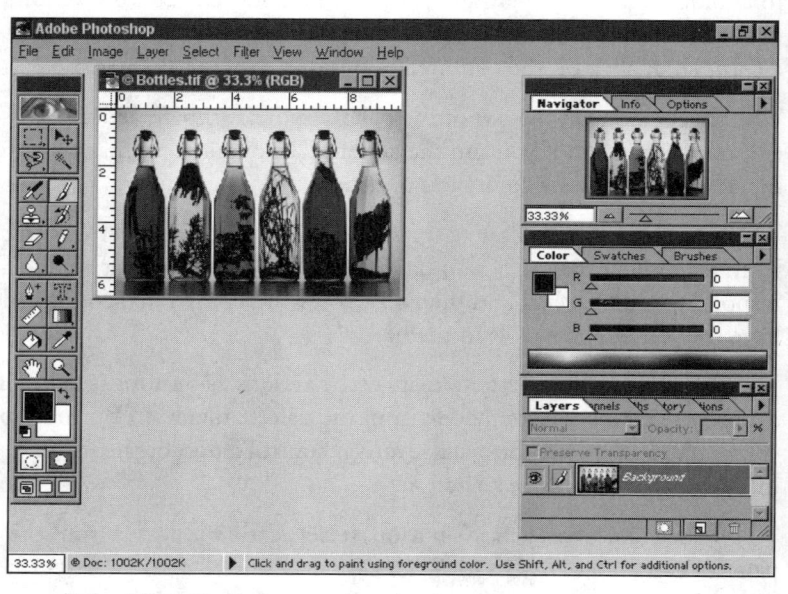

Figure 3.18 The Windows application window, with the status bar at the bottom.

Figure 3.19 The Mac image window, with the status bar at the bottom.

Photoshop Basics   47

In Windows, you also see tips or brief instructions about the active tool.

To turn off the status bar (only in Windows), choose Window|Show/Hide Status Bar.

If you hold your mouse down on the black options arrow on the status bar, you activate the status bar's menu (see Figure 3.20). The selections and their options are as follows:

- **Document Sizes** Shows the size of the image file if saved as a flattened, merged file (first number) and the size if saved with all channels and layers separate.

- **Scratch Sizes** Shows the amount of RAM being used by Photoshop for all buffers, including all open images with their channels and layers, the History palette and Undo, saved patterns and snapshots, and the contents of the clipboard. The second number is the total amount of RAM available to Photoshop.

- **Efficiency** Shows whether Photoshop is using scratch disk space to perform operations. A value less than 100 percent indicates that Photoshop is relying on scratch disk space, rather than RAM, which is probably slowing performance.

- **Timing** Shows the time it took to perform the last operation.

- **Current Tool** Shows the name of the currently active tool.

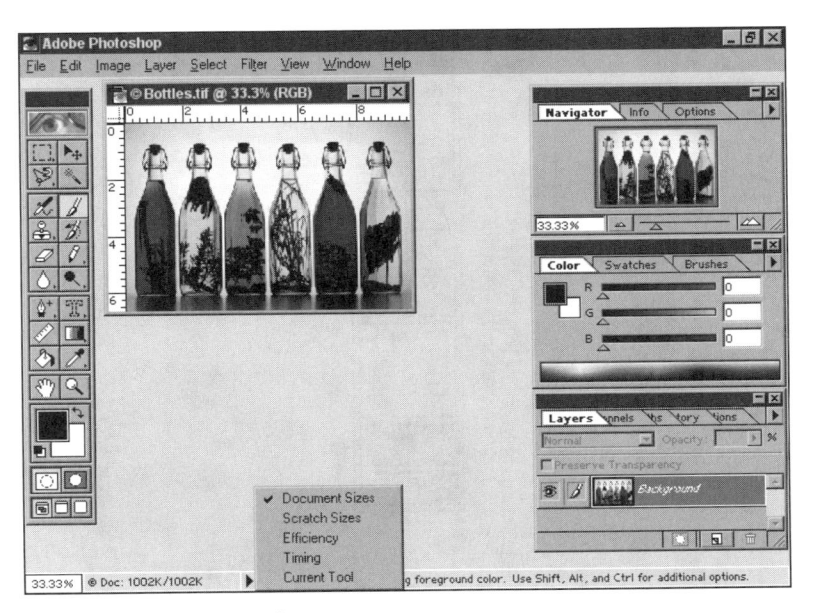

Figure 3.20   The status bar menu.

The Toolbox

Knowing how to navigate quickly through the Toolbox, as well as knowing common keyboard shortcuts, is important. The Toolbox (see Figure 3.21) provides access to Photoshop's selection, moving, painting, measuring, typing, color selection, magnification, and screen modes—as well as Adobe Online Help.

> **STUDY ALERT:** Remember that you can hide or show the Toolbox by using the Window|Show Tools command or by pressing Tab.

Toolbox Basics

The following are some important tips about using the Toolbox:

➤ You can move the Toolbox anywhere on the screen. Simply drag its title bar.

➤ Click on a tool to select that tool.

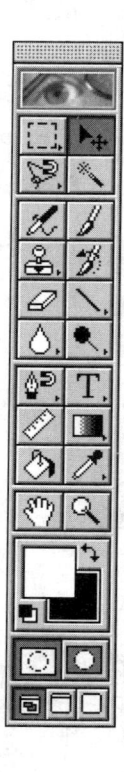

Figure 3.21 The Toolbox.

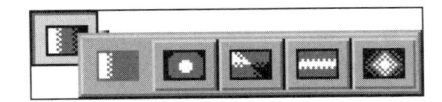

Figure 3.22 Hold down the cursor on a tool to expose its hidden tools menu.

➤ If a tool's icon also has a black triangle, click and hold to display the menu of hidden tools (see Figure 3.22).

➤ Double-click on a tool to open its Options palette.

> You can also access the hidden tools by Option+clicking/Alt+clicking on a tool's icon, or by pressing Shift and the tool's keyboard shortcut. This action cycles you through that tool's available hidden tools.

Keyboard Shortcuts

You can access all the tools from the keyboard.

> Knowing the keyboard shortcuts by heart is a good idea. Most of them are identified by a letter that appears in their name, but not necessarily the first letter. Table 3.2 lists the available keyboard shortcuts. (The keyboard shortcut, if in the word, is printed in bold.)

> If you are working with a 16-bit-per-channel image, you can use only the following tools:
>
> ➤ Marquee
>
> ➤ Lasso
>
> ➤ Crop
>
> ➤ Measure
>
> ➤ Zoom
>
> ➤ Hand
>
> ➤ Pen
>
> ➤ Eyedropper
>
> ➤ Color Sampler
>
> ➤ Rubber Stamp

Table 3.2 Available keyboard shortcuts.

Shortcut	Description
M	Rectangular Marquee
C	Crop
V	Move
L	Lasso
W	Magic Wand
J	Airbrush
B	Paintbrush
S	Rubber Stamp
Y	History Brush
E	Eraser
N	Pencil
R	Blur
O	Dodge
P	Pen
T	Type
U	Measure
G	Linear Gradient
K	Paint Bucket
I	Eyedropper
H	Hand
Z	Zoom
X	Switch colors
D	Default colors
Q	Standard/Quick Mask mode
F	Viewing modes: Standard/Full with menu bar/Full

Foreground/Background Colors

The following are some tips for working with foreground and background colors:

➤ To select a new foreground or background color, click on the color's square in the Toolbox to open the Color Picker.

Photoshop Basics   51

➤ To reverse the existing foreground and background colors, press X or click on the bent arrow icon in the foreground/background color area of the Toolbox.

➤ To reset the foreground/background colors to their defaults (black/white), press D or click on the miniature foreground/background color icon.

Viewing Modes

At the bottom of the Toolbox, along with the buttons used to switch between Standard editing mode and Quick Mask editing mode (shortcut = Q), as shown in Figure 3.23, are the buttons used to switch between viewing modes (shortcut = F). The Standard and Quick Mask buttons are shown in Figure 3.24.

> **STUDY ALERT:** The keyboard shortcuts for these viewing modes are toggles. Press Q to switch between Standard and Quick Mask. Press F to cycle through Standard, Full with menu bar, and Full.

The viewing modes images are as follows:

➤ **Standard screen mode** This mode shows the default image window appearance: a title bar at the top, scroll bars on the side, and (on the Mac) the status bar at the bottom.

➤ **Full screen mode with menu bar** This mode centers the image and displays it full screen (if the magnification is high enough), without a title bar or scroll bars. The application menu bar remains on the screen.

➤ **Full screen mode** This mode centers the image and clears the menu bar, title bar, and scroll bars.

> **STUDY ALERT:** The Toolbox and palettes remain on the screen in all these modes. Remember that you can press Tab to hide or show all of them. Alternatively, you can press Shift+Tab to hide or show only the palettes.

Changing Tool Pointers

For most of the tools, you can alter the appearance of the pointer that you use to guide yourself in the image. By default, the cursor takes on the appearance

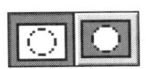

Figure 3.23 The Standard and Quick Mask buttons.

Figure 3.24 The viewing mode buttons.

of the tool. If you want to use the pointers that show you exactly where you are painting or drawing and what shape you are painting or drawing, change the tool pointers in the Preferences.

To change the tool pointers, choose File|Preferences|Display & Cursors. Painting Cursors and Other Cursors are the two cursor pointers options boxes. Notice that the Other Cursors box has only two of the three pointer options.

The Painting Cursors box sets the pointers for the following:

- Eraser
- Pencil
- Airbrush
- Paintbrush
- Rubber Stamp
- Pattern Stamp
- Smudge
- Blur
- Sharpen
- Dodge
- Burn
- Sponge

The Other Cursors box sets the pointers for the following:

- Marquee
- Lasso
- Polygon Lasso
- Magic Wand
- Crop
- Eyedropper
- Pen
- Gradient
- Line
- Paint Bucket
- Magnetic Lasso
- Magnetic Pen
- Measure
- Color Sampler

The tool pointer options are as follows:

- **Standard** Displays the pointers as the tool's icon
- **Precise** Uses more precise crosshairs for the pointer
- **Brush Size** Uses the shape and pixel size of the selected brush

You can use the Caps Lock key to swap between pointer options quickly, depending on which option you have selected in Preferences. As long as Caps Lock is locked down, the swap will remain.

- If you have Standard selected, Caps Lock gives you Precise.
- If you have Precise selected, Caps Lock gives you Brush Size.
- If you have Brush Size selected, Caps Lock gives you Precise.

Figure 3.25 An exposed contextual menu.

Contextual Menus

As you work in Photoshop, you can bypass moving to options palettes and other command dialog boxes by using contextual menus. These menus are relative to the tool you're using and what you're doing. For example, if you're painting with the Paintbrush tool, and you access the contextual menu, you see a menu that allows you to cycle through the Brushes palette or select a Blending mode. If you use the Zoom tool, you are offered several view options (see Figure 3.25).

Access contextual menus by pointing your tool over an area of the image or over an item in a palette list. Then, on the Mac, hold down Control and hold down the mouse button. In Windows, click with the right mouse button.

The Canvas

Photoshop's canvas is the size of the image you're editing. Unlike page layout programs such as QuarkXPress, Photoshop doesn't have a "pasteboard," and you can't work outside the actual image area of the file. If you want to perform an edit that requires you to do something outside the area of the saved image, you must use the Canvas Size command to enlarge the file's area. Remember that you increase the image's file size at the same time. You can also use the Canvas Size command to crop an image (but using this command isn't very precise).

> Don't confuse Image Size and Canvas Size. The Canvas Size command enlarges an image's editable area by adding an area of new pixels, whereas the Image Size command affects an image's final size and resolution.

Access the Canvas Size dialog box by selecting Image|Canvas Size. The upper area of the dialog box (see Figure 3.26) shows you the current size of the image's canvas, based on the resolution specified in the Image Size dialog box and the measurement units specified in the lower area of this box. If you change the measurement units in the lower area to points, for example, the width and height info above change to points also.

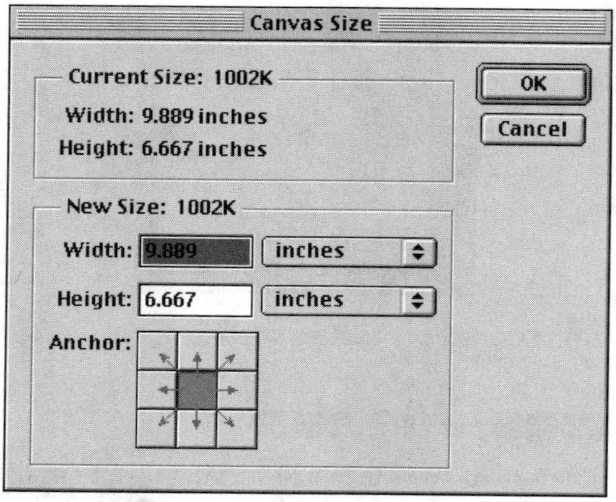

Chapter 3

Figure 3.26 The Canvas Size dialog box.

The Canvas Size dialog box also tells you what the new file size of the image will be after this operation.

In the dialog box, you can pull down the measurements unit box (see Figure 3.27) to change the canvas size based on several measurements, including the following:

- Percent
- Pixels
- Inches
- Centimeters (cm)
- Points
- Picas
- Columns

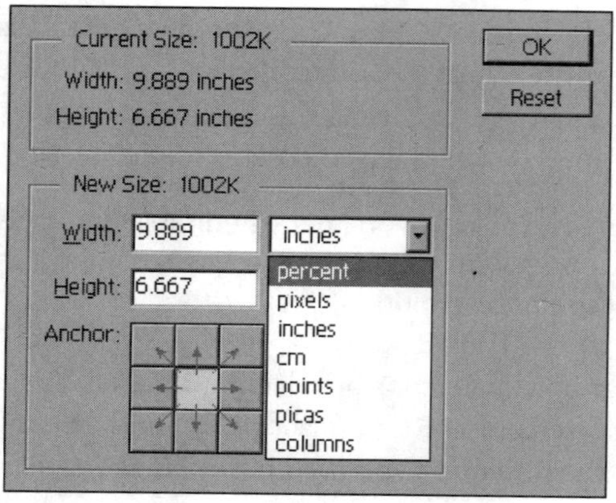

Figure 3.27 The Canvas Size measurement options.

Using the Anchor box, you can select where you want Photoshop to add the new editable area by clicking on one of the nine squares. For example, if you leave this area at the default, centered position, Photoshop adds a new area, made up of pixels filled with the currently selected background color, all around the existing image. If, on the other hand, you click on any other box, Photoshop places the existing image in that position on the new area. Figures 3.28 and 3.29 show an example.

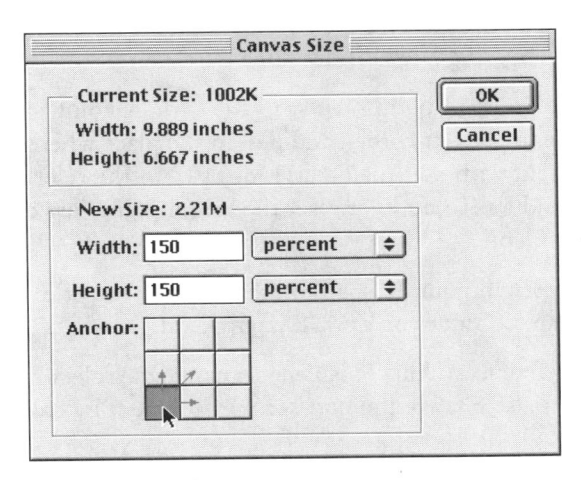

Figure 3.28 Select an anchor spot.

Figure 3.29 The resulting canvas.

> **STUDY ALERT:** Because the Canvas Size command fills the newly created area with the current background color selection, you should make sure that you select the desired color before you use this command.

Rulers And Measuring

You should know how to manage the rulers, even if you don't use them, because they affect the underlying grid. You can activate the rulers, as shown in Figure 3.30, by choosing View|Show Rulers.

To move the rulers' zero point, just grab the Origin Point icon (the dotted crosshair) in the upper-left corner, and pull to the place where you want it. It snaps to alignment with the small marks, or ticks, of the ruler if you hold the Shift key as you drag. To undo or reset the origin point, just double-click on the Origin Point icon.

If you want the origin point to snap to the guides or the grid as you move it, select View|Snap to Guides or View|Snap to Grid.

Choose File|Preferences|Units & Rulers to change the rulers' settings in Preferences. You can also change the units of measurement by changing them in the Info palette.

The Measure Tool

The Measure tool—one new feature of Photoshop 5—is easy to use. Simply select the Measure tool from the Toolbox, and then click on a spot in your image. Drag across the distance you want to measure, and let go. The distance is displayed as "D:" in the Info palette (see Figure 3.31). (You don't have to remember to show the Info palette; it pops open automatically as you measure.)

Figure 3.30 An image window with rulers visible.

Photoshop Basics

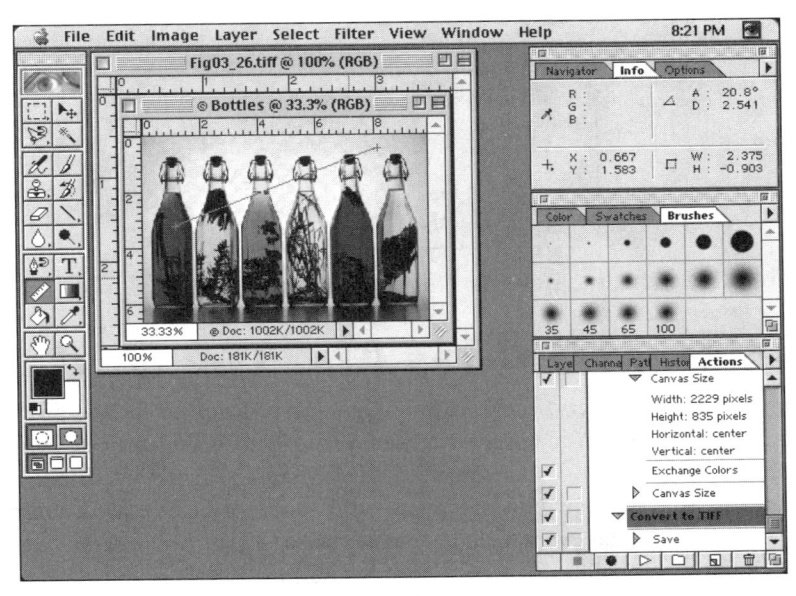

Figure 3.31 Using the Measure tool.

Notice that the angle of your measuring line is also displayed in the Info palette as the "A:" directly above the distance measurement.

You can move either point of this line simply by dragging one. You can move the entire line by grabbing it between the end points.

To delete the line, grab it between the end points, and drag it out of the image window.

The X and Y values represent the starting point of your line. The horizontal and vertical distances between the two points are displayed as the W (horizontal) and H (vertical) values.

Holding the Shift key as you drag constrains the tool's line to multiples of 45 degrees.

> **STUDY ALERT**
>
> To use the protractor feature of the Measure tool, draw your first, or base, line. Then, hold down Option/Alt, and click on an existing point. The pointer changes to the protractor icon when you are ready; then drag to another point, and let go. Holding down the Shift key restricts the line to multiples of 45 degrees.
>
> The angle value in the Info palette (see Figure 3.32) changes to display the angle between the two lines. Another "D:" value is added to show the distance measurement of the second line.

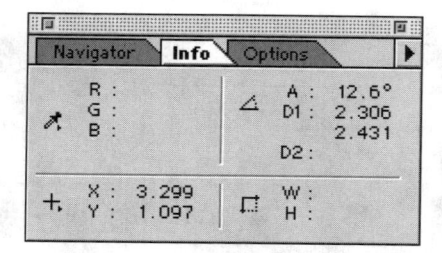

Figure 3.32 The Info palette after using the protractor feature.

Basics Of Guides And The Grid

Using guides and the grid can help you align and position selections precisely as you edit an image. You specify the size of the grid in Preferences, and you create and position guides as you need them. Keep in mind that neither of them print. You can lock guides, move them around, or delete them, and they are specific to the image in which you create them. On the other hand, the grid is fixed and universal, so after you specify the grid's measurement unit and spacing, that grid is used for all images until you change the Preferences again. However, you can specify within each image the visibility of guides or the grid.

You can choose to have tools and selections snap to the grid or to the guides, or you can turn off this feature for either by selecting View|Snap To Guides or View|Snap To Grid. Guides you create also snap to the grid if you have Snap To Grid selected.

Set the guide and grid preferences by choosing File|Preferences|Guides & Grid. You have these options for both:

- **Color** Set the color used to display the guides and grid. Use the same for both, or choose separate colors.
- **Style** Select between lines or dashed lines for guides; and lines, dashed lines, and dots for the grid.

You also have these options for the grid:

- **Gridline Every** Set the distance between the grid lines and the measurement units to use.
- **Subdivisions** Set the number of intermediate lines that will appear between the main grid lines.

To create a guide, first show the rulers (by choosing View|Show Rulers), and then drag from either the horizontal ruler or the vertical ruler to pull out a guide. If you hold down the Shift key as you drag, the guide snaps to the ruler ticks. If the grid is visible, and you have selected Snap To Grid, the guide also snaps to the grid. Hold down Option/Alt to switch to a vertical guide from the horizontal ruler or a horizontal guide from the vertical ruler. The cursor turns into a guide icon when you are moving a guide. Even if you have hidden the guides, as soon as you let go of the guide you've just created, Photoshop shows all the guides.

To move an existing guide, use the Move tool to grab it and drag.

To change an existing guide from a horizontal to a vertical guide, or vice versa, hold down Option/Alt as you move the guide.

Remove guides individually by dragging them off the image window, or remove all the guides by selecting View|Clear Guides.

Creating, Opening, And Placing Files

Before you can get to work in Photoshop, you must have a file to work in. You can either start from scratch and create a new file, import a new scan or PICT resource, or open an existing file. You can also place one file as a new layer in an open file. (Opening and importing files are covered in detail in Chapter 5.)

Creating A New File

To create a new file, select File|New to access the New dialog box (see Figure 3.33). Enter the width, height, and resolution values you want. Select the measurement units and the color mode from the options menus.

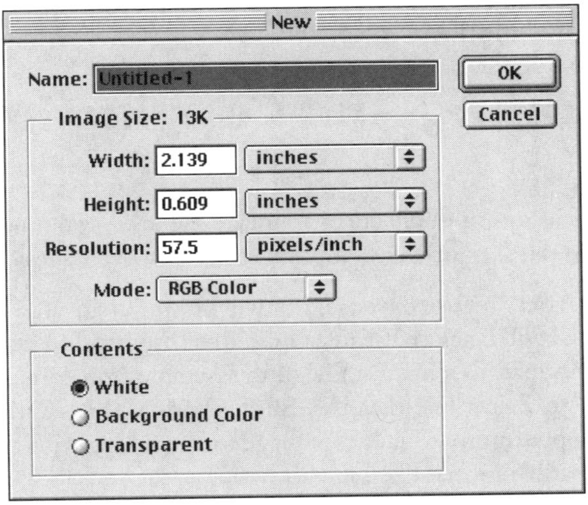

Figure 3.33 The New dialog box.

You can choose to create a file with a background of white, the current background color selection, or transparency.

Opening A File

To open a file, select File|Open, and browse the resulting dialog box to find the file you want to open. If the file is of a specific format, and you want Photoshop to open it in that format, choose File|Open As in Windows, and select the format before browsing for the file. On the Mac, choose File|Open, select Show All Files, and then select a format and open a file.

Importing A Scan

You must have a scanner attached to your computer and the appropriate import plug-in installed in Photoshop to use the Import command. When you select File|Import, you see the available import plug-ins. Select the one you want and proceed.

On the Mac, you see listed with the import plug-ins the command PICT Resource. PICT resources are picture files embedded in other files. For example, if you select this command and then open the Adobe Photoshop installer file, you see a dialog box that shows how many picture files are in the installer file and what they look like.

Employing The Place Command

If you have ART files from Adobe Illustrator, Adobe Acrobat PDF, or EPS files that you want to paste into an open Photoshop file as a new layer, you can use the Place command. Just choose File|Place, and then browse the resulting dialog box to find the file.

Duplicating And Copying Image Files

You can create a copy or duplicate of an image file in several ways. Each of the following methods has different advantages and disadvantages:

➤ **Save As** After you use Save As, you will be working in the new file, and the original will be closed. You can use this command to save a copy to a different format, to rename a file, or to save an original image in a certain state. Select File|Save As (Shift+Cmd+S/Shift+Ctrl+S). You have the opportunity to save the image to any folder, with any name, and in a compatible format.

- **Save A Copy** This command creates a copy of the file, but you continue working in the original file. This command can also be good for creating copies of steps or states as you work. You have the options of saving to any folder, with any name, and in a compatible format. This command also allows you to flatten the image file as the copy is made and to include or exclude the alpha channels and/or the nonimage data (everything but pixels). In certain formats, you also choose what, if any, preview icons to include. Choose File|Save A Copy (Option+Cmd+S/ Alt+Ctrl+S).

- **Duplicate** This command creates a quick copy, while you continue working in the original file. It also allows you to merge layers as you copy. To use it, choose Image|Duplicate.

- **New View** This command creates a new image window with an exact copy of the file in which you're working. The file is an active copy, in that it is updated as you work in the original. You can use this command to work on an enlarged detail area on one window, while you watch the entire image in the other window. To use it, choose View|New View.

- **History Palette** You can use the New Document button in the History palette to create a new file based on the selected state. (The History palette is presented in detail later in this chapter.)

Working With Selections

After you select part of an image, you can do a lot with that selection. (For more on selecting, see Chapter 7.) Understanding these operations is essential.

Moving Selections

Photoshop features several ways to move selections: by clicking on a tool, by using a keyboard shortcut, and by using numeric transform.

Using The Move Tool

To move a selection with the Move tool, select the Move icon (see Figure 3.34) from the Toolbox, or press Cmd/Ctrl while in most other tools.

Figure 3.34 The Move tool.

Chapter 3

> **STUDY ALERT**
>
> You cannot use the Cmd/Ctrl shortcut to activate the Move tool from these tools:
> - Pen
> - Direct Selection
> - Hand
> - Magnifying Glass
> - Anchor Point

The following are the basic Move tool operations:

- To move a selection with the Move tool, simply click, hold, and drag.
- To restrict the movement to 45-degree angles, hold the Shift key as you drag.
- By default, when you move a selection, you are actually performing a cut and paste; you leave a hole in the image where your selection was. To copy a selection as you move—leaving the original image intact—hold Option/Alt as you drag. You can use this option even if you are activating the Move tool with the Cmd/Ctrl button; just hold them both at the same time.

> **STUDY ALERT**
>
> Let me remind you of one important aspect of using the keyboard and cursor shortcut to copy a selection: The selection is not copied to the clipboard. This result would be fine unless you intended to paste the selection after deselecting it. It would also be beneficial if you had something on the clipboard that you were waiting to paste: This operation would allow you to copy and paste something else without disturbing the clipboard's contents.

> **STUDY ALERT**
>
> If you are working with another application—such as Adobe Illustrator—chances are that you can drag and drop between that application and Photoshop. Simply configure your desktop so that you can see both windows you're working on, and drag from one to the other.
>
> If you are dragging vector artwork from another application to Photoshop and don't want it converted to a bitmap image, hold down Ctrl (Windows only) as you drag and drop. This way, you can import the vector artwork into Photoshop as a path.
>
> On the Mac, the application must support Macintosh Drag Manager, and in Windows, the application must be OLE-compliant.

You can set the two Move tool options in its Options palette:

- **Pixel Doubling** This option speeds preview by lowering the resolution of the dragged image.

- **Auto Select Layer** If you have several transparent layers, and you are trying to move a selection from one of them, but it is not the active layer, this option allows you to complete the move without having to select the actual layer you're trying to move. The cursor moves the visible pixels from whatever layer is directly beneath the cursor.

Moving With The Keyboard

After you make a selection, simply press the arrow keys in the direction you want. This method moves the selection 1 pixel at a time. To move the selection 10 pixels at a time, press the Shift key as you press the arrow keys.

To copy a selection as you move it this way, hold the Option or Alt key to create and move a duplicate of the selection 1 pixel. You can press Shift+Option/Alt to create and move a duplicate 10 pixels.

Moving With Numeric Transform

You also can move a selection by selecting Edit|Transform|Numeric. (See Chapter 9 for more information on transforming images.) When the Numeric Transform dialog box opens, you can click on the Position checkbox and set values in the X: box to move the selection horizontally and in the Y: box to move the selection vertically. You can also choose the measurement unit by which to move the selection by pulling down the option box next to the values.

If the Relative checkbox under the values is selected, you move the selection relative to its current position. If the checkbox is deselected, you move the selection to the screen position you have entered as values.

Copying Selections

Copying a selection is as easy as holding down Option/Alt as you drag with the Move tool. You also can hold down Option/Alt or Shift+Option/Alt as you press arrow keys, or you can choose Edit|Copy (Cmd+C/Ctrl+C) after you make a selection. (Remember that the keyboard/cursor shortcuts do not copy the selection to the clipboard.)

If you use Edit|Copy, you copy from the active layer. If you want to copy the shape of the selection from all visible layers, choose Edit|Copy Merged (Shift+Cmd+C/Shift+Ctrl+C) instead.

Cutting Selections

You cut a selection if you grab it with the Move tool and drag it or if you use the arrow keys. Alternatively, you can choose Edit|Cut (Cmd+X/Ctrl+X), which is the only way to cut the selection from the image and copy it to the clipboard for pasting.

> When you cut or copy a selection to the clipboard and then quit Photoshop, the program automatically converts the clipboard contents to a bitmap image (if it's not already a bitmap image) and saves it, in case you want to paste it into a different application. Saving all these images can take up considerable memory if you have large images, so if you want to prevent filling up memory, you can do one of two things:
>
> ➤ Before you quit Photoshop, choose Edit|Purge|Clipboard to delete the contents of the clipboard.
>
> ➤ Select File|Preferences|General and deselect Export Clipboard in the dialog box. Photoshop then deletes its clipboard as it quits.

Pasting Selections

After you cut or copy a selection, it is stored in the clipboard until you paste it somewhere. To paste, choose Edit|Paste (Cmd+V/Ctrl+V).

Using Paste Into

Photoshop also allows you to paste one selection into another. First, select the image area you want to paste; then cut or copy the selection to the clipboard. Then, select another area (in the same or a different image), and choose Edit|Paste Into (Shift+Cmd+V/Shift+Ctrl+V). The contents of the clipboard are pasted into the selection and a new layer is created with a layer mask in the shape of that selection.

Pasting From A Different PostScript Application

If you need to paste an image from another PostScript application, copy it to the clipboard in the other application, and then select Edit|Paste (Cmd+V/Ctrl+V). You then see a dialog box with the following options:

➤ **Paste As Pixels** If you want Photoshop to rasterize the image to pixel data like a Photoshop image, choose this option. If you do, you also need to decide whether to keep the anti-aliasing of the imported image.

➤ **Paste As Paths** This option allows you to import the vector artwork as a vector-based path.

Matting

If you are cutting or copying a selection from a high-contrast background, when you paste the selection, it may show some ugly artifacts along its edges. You can diminish this by using the following Matting commands. These commands look at an image and compare its edge pixels. If they seem vastly different, Photoshop changes them.

➤ **Defringe** Changes the contrasting edge pixels to match the more solid edge colors for a more even-looking edge

➤ **Remove Black Matte/Remove White Matte** Removes contrasting edge pixels so that the selection blends with the background

Deleting Selections

If you want to delete a selection, with no intention of pasting it, press Delete or choose Edit|Clear. If you intend to paste the deleted selection, you must choose Edit|Cut (Cmd+X/Ctrl+X) to save it to the clipboard.

To delete a selection and fill the area it vacates with the background color, hold the Cmd/Ctrl key as you press Delete. To fill that area with the foreground color, hold Option/Alt as you press Delete.

If you are deleting a selection from a transparent layer with Preserve Transparency selected, the background color will fill the area vacated by the selection. If you want to delete the selection and leave nothing in its place, deselect Preserve Transparency.

Correcting Mistakes

Photoshop has long had an Undo command, but it was limited to recalling one previous state of the image. That Undo command is still available in Photoshop 5, but now it is supported by the History palette, which opens up the possibility of returning to as many as 100 previous states.

Undo/Redo

To undo your last operation, simply select Edit|Undo (Cmd+Z/Ctrl+Z). The command is available only if it's possible to undo what you just did. After you "undo" the last operation, the Undo command toggles to Redo, and you can—surprise—redo the operation. This operation is effective for comparing before and after states.

History Palette

Now comes the good part. In Photoshop 5, Adobe has introduced the History palette. This powerful palette, shown in Figure 3.35, allows you to save previous steps of your work on an image file, keeps a list of previous steps that you can skip to and from, and provides states that you can use to paint or erase with.

Navigating The History Palette

The following are some tips for navigating the History palette:

➤ The thumbnail at the top of the palette is a snapshot of the document as it looked when you opened it.

➤ The History Brush icon in the box to the left of the thumbnail signifies that you would be painting or erasing from that state. You can click on any state's little box to move the History Brush icon to that state.

➤ Beneath the gray bar are the steps you've taken as you worked. They are called "states" and are listed with the oldest state at the top and most recent at the bottom. Each is labeled with the command that was used in that state.

➤ The little pointer at the left of each state's name is a slider that you can grab to quickly fast-forward or fast-backward between states.

Figure 3.35 A loaded History palette.

- The little dialog box button at the bottom of the palette is the New Document button, which creates a new file that is a duplicate of the currently selected state.

- The middle button is the New Snapshot button, which creates a snapshot of the currently selected state.

- The trash button deletes the currently selected state—and all states after it. (Selecting the Allow Non-Linear History option in the History options will allow you to delete only the selected state.)

Using The History Palette

The following are some tips for using the History palette:

- You can skip back to any previous state simply by doing the following:

  - Clicking on that state in the History palette

  - Sliding the slider

  - Choosing Step Forward/Backward from the palette menu

  - Pressing Shift+Cmd+Z/Shift+Ctrl+Z to move one state forward or Option+Cmd+Z/Alt+Ctrl+Z to move back one state

- If you go back to a previous state and start to work from there, all states after that state are deleted. (However, if that was a mistake, the trusty Undo command will save you if you use it after only one operation. Also, selecting the Allow Non-Linear History option in the History options will allow you to delete only the selected state.)

- Grab the slider and glide through several states, comparing the image at those states.

- You can delete a state or a snapshot by dragging it to the trash, by clicking on its name and then the trash button, or by clicking on its name and using Delete from the palette menu.

- If you delete a state, all states after it are deleted unless you choose the Allow Non-Linear History option from the palette menu.

- To delete all the states without changing the image, choose Clear History from the palette menu. Choosing this option deletes all but the last state from the palette but leaves them in memory (allowing you to use Undo). If you want to delete the states and clear memory, hold down the Option/Alt key as you choose Clear History, or select Edit|Purge|Histories. This process cannot be undone.

➤ If you think you might want to return to a state later, make a snapshot of it. This way, you can name the state and quickly return to it. Making a snapshot is a good backup practice to follow before trying some extensive operation you might not want to keep. You can make a snapshot by clicking on the name of a state and then the New Snapshot button or by dragging a state to the button. You have several options:

   ➤ **Full Document** Creates a snapshot of all the layers

   ➤ **Merged Layers** Creates a snapshot after merging all the layers up to that state

   ➤ **Current Layer** Creates a snapshot of only the currently selected layer

➤ After you close the file, all states and snapshots are deleted. If you want to preserve some of these states, use the New Document button.

➤ If you want to close an image but not lose the snapshots, you can make individual files from the snapshots with the New Document button. Later, you can add them back to the original image's history palette by dragging the initial snapshot from their History palette to the original image's image window.

> The History palette saves 20 states by default. Although you can specify the number of states (up to 100) saved in the History palette by selecting History Options from the palette menu, this number is limited by the amount of available memory and the file size of the image.

Painting From The History Palette

You also can use the History palette to "paint" back to an earlier state. You can do so by using the History Paintbrush tool or the Eraser tool.

➤ To use the History Paintbrush tool, select the tool from the Toolbox, and select a brush size from its Options palette. Then, select a state from the History palette. You paint just as you would with any other tool, but you paint over one state with the other state.

➤ To use the Eraser tool, select the tool from the Toolbox, and select Erase To History from the tool's Options palette. Instead of erasing and filling with the background color, now you can "painting" with a previous state.

Stopping An Operation
If you've already clicked on OK and an operation is proceeding, you can stop it by holding the Escape key (or Cmd+Period on the Mac) until it stops.

Reverting
You can select File|Revert to return to the last saved version of the image file. This action deletes everything you may have done since that last save, and it cannot be undone.

Saving Files
You can choose File|Save (Cmd+S/Ctrl+S) for simple saves. (Saving and exporting files are explained in detail in Chapter 5.) To make a copy, change the name of the file, or change its format, choose File|Save As. If you are working with layers, you cannot save as anything other than a Photoshop file. (The other methods for saving and duplicating files are discussed earlier in this chapter.)

Getting The Help You Need From The Program And From Adobe
As you work in Photoshop and need assistance with operations, tools, commands and so forth, you can turn to the application for help or go online to seek information.

Online Help
Adobe has supplied a comprehensive Help file (see Figure 3.36) that you access by pulling down the Help menu or (in Windows) by pressing F1 or Shift+F1. If you use Shift+F1, the cursor turns into a question mark, and you can then click on a tool or command to jump right to that section of the Help file.

> Don't confuse Online Help and Adobe Online. Online Help is the Help file loaded into your computer that you can access as you work in Photoshop. Adobe Online is the site on the World Wide Web where you can access additional Photoshop and Adobe information.

You can access these Help options:

➤ **Tool Tips** These little boxes that tell you the names of tools, buttons, and other options pop open when you hold the mouse cursor over an appropriate area. Turn this feature on and off by choosing File|Preferences|General.

Figure 3.36 The Help window.

➤ **Help Contents (Mac) or Contents (Windows)** This option opens the Help file to the Contents tab in the Topics window (see Figure 3.37). Here, you can quickly scan the Help file's contents. In this window, you can also choose the Index and Find options. Index is like a quick topic search, and Find is a search tool.

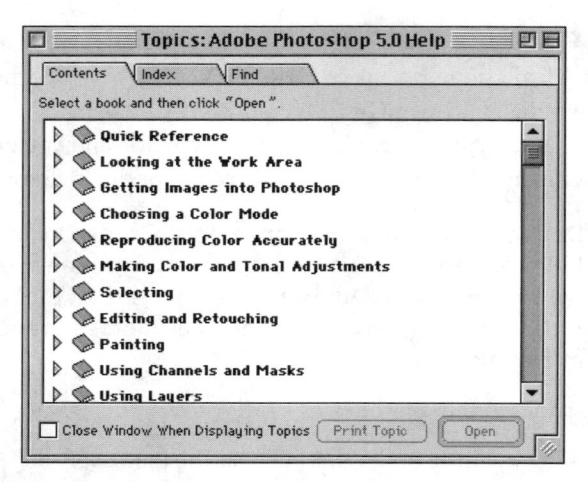

Figure 3.37 The Help File's Topics window.

➤ **Keyboard** This option opens the Quick Reference Help window. On the Mac, this window also contains navigation buttons for the entire Help file and the Keyword search dialog box.

➤ **How To Use Help** Here, you can find help for Help.

In Windows:

➤ **Search For Help On** This option opens the Help index.

On the Mac:

➤ **Balloon Help** This is the Mac operating system's balloon help and can actually be quite annoying while working in Photoshop.

Adobe Online

At Adobe Online, you can register your product, access the tech files and support databases, read the tips, check out other Adobe products, find out about upgrades, and download plug-ins.

The little Adobe Online icon at the top of the Toolbox (see Figure 3.38) first opens the Adobe Online Welcome window. From this window, you can automatically open your Web browser and connect directly to the Adobe corporate Web site. (Or, you can select File|Adobe Online.) Obviously, you must have an Internet connection and a browser. You also need enough RAM to open both your browser and Photoshop.

Here, you can click on Configure. In the resulting dialog box, you can select from several options, including how often to have Adobe Online automatically update your Adobe Online files, connection protocols, and which browser to use.

If you click on Update in the Adobe Online window, the program downloads the most recent files and reconfigures your Adobe Online file. You'll see a new Adobe Online screen from now on, as shown in Figure 3.39. It acts just like a browser window: Just click on the different links, and off you go.

Figure 3.38 The Adobe Online button.

Figure 3.39 The Adobe Online window.

Every time you click on one of the buttons in the Adobe Online window, that window closes as it sends you to the browser. So, if you want to come back and click on another button, you have to select Adobe Online again.

Practice Questions

Question 1

> If you want to select the unselected pixels of an image, which command should you use?
>
> ❍ a. Select|Image|Unselected
>
> ❍ b. Select|Pixels|Unselected
>
> ❍ c. Select|Inverse
>
> ❍ d. Image|Adjust|Invert

Answer c is correct. Use the Inverse command, under the Select menu.

Question 2

> You are working with a 16-bit-per-channel image in RGB mode. What is the keyboard shortcut to use to access the Measure tool?
>
> ❍ a. U
>
> ❍ b. M
>
> ❍ c. You can't use the Measure tool with 16-bit-per-channel images.
>
> ❍ d. Because you are in RGB, you can access tools only from the Toolbox.

Answer c is correct, because you can't use the Measure tool at all with 16-bit-per-channel images. If you had an image with anything less than 16-bits-per-channel, you would use U to access the Measure tool.

Question 3

> You are working with the Paintbrush tool, and you want to switch between two of the tool pointer options. If you use Caps Lock to switch between the tool pointer options, and one of them is the Precise tool pointer option, which other tool pointer option must you start with? (Select all that apply.)
>
> ☐ a. Standard
>
> ☐ b. Precise
>
> ☐ c. Brush Size
>
> ☐ d. Neither; the Paintbrush tool doesn't support tool pointer options.

Answers a and c are correct. You can use Caps Lock to toggle between two tool pointer options. Standard toggles to Precise. Precise toggles to Brush Size. Brush Size toggles to Precise.

Question 4

> If you have only one guide on your image, and you want to switch it from a vertical to a horizontal guide, what should you do?
>
> ○ a. Hold down Option/Alt as you drag the zero point.
>
> ○ b. Hold down Option/Alt as you drag the guide.
>
> ○ c. Hold down the Shift key as you drag.
>
> ○ d. Make sure you have turned off Snap To Grid.

Answer b is correct. Hold down Option/Alt as you drag the guide.

Question 5

> You need to save a copy of your image file, and you want to keep working in the original file. Which command should you use? (Select all that apply.)
>
> ❏ a. Image|Save A Copy
> ❏ b. Image|Duplicate
> ❏ c. View|New View
> ❏ d. Image|Save As

Trick! question

Answer b is the only correct answer. You might easily get this one wrong if you don't read it carefully. You could use Save A Copy, but because that command is actually under the File menu and not the Image menu, answer a is incorrect. Because View|New View only opens another window with the same image, answer c is incorrect. Because Save As opens a new file and closes the original, answer d is incorrect. Therefore, you should use Image|Duplicate.

Question 6

> If you are trying to drag and drop between another application and Photoshop, and the procedure isn't working, what might be the reason?
>
> ○ a. Photoshop does not support drag and drop between applications.
> ○ b. You haven't turned on Drag And Drop Capable in the General dialog box (which you open by selecting File|Preferences|General).
> ○ c. The other application is not OLE-compliant.
> ○ d. The other application is not an Adobe product.

Answer c is correct. Photoshop supports drag and drop between any other application that is OLE-compliant in Windows and that supports Macintosh Drag Manager on the Mac.

Question 7

> If you don't want Photoshop to convert a large clipboard file for export as Photoshop closes, what should you do? (Select all that apply.)
>
> ☐ a. Turn off Export Clipboard in the General dialog box (which you open by selecting File|Preferences|General).
>
> ☐ b. Turn off Export Clipboard in the Clipboard Options palette.
>
> ☐ c. Select File|Purge|Clipboard.
>
> ☐ d. Hold down the Escape key as you Quit or Exit.

The only correct answer is a. Be careful here. Read these answers closely. Again, you must be careful about which commands are associated with which menus. Because you should turn off Export Clipboard in the Preferences, a is correct. You also might be tempted to select two answers for this question, but only one is correct. Sure, you can purge the clipboard, but you don't do it under the File menu; you do it under the Edit menu.

Question 8

> How can you return to a previous state of an image file? (Select all that apply.)
>
> ☐ a. Click on a state in the History palette.
>
> ☐ b. Choose Step Backward from the History palette menu.
>
> ☐ c. Open a document you created with the New Document button on the History palette.
>
> ☐ d. Select File|Revert.
>
> ☐ e. Select the Eraser tool and Erase to History in its options palette; then select a state from the History palette, and erase the entire image.

All of these answers are correct.

Question 9

> What is Pixel Doubling?
>
> ○ a. Photoshop performs this process on a vector graphic when it rasterizes the graphic on import.
>
> ○ b. It is an option that speeds preview.
>
> ○ c. Photoshop performs this process on an image when the Canvas Size command is used.
>
> ○ d. Selecting twice as many pixels as normal.

Answer b is correct. Pixel Doubling is an option for the Move tool that halves the resolution of dragged selections, speeding preview.

Question 10

> If you are using the Measure tool, what does D2: signify in the Info palette?
>
> ○ a. It shows that you are pixel doubling.
>
> ○ b. It is the distance from the first point to the second point.
>
> ○ c. It is the angle between the first line and the second line.
>
> ○ d. It is the length of the second line you drew using the protractor feature.

Answer d is correct. When you use the protractor feature, the Info palette changes to show the angle between the two lines (A), the distance of the first line (D1:), and the distance of the second line (D2:).

Need To Know More?

McClelland, Deke: *Photoshop 5 for Macs for Dummies*. IDG Books Worldwide, Inc. ISBN 0-7645-0391-X.

McClelland, Deke: *Macworld Photoshop 5 Bible*. IDG Books Worldwide, Inc. ISBN 0-7645-3231-6.

Working With And Understanding Photoshop's Color

4

Terms and concepts you'll need to understand:

- √ Color modes
- √ Color models
- √ Color space
- √ Gamut
- √ Color channels
- √ ICC profile
- √ CLUT
- √ Dither
- √ Calibration
- √ Gamma
- √ Transfer functions
- √ Color separation
- √ Dot gain

Techniques you'll need to master:

- √ Converting image bit depth
- √ Converting image modes
- √ Selecting colors
- √ Using Color Samplers
- √ Calibrating monitors
- √ Installing ICC profiles
- √ Setting separation options
- √ Selecting colors with the different Color Pickers
- √ Converting color spaces of open images

You must understand Photoshop's color system to use Photoshop effectively and to succeed with this exam. For example, you need to know basic color theory and the difference between color models, color modes, color channels, gamuts, and file formats. You should know how to calibrate your system to display an image representation that is as close as possible to your final output. You should also know what models and modes work with which Photoshop features and file formats.

Understanding The Different Color Modes And Models

> A color model is a method of describing color objectively so that it can be generally reproduced on a monitor or on paper. A Photoshop color mode is a numeric system used by the application for reproducing a specific color model. You don't have to use the color model with the same name as the color mode you are using (in fact, no HSB mode even exists). For example, when you open an image in RGB mode, you can still use the CMYK model to define colors.

Color Models

Color models are the different ways that we describe colors.

HSB Model

The HSB model is the model that is closest to the way you see and describe colors. If you see an apple, you might say that it looks "bright red." In this case, you're using a subjective description, but it can be objectively, numerically translated to color using the HSB (Hue, Saturation, Brightness) model, where pure colors are spread around a flat circle of color—the color wheel. This wheel has the visible spectrum of colors spread around its edges to encompass 360 degrees—like a round rainbow. At the center of the wheel, you just see white. As you move out from the center, the colors begin to "have more color," or saturation. Brightness could be represented if this color wheel was then rendered in three dimensions—into a cylinder, where colors with no light would be at the base of the cylinder (0) and colors with a lot of light would be at the top surface of the cylinder (100).

You can then use the HSB model to describe the color using the following three components:

➤ **Hue** Describes the pure color, such as red, green, or blue, that is the base of the color. The value of Hue is denoted with a degree (°) symbol because it describes the location of the color around the 360-degree wheel.

➤ **Saturation** Describes how pure or undiluted the color is. If it is just barely red, for example, it has a low saturation. If it is solid red, it is highly saturated. The Saturation value is a percentage, from 0 to 100%, representing how far out the color is from the center (0%) of the wheel.

➤ **Brightness** Describes how light a color is—like a *bright* red apple. This value is also represented as a percentage (of white). Therefore, if a color has no brightness (0%), it is black.

Example: Bright pink would have a Hue of 0° (it is in the Red portion of the wheel), a Saturation of maybe 50% (not fully red—that's what makes it pink), and a Brightness of 100% (very light, or bright).

RGB Model

RGB is the color model that is universal to color computer monitors and television screens. As the three additive primary colors are "shined" together in various brightness combinations, they add their colors together to create other colors.

The RGB colors are "additive," resulting in white when mixed together equally at full strength. When two additive colors mix, they create one of the subtractive primary colors, either cyan, magenta, or yellow.

In Figure 4.1, you can see the color combinations that are created by the mixture—or addition—of colors.

CMYK Model

CMYK is the color model used by commercial printers to create colors with ink on paper. C is for cyan, M is for magenta, Y is for yellow, and K is for black. Four colors are used, rather than just the three complementary colors, because when they are mixed together equally at full strength, they create a muddy brown rather than black. So, a black ink is added. This process is referred to as *four-color process printing*.

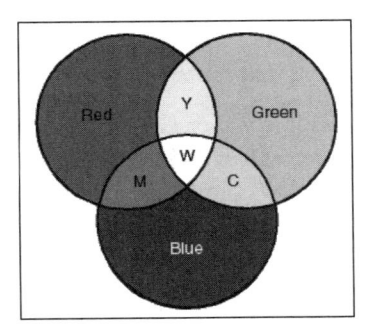

Figure 4.1 The additive colors.

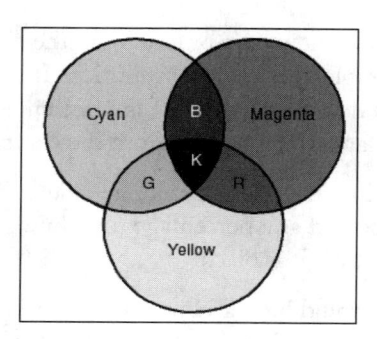

Figure 4.2 The subtractive colors.

Cyan, magenta, and yellow are the subtractive primary colors and absorb color rather than add it. Theoretically, when two subtractive primaries are added, they create one additive primary color, either red, green, or blue.

As you can see in Figure 4.2, the subtractive colors mix to create the additive colors and, theoretically, create black when added together equally at full strength.

> Here's a tip for remembering the difference between additive and subtractive colors: Think of adding light and subtracting light. If you add light, things get lighter—or whiter. If you subtract light, things get darker—or blacker. So, the three additive colors add light to create white, and the subtractive colors subtract light to create black.
>
> Then, if you have trouble remembering which of the two models creates white—constituting the additive colors—and which creates black—constituting the subtractive colors—just remember that in the two models, black is with the colors that create it. Therefore, CMYK is the subtractive color model.

L*a*b Model

The CIE L*a*b color model is an international standard for creating consistent color across all device platforms that contains every color visible to the human eye.

L*a*b color is defined by its luminance (L) value—think of this as its brightness—and two color values: *a*, which defines its green to red color component, and *b*, which is its blue to yellow color component.

Color Modes

Color modes are methods of using color models to manage how the computer represents color.

RGB Mode

On the computer, each individual pixel comprising the monitor's screen display is assigned a color value. An RGB value is described as a number from 0 to 255 (256 colors). When all three color values are zero, the result is black. When all three color values are 255, the result is white. Medium gray would be values of 127.

> RGB mode images are 24-bit images: They have 8 bits of information for each of the three color channels, for a total of 24 bits and 16.7 million possible on-screen colors.

> RGB mode images can be 16-bit-per-channel images, also. They would be 48-bit images because they would have 16 bits in each of the three channels (16+16+16=48). Limited editing is available with 16-bit-per-channel images.

> Because computer monitors always use the RGB color model and mode to display images, editing in RGB mode is preferable—even if you will eventually convert your image to CMYK for output. Probably for this same reason, the default mode for images created in Photoshop is RGB.

> While in RGB mode, you can preview what your image will look like in CMYK by choosing View|Preview and selecting one of the options. You can also use the Color Sampler tool to check the color values of your image if it is in CMYK.

CMYK Mode

Remember that your computer monitor uses a three-color model and that CMYK is a four-color model. Consequently, for this mode, Photoshop must jump through some serious digital hoops to get the color converted as an image file and then again back to RGB for display. As a result, you will find editing in CMYK slow. This mode is best for working with images that have been imported from high-end scanners as CMYK images. Otherwise, try to convert images to CMYK as a last step, only after you have completed your editing.

The four color values are entered as percentages of 100, with less ink providing less color.

Because ink-on-paper color printing presses are the only four-color output devices, CMYK images are practical only for printing to separations for color printing presses. For example, if you were to work in RGB, convert to CMYK, and then print to a laser printer, Photoshop would have to convert the file twice for output.

> CMYK mode images are 32-bit images: They have 8 bits of information for each of their four color channels, for a total of 32 bits.

> CMYK mode images can be 16-bit-per-channel images, also. They would be 64-bit images because they would have 16 bits in each of the four channels (16+16+16+16=64). Limited editing is available with 16-bit-per-channel images.

Lab Mode

Often used by professionals because of its color range, the Lab mode is as fast as RGB for editing. You can print Lab mode images to PostScript Level 2 and 3 printers. Lab mode is also recommended for editing Kodak Photo CD images.

> Because the L*a*b model separates color values from their luminance value, the Lab mode can be useful for adjusting colors without affecting their brightness.

The luminance, or lightness, component value is entered as a number from 0 to 100. The color components *a* and *b* can be entered as values from +120 to -120.

> Some professionals figure that working in Lab mode makes sense because it is Photoshop's internal color mode. In fact, if you convert an image from RGB to CMYK, Photoshop actually converts the image to Lab mode before converting it to CMYK.

> Lab mode images are 24-bit images: They have 8 bits of information for each of their three color channels, for a total of 24 bits.

Bitmap Mode

Bitmap mode images are made up of only two colors: black and white. Bitmap is best used for high-contrast images (see Figure 4.3) or line art. If you want to edit a Bitmap mode image extensively, you should convert it to grayscale first. (Grayscale is the only mode available when you're converting bitmap images.)

> Bitmap mode images are 1-bit images: They have only 1 bit of information for one color channel, for a total of 1 bit.

Working With And Understanding Photoshop's Color 85

Figure 4.3 A bitmap image.

> Only limited editing tools are available in Bitmap mode. Bitmap mode does not support the following:
>
> - Magic Wand tool
> - Blur tool
> - Sharpen tool
> - Smudge tool
> - Burn tool
> - Dodge tool
> - Sponge tool
> - Gradient tool
> - Paint Bucket tool
> - Quick Mask
> - Layers
> - Filters
> - Channels

Grayscale Mode

Although Grayscale mode is similar to RGB mode, it uses only shades of black (gray) rather than colors. You can convert both Bitmap mode images and color images to grayscale, and you can convert grayscale images to color modes.

Gray values are defined like RGB color values: 0 (black) to 255 (white).

All editing features are available in Grayscale mode.

> Grayscale mode images are 8-bit images: They have 8 bits of information for one color channel, for a total of 8 bits.
>
> Grayscale mode images can be 16-bit-per-channel images, also. They would be 16-bit images because they would have 16 bits for their one channel (16=16). Limited editing is available with 16-bit-per-channel images.

Duotone Mode

Using Duotone mode, you can create special "colorized" images. You can create monotone, duotone, tritone, and quadtone images.

Duotone mode images can be saved only as Photoshop (PSD), Photoshop EPS, DCS 2.0 (after conversion to multichannel mode), and PICT files.

Indexed Color Mode

Because the Indexed Color mode is effective for reducing file sizes, it is used primarily for multimedia and Web images. Photoshop allows you to set the bit depth from 3-bits-per-pixel to 8-bits-per-pixel for a maximum of 256 colors.

When converting to Indexed Color, Photoshop analyzes the colors in the image and—if necessary—discards colors to get in under the 256-color limit. This conversion can result in a loss of display quality in images with extensive colors.

A *color lookup table* (CLUT), which serves as the index of colors available to display the image, is generated.

> Indexed Color images are single-channel images that can have up to 8 bits per pixel, for a maximum of 256 colors.

> Indexed Color also offers limited editing capability. Consequently, you should convert image files to Indexed Color only after you have completed editing.

The following features are not supported:

- History Paintbrush tool
- Blur tool
- Sharpen tool
- Smudge tool
- Burn tool
- Dodge tool
- Sponge tool
- Gradient tool
- Layers
- Filters

You can save Indexed Color images only as these file types:

- Photoshop (PSD)
- BMP
- EPS
- GIF
- PCX
- PDF
- PICT
- PNG
- TIFF

Multichannel Mode

In Multichannel mode, the color channels contain independent color information. These channels are essentially spot color channels, made up of grayscale channels of 256 colors. Unlike the colors in RGB or CMYK channels, the colors in these channels can be edited without affecting the other channels. As a result, multichannel mode is excellent for creating duotones and duotone effects.

You can convert grayscale, duotone, RGB, and CMYK images into Multichannel mode images, and/or you can create new Multichannel mode images.

If you delete a channel from either an RGB, CMYK, or Lab image, it is automatically converted to Multichannel mode.

You can save, export, or print Multichannel mode images only as Photoshop (PSD) or DCS 2.0 files. You cannot directly print a Multichannel mode image as a color composite.

> Multichannel images are 8-bit-per-pixel images.

Color Gamuts

A *gamut* is the total range of colors available in or on any color reproduction system. The human eye has the widest gamut, and in this Photoshop environment, L*a*b has the widest gamut, RGB is narrower, and CMYK has the most narrow gamut. So, you can see and edit some colors in Lab mode or RGB mode that you would not be able to print in CMYK.

In Photoshop, a color that cannot be reproduced by the CMYK printing process is said to be out-of-gamut.

If you convert an image to CMYK, Photoshop automatically changes all out-of-gamut colors to colors that fall within the CMYK gamut. In so doing, it may change the colors in ways you don't want, so you can check for out-of-gamut colors before you convert the file and change them.

You can check for out-of-gamut colors in several ways:

➤ **Gamut Warning** The Gamut Warning command highlights all out-of-gamut colors in an image. Turn it on by choosing View|Gamut Warning. You can change the highlight color in the Transparency & Gamut dialog box, which you open by choosing File|Preferences|Transparency & Gamut.

- **Info palette** You can set one of the color value boxes to be CMYK and then place the Eyedropper tool over a spot on the image. Out-of-gamut colors are identified by an exclamation point.

  To use a Color Sampler and the Info palette, place a Color Sampler in the image, and change the color model in the associated Info palette box to CMYK.

- **Color Picker** An alert triangle appears next to the color swatches in the upper-right corner. The small color swatch beneath it is the closest color within the gamut. If you want this color, click on the alert triangle or the little color swatch.

- **Color palette** The alert triangle and the in-gamut color sample appear beneath the foreground/background color boxes. As you do with the Color Picker, just click on the triangle or the color sample to accept that color.

> *Color space* is a term applied to the range of colors (or gamut) that a specific device can display or print. So, color space is sometimes used to mean gamut. Color space is separate from color model or color mode. For example, your monitor may have one color space (RGB), but you could still be working in a different Photoshop color mode (Lab), while selecting colors using a different color model (CMYK).

Color Channels

Color channels are the separations that Photoshop makes of the individual primary colors in an image. If you are in RGB mode, Photoshop will create three color channels: one each for red, green, and blue. In CMYK, one channel each is available for cyan, magenta, yellow, and black. In both of these modes (and Lab mode), a composite display channel is also included in the Channels palette. No composite channel is available in Bitmap, Grayscale, Duotone, or Multichannel mode. (Using channels is discussed in detail in Chapter 10.)

> Photoshop images can have up to 24 channels.

Selections in an image can be saved as *alpha channels*, which are additional channels that are used to create masks and spot color channels.

Monitors And Color

Just as the bit depth of images affects the amount of color in an image, the video display bit depth of a computer/monitor system affects how much color information is used to present an image on screen. Monitor bit depth, then, can affect how you edit an image and could affect your choice of file formats—especially if you are producing images primarily for screen display. You don't need to save an image as a 24-bit RGB file (16.7 million colors) if it is only going to be displayed on an 8-bit monitor that supports only up to 256 colors.

If a file contains more bits-per-pixel than a monitor can display, Photoshop resorts to *dithering* the image for display. Dithering is a technique of applying an approximate gradation from one color to another.

> Don't confuse the display dithering with the dithering that Photoshop does when converting to Bitmap mode and Indexed Color images. This dithering affects only how images with more than 8-bits-per-pixel—no matter what their file format or mode—are displayed on 8-bit monitors and has no effect on the saved data of the file.

Photoshop has two display dithering options that you access or change by choosing File|Preferences|Display & Cursors:

- **Pattern Dithering** This option is the Photoshop default and can result in some pretty ugly, distinct banding of colors.

- **Diffusion Dithering** This option gives a more even-looking transition from color to color.

If you are working on 8-bit monitors, another display option to be aware of is Use System Palette, also in the Display & Cursors dialog box. This option affects the specific colors available to Photoshop for displaying an image. By default, this option is turned off. When turned on, it restricts Photoshop to the system palette (the palette provided by the operating system) for displaying an image. Using this palette may help speed some redraws and may prevent some screen fluctuations, but it may not be a good palette for a particular image.

Converting Images

Converting images from one mode to another may be as easy as pulling down a menu and selecting a mode, but you have some important considerations before undertaking conversion. In many cases, data will be lost or altered, limited editing may be available, and/or color values may be adversely affected. (Converting images to CMYK for printing is discussed in detail in Chapter 12.)

To change image modes, choose Image|Mode and select the mode you want.

> **STUDY ALERT:** If you convert between these modes, Photoshop will flatten the file (a dialog box will ask for your approval, and you must approve or the conversion will not proceed). Here are the available selections:
>
> - RGB to Indexed Color
> - RGB to Multichannel
> - CMYK to Multichannel
> - Lab to Multichannel
> - Lab to Bitmap
> - Lab to Grayscale
> - Grayscale to Bitmap
> - Grayscale to Indexed Color
> - Grayscale to Multichannel
> - Duotone to Bitmap
> - Duotone to Indexed Color
> - Duotone to Multichannel

Between Bit Depths

Keep in mind that 16-bit-per-channel images contain much more pixel data, so their potential color reproduction is much higher than 8-bit-per-channel images. However, the 16-bit-per-channel file sizes are much larger, and Photoshop supports limited editing with 16-bit-per-channel images, so you have to consider the trade-offs.

You can convert 8-bit-per-channel images to 16-bit-per-channel images by first flattening the image and then choosing Image|Mode|16 Bits/Channel. You can convert 16-bit-per-channel images to 8-bit-per-channel images by simply choosing Image|Mode|8 Bits/Channel.

> **STUDY ALERT:** Remember that when working with 16-bit-per-channel images, you can use only the following tools:
>
> - Marquee
> - Lasso
> - Crop
> - Measure
> - Zoom
> - Hand
> - Pen
> - Eyedropper
> - Color Sampler
> - Rubber Stamp

You also can use only the following commands:

- Duplicate
- Feather
- Modify
- Levels
- Auto Levels
- Curves
- Hue/Saturation
- Brightness/Contrast
- Color Balance
- Equalize
- Invert
- Channel Mixer
- Image Size
- Transform Selection
- Rotate Canvas

Between Modes

The most important point to remember about converting images between modes is that the changes to the color values are permanent. This consideration can be important if you are converting RGB files to CMYK and have many out-of-gamut colors. Those colors' values are altered by Photoshop, and if you need to convert back to RGB for more editing, you cannot recover those original color values. Also, blending modes affect colors on conversion, so you should flatten images before conversion.

Follow these basic guidelines when you convert images from one mode to another:

- Perform most of your editing work in the image's original mode.
- Convert a copy of the image rather than the original.
- Flatten the file before conversion.
- Convert only once to preserve image quality.

Grayscale To Bitmap

Before you convert any image to Bitmap mode, you must first convert it to grayscale. (Remember that limited editing is available in Bitmap mode, so complete your editing in the original mode or in grayscale before converting to Bitmap.)

To convert from grayscale to bitmap, select Image|Mode|Bitmap. You are first asked to approve the discard of all color data. Then, the Bitmap dialog box opens, in which you enter a resolution value for final output and select a conversion method.

For a conversion method, select from one of the following options:

- **50% Threshold** Creates a high-contrast conversion that splits the grays at 50 percent and turns all those below 50 percent to white and all those above to black. Figure 4.3 on page 85 was converted with this method.
- **Pattern Dither** Creates a strange-looking conversion to geometric patterns of black-and-white dots, as shown in Figure 4.4.
- **Diffusion Dither** Creates an image that looks like highly enlarged film, with a grainy texture, as shown in Figure 4.5.
- **Halftone screen** Creates a simulated screened image (which may produce moiré patterns when printed). If you select this method, another dialog box opens with these options:
  - **Frequency** A measurement unit and a value from 1 to 999 that will imitate a halftone line screen's density.
  - **Angle** The angle of the lines on the image.
  - **Shape** The shape of the dots. Choose from Round, Diamond, Ellipse, Line, Square, and Cross.
- **Custom Pattern** Create a pattern of your own, and apply it to the image as a screen. To use this method, you must first define a pattern.

Figure 4.4 A Pattern dither.

Figure 4.5 A Diffusion dither.

Indexed Color

Indexed Color is probably most widely used for reducing the file sizes of images destined for the Web or multimedia presentations. This mode reduces the total number of colors in an image to a maximum of 256 (8-bit). Limited editing is available for Indexed Color images. You can specify the color palette you want for the image, or you can create a custom palette of colors you want in the file's color lookup table (CLUT).

Convert an RGB image to Indexed Color by choosing Image|Mode|Indexed Color. If the image has layers, you are prompted to flatten them. You then need to select a color palette and specify the bit depth and the dithering method.

> Indexed Color is not a conversion option from Bitmap, CMYK, or Multichannel modes.

Select from these palette choices:

- **Exact** This palette is available only if the image contains 256 or fewer colors, like an image containing mostly shades of one color range. If the image does have 256 or fewer colors, this choice comes up as the default.

- **System (Windows)** This palette uses the default 8-bit palette of the Windows system. (Selecting this palette can be risky for multiple-platform presentations.)

- **System (Mac)** This palette uses the default 8-bit palette of the Mac operating system. (Selecting this palette can be risky for multiple-platform presentations.)

- **Web** This palette was created specially for use with the common graphical Web browsers and actually contains only 216 colors. Even though this palette is supposedly best for Web images, it often results in a loss of image quality on higher-resolution displays.

- **Uniform** Photoshop creates a color palette based on uniform values from the spectrum.

- **Adaptive** This choice is the best for most images because of the sensible way it works. It samples the colors in the image and creates a CLUT based on the most common colors in the image. For example, if you are converting a picture of an apple, the adaptive palette for it is likely almost all red colors. For that reason, this palette may result in the best gradations between the dominant colors in the image.

  You can also select an area of the image before conversion, and Photoshop will favor those colors when building the CLUT.

- **Custom** Selecting this option opens the Color Table dialog box, with an adaptive palette loaded. You can then edit this table, save it for another image, select a predefined table from the Table menu, or load a saved table from another image.

The predefined color tables are as follows:

- **Custom** This table allows you to create your own color table.

- **Black Body** This table provides a palette of colors created when a "blackbody radiator" is heated. It looks mostly like the colors of fire.

- **Grayscale** This table provides 256 grayscale levels.

- **Spectrum** This table is based on the visible spectrum.

- **Windows System**

- **Macintosh System**

- **Previous** This option allows you to use whatever palette you used for the most recent conversion.

Next, specify a color depth (bit depth). At this point, you can experiment to really reduce file sizes. You can select from the menu options of 3, 4, 5, 6, 7, or 8 bits per pixel or you can specify a number of colors (using Other).

Finally, you have the option to dither or not and which method of dithering to use:

➤ **None** Without dithering, the transitions between colors may be drastic.

➤ **Diffusion** This option provides the smoothest-looking transitions between colors.

➤ **Pattern** This option is available only if you've used the Web, Mac, or Uniform palettes. It creates a dithering resembling that strange-looking geometric pattern (refer to Figure 4.4).

You also can choose from these color-matching options:

➤ **Best** Photoshop takes the time to find the best possible match for each pixel. (This option is not available with Pattern dithering.)

➤ **Faster** With this option selected, Photoshop takes less time to decide on color matches, so it is not as reliable. (It is not available with Pattern dithering.)

➤ **Preserve Exact Colors** This method (available only with Diffusion) preserves areas of solid color. It can be good for text and fine lines.

You can edit the color table of an Indexed Color image any time by choosing Image|Mode|Color Table.

Selecting And Monitoring Colors

Photoshop offers several different methods of selecting and changing colors. You can choose from the different color models and from the different Color Pickers and palettes.

Foreground/Background Colors

The selected foreground and background colors are displayed in the color selection area of the Toolbox (see Figure 4.6) The top color is the foreground color, and the bottom color is the background color. By default, the foreground color is black, and the background color is white.

> While an alpha channel is active, the default colors are white for the foreground and black for the background.

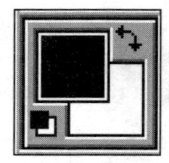

Figure 4.6 The color selection area of the Toolbox.

The selection of the foreground and background colors is important because many of the tools and commands fill or paint with one or the other.

- To select a new foreground or background color with the Color Picker, click on the color's square in the Toolbox, or click on the active color's square in the Color palette to open the Color Picker.

- To select a new foreground or background color with the sliders, value boxes, or the color bar in the Color palette, activate the color's square in the Color palette by clicking on it. (If it is already active, this step opens the Color Picker.)

- To reverse the existing foreground and background colors, press X or click on the bent arrow icon (the Switch Colors icon) in the color selection area of the Toolbox.

- To reset the foreground/background colors to their defaults (black/white), press D or click on the miniature foreground/background color icon (the Default Colors icon).

Photoshop uses the foreground color to do the following:

- Paint

- Fill: with the Option+Delete (Mac)/Alt+Delete (Windows) keys

- Fill: when selected in the Fill dialog box opened by choosing Edit|Fill

- Make gradient fills

- Stroke

Photoshop uses the background color to do the following:

- Fill: with the Delete (Mac)/Backspace (Windows) key

- Fill: when selected in the Fill dialog box opened by choosing Edit|Fill

- Fill: with the Edit|Clear command

Working With And Understanding Photoshop's Color   97

> Fill: with the Eraser tool
> Fill: new canvas areas created by the Canvas Size command
> Make gradient fills

Using The Color Picker

The Color Picker, shown in Figure 4.7, allows you to select and edit colors by the following methods:

> Clicking on a color in the color field
> Dragging the color selection marker around in the color field
> Clicking on a color in the color bar
> Sliding through the color range on the color bar
> Entering numerical values for one of the four color models (HSB, RGB, L*a*b, CMYK)

Access the Color Picker by clicking on either the foreground or the background color selection box in the Toolbox or by clicking on the active color box in the Color palette.

STUDY ALERT: You can use the Color Pickers for the Mac or Windows operating systems by selecting the respective picker in the General dialog box, which you open by choosing File|Preferences|General. By default, the Photoshop Color Picker is selected.

The large square color field in the Color Picker represents the brightness and saturation of a pure color. The pure colors are represented in the color bar.

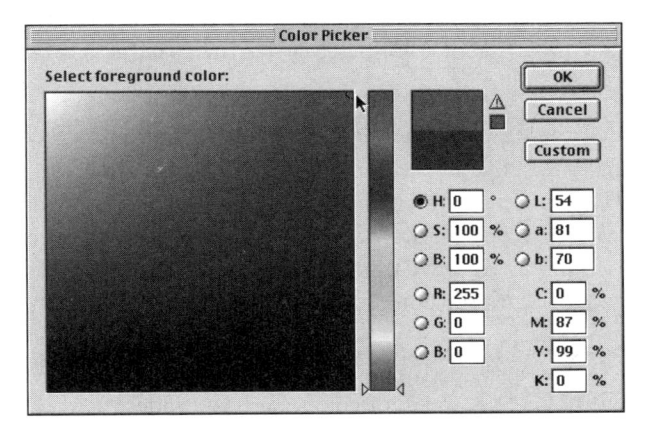

Figure 4.7   The Color Picker.

The radio buttons beside the HSB, RGB, and L*a*b letters allow you to change the displays for the color bar and the color field. Clicking on one of them changes the color bar to the field to display the range of colors available for that particular component. Then, the color display shows the other two components. For example, if you click on the R: radio button, you see the available range of red colors displayed in the color bar. The color display then shows the other colors (green and blue) on one axis or the other. Or, clicking on the H: radio button displays all the possible hues in the color bar and their possible saturation (S:) and brightness (B:) as the axes of the color display.

You must enter the values appropriate to the specific color model you choose:

➤ **HSB** Hue (H:) is entered as the degrees (°) around the color wheel, whereas saturation (S:) and brightness (B:) are entered as percentages.

➤ **RGB** Each of these values is entered in the range of 0 to 255 (256 colors).

➤ **L*a*b** Lightness (L:) is entered in the range of 0 (dark) to 100 (light); green to magenta (a:) and blue to yellow (b:) are entered as values from -128 (green/blue) to +127 (magenta/yellow).

➤ **CMYK** Each of these values is entered as a percentage.

The alert triangle next to the before and after color samples in the Color Picker signifies that the new color is out-of-gamut and is not printable using the four process colors (CMYK). The small color sample beneath the alert triangle is Photoshop's suggestion for the closest printable color. If you approve of this color, click on the alert triangle or the color sample, and that color is selected.

The Custom button in the Color Picker opens the Custom Colors dialog box and toggles between Custom and Picker when you are in the Color Picker and the Custom Colors dialog box, respectively. In the Custom Colors dialog box, you can select from different color palettes that are specific to several commercial color systems.

To select one of the supplied color systems, pull down the Book option menu. If you have a printed copy of the book you're using, you can select a color from that book by typing the number. (If you don't see an entry box for this number, all you have to do is type it.) Alternatively, you can browse the book's colors by sliding the triangles up or down or by clicking on the up or down arrow on the color bar. Then, click on the color sample you want.

The following custom color systems are supported by Photoshop:

➤ **PANTONE** CMYK specs for colors from the widely used PANTONE system of color specs for printing inks. The system includes the following:

➤ PANTONE Coated

- ► PANTONE Uncoated
- ► PANTONE Process
- ► PANTONE ProSim custom colors
- ► **TRUMATCH** CMYK specs for colors that are computer-generated and then printed.
- ► **FOCOLTONE** English system of 763 CMYK colors.
- ► **TOYO Color Finder 1050** Colors from the most widely used printing inks in Japan.
- ► **ANPA-COLOR** A system of 33 process colors and 5 spot colors most commonly used by newspaper printers. This system was created by the Newspaper Association of America (when it was the American Newspaper Publishers Association).
- ► **DIC Color Guide** More colors from printing inks used in Japan.

Using The Color Palette

You can use several methods in the Color palette (see Figure 4.8) to change the foreground and background colors. For each, you should first select the color model you want to use from the palette menu and make sure that either the foreground color or background color is active (denoted by the border around its color box).

Hide or show the Color palette by choosing Window|Show Color. Select the Color palette from an open palette group by clicking on its tab.

To change the foreground or background color from the Color palette, you can do the following:

- ► Drag the color sliders one way or the other.
- ► Enter a color value in the box next to the sliders.
- ► Click on the active color's icon to activate the Color Picker.

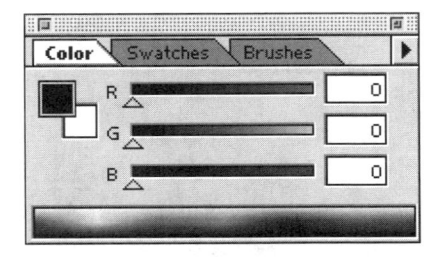

Figure 4.8 The Color palette.

➤ Click on a color in the color bar at the bottom of the palette to select a color.

To change the available selection of colors in the Color palette's color bar, select Color Bar from the palette menu, and select one of the listed options (Current Colors displays the range of colors represented by the current foreground and background color selections). Cycle through these options by Shift+clicking.

You see the colors under the sliders change as you drag the sliders. This setting is the default, but if it seems to degrade performance, turn off Dynamic Color Sliders under File|Preferences|General.

If a selected color is out of gamut, a warning triangle appears in the lower-left part of the Color palette, next to a swatch of the nearest color within the gamut. If you approve of that color, click on the swatch to transfer its values to the active color. You can edit this color after it is selected.

Swatches Palette

The Swatches palette (see Figure 4.9) shows a selection of colors (little swatches) you can quickly choose as the foreground or background color. You can replace the default set of colors completely or just replace a few colors. You can also create a completely new set of colors, load a swatch from another image file, or save a swatch to load into another image file.

Hide or show the Swatches palette by choosing Window|Show Swatches. Select the Swatches palette from an open palette group by clicking on its tab.

To use the Swatches palette, do the following:

➤ To choose a foreground color from a swatch, simply click on a color.

➤ To select a background color, press Option/Alt and click on a color.

➤ To change an existing color in the Swatches palette, select a color in the foreground color box. Then, hold down the Shift key, and position the cursor over the swatch you want to change. The cursor changes to the

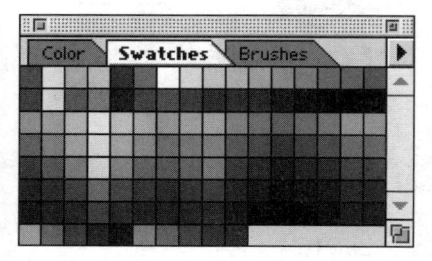

Figure 4.9 The Swatches palette.

Paint Bucket tool and fills that swatch with the color from the foreground color box.

➤ To add a color to the Swatches palette, select a color in the foreground color box. Then, click on an empty swatch at the bottom of the palette. The cursor changes to the Paint Bucket tool and fills that swatch with the color from the foreground color box.

➤ To insert a swatch next to an existing one, click on a swatch while holding Shift+Option/Shift+Alt.

➤ If no empty swatches appear at the bottom of the palette, simply insert a new swatch anywhere in the Swatch palette, and you'll add a whole new row of empties. To insert a swatch, click on a swatch while holding Shift+Option/Shift+Alt.

➤ Delete swatches by holding down Cmd/Ctrl and clicking on the swatch. The cursor changes to the scissors icon.

The palette menu options for the Swatches palette are as follows:

➤ **Reset Swatches** Choosing this option opens a dialog box that allows you either to replace the current swatch set with the default set or to append the default set to the current set.

➤ **Load Swatches** This option allows you to add to the current set of swatches a previously saved set of swatches.

➤ **Replace Swatches** This option allows you to replace the current set of swatches with a previously saved set of swatches.

➤ **Save Swatches** This option allows you to name and save the current set of swatches.

The Eyedropper Tool

You can select colors from within an image by using the Eyedropper tool (see Figure 4.10).

➤ When you click the Eyedropper tool on an image, the color underneath is automatically selected as either the foreground or background color.

➤ To select a color as the foreground color, just click with the Eyedropper tool.

Figure 4.10 The Eyedropper tool icon.

- ➤ To select a color as the background color, hold down Option/Alt and click with the Eyedropper tool.

- ➤ You can click on an image in a background window with the Eyedropper tool without changing it to the active window.

- ➤ When you drag with the Eyedropper tool, you see the foreground or background color changing as the colors under the tool change.

- ➤ You can activate the Info palette to see the color values under the Eyedropper tool.

- ➤ You can temporarily activate the Eyedropper tool while using any painting tool by holding down Option/Alt.

To change the size of the sampling area of the Eyedropper tool, first activate the tool's Options palette by double-clicking on the tool's icon in the Toolbox or by clicking on the Options palette tab. Then, select from these options:

- ➤ **Point Sample** Samples only one pixel at a time

- ➤ **3 by 3 Average** Samples a 3×3-pixel square and averages the color values

- ➤ **5 by 5 Average** Samples a 5×5-pixel square and averages the color values

The New Color Samplers

Photoshop's new Color Samplers (see Figure 4.11) provide a means of sampling the color of pixels in four areas of an image. These samplers don't print, but they are saved with the image. They can be moved and their sample area adjusted. The Color Samplers act like fixed Eyedropper tools. You place them where you want, and there they stay until you delete or move them.

You can access Color Samplers in one of these three methods:

- ➤ Hold down the Eyedropper tool icon in the Toolbox to open the Eyedropper tool's hidden tools menu. Slide over to the Color Sampler icon (the rightmost icon on the hidden menu) and let go.

- ➤ Press Shift+I while in the Eyedropper tool.

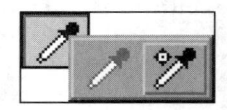

Figure 4.11 The Color Samplers are hidden tools, under the Eyedropper tool.

Working With And Understanding Photoshop's Color

➤ To use the Color Sampler icon temporarily, hold down the Shift key while clicking on the Eyedropper tool. (This technique works any time the Eyedropper tool is active—for most other dialog boxes or palettes.)

Clicking on an image with the Color Sampler icon places a numbered "target" icon on the image (see Figure 4.12). Subsequent clicks create additional samplers. The color values under the samplers are displayed by number in new, numbered boxes in the Info palette (see Figure 4.13).

You can adjust the area sampled by the Color Samplers (just like the Eyedropper tool) by selecting one of the sample sizes in the tool's Options palette. This selection is then applied to all placed samples and can be changed as often as you wish.

Figure 4.12 The Color Sampler icon and Color Samplers on an image.

Figure 4.13 The Info palette displays the color values under the samplers.

To preview in different color spaces the color values under samplers, change a sampler's color space by pulling down the menu accessed on the eyedropper icon in that sampler's value box in the Info palette. The Info palette expands to include all four possible sampler value boxes. In Figure 4.13, notice the out-of-gamut colors under sampler #2, signified by the exclamation points following the color values.

If the Info palette becomes too large while the sample values are displayed, you can hide the additional value boxes by selecting Hide/Show Color Samplers from the Info palette menu.

If you need one more sample, just use the cursor for a temporary fifth sample. To move a Color Sampler, you can do either of the following:

➤ Select the Color Sampler icon and drag the placed Color Sampler to the place where you want it.

➤ Hold down Shift while dragging with the Eyedropper tool.

Delete Color Samplers by first selecting the Color Sampler tool and then use one of the following procedures:

➤ Drag the sampler out of the image window.

➤ Option+click/Alt+click on the sampler.

Accurately Reproducing Colors From The Monitor Display To Output

You hope to better ensure accurate color reproduction by calibrating your system. This process involves setting your monitor, Photoshop's color conversion settings, and your output devices so that when you work on a color on your screen, you actually get that color when you output your image.

> Adobe emphasizes that calibration is the most important step in reproducing the colors you have worked on in your computer system and expect to see in the final output. This calibration step starts with calibration of the monitor.

The possible "workflow" or process of calibration and the associated Photoshop utilities include the following:

1. Calibrating the monitor (gamma)
2. Setting the RGB color space information (RGB Setup)
3. (For CMYK output) setting the CMYK output information (CMYK Setup)

4. Setting the grayscale color space information (Grayscale Setup)

5. Setting the color space definitions for your various devices (Profiles Setup)

6. (For CMYK output) printing a color proof for fine-tuning the CMYK (CMYK Setup)

After this workflow is completed, then Photoshop's normal workflow is as follows:

1. Opening the file

2. Comparing file data with defined color spaces

3. Converting color, if necessary, to match defined color spaces

4. Automatically saving the color space data used for working on the file, as the file is saved

ICC Profiles

In Photoshop 5, calibration is enhanced by the support of International Color Consortium (ICC) profiles. An *ICC profile* is data that describes the color space of a particular device, such as a monitor or output device. The data—or profile—about the color spaces of the computer system where the file was created or edited is saved with the image file and is read by a Color Management Module (CMM), which converts the colors in the image to match when the image is moved from one device (such as your monitor/system) to another device (such as another monitor/system or the final output printer/imagesetter).

ICC profiles are supplied by many device manufacturers, or you can create your own for specific devices. Adobe recommends that you have an ICC profile for each different output device you use and that you change to that ICC profile when printing to that device.

Color Management Modules (CMM)

Photoshop 5 supports any CMM you install in your system, and you can select which one to use in the Engine option menu of the ICC profile options in the CMYK Setup dialog box.

Calibrating Monitors

You can use the Adobe Gamma utility to set up monitors for use with Photoshop, or you can use third-party calibration utilities in conjunction with an ICM 2-compatible or ColorSync-compatible ICC profile generator. Regardless of the calibration utility you use, you need to calibrate the monitor only once—unless you change the lighting environment or the monitor's brightness and contrast controls. Note that gamma settings from earlier versions of Photoshop and from the Windows Monitor Setup Utility are not supported by this version of Adobe Gamma.

This utility helps you eliminate color casts by adjusting contrast, brightness, the midtone colors (gamma), the color balance, and the white point of the monitor. The utility saves these settings as an ICC profile for the monitor.

Before you calibrate a monitor, make sure that you take into account the following considerations:

➤ Make sure that the monitor is properly warmed up (by being turned on for more than 30 minutes).

➤ Make sure that the lighting in the work area is what you normally experience while working.

➤ Change the desktop pattern/wallpaper on your computer to a light gray.

➤ Turn up the brightness and contrast controls on the monitor to their highest settings.

On the Mac, the Adobe Gamma utility is located in the Photoshop/Goodies/Calibration folder. In Windows, it is in the Photoshop/Calibrate folder. On both systems, the utility is also loaded into the Control Panels folders for easy access.

The two options for proceeding with Gamma are Step By Step and Control Panel. The Step By Step choice (see Figure 4.14) is an assistant/wizard that guides you through the process. Control Panel (see Figure 4.15) is a single dialog box, where you can select the settings in one step.

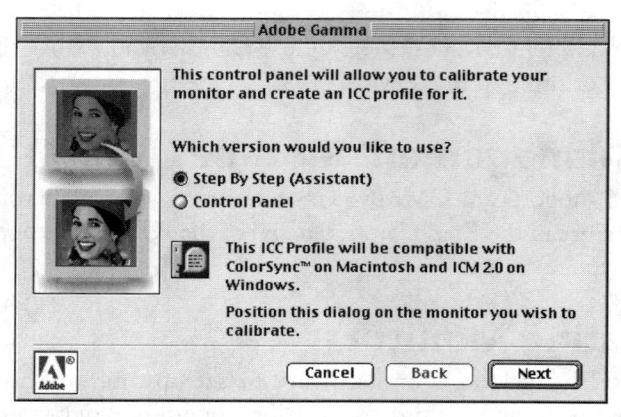

Figure 4.14 The Adobe Gamma assistant/wizard.

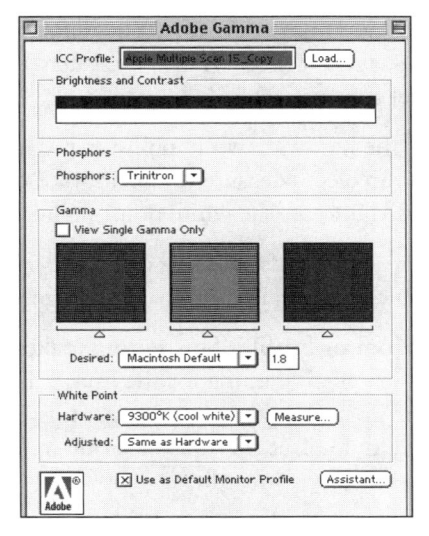

Working With And Understanding Photoshop's Color   107

Figure 4.15 The Adobe Gamma control panel.

The following are the options/adjustments in Adobe Gamma:

- **Load** The utility shows you the current ICC profile in use to describe your monitor. If it is correct, move on. If not, click on Load and locate the appropriate profile.

- **Brightness and Contrast** In the utility's assistant/wizard, you see a display of boxes in boxes. The outer box is white, and the two inner boxes are black. The display in the control panel is a white bar under a bar of alternating black and gray squares. Adjust the brightness control of the monitor so that the outer box/white bar remains a bright white, while trying to get the inner box/gray squares as dark as possible without being full black.

- **Phosphors** Select the appropriate phosphor profile for the monitor. (You may need to consult the monitor's documentation.)

- **Gamma** This option is similar to the Brightness and Contrast option but is used for setting the midtones—the colors between black and white. You can choose View Single Gamma Only, which allows you to refine the grayscale gamma, or you can deselect this option and refine the three monitor colors (RGB) individually. Move the sliders left or right to get the inner boxes to appear the same color as the outer boxes. (Adobe recommends that you squint or step back from the screen to see this effect better.)

- **Desired** Select a desired target gamma. The default target gamma for the Mac OS is 1.8, and for those Windows systems that can control the monitor, the target gamma is 2.2.

- **Hardware** Select the hardware white point; may be one of the offered options. You also can elect Measure to use another calibration assistant/wizard that allows you to set the white point manually.

- **Adjusted** Adobe recommends that this option be set to the color temperature at which the final output of the image will be viewed.

- **Use As Default Monitor Profile** This setting makes this gamma you have worked on the default gamma for the image files you edit. This choice may be fine if you have one monitor, but if you have multiple monitors, you should deselect this option for the monitor you don't use for displaying the images as you edit.

RGB Setup

Adobe recommends that you use the default RGB settings, unless you specifically need to define a separate color space for editing images. Access the RGB Setup dialog box by first choosing File|Color Settings. You can load a previously saved profile or save the profile you create from this dialog box.

The options menu of RGB color spaces includes the following:

- **sRGB** Standard RGB, which is the Photoshop default.

- **Apple RGB** The old Photoshop default, recommended for images to be displayed only on Mac systems.

- **CIE RGB** A color space defined by the Commission Internationale d'Eclairage. This option does not display cyan well.

- **ColorMatch RGB** A color space designed by the monitor manufacturer Radius for use with its Pressview monitors.

- **NTSC (1953)** The original color-television standard.

- **PAL/SECAM** The color television standard for many countries in Europe and other parts of the world.

- **SMPTE-240M** The new standard for high-definition television (HDTV).

- **SMPTE-C** The current color television standard for the U.S.

- **Wide-Gamut RGB** Oddly conceived color space that includes many colors that can neither be printed nor displayed on monitors.

► **Custom** A custom profile. This option allows you to set values for the gamma, white point, and phosphors.

CMYK Setup

Setting up CMYK is an important step when you're creating or editing files that will be printed on four-color process printing presses. Here, you define the color space information that Photoshop will use when displaying images so that they will appear on screen as you expect them to appear when the image is finally printed.

If you are familiar with previous versions of Photoshop, you will notice that the Printing Inks and Separation dialog boxes are no longer available. Those options are now incorporated in the CMYK Setup dialog box. You can access the CMYK Setup dialog box by choosing File|Color Settings|CMYK Setup.

In the CMYK Setup dialog box, you can specify the type of color space definition to use:

► **Built-in** Set properties for the paper and inks that will be used for printing.

► **ICC Profiles** Select a profile defined for the printer you will use.

► **Tables** Save the CMYK setup information as a profile that you can load for other images, in other programs, and on other systems.

Using The Built-in Color Space

To use the built-in color space, click on the Built-in radio button on the CMYK Setup dialog box. The entry options are as follows:

► **Ink Options** Select an ink type from the option menu, or define a custom ink. (See "Custom Ink Colors," later in this chapter.)

► **Dot Gain** Set the dot gain here after printing a color proof or after your printer has given you a value to enter. (See "Calibrating With The Color Proof," later in this chapter.)

► **Separation Options** Choose the appropriate type of separation (GCR or UCR). Set the amount of black generation, ink limits, and the amount of undercolor addition. (See "Separation Options," later in this chapter.)

Of course, you can also save these settings as an ICC profile and/or load another saved profile from this dialog box, as well.

Using The ICC Color Space

To use the ICC color space, click on the ICC radio button on the CMYK Setup dialog box. The entry options are as follows:

- **Profile** Specifies the ICC profile of the printer that will be used for output.
- **Engine** Allows you to select the Color Management Module (CMM) to use.
- **Intent** Affects the conversion of colors for output. You have these options:
  - **Perceptual (Images)** Preserves the "look" of the colors, even though the numerical values may change.
  - **Saturation (Graphics)** Preserves the saturation levels but converts out-of-gamut colors to the closest in-gamut color with the same saturation.
  - **Relative Colorimetric** Preserves the color values of all colors within the gamut. Out-of-gamut colors are converted to colors within the gamut that have the same lightness value.
  - **Absolute Colorimetric** Disables white point matching. (Not recommended.)
- **Black Point Compensation** Tells Photoshop to match the darkest neutral color on the image to the darkest neutral color of the output device's color space rather than black.

Using The Tables Color Space

To use the Tables color space, click on the ICC radio button on the CMYK Setup dialog box. You then see the "from" and "to" CMYK tables that are currently loaded. You can load a different profile or save this profile from here.

Separation Options

Separation Options refers to the options for converting the colors of the areas in an image that are intended to be black. As described in Chapter 2, the three subtractive primaries theoretically combine to create black but, in practice, combine to create a muddy brown. The black ink that is added to the press run to create the actual black color can be added to the image in various ways, depending on a specific printers' specifications. Enter values for these options only after consulting with the printer.

The Separation Options are as follows:

Working With And Understanding Photoshop's Color

> **GCR (gray component replacement)** This option replaces the subtractive primaries with black in areas where the three are to be applied in equal amounts, regardless of the color of the image area. This replacement improves the reproduction of darker colors and helps the press hold the gray values.

> **UCR (undercolor removal)** This option replaces the subtractive primaries with black only in neutral-colored areas where the three are to be applied in equal amounts. These equal amounts would (theoretically) combine to produce various shades of gray, so replacing them with black ink not only produces better blacks and grays and better definition in shadow areas, but also results in less ink coverage. Use of this option is recommended for more porous paper stocks, such as newsprint and uncoated papers.

> **Black Generation** This option is available only if you select the GCR separation type and set the amount of black Photoshop will add to the separations. Choose None, amounts from Light to Maximum, or Custom to define a specific number by using a curves representation.

> **Black Ink Limit/Total Ink Limit** These options define the amounts of ink—the ink density—that a particular printing press can support. Set these values according to the printer's directions.

> **UCA (undercolor addition) Amount** Available only in GCR separations, this option actually adds some of the three subtractive primary colored inks to the black ink in areas of neutral color. This addition enhances the shadow areas and can prevent posterization in these areas.

> Understand these separation options. Remember that GCR adds black to areas of equal CMY density—regardless of color—and that UCR adds black only to neutral areas of equal CMY density. Remembering that UCA adds black to the neutral areas and is available only in GCR separations can help you remember the difference between GCR and UCR.

Color Proof

You cannot properly calibrate your system without printing a color proof to compare the screen representation of colors with the output colors. The following are some basic guidelines for printing color proofs:

> Use an image file that shows samples of all the CMYK combinations.

> Use the Testpict.jpg supplied with the Windows version or the Olé No Moire file supplied with the Mac version.

- Do not print an RGB image converted to CMYK in Photoshop.
- Use an image saved in CMYK without an ICC profile that has been created in CMYK mode.

Calibrating With The Color Proof

After you have the color proof, you can check it against the image on the screen. If it does not match, and you have used the Built-in color model, you may need to adjust some of your CMYK Setup values and selections, such as dot gain, custom ink characteristics, and color casts.

If you have used ICC profiles, and the proof and screen representation don't match, you may need to do some troubleshooting:

- Check the calibration of the output device.
- Replace the ICC profile.
- Create a new ICC profile with a third-party profile-creation product.
- Adjust the dot gain via transfer functions to compensate for dot gain between the on-screen image and the film output.
- Use the Built-in option instead of ICC profiles.

Dot Gain

Dot gain, the spread of ink into the paper that creates larger dots and thereby darkens images, varies from paper to paper and ink to ink. Photoshop's default dot gain setting represents the amount of spreading that can be expected of the pixels that contain 50 percent coverage, from the original image to the final printing. Any changes you make to the dot gain setting affect only the display of the image, not the file data.

You need a reflective densitometer to measure the density of the ink coverage. Measure a dot to get its actual size. The difference between that size and its intended size represents the dot gain.

Specify dot gain in the CMYK Setup (Built-in) dialog box in one of these ways:

- For Standard, use the densitometer to measure the ink coverage at the 50 percent mark of the calibration bar on the proof. Enter the difference between that number and 50 percent in the % box.
- For Curves, use the densitometer to measure the ink coverage on the calibration bar at one or more of the 13 values displayed in the Dot Gain Curves dialog box. Enter the difference between the densitometer

readings and the corresponding value in the appropriate % box. By clicking on the All Same checkbox, you can choose to enter values separately for the four colors.

Previewing Dot Gain In Grayscale Images

You can change the dot gain settings for grayscale printing in the Grayscale Setup dialog box, which you access by choosing File|Color Settings. In this dialog box, the options are as follows:

- **RGB** Leaves the RGB display of the grayscale image undisturbed.

- **Black Ink** Changes the display to represent final output by using the dot gain settings that have been specified in CMYK Setup.

Setting Transfer Functions

> Transfer functions are a last-resort option for dot gain problems, such as those produced by a miscalibrated imagesetter, that have no other apparent solution. Transfer functions work much the same way as other dot gain settings, but they affect only the dot gain that may occur from the image on-screen to the output of a miscalibrated printer or imagesetter. In other words, if the output to a printer or imagesetter doesn't match the image on-screen and you have completed all other troubleshooting without success, transfer functions may be the solution.
>
> It is important not to think of transfer functions as a remedy for any dot gain problems that may occur from film output to final printed piece. Use the CMYK Setup dot gain curves in this case.

To set transfer functions, first access the Transfer Functions curves dialog box by choosing File|Page Setup. Click on the Transfer button to open the dialog box. Use a densitometer to read the output of the printer or imagesetter, then enter values in the various coverage areas (see the section on dot gain, previously in this chapter, for more details on this type of curves dialog box).

> If you want to export the transfer functions along with a file, select the Override Printer's Default Functions checkbox. Then, you must save the file as a Photoshop EPS or DCS file and select the Include Transfer Function checkbox in the EPS Options dialog box.

Hold down Option/Alt while you're in the Transfer Functions dialog box. Doing so changes the Save button to ->Default, which allows you to save the current settings as the default, and changes the Load button to <-Default, which loads the defaults as the current settings.

Custom Ink Colors

You set custom ink colors in the Built-In option of the CMYK Setup dialog box, which you access by choosing File|Color Settings. Select Custom in the Ink Color options menu to open the Ink Colors dialog box.

Custom ink settings should be obtained from your printer or can be determined for specific colors by using a spectrophotometer or colorimeter. By default, the color values are entered as Y (lightness), x, and y. You can override this setting by clicking on the L*a*b Coordinates button to enter L, a, and b values.

Using The Profiles Dialog Box To Manage ICC Profiles In Files

To ensure that an image file will be accurately rendered on another system or in another ICC-aware application, that file should have its ICC profile data embedded in it. In the Profile Setup dialog box, you define how Photoshop will use the ICC profile data it finds when it opens a specific file.

Embedding profiles increases the file size, but provides color consistency.

You can embed ICC profiles in files saved in the following formats:

- EPS
- JPEG
- PCT
- PDF (for RGB and Grayscale images only)
- PSD (Photoshop)
- TIFF

The Profile Setup options are as follows:

- **Embed Profiles** Select whether to embed ICC profile data in RGB, CMYK, Grayscale, and/or Lab mode images.

- **Assumed Profiles** Select the ICC profiles used to define the RGB, CMYK, and Grayscale color spaces used when opening files without ICC profile data.

- **Profile Mismatch Handling** Select how Photoshop opens a file that contains ICC profile data that doesn't match the profiles specified in the RGB Setup, Grayscale Setup, and CMYK Setup dialog boxes.

Converting Open Images To Other Color Spaces

Use the Profile To Profile command under Image|Mode to convert an open image to another color space. This technique may be useful following a change from one color space to another in the RGB Setup dialog box because open images are not affected by this change until they are closed and reopened.

The options for Profile To Profile are as follows:

- **From** Define the image's current color space.

- **To** Choose a new color space.

- **Engine** Choose a Color Management Module (CMM).

- **Intent** Select a rendering intent. (See "Using The ICC Color Space," previously in this chapter, for descriptions of the different options.)

- **Black Point Compensation** Convert the darkest neutral color in the current color space to the darkest neutral color in the new color space, if selected.

Practice Questions

Question 1

> Select all the color modes from the following list.
> - a. RGB
> - b. L*a*b
> - c. CMYK
> - d. HSB

Answers a and c are correct; RGB and CMYK are color models and color modes. Each of the other responses is a color model, but only two of them are color modes. L*a*b is a color model, after which the Lab mode is modeled, but no L*a*b mode exists. HSB is a color model, but not a color mode.

Question 2

> If you want to use the HSB model to make a pink color more red, which component would increase the red?
> - a. H
> - b. S
> - c. B

Answer b is correct. Saturation (S) is the amount of pure color (hue) in a color.

Question 3

> Which color model is used to display colors on computer monitors?
> - a. HSB
> - b. RGB
> - c. CMYK
> - d. L*a*b

Answer b is correct. Computer monitors and televisions create color by mixing the additive primary colors of red, green, and blue.

Question 4

> Which of the following is a process color? (Select all that apply.)
> ❏ a. Cyan
> ❏ b. Magenta
> ❏ c. Yellow
> ❏ d. Black

Answers a, b, c, and d are correct. The four process colors used to print colors on paper are referred to as CMYK: cyan, magenta, yellow, and black.

Question 5

> What mode(s) would you not want to use if you wanted to use the Paint Bucket tool to edit an image? (Select all that apply.)
> ❏ a. Bitmap
> ❏ b. RGB
> ❏ c. Grayscale
> ❏ d. Indexed Color

Trick! question

The only correct answer is a. Two of the modes listed have limited editing capabilities: Bitmap and Indexed color. Only one of them does not support the Paint Bucket tool: Bitmap.

Question 6

> Which statement is not true about Lab mode?
> ○ a. Lab mode can be useful for adjusting colors without affecting their brightness.
> ○ b. Lab mode is the Photoshop internal color mode.
> ○ c. Lab mode images can be 8-bit-per-channel or 16-bit-per-channel images.
> ○ d. You can print Lab mode images to PostScript Level 3 printers.

Answer c is correct. However, answers a, b, and d are true statements. Although Lab mode images are 8-bit-per-channel images, they cannot be 16-bit-per-channel images.

Question 7

> Which type of file contains at least 256 colors and can be saved as a JPEG file?
>
> ○ a. Bitmap
> ○ b. Grayscale
> ○ c. Indexed Color
> ○ d. Multichannel

Trick! question

Answer b is correct. Be careful here; it's true that Indexed Color images have 256 colors, but they can't be saved as JPEG. Multichannel colors have at least 256 colors, but they can't be saved as JPEG. Bitmap mode images have only two colors. Grayscale images have 256, and they can be saved as JPEG.

Question 8

> Which has the wider gamut?
>
> ○ a. L*a*b
> ○ b. RGB
> ○ c. CMYK

Answer a is correct. The L*a*b has the widest gamut; CMYK has the narrowest.

Question 9

> What is the maximum number of color channels a Photoshop image can have?
>
> ○ a. 12
> ○ b. 100
> ○ c. 24
> ○ d. 16

Answer c is correct. A Photoshop image can have 24 color channels.

Question 10

Which of the following statements are true about converting images to different modes? (Select all that apply.)

- ❏ a. You should perform most of your editing work in the image's original mode.
- ❏ b. You should convert a copy of the image rather than the original.
- ❏ c. You should not flatten the file before conversion.
- ❏ d. You should convert only once to preserve image quality.

Answers a, b, and d are correct. All of these answers are true except c. You *should* flatten the file before conversion.

Question 11

For which of the following operations can either or both the foreground or background color be used? (Select all that apply.)

- ❏ a. Painting
- ❏ b. Filling the new areas created by the Canvas Size command
- ❏ c. Making gradient fills
- ❏ d. Erasing with the Eraser tool

Answer c is the only correct answer. You use both the foreground color and the background color to make gradient fills, so this answer is correct. You can paint with the foreground color, but not with the background color. Creating new areas with the Canvas Size command fills those areas with the background color. You can erase to the background color, but not the foreground color.

Question 12

If the H radio button is selected in the Color Picker, which two components would be displayed in the color field? (Select two answers.)

❏ a. Lightness

❏ b. Saturation

❏ c. Red

❏ d. Brightness

Answers b and d are correct. The color bar of the Color Picker displays the range of color available, based on the selection of a component from one of the available models. The color field then displays the other two components. H is the color component of the HSB model. The other two components are saturation (S) and brightness (B).

Question 13

You can temporarily activate the Eyedropper tool from any painting tool by using what keystroke?

○ a. Cmd/Ctrl

○ b. Shift

○ c. Option/Alt

○ d. Shift+Option/Shift+Alt

Answer c is correct. Use the Option/Alt key.

Question 14

While you're using Color Samplers, how many different areas of an image can you sample?

○ a. 2

○ b. 4

○ c. 5

○ d. 8

Trick! question

Answer c is correct. Be careful on this one. You can place only four Color Samplers, but you can then sample another area with the Color Sampler icon.

Question 15

Which monitor calibration utilities are supported by Photoshop 5? (Select all that apply.)

❏ a. CMYK Setup

❏ b. Adobe Gamma

❏ c. Monitor Setup

❏ d. Monitor Calibrator

Answer c is correct. Photoshop 5 does not support settings from earlier versions of Photoshop or from the Windows Monitor Setup Utility.

Question 16

What is the default Photoshop color space?

○ a. sRGB

○ b. Apple RGB

○ c. CIE RGB

○ d. Color Match RGB

Answer a is correct. sRGB is the default color space in Photoshop.

Question 17

What is dot gain?

○ a. When the separation process inadvertently creates too many dots in converting the image for printing.

○ b. The addition of extra-sized dots for enhanced printing on low-end printers.

○ c. The frequency of dots printed from wide-gamut RGB.

○ d. The spreading out of printed dots on paper, as a result of the ink soaking into the paper.

Answer d is correct. When ink is applied to porous paper, the ink soaks in and spreads out.

Question 18

> Which of these separation options will add black ink to the neutral-colored areas covered by equal amounts of cyan, magenta, and yellow?
>
> ○ a. GCR (gray component replacement)
> ○ b. UCR (undercolor removal)
> ○ c. Black Generation
> ○ d. UCA (undercolor addition)

Trick! question

Answer d is correct. GCR adds black to the areas of even cyan, magenta, and yellow density, regardless of the color of the area. Although both UCR and UCA involve printing black ink in areas of equal cyan, magenta, and yellow density, UCR *replaces* the three subtractive inks with black. UCA is the only one that *adds* black to the neutral areas.

Question 19

> You have completed the calibration workflow and have done all the troubleshooting possible, but you are still having dot gain problems with grayscale (black and white) images printed on a laser printer. What option(s) could you use to correlate the output with the on-screen image? (Select all that apply.)
>
> ❏ a. Transfer functions
> ❏ b. Rendering Intent
> ❏ c. Black Generation
> ❏ d. UCA (undercolor addition)

Answer a is correct. Transfer functions are a possible solution to screen image-to-output dot gain problems that cannot be fixed any other way.

Need To Know More?

McClelland, Deke: *Photoshop 5 for Macs for Dummies*. IDG Books Worldwide, Inc. ISBN 0-7645-0391-X.

McClelland, Deke: *Macworld Photoshop 5 Bible*. IDG Books Worldwide, Inc. ISBN 0-7645-3231-6.

Managing Image Files In Photoshop

5

Terms and concepts you'll need to understand:

- ✓ File format
- ✓ GIF
- ✓ EPS
- ✓ JPEG
- ✓ PDF
- ✓ PICT
- ✓ Image resolution
- ✓ Scanning resolution
- ✓ Screen frequency
- ✓ Anti-alias
- ✓ Digimarc
- ✓ Lossy compression
- ✓ Lossless compression
- ✓ LZW
- ✓ Clipping paths
- ✓ File format
- ✓ Place command

Techniques you'll need to master:

- ✓ Selecting file formats for saving files
- ✓ Determining the optimum scanning resolution for images
- ✓ Creating new image files
- ✓ Opening image files
- ✓ Importing image files
- ✓ Opening PDF files
- ✓ Saving files
- ✓ Saving copies of files
- ✓ Reducing file sizes
- ✓ Setting the preferences for saving files
- ✓ Exporting GIF89a files
- ✓ Exporting Photoshop paths to Adobe Illustrator
- ✓ Creating and saving clipping paths

Managing image files in Photoshop involves creating new files, saving files, copying files, understanding what file formats are and which are appropriate for certain applications, scanning files at appropriate resolutions, importing files, and exporting files.

The File Formats

ALERT: File formats are separate and different from modes. This concept is confusing sometimes because people often refer to files either by an image mode type or by file format type. File formats are the different formats for saving data in files that you can open, save, export, and import from Photoshop and other applications.

Not all file formats are compatible with all applications and platforms. You need to know how an image file is to be used so that you can decide in which file format to save that file.

Photoshop (PSD)

PSD is the default file format for images created in Photoshop and is the only file format from which you can work with every one of Photoshop's features. These files save all Photoshop non-image data, such as layers, channels, effects—everything you can do to a file in Photoshop.

Photoshop files open, save, and compress in Photoshop faster than any other file formats.

Note that Photoshop files created and/or edited in Photoshop 5 are not backward compatible with earlier versions of Photoshop. Any data regarding Photoshop 5's new features, such as editable type layers or spot channels, is lost if you open the files in previous versions of Photoshop.

ALERT: The Photoshop file format is the only format in which you can save files and retain their layer information. If you open a file from any other format and then create layers in that file, before you save it, you will have to flatten the layers; otherwise, the Save As dialog box opens, and you have to save it as a Photoshop file.

Photoshop 2.0

The Photoshop 2.0 format (available only on the Mac) allows applications that don't support Photoshop's layers to use Photoshop files.

Amiga IFF

Developed for the defunct Amiga computer, the Interchange File Format (IFF) is useful only if you have old Amiga files or work with the few applications that still support this format.

BMP

BMP is the default format for image files used by many Microsoft/Windows applications. Photoshop supports BMP files up to 24-bit depth. Note that 4- and 8-bit BMP files can use RLE compression.

This format does not support alpha channels and supports only the following Photoshop modes:

- RGB
- Indexed Color
- Grayscale
- Bitmap

CompuServe GIF

The Graphic Interchange Format (GIF) was developed by Unisys specifically for image files prepared for display on the Web. The format uses LZW compression and limits files to 256 colors. The reduced file sizes transfer relatively quickly over slow Internet connections.

The two types of GIF files are as follow:

- **CompuServe GIF (87a)** This format creates GIF files from the Bitmap, Grayscale, or Indexed Color modes, but does not support transparent pixels. You cannot save alpha channels, but you can specify interlacing.
- **GIF89a** This format, which supports interlacing and a single alpha channel, is popular because you can export GIF files that have transparent pixels. Choose File|Export|GIF 89a Export to create these files and define the pixels you want to be transparent.

Photoshop DCS 1.0/2.0

DCS, which is a type of EPS (Encapsulated PostScript) format, stands for Desktop Color Separations. CMYK files saved in these formats automatically separate an appropriate number of color plates. DCS 1.0 saves CMYK files only with four channels, but 2.0 saves multichannel files, CMYK files with spot channels, and one alpha channel. Photoshop clipping paths are compatible with both 1.0 and 2.0.

EPS

Based on Adobe's PostScript printing language, Encapsulated PostScript (EPS) files are most commonly used in vector-oriented drawing programs. They are used primarily for transferring graphics files to output devices and between applications. EPS files can contain either vector graphics for bitmap image data—or both. Photoshop rasterizes the vector graphic data when it opens the file. (For more information about opening EPS files, see "Creating, Opening, and Importing Images," later in this chapter.)

EPS files support clipping paths but do not support alpha channels. They support only these Photoshop modes:

- Bitmap
- Grayscale
- Duotone
- Indexed Color
- RGB
- CMYK
- Lab

When saving files as EPS, you create a Photoshop EPS file. If you open an EPS file that is not a Photoshop EPS file (such as an Adobe Illustrator EPS file), Photoshop opens the Rasterize Generic EPS Format dialog box, which allows you to specify several options for Photoshop to use when rasterizing the file.

EPS PICT Preview/EPS TIFF Preview

EPS PICT Preview and EPS TIFF Preview "formats" are displayed as options only in the Open and Open As dialog boxes. They are supplied as possible "workarounds" to difficulties encountered when you try to open files that may have been saved in formats not supported by Photoshop. If, for example, you encounter a file that doesn't appear as an available file in the Open or Open As dialog boxes, you could try to open the file's preview. EPS TIFF Preview is available only on the Mac.

Filmstrip

The Filmstrip file format is used to exchange images between Photoshop and Adobe Premiere. Premiere is a movie-editing application that has limited image-editing capability. So, for image editing, a movie can be saved as a Filmstrip file and opened in Photoshop for editing. However, if a Filmstrip file is resized or resampled, if any alpha channels are removed, or if the color mode or format is changed, it can no longer be saved in the Filmstrip format.

FlashPix

FlashPix is a new format developed by Kodak specifically for digital photographic images. Similar to Kodak's Photo CD files, FlashPix image files contain multiple resolutions of the same image.

Although Photoshop both opens FlashPix files and saves to the FlashPix format, FlashPix is not automatically installed with Photoshop. You must select Custom Install from the Adobe Photoshop Installer and then select FPX with Microsoft OLE 2.08. OLE is required for using the FlashPix format.

JPEG

JPEG stands for Joint Photographic Experts Group, the body that developed this format. Primarily used for preparing photo files for display over the Internet, JPEG compresses files as it saves them, allowing various levels of compression, from 0 to 10. (Oddly, these numbers don't refer to the amount of compression, but the level of quality. The number 0 is minimum quality, and 10 is maximum quality.)

Unlike the GIF format, JPEG retains the full color space of images. The tradeoff is that JPEG is a lossy form of compression, discarding varying amounts of image data, depending on the compression amount. However, you can expect very little image quality loss at the upper levels of the JPEG quality scale, even though you see considerable reductions in file size.

You can save to JPEG from CMYK, RGB, and Grayscale modes, without alpha channels.

Options for JPEG images include the following:

➤ **Baseline** Specifies the safest format for greater compatibility with Web browsers.

➤ **Baseline Optimized** Produces higher-quality color while producing a smaller file, but it is not compatible with all Web browsers.

➤ **Progressive** Displays the file gradually as it loads. This option is not supported by all Web browsers.

> **STUDY ALERT:** Remember that each time a file is compressed with JPEG, the file's image quality degrades. For this reason, files should be compressed only once with JPEG, after all editing is completed. You should save a copy of the original file for later editing.

Kodak ICC Photo CD

Photoshop opens image files from Kodak Photo CDs, but does not save files in the Photo CD format.

PCX

PCX is a format used by the application PC Paintbrush. You might never see a file in this format, unless you use these old DOS files.

PDF

PDF, which stands for Portable Document Format, is the format used by Adobe Acrobat and other applications that create this type of cross-platform document file. Usually, the appropriate "reader" application is necessary to view these files, but Photoshop can now import them as image files.

Like EPS files, PDF files can contain vector graphics and bitmap images. Unlike EPS files, they can also contain Web-like links and navigation buttons.

PDF files created and edited in Photoshop PDF format support RGB, Indexed Color, CMYK, Grayscale, Bitmap, and Lab modes, without alpha channels. You can compress these files with JPEG or ZIP, but Bitmap mode PDF files are compressed using CCITT Group 4 compression.

> **STUDY ALERT:** One of Photoshop's new automation assistants/wizards imports PDF files and converts them to PSD files. To find it, choose File|Automate|Multi-page PDF To PSD. This assistant/wizard opens the PDF file and creates a new Photoshop file for each page of the PDF, or only the pages you specify.

PICT File

Apple developed the PICT format for use with the Macintosh operating system. Although this format is widely used on the Mac, you might have trouble using PICT files in Windows applications if the files have been compressed with the QuickTime JPEG compression supported by the PICT format.

PICT files can be RGB, Indexed Color, Grayscale, or Bitmap mode, but they support only alpha channels (and only one) in RGB.

PICT Resource

Available only on the Mac, PICT Resource is a File|Import option that allows you to open a file to search for PICT files that may be used in the file. For example, you can open an application and find its startup screen.

You can save files as PICT Resource files for use as startup screens. You can also open images from the Scrapbook with this option.

PIXAR

The PIXAR format is for files to be saved for PIXAR's proprietary graphics animation workstations. PIXAR, the computer-animation company founded by Steve Jobs, produces movies, such as *Toy Story*.

You can save RGB and Grayscale mode images with one alpha channel as PIXAR format files.

PNG

Developed for Web images as a 24-bit and 48-bit freeware alternative to the patented 8-bit GIF format, PNG is not yet widely used and may not be compatible with some Web browser applications. PNG files can be saved from RGB and Grayscale modes with one alpha channel, or Bitmap and Indexed Color modes without channels.

To save PNG files with transparency, create a mask/alpha channel and save only that channel with the file. When you're saving PNG files, compression is automatic and not as drastic as JPEG compression, but it is also lossless. You can choose to interlace on download with the Adam7 method, which loads the image gradually. You can also select from several complicated filtering methods designed to provide more control over the compression process.

Raw

The Raw format is primarily used to import and export image files to and from mainframe computers.

Scitex CT

CT stands for continuous tone. Scitex is the manufacturer of high-end scanners and imaging systems used by commercial printers and production houses.

These files are often very large and of very high quality. Photoshop can save Scitex CT files without alpha channels from RGB, Grayscale, and CMYK modes.

Targa

Most often used for video and multimedia production, the Targa format was developed for use on systems equipped with certain TrueVision video boards.

TIFF

TIFF (Tag Image File Format) is another of the most popular and widely compatible file formats. TIFF images can be used on nearly all graphics programs. TIFF files are nearly as compatible with Photoshop as are Photoshop-native files. You can save TIFF files—with unlimited alpha channels—from RGB, Grayscale, and CMYK images, or without alpha channels from Bitmap, Indexed Color, and Lab files.

When saving TIFF files, you must specify whether Photoshop should prepare the image for the PC or the Mac. The format is largely compatible with most relevant applications on both platforms, regardless of this decision, but for insurance, you should select the platform on which the file will most likely be used.

You also can select LZW compression for TIFF files. Because LZW is lossless, the only reason not to choose this format is that it may slightly slow the opening and saving of the file.

Determining The Appropriate Scanning Resolution

Remember that resolution and file size are interrelated and that more pixels are needed for higher resolution and more pixels mean larger files. Larger files take more time, memory, storage space, and computing power to open, save, and edit. Consequently, you should create and save files that are both optimally scanned and only as large as necessary to produce the image quality you need at final output. You need to determine an optimum scanning resolution that is neither too high nor too low for your needs. Three factors influence this determination for printed images:

➤ Original image size

➤ Final image size

➤ Halftone screen frequency of destination publication

Managing Image Files In Photoshop 133

Publishing professionals rely on a simple formula for determining the optimum scanning resolution of an image. Your goal is to produce an image resolution 1.5 to 2 times the halftone screen frequency of the printed publication. (The numbers 1.5 to 2 are part of what are called *sampling ratios*, and can also be shown as 1.5:1 or 2:1.)

You need to understand the difference between pixel dimensions, image resolution, monitor resolution, scanning resolution, printer resolution, and screen frequency. The following list provides a breakdown of these principles:

➤ **Pixel Dimensions** Refers to the number of pixels that an image has along its two dimensions. An image with a pixel dimension of 72x72 is 72 pixels tall and 72 pixels wide. These numbers alone have little bearing on the print quality of an image because the print quality of an image is dependent on how many pixels are printed per unit of measurement.

However, when you're working with the display of images on the computer screen, these numbers are much more important. The pixel dimensions of an image determine how large the image will appear on screen, without regard to any image resolution setting.

➤ **Image Resolution** Is related to printer resolution and refers to the number of pixels that are available to display the image at its intended size. This resolution is usually described in pixels-per-inch (ppi). So, if a 1-inch-square image is planned for printing at 144 ppi/dpi, it is said to have a resolution of 144 ppi/dpi; it needs 144 pixels along its width and its height to print 1-inch square at that resolution. (That 144x144 could be referred to as its *pixel dimensions*.) A 2-inch-square image at 144 dpi has 288 pixels along its width and its height, a 4-inch-square image has 576 pixels on each dimension, and so on.

➤ **Monitor Resolution** Refers to the number of pixels (or dots) per inch that are displayed on a computer monitor. The most common resolutions of monitors are 96 dpi for many PC monitors and 72 for Mac monitors. Monitor resolution and pixel dimensions combine to determine the on-screen size of an image. A 1-inch-square image with an image resolution of 72, displayed on a 72-dpi monitor, appears approximately 1-inch square.

If, however, that 1-inch-square image has an image resolution of 144, it appears twice as large on screen. You see this result because the monitor resolution can't change (it stays at 72 dpi), nor can the number of pixels in the image change, so the image appears larger. Therefore, images in Photoshop with higher image resolutions may have tremendous pixel dimensions and appear very large on screen; because all of the pixels are spread out at 72 or 96 dpi.

➤ **Scanning Resolution** Is the number of pixels that are captured and stored by a particular scanning device. A scanner creates a digital image of a photograph, for example, by taking a tiny picture of the image every so often and then converting the tiny picture into a number and tucking it away to be used when the image is displayed on the screen or printed. These tiny pictures are referred to as either samples-per-inch (spi) or, more commonly, pixels-per-inch. The maximum number of times per inch that the scanner can stop and take a tiny picture is its maximum optical scanning resolution. A higher scanning resolution produces more samples per inch, more pixel data (hence, higher pixel dimensions), and higher image resolutions.

➤ **Printer Resolution** Refers to the number of dots per inch an imagesetter or printer can produce. A printer's resolution determines how much detail it can print. A higher resolution means that it can print more dots per inch to produce more colors per inch. Whereas a decent-quality laser printer in an office setting today might have a printer resolution of about 600 dpi, imagesetters that are used for printing high-quality negatives for making printing plates commonly have printer resolutions of up to 2,800 to 4,800 dpi.

➤ **Screen Frequency** Is the number of rows and columns of halftone dots per inch on a specific halftone screen. *Halftone* describes the process of converting continuous-tone images (photographs) for printing on paper. Because you cannot print continuous-tone images with ink on paper, the images are converted to millions of big and small dots. Areas with a lot of small dots appear lighter; areas with a lot of big dots appear darker. (You can see these dots for yourself with a magnifying glass and a newspaper.)

Traditionally, this conversion was accomplished by laying a film-like screen of millions of clear dots over a photograph and taking another photograph of the photograph. The film-like screen, called a halftone screen, was etched with a grid of a specific number of rows and columns of dots. The number of these rows and columns—referred to as lines—per inch determined the screen's frequency. If the screen had 133 rows of dots per inch, it had a screen frequency of 133 lines-per-inch (lpi).

Screen frequency is important in printing images because various papers and printing presses can support various screen frequencies. For example, you can almost see with the naked eye the halftone dots of a photograph printed in a newspaper, whereas you really need a magnifying glass to see the dots of a photograph printed in a four-color, glossy magazine. In very simplified terms, porous newsprint soaks up more ink, creating more dot gain, requiring a coarser screen than the fine screen used for the magazine photos that are printed on less-porous paper.

The following are the common halftone screen frequencies used for various publications:

Low-quality jobs on porous paper
65 lpi

Newspapers
85 lpi

Four-color magazines
133 lpi

High-quality jobs (fine art publications, annual reports, and so on) on coated paper
177 lpi

Consult your publication's printer/production house/service bureau for the recommended lpi of your printing project.

Follow these steps to determine the optimum scanning resolution of an image printed on paper:

1. Measure the original image.
2. Determine the size the image will be when printed.
3. Determine the percentage of enlargement or reduction of the original image that will be necessary to reach the intended printing size. You can use a proportion wheel or divide the intended size measurement by the original size measurement.
4. Obtain or decide on the halftone screen resolution for the publication.

5. Multiply the screen frequency number by the enlargement or reduction percentage.

6. Multiply that result by sampling ratio amounts of either 1.5 for adequate quality or 2 for higher quality.

By following these steps, you can find the scanning resolution that will result in an image file that has the resolution needed to produce a quality printed image.

Here's an example: You are starting with an original image that is 3 inches by 3 inches. It is to be printed in a four-color magazine (133 lpi) at 3 inches by 3 inches (100%), and you want a 2:1 sampling ratio. Multiply the enlargement or reduction percentage (100%=1.0) by the screen frequency number (133). Multiply the result (133) by your sampling ratio (2). The result (266) is the optimum scanning resolution for that particular image.

Creating, Opening, And Importing Images

The first step in editing image files in Photoshop is to open an existing file, create a new file, or import a file from a scanning device or another application.

Creating A New File

To create a new file, choose File|New to access the New dialog box (see Figure 5.1). You have three options for automatically sizing a new image canvas:

➤ By default, the New dialog box opens and displays a size based on the size of the contents of the clipboard.

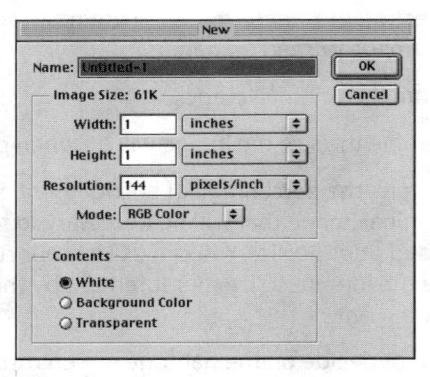

Figure 5.1 The New dialog box.

> Hold down Option/Alt when you're choosing File|New, and the New dialog box displays the last entered size values or the default values.

> To copy the size of an image that is currently open, choose File|New and then select the name of the open image from the Window menu.

After the New dialog box opens, you can give the new file a name or leave it untitled. In the Image Size option area, you can specify the size of the new image, the measurement units to use, the image resolution, and the editing mode. The size of the file, based on the size and resolution values you enter, is displayed next to Image Size. In the Contents option area, you can choose whether to fill the empty canvas with white, the current background color, or to leave the canvas transparent.

Opening An Existing Image

To open an existing image, choose File|Open to access the Open dialog box (see Figures 5.2 and 5.3). From here, you can browse your drives to find compatible existing files to open. Highlighting a file's name displays its file size and, if it was saved with a preview, displays a thumbnail of the file. On the Mac, you can turn off this option by clicking on the Show Thumbnail checkbox, and you can create a thumbnail for a file that does not have one by clicking on the Create button.

In Windows, use Files Of Type in the Open dialog box to view only files saved in certain file formats or to view all files in a folder. On the Mac, you can choose only between viewing all the available files or all the files in a folder by using the Show All Files checkbox.

To open a file as a specific file format different from the file format in which it was saved, choose File|Open As (this menu option is available only in Windows), select a file, and specify in the Open As option menu which format to use. On the Mac, clicking on the Show All Files checkbox changes the Open

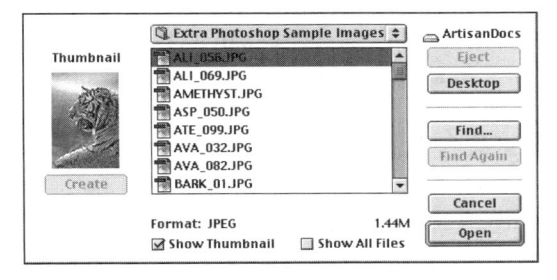

Figure 5.2   The Mac Open dialog box.

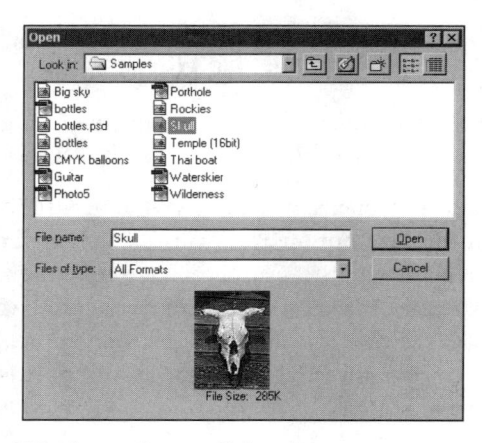

Figure 5.3 The Windows Open dialog box.

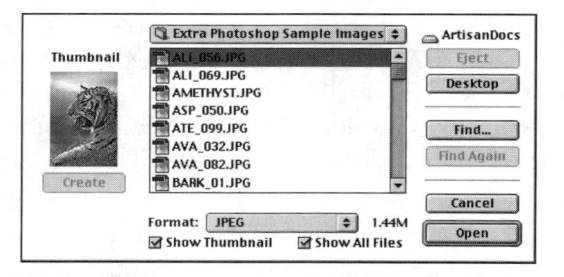

Figure 5.4 The Mac Open dialog box with the Format option available.

dialog box to show the Format option menu (see Figure 5.4), which you can use to open a file as a specific file format.

Opening A Kodak Photo CD Image File

To open a Kodak Photo CD image file, choose File|Open and browse to find the location of the Photo CD file. When the Photo CD dialog box opens, you can specify which resolution of the image to open (Resolution), the source type (Source), and in which editing mode to open it (Destination). The Image Info button displays additional information about the file's source.

Importing An Image

Importing is the term used in Photoshop to refer to bringing in any image that is either new from a scanner or digital imaging device, or a file containing vector graphics. To import files, either choose File|Import or File|Open.

Managing Image Files In Photoshop   **139**

When you choose File|Import, you can select from the following options and default import plug-ins:

- **Anti-aliased PICT (Mac only)** Use this option to open a PICT file using anti-aliasing when you have turned off the Anti-alias PostScript option in the General dialog box (which you access by choosing File|Preference|General).

- **PICT Resource (Mac only)** Use this option to find an embedded PICT file (such as a welcome screen) in another application's resource file.

- **Quick Edit (Mac only)** Use this option to import only part of an existing Photoshop 2, Scitex CT, or TIFF image. After you choose this option, the Quick Edit dialog box opens, allowing you to select a small portion of the image, which is then imported as a file of its own. This option does not work with compressed TIFF files.

- **TWAIN Acquire (Mac) or TWAIN_32 (Windows)** Use this option to import images directly from a scanner or other digital imaging device that supports the TWAIN interface.

- **TWAIN Select (Mac) or Select TWAIN_32 Source (Windows)** Use this option to select the specific TWAIN device if you have more than one connected.

You can install additional import options by placing their plug-ins in the Import/Export folder of the Plug-Ins folder.

When opening or importing Adobe Illustrator, PDF, or EPS files, you can either open them as Photoshop files or place them in an existing Photoshop file. You can also paste or drag and drop Adobe Illustrator artwork directly from Illustrator to an existing Photoshop file.

> Anti-aliasing is the process of smoothing the edges of imported graphics. In some cases, these graphics may have jagged or "pixelated" lines, corners, circles, or other shapes. Anti-aliasing smoothes these imperfections by adding pixels of varying shades of gray or color. Unfortunately, anti-aliasing may also make some graphics, such as type, appear fuzzy, so you might need to experiment with it to determine whether it is optimum for a particular image.

Opening Adobe Illustrator, PDF, Or EPS Files
You can open Adobe Illustrator, PDF, or EPS files by choosing File|Open. Follow the typical procedure for opening files (discussed previously in this chapter).

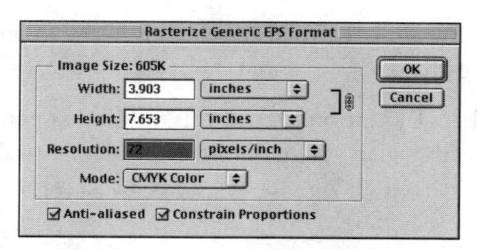

Figure 5.5 The Rasterize Generic EPS Format dialog box.

If you are opening Illustrator or EPS files, you see the Rasterize Generic EPS Format dialog box (see Figure 5.5). This dialog box opens with the values Photoshop obtains from the file's resource information. You can change these values—with or without constraining the proportions—and you can select anti-aliasing for the file.

> **STUDY ALERT** Rasterizing is the process of converting vector-based image information to pixel-based data. Because the image quality of vector-based graphics is not resolution-dependent, you can resize files that contain no bitmap graphics by using the Rasterize Generic EPS Format dialog box without concern for losing image quality. In fact, in some cases, you may find that increasing the resolution of vector-based graphics on rasterization improves the image quality after the image is imported into Photoshop.

> **STUDY ALERT** Photoshop can open PDF files only one page at a time. If you are opening single-page PDF files, the typical file opening procedure still works. When you're opening PDF files with multiple pages, you see a dialog box that allows you to select a specific page to open; you need to repeat this process for each page you want to open.
>
> However, Photoshop includes an automation assistant/wizard that automatically opens all the pages of a multiple-page PDF document. Choose File|Automate|Multi-Page PDF to PSD. The Convert Multi-Page PDF to PSD dialog box then opens (see Figure 5.6). Here, you choose the file to open (Source PDF), the pages to open (Page Range), the resolution and mode with or without anti-aliasing (Output Options), and the base name of the files to be created (Destination). Photoshop opens a new file for each page of the document and names it according to the base name, adding a numerical suffix to that name for each page.

Managing Image Files In Photoshop

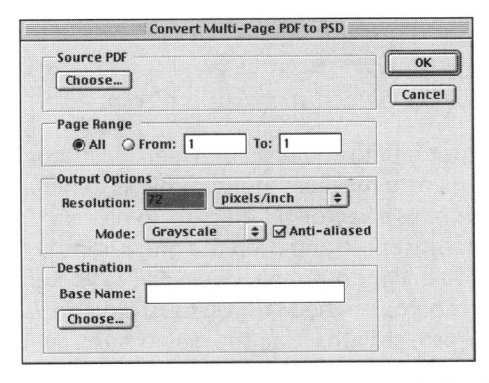

Figure 5.6 The Convert Multi-Page PDF To PSD dialog box.

Placing Adobe Illustrator, PDF, Or EPS Files

Use the Place command (File|Place) to insert Illustrator, PDF, or EPS files or graphics into open Photoshop files. Photoshop rasterizes these images as it imports them. An imported image appears on a new layer in the Photoshop image, in a bounding box that defines its size and shape. You then can adjust the imported image to place it where you want and at what size and attitude.

Control the bounding box with these commands/actions:

- Move the imported image by dragging inside the bounding box.

- Scale the imported image by dragging any corner or side handle of the bounding box. Constrain the proportions by pressing Shift as you drag a handle.

- Rotate the imported image by placing the cursor anywhere outside the bounding box and then dragging when the cursor changes to the bent arrow. Dragging the circle at the center of the bounding box moves the rotation axis.

- Skew the imported image by holding Cmd/Ctrl while dragging one of the bounding box's side handles.

- Confirm placement by pressing Return/Enter or double-clicking inside the bounding box.

- Cancel the placement by pressing Esc.

Pasting Adobe Illustrator Artwork

You also can paste vector graphics from Adobe Illustrator into open Photoshop files by choosing Edit|Paste or by dragging and dropping. Cut or copy the graphic from the open Illustrator file, switch to Photoshop, and then paste the graphic. Alternatively, you can select the graphic and drag it onto the window of the Photoshop file into which you want it placed.

> When using drag and drop between Illustrator and Photoshop, you can paste the Illustrator graphic as either a rasterized bitmap graphic or as a vector-based path. To paste graphics as bitmap graphics, just drag and drop the graphic into Photoshop. To paste as a path in Windows, hold down Ctrl as you drag and drop. To paste as paths on the Mac, you must use the Paste command and select Paste as Paths from the dialog box that opens.

Copyright And File Information

Pertinent file information can be read and/or attached to files in Photoshop. This file information includes ANPA-style file information and Digimarc copyright information.

ANPA File Information

The Newspaper Association of America and the International Press Telecommunications Council developed this standard for including extra information such as captions, credits, and index information on images that were likely to be transmitted and/or exchanged between newspapers and other publications. The File Info feature is available for all file formats on the Mac and for Photoshop, TIFF, JPEG, EPS, and PDF files in Windows.

You can access the File Info dialog box by choosing File|File Info. Here, you can choose to enter information for the following options:

➤ Caption (Cmd+1/Ctrl+1)

➤ Keywords (Cmd+2/Ctrl+2)

➤ Categories (Cmd+3/Ctrl+3)

➤ Credits (Cmd+4/Ctrl+4)

➤ Origin (Cmd+5/Ctrl+5)

➤ Copyright & URL (Cmd+6/Ctrl+6)

You can access these options either by selecting one from the Section option menu, by using the Prev or Next buttons, or by pressing the keyboard shortcut.

You can choose to replace the file info for a file by using the Load button and selecting another File Info file. You can save the current file info to a File Info file for later use with other images by using the Save button. Use the

Append button to add file information from a File Info file to the current information.

Digimarc

Digimarc is a third-party vendor of copyright protection services. The Digimarc process embeds digital information in an image that contains data regarding the author and/or copyright owner of an image. Photoshop scans every file that is opened for Digimarc copyright information using the Digimarc Detect Watermark plug-in. The presence of a copyright is signaled by the appearance of a copyright symbol in the title bar of the image's window. You can find the specific copyright information about an image by choosing File|File Info|Copyright & URL.

Saving And Exporting Images

Photoshop provides several options for saving and exporting image files.

Compression

Compression is the reduction of a file's size by reducing the amount of stored data in a file. The two types of compression are *lossy* and *lossless*. Lossy compression techniques compress files while discarding some image data, resulting in a loss of image quality. Lossless compression techniques accomplish reduction of the file size without discarding image data, protecting the quality of the image.

The following are the compression types that you may encounter in Photoshop:

- Lossless:
    - RLE (Run Length Encoding)
    - LZW (Lemple-Zif-Welch)
    - CCITT
    - ZIP
- Lossy:
    - JPEG (Joint Photographic Experts Group)

> Although JPEG is a lossy compression type, it's one of the more popular file formats and is considered the best format for compressing photographic image files. When saving image files to JPEG, you can specify the amount of compression, which, in turn, affects the amount of image degradation.
>
> Each time you save a file to JPEG, the file is compressed again, resulting in at least minor image degradation each time it is

> compressed. For this reason, you should save image files to JPEG only once, after you have completed all editing. Keeping a copy of the original image file in its native format is also advisable, in case you need to edit the image again later.

Flattening Layers

Before saving in any file format except Photoshop, you must flatten the image. You do so either by choosing Layer|Flatten Image or by choosing Flatten Image in the Layers palette menu. Remember that only visible layers are incorporated in the flattened image. (For more information about using layers, see Chapter 9.)

When you use the Save A Copy command to save a Photoshop file as another Photoshop file, the Save A Copy dialog box allows you to choose to flatten the file upon copying.

Reducing File Sizes

Reducing a file's size as much as possible may be necessary, particularly when you're producing images for the World Wide Web. Several techniques reduce a file's size:

➤ Use the Save A Copy command and select Exclude Non-Image Data. This option removes all the data that is not used specifically for reproducing the image, including file information, paths, guides, grids, and so on.

➤ Choose File|Preferences|Saving Files and select Never Save or Ask When Saving from the Image Previews option menu before saving the image. Saving a file without image previews sometimes drastically reduces its file size.

Preferences For Saving

The preferences for saving files can help speed your work in some cases by automatically assuming some characteristics for saved files. After you choose File|Preferences|Saving Files, you can set preferences for the following:

➤ **Image Previews** You can set Photoshop to never save the previews, always save the previews, or to ask every time if you want to save the previews.

On the Mac, this preference affects the saving of icons, the thumbnail previews (which appear in the Open dialog box), and the full-size 72 ppi preview image. If you choose Ask When Saving, the Save As dialog box expands to allow you to choose which of the previews to save.

In Windows, this preference affects the saving of the thumbnail preview only. To create and save a thumbnail icon (that will show up on the desktop and in file lists) for a Photoshop (PSD) file, open its properties dialog box from the file list with the right mouse button, and click on Photoshop Image. Click on the Generate Thumbnails checkbox, and then click on OK.

➤ **(Append) File Extension** This preference is different between the two platforms. Because the Windows version always saves the three-character file extension when saving files, the choice here is only whether to use upper- or lowercase letters for the extension.

On the Mac, you have the option of not saving the file extension at all, so you can tell Photoshop to always or never add the file extension, or to ask whether to do so each time you save. If you choose to add the file extension, you can select upper- or lowercase characters.

➤ **File Compatibility** This option provides a means of saving Photoshop files that will be compatible with applications that don't support Photoshop layers. This option can drastically increase the file size. The default is on, but if you don't think you'll need it, click on the Include Composited Image With Layered Files checkbox to turn it off.

Save

After you create and name a new image file or open an existing file, you can save changes made to the image file by choosing File|Save (Cmd+S/Ctrl+S).

Save As

If you need to save a copy of a file or save a file in a different file format, you can choose File|Save As (Shift+Cmd+S/Shift+Ctrl+S). Remember, though, that after you use Save As, you will be working in the new file, and the original will be closed. You have the opportunity to save the open file to any folder, with any name, and in any compatible format.

Save A Copy

You can also choose File|Save A Copy (Option+Cmd+S/Alt+Ctrl+S) to copy or rename a file or change it to a different format. The difference between Save A Copy and Save As is that Save A Copy creates a copy of the file, while leaving you in the original file. Save A Copy can also be good for creating copies of steps or states as you work. You have the options of saving to any folder, with any name, and in a compatible format. SaveS Copy also allows you to flatten the image file as the copy is made and to include or exclude the alpha channels and/or the non-image data (everything but pixels). In certain formats, you also choose what, if any, preview icons to include.

Saving Files As Photoshop EPS Or DCS

Image files destined for use in other applications are often saved as Photoshop EPS or DCS files. EPS files are useful for exporting image files to other applications, and DCS files are useful for producing color separations for printing. The DCS 2.0 format supports spot channels and single alpha channels.

> **For image files exported to Adobe Illustrator or PageMaker for eventual printing on paper, Adobe recommends saving the files as Photoshop EPS or TIFF files, from the CMYK mode. The colors in TIFF files can be managed even after placement in Illustrator 7 or PageMaker 6.5.**

Save files as Photoshop EPS or DCS files by first choosing File|Save As or File|Save A Copy. If the file has been flattened, you can choose Photoshop EPS, Photoshop DCS 1.0, or Photoshop DCS 2.0 from the Format option menu.

If you select Photoshop EPS, the EPS Options dialog box opens. The EPS Options dialog box options are as follow:

- **Preview** Select a type of Preview to be saved with the file. If you intend to export the file for use in another application, you must save a preview if you want to be able to see the image in the other application.

- **Encoding** Select an encoding option. The optimum encoding method is determined by the platform you are working on and whether you need to compress the file at all. You should consult your printer or service bureau before you select an encoding option.

- **Include Halftone Screen** Select this option if you are sending the file to an application that can read the custom halftone screen information you may have entered for the file.

- **Include Transfer Function** Choose to include any transfer functions settings you have used to improve the file's output. (For more information on transfer functions, see Chapter 4.)

- **PostScript Color Management** Select this option if you are printing to a PostScript printer and you have not yet converted the file's colors to the printer's color space.

If you are saving the file as a DCS file, you have the same options, except you don't have the PostScript Color Management option. You also need to select the type of DCS file to produce from the DCS option menu.

Export

Images and supporting features can be exported from Photoshop to other applications. The Export commands, which you access by choosing File|Export, are necessary for creating GIF images and exporting vector-based paths to Adobe Illustrator. On the Mac, you can also save a file you created by choosing File|Import|Quick Edit.

In addition, from the Paths palette you can create and export clipping paths, which help preserve an image's transparency when you're printing from another application.

You can install additional export options by placing their plug-ins in the Import/Export folder of the Plug-Ins folder.

GIF Files

GIF files can be either GIF87a or GIF89a. GIF87a files do not support transparency, but GIF89a files do. Whereas you can save GIF87a files from many Photoshop modes by choosing File|Save As, you can save GIF89a files only from the RGB and Indexed Color modes.

If you want to export an image as a GIF89a file with transparency, you have two options. You can create an image with background transparency in RGB mode and export the file from RGB mode, or you can convert an image without background transparency to Indexed Color mode and define the transparency when exporting.

To export an image as a GIF89a file from RGB, follow these steps:

1. Create a file with a foreground image on a background transparency.

2. Choose File|Export|GIF89a Export. The GIF89a dialog box opens (see Figure 5.7).

3. Select or load a Palette type, specify an exact number of colors (from 2 to 255) or a bit depth, and select interlacing and whether to include caption information with the file. You can preview the file using the Preview button, which opens the Preview dialog box.

To export an image as a GIF89a file from Indexed Color, follow these steps:

1. Select File|Export|GIF89a Export. A different GIF89a dialog box opens; this one is more like the Preview dialog box of the RGB export process (see Figure 5.8).

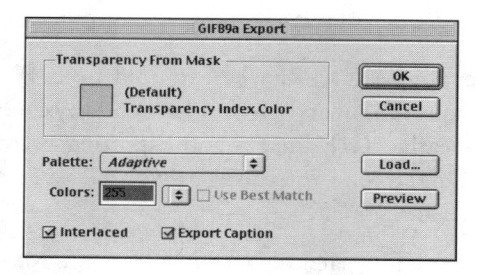

Figure 5.7 The GIF89a dialog box when opened from an RGB file.

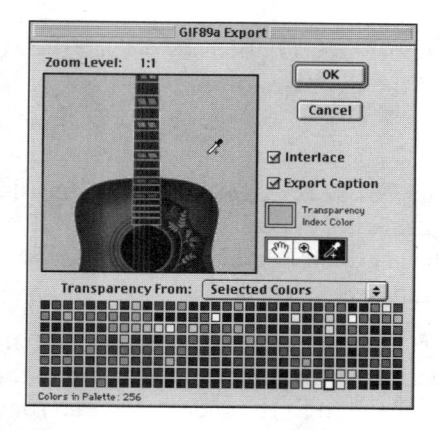

Figure 5.8 The GIF89a dialog box when opened from an Indexed Color file.

2. From this dialog box, you have the same options as described in the RGB process, but you also need to select a transparency color using the Eyedropper tool in the dialog box. When you click on a color in the preview area of the dialog box, that color becomes transparent. That transparent color's swatch is outlined in the grid of color swatches at the bottom of the dialog box. If you need to remove a color from transparency, toggle the Eyedropper tool with Option/Alt, and click on the color's swatch.

Note: You can also define the transparency of an Indexed Color GIF89a file by first creating an alpha channel mask for the file and then selecting the name of that mask in the Transparency From option menu.

Creating And Saving Clipping Paths

> Another way to create transparency for an image is to use clipping paths. *Clipping paths* define an area that will not appear when an image is printed from another application. Don't confuse this term with *clipping groups*, which are a feature of layers.

Create clipping paths by choosing Clipping Path from the Paths palette menu. The Clipping Path palette opens, and you can select a pathname from the Path option menu.

When an image with a clipping path is printed from another application, the PostScript printer reproduces the path using only straight lines. *Flatness* is a reference to how many straight lines it will use to create the clipping path; flatness values can range from 0.2 to 100. If the path is very circular, you would want the printer to use fewer straight lines to more smoothly approximate the curves and you would enter a lower flatness value. Clipping paths is another feature that can cause printing problems, so consult with your printer or service bureau for optimum settings information.

If the file is to be printed on a PostScript printer, you should save it as Photoshop EPS or DCS. If it is to be printed on a non-PostScript printer, it works only if you export it as a TIFF file to Adobe PageMaker 5 or higher.

> If a file with a clipping path causes printing errors, you might need to simplify the original path used to define the clipping path. Manually reduce the number of anchor points on the path, or increase the tolerance setting when creating the path. (See Chapter 7 for more information about paths.)

Exporting Paths To Adobe Illustrator

If you need to export vector-based paths to Adobe Illustrator, select File|Export|Paths To Illustrator. You are then prompted to choose a destination with the path for the new file that will be created. On the Mac, you also need to tell Photoshop which path to export in the Write option menu.

When you open the file in Illustrator, it is the size of the file from which you exported the path, and the path is in the same respective position as it was in the original. As long as you don't move it, it remains there, so you can exchange it back to Photoshop more easily.

Object Linking And Embedding

OLE, which stands for Object Linking and Embedding, is a feature of Windows 95 and Windows NT 4.0 and higher applications. It allows you to associate an image with Photoshop while it is in another application. A similar feature available on the Mac is called Edit Graphic Object (EGO).

Practice Questions

Question 1

> Which of these file formats supports layers? (Select all that apply.)
>
> ❏ a. PSD
> ❏ b. PICT
> ❏ c. TIFF
> ❏ d. EPS

Answer a is correct. PSD is the suffix for the Photoshop file format. It is the only format that supports layers.

Question 2

> If you are working on a file in Lab mode, in which of these file formats could you save it? (Select all that apply.)
>
> ❏ a. PSD
> ❏ b. BMP
> ❏ c. JPEG
> ❏ d. TIFF

Answers a and d are correct. Neither BMP nor JPEG support Lab mode files.

Question 3

> If you want to compress a file without losing image quality, which of these compression techniques should you not use?
>
> ○ a. LZW
> ○ b. JPEG
> ○ c. RLE
> ○ d. ZIP

Answer b is correct. JPEG is a lossy compression technique.

Question 4

Which of these abbreviations can represent image resolution? (Select all that apply.)

- ❑ a. ppi
- ❑ b. rip
- ❑ c. lpi
- ❑ d. rsi

Answer a is correct. ppi is short for pixels-per-inch. lpi is short for lines-per-inch and refers to halftone screen frequencies only.

Question 5

What is an acceptable sample ratio for scanning an image? (Select all that apply.)

- ❑ a. 1:1
- ❑ b. 1.5:1
- ❑ c. 2:1
- ❑ d. 2.5:1

Answers b and c are correct. You should scan images at a resolution that is 1.5 to 2 times the value of the halftone screen frequency of the target publication.

Question 6

If I'm printing with a screen frequency of 85 lpi, what type of publication am I likely printing in?

- ○ a. Magazine
- ○ b. Glossy brochure
- ○ c. Newspaper
- ○ d. Annual Report

Answer c is correct. Newspapers usually print with a line screen of 85 lpi.

Question 7

What is *rasterizing*?

○ a. Converting to a particular Jamaican religion

○ b. Converting pixel-based data to vector-based data

○ c. Converting vector-based data to pixel-based data

○ d. Importing paths from Adobe Illustrator

Answer c is correct. Rasterizing is the process of converting vector-based data to pixel-based data that Photoshop must use when importing EPS, PDF, or Illustrator files.

Question 8

If you import a 10-page PDF file by choosing File|Open, how many Photoshop files will you wind up with?

○ a. 1

○ b. 10

○ c. However many you choose from 1 to 10

○ d. None; you can't choose File|Open to import PDF files.

Answer a is correct. When you choose File|Open to import a PDF file, you can choose which page of the 10-page PDF file to open, but you can open only one of these pages at a time. If you want to open more of the pages at one time, you should choose File|Automate|Multi-Page PDF To PSD.

Question 9

Select the different methods for using Adobe Illustrator images in Photoshop. (Select all that apply.)

❏ a. File|Open

❏ b. Drag and drop

❏ c. File|Place

❏ d. Edit|Paste

All the answers are correct. You can open an Illustrator file, you can drag and drop from Illustrator, you can place an Illustrator file, and you can paste Illustrator graphics cut or copied from Illustrator to the clipboard.

Question 10

> Where can you see an indication that a file has a Digimarc watermark? (Select all that apply.)
>
> ❏ a. A copyright symbol in the image window title bar
> ❏ b. A copyright symbol in the lower-left corner of the image window
> ❏ c. In the Copyright & URL dialog box, which you open by choosing File|File Info\Copyright & URL
> ❏ d. Under Digimarc Info when you choose View|Digimarc Info

Answers a and c are correct. The Digimarc Detect Watermark plug-in scans every file you open in Photoshop. and if a file has a watermark with copyright information embedded, Photoshop displays a copyright symbol in the title bar and the copyright information in the Copyright & URL dialog box.

Question 11

> Which of the following can increase a file's size, and which of them can you exclude from an image to decrease the file's size? (Select all that apply.)
>
> ❏ a. File information
> ❏ b. Image previews
> ❏ c. Paths
> ❏ d. Image data

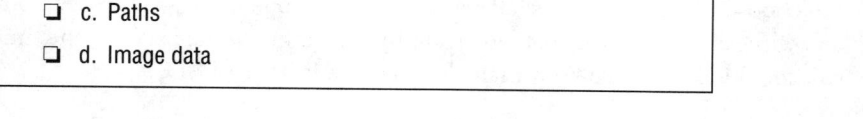

Trick! question

All the answers are correct. All these factors can increase a file's size. You can exclude file information and paths with the Exclude Non-Image Data option in the Save A Copy dialog box. You can choose not to save Image Previews. You also could use JPEG to compress the file, which would discard some image data.

Question 12

> If you want to create a copy of the image file you are currently editing, and you want the original file to remain open after you make the copy, which command do you use? (Select all that apply.)
>
> ❏ a. File|Save
>
> ❏ b. File|Save As
>
> ❏ c. File|Save A Copy
>
> ❏ d. Image|Duplicate

Answers c and d are correct. Save doesn't create a copy. Save As creates a copy but closes the original. Save A Copy creates a copy but doesn't open it, leaving you in the original. Duplicate creates a copy and opens it, leaving the original open on the desktop.

Question 13

> From which of these modes can you create GIF files? (Select all that apply.)
>
> ❏ a. Grayscale
>
> ❏ b. RGB
>
> ❏ c. Indexed Color
>
> ❏ d. CMYK

Answers a, b, and c are correct. You can Save As from Grayscale, RGB, and Indexed Color to create a GIF87a file, and you can Export from RGB and Indexed Color to create GIF89a files.

Question 14

> Which of the following flatness values creates a smoother clipping path curve when printed?
>
> ○ a. 0.1
> ○ b. 10
> ○ c. 89
> ○ d. 200

Answer b is correct. It is true that the lower the flatness value, the smoother the curve, but flatness values must range from 0.2 to 100.

Need To Know More?

Blatner, David & Steve Roth: *Real World Scanning and Halftones*. Peachpit Press. ISBN 1-56609-093-8. In-depth information about resolution and scanning.

McClelland, Deke: *Macworld Photoshop 5 Bible*. IDG Books Worldwide, Inc. ISBN 0-7645-3231-6.

Adjusting Images

Terms and concepts you'll need to understand:

- ✓ Color table animation
- ✓ Histogram
- ✓ Image cache
- ✓ Levels
- ✓ Curves
- ✓ Threshold
- ✓ Sharpening
- ✓ Unsharp Mask
- ✓ Crop
- ✓ Image size
- ✓ Resampling
- ✓ Interpolation

Techniques you'll need to master:

- ✓ Reading a histogram
- ✓ Using the Levels dialog box
- ✓ Using the Auto Levels command
- ✓ Using the Curves dialog box
- ✓ Using the Variations dialog box
- ✓ Applying the Unsharp Mask filter
- ✓ Changing an image's size and resolution

After you open a file in Photoshop, you can edit or adjust its colors, sharpness, and size and shape. This chapter deals with the tools and commands for making those adjustments.

Adjusting Colors And Tones

When you make adjustments to the colors and tones of an image, you can make those adjustments to the entire image or to individual channels, to an individual layer, or to an adjustment layer. (See Chapter 10 for more information on channels and Chapter 9 for more information on layers.)

Photoshop provides many tools for adjusting the colors and tonal ranges of an image, including the following:

- Levels
- Curves
- Auto Levels command
- Color Balance command
- Hue/Saturation command
- Replace Color command
- Selective Color command
- Variations command
- Invert command
- Equalize command
- Threshold command
- Posterize command
- Desaturate command

Previewing Colors And Color Adjustments

Remember that the methods for previewing colors (as presented in Chapters 3 and 4) include the following:

- Showing and using the Info palette
- Using color samplers and the Info palette
- Showing and using the Color palette

You can monitor out-of-gamut colors, as presented in Chapter 4, by choosing View|Gamut Warning or by watching the color values in the Info palette.

You can preview the on-screen appearance of colors that will be converted to CMYK by selecting View|Preview and then selecting CMYK for the composite image, CMY for just the three subtractive primaries, or the individual color components. You can preview both the RGB image and its CMYK equivalent by choosing View|New View. This command opens a new window for the image that changes as you edit the other (or vice versa); you can set one of the windows to preview CMYK and leave the other in RGB.

Color Table Animation

If you make a color or tonal adjustment to an image that has a Preview option in its dialog box, and you have the option selected, Photoshop changes the colors of your entire monitor to show the preview of the changes. This process happens while you are still in the dialog box, before you have accepted the adjustment with the OK button. After you approve the adjustment, the changes are made to the image only, and the monitor reverts to its "normal" colors. This process, called *color table animation*, can be annoying if the preview is inaccurate.

You can turn color table animation on and off by choosing File|Preferences|Display & Cursors and then selecting the Video LUT Animation checkbox. This option is on by default on the Mac, but it doesn't work in many cases if the monitor is not set to 256 colors. The same is true for Windows, where the option is off by default.

Histograms

You can view distribution of the brightness levels of the pixels in an image by viewing its *histogram*.

> A histogram is a bar chart that shows the distribution of the brightness levels of the pixels in an image (see Figure 6.1). The brightness values are spread across the histogram, from zero at the left to 255 at the right. The height of the bars indicates how many pixels in an image have brightness values in the range where the bar is located. If an image has a lot of dark areas, you see tall bars at the left of the histogram. The histogram of a light image would have taller bars on the right side. In the case of the image displayed in the histogram in Figure 6.1, you can see that the image (shown in Figure 6.2) has many pixels with values in dark areas and many pixels with values in light areas. The remaining pixels spread out fairly evenly across the middle values.

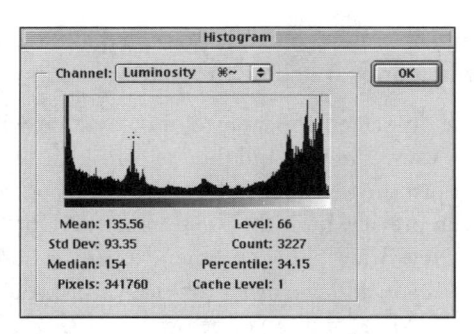

Figure 6.1 The Histogram dialog box

Figure 6.2 The image that is represented by the histograms in Figures 6.1 and 6.3.

You can view a histogram for an image at any time by choosing Image|Histogram. Histograms are also displayed when you use Levels or the Threshold command.

Selecting an area before choosing Image|Histogram creates a histogram based only on the pixels in the selected area.

You can choose to view the histogram of the image's luminosity (Luminosity) or of any of the color components by selecting one in the Channel option menu of the Histogram dialog box.

Placing the cursor (the crosshair icon shown in Figure 6.1) over an area on the histogram displays the following information:

- **Mean** The average brightness value of the image
- **Std Dev** The standard deviation of the values
- **Median** The middle level of brightness of the image's pixels
- **Pixels** The number of pixels on which the histogram is based
- **Level** The brightness level where the cursor is located (from 0 through 255)
- **Count** The number of pixels at the level where the cursor is located
- **Percentile** The percentile of the level where the cursor is located (where 0 percent is the darkest level in the image and 100 percent is the brightest level).
- **Cache Level** The number of the downsampling used to create the histogram

The Image Cache

Photoshop can save up to eight downsamplings of an image in a RAM cache to help speed up previews. This process is called *image caching*, and the downsamplings are progressively smaller copies of the image. The default setting is four, so Photoshop saves to RAM copies of the image at 100, 50, 25, and 12.5 percent of its size.

You set the number of cached images you want Photoshop to save by choosing File|Preferences|Image Cache and entering a number from 1 through 8. Obviously, if Photoshop is sending data to RAM for the image cache, it is using up available RAM, which might be a consideration on systems with less RAM. On these systems, you might want to set a lower number of downsamplings.

The Use Cache For Histograms checkbox in the Image Cache preference box tells Photoshop to base histograms on the downsampling that is closest to the display size of the image. This option may speed the creation of histograms in some cases, but a histogram based on any downsampling other than the 1, or 100 percent, downsampling, may not be accurate.

If the Cache Level info area at the lower right of the Histogram dialog box (refer to Figure 6.1) has a 1 in it, the histogram is based on the full-sized image copy. A number 4 means the histogram is based on the smallest, 12.5 percent-sized copy.

The Levels Dialog Box

Levels is an adjustment option that allows you to view a histogram of an image's colors and make adjustments to the image's highlights, midtones, and/or shadows. You can adjust all the color channels simultaneously, individually, or in groups of your choosing. However, the options displayed on the right of the Levels dialog box affect all channels simultaneously.

Access Levels by choosing Image|Adjust|Levels (Cmd+L/Ctrl+L). Selecting Levels opens the Levels dialog box (see Figure 6.3). A histogram of the image or a selected area of the image appears in the Levels dialog box.

You can make adjustments to the image by manipulating these options and values in the Levels dialog box:

➤ **Channel** Select the color channel you want the histogram to map. If you want to edit more than one channel at a time, you must select multiple channels by Shift+selecting in the Channels palette before you open the Levels dialog box.

➤ **Input Levels** Increase the overall contrast of an image by adjusting the white point level, the gamma (midtones), and the black point level. Use either the numerical values boxes or the sliders under the histogram.

Possible numerical values range from 0 through 255. All pixels at levels below the value entered in the first box are black, and all pixels at levels above the value entered in the last box are white. Entering a value in the middle box sets the gamma, or middle gray, position. Gamma values range from 0.10 through 9.99, and the default, or "true," middle gray value is 1.00.

The sliders are colored to correspond to their adjustment. Sliding the black slider to the right maps all pixels to the left of the slider as black.

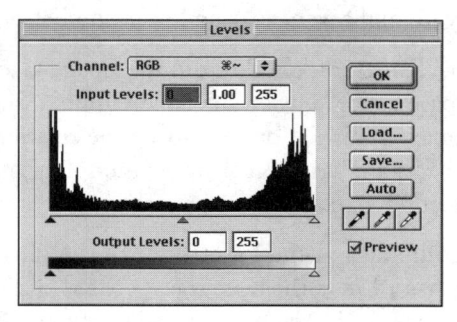

Figure 6.3 The Levels dialog box.

Sliding the white slider to the left maps all pixels to the right of the slider as white. Sliding the gray slider moves the middle gray value, lightening or darkening the midtones without affecting the highlights and shadows.

You can also adjust the Input Levels up and down by 1 by pressing the arrow keys and by 10 by holding the Shift key as you press the arrow keys.

➤ **Output Levels** Decrease the overall contrast of an image by adjusting the levels of the brightest and darkest pixels in the image. Whereas the Input Levels allow you to spread out an image's pixels over a greater range of brightness, Output Levels allow you to foreshorten that range of brightness. Again, you enter numerical values or slide the shadow or highlight sliders. Entering a higher number in the first values box or sliding the black slider to the right maps the darkest pixels to a higher, or more gray, brightness. Entering a lower number in the second values box maps the lightest pixels to a darker, more gray, brightness.

➤ **Cancel/Reset** Close the Levels dialog box without accepting any changes, or reset the original values. Hold the Option/Alt key to toggle the button to Reset.

➤ **Load** Load previously saved values.

➤ **Save** Save to disk the values currently entered in the Levels dialog box.

➤ **Auto/Options** Select the Auto Levels command (described in the next section), or open the Options dialog box for the Auto Levels command by pressing the Option/Alt key.

➤ **Eyedroppers** Set the white, gamma, and black points of an image by selecting a specific color in an image. While the Levels dialog box is open, clicking on a color with the black-tipped eyedropper (as shown in Figure 6.4) selects that specific pixel's brightness level as the black point. All pixels at lower brightness levels become black. The middle, or gray-tipped, eyedropper sets the middle gray level, and the white-tipped eyedropper sets the white point, the brightness level above which all pixels will become white.

Figure 6.4   The Eyedropper icons in the Levels dialog box.

➤ **Preview** Toggle on and off the preview option. If the Video LUT Animation checkbox is checked (on) in the Display & Cursors dialog box, selecting Preview applies the appearance of Levels adjustments to the image window only. Deselecting Preview applies the adjustments to the entire monitor. (When Video LUT Animation is active and Preview is deselected, clicking on the title bar of the Levels dialog box toggles between the entire screen preview and no preview.) If the Video LUT Animation checkbox is not checked (off) in the Display & Cursors dialog box, no preview of any kind is displayed.

In RGB and Grayscale modes, you can also use the Threshold mode (described later in this chapter) from the Levels dialog box to determine the extreme light and dark areas of an image. Make sure Preview is deselected and hold down Option/Alt while you drag the white or black Input Levels triangle to change to the Threshold mode of the Levels dialog box.

The Auto Levels Command

The Auto Levels command automatically performs the same contrast adjustment that you can do manually with the Levels dialog box. Auto Levels automatically maps the lightest pixels in an image as white and the darkest pixels as black and then spreads out the midtones between them. Auto Levels performs this operation individually to each color channel. Figures 6.5 and 6.6 show histograms for the same image, before and after using Auto Levels.

The Auto Levels command clips the pixel values at each extreme of the histogram by a value you set with the Options button in the Levels dialog box. The default value is 0.5%. Access the Options button in the Levels dialog box by pressing the Option/Alt key, which toggles the Auto button to Options.

The Curves Dialog Box

The Curves adjustment is an alternative to the Levels adjustment. Whereas you can adjust only the highlights, gamma, and shadows of an image with

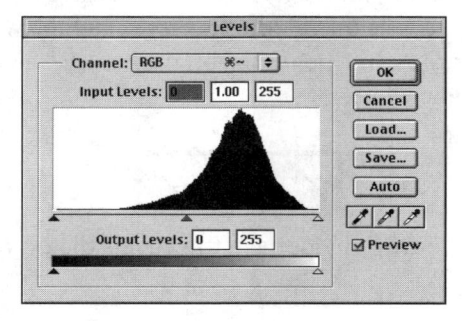

Figure 6.5 An uncorrected histogram.

Adjusting Images

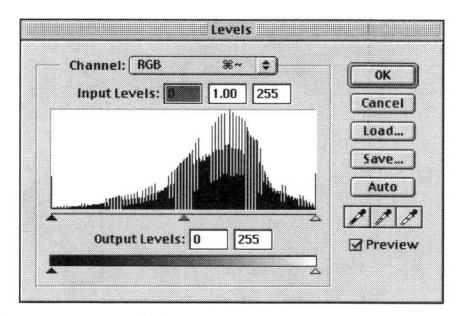

Figure 6.6 The histogram for the same image as in Figure 6.5, after using Auto Levels.

Levels, you can adjust pixel levels at up to 16 points with the Curves command. Open the Curves dialog box (shown in Figure 6.7) by choosing Image|Adjust|Curves (Cmd+M/Ctrl+M). As with the Levels dialog box, those options displayed down the right side of the Curves dialog box perform operations on all color channels simultaneously.

The Curves dialog box has several of the same features, with the exception of the adjustment operation itself, and works much the same way as the Levels dialog box. Use the Channel option menu, the Cancel/Reset button, the Load/Save buttons, the Auto/Option button, and the Preview button as you would in the Levels dialog box.

> Remember that in both the Curves and Levels dialog boxes, you can choose to define adjustments to individual or all color channels. If all the channels are selected in the Channels palette before you open the dialog box, the RGB or CMYK channel is the default selection in the Channel option menu, depending on the mode.
>
> If you want to edit one of the other channels, select a specific channel in the Channel option menu to make a change only to that one specific channel.
>
> To edit multiple channels—but not all the channels—simultaneously, close the dialog box and Shift+click in the Channels palette to select the multiple channels to edit. Choose the Levels or Curves command again, and you will see the initials of the channels you selected listed together in the dialog box. Only those channels that you selected in the Channels palette are then available in the dialog box, and you can edit their composite or the channels individually. Spot channels are not included in the composite, nor is there a composite curve when multiple spot color channels are selected.

Chapter 6

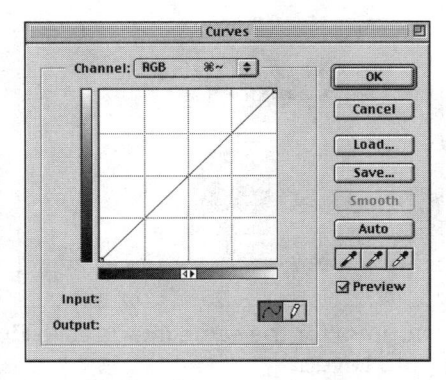

Figure 6.7 The Curves dialog box.

In other words, if you want to define a point on the brightness curve for only the green channel, you Shift+click the green channel in the Channels palette and then open the respective dialog box. If you want to edit both the blue and green channels at the same time, you do the same thing, but you Shift+click both channels in the Channels palette before you open the respective dialog box.

The Curves dialog box also has an Auto button, which performs the same operation as the Auto button in the Levels dialog box and the Auto Levels command.

The other features and options of the Curves dialog box are as follows:

▶ **Brightness Graph** Displays the line, or brightness curve, from the dark values (in the lower left) to light values (in the upper right) when in RGB and displays the ink percentages with 0 percent on the left and 100 percent on the right when in CMYK. Reverse the display of the curve by clicking on the double arrow on the brightness bar under the graph.

Displayed from left to right, Input Levels are the original brightness levels of the pixels in the image, effective when you open the Curves dialog box. Output Levels are the brightness values that will exist if you approve the operation by clicking OK. RGB brightness values range from 0 to 255 and CMYK values range from 0 to 100.

Toggle the grid between one-quarter divisions and one-tenth divisions by pressing Option/Alt while clicking in the grid.

▶ **Brightness Bar** Displays the light-to-dark direction of the curve. Click on this brightness bar to reverse the display direction of the curve.

▶ **Input/Output** Displays the numerical values for an individual point on the brightness curve. Clicking on a point activates that point and displays that point's input and output values. You can then change the

Adjusting Images   **169**

point's values by entering numerical values in these boxes. If the curve has multiple points, the active point, or the one whose Input/Output values are displayed, is signified by a black square. The inactive points are white squares.

➤ **Curve Tools** Change the brightness values of up to 16 different points in the image's brightness range or draw arbitrary curves.

Use the Point tool to add a point to the curve, and the drag the point to change its values. Dragging any one point doesn't affect any other existing points.

Use the Pencil tool to draw a free-form, arbitrary curve. Click and drag anywhere in the graph along the line, and the curve will connect to that point. Pressing Shift as you drag constrains the curve to a straight line.

> After a point is set on the curve, you can delete it simply by activating it and pressing Delete. Alternatively, you can drag it off the graph, or press Cmd/Ctrl and click on the point.
>
> To remove all the points on a curve, hold Option/Alt to toggle the Cancel button to Reset, and click on the button.

➤ **Smooth** Automatically smooths the curve for better transitions between colors in the image. Available after using the Pencil tool to draw an arbitrary curve.

➤ **Eyedroppers** Set the white point, middle gray point, and the black point. These eyedroppers operate much the same way as the eyedroppers in the Levels dialog box, with some differences. After you set a point with the eyedroppers, you can drag that point to adjust its brightness.

If one of the Eyedropper tools is already selected, click on its icon to activate the regular Eyedropper tool. Then, you can go outside the dialog box to the image window to obtain the Input/Output values of specific colors in the image. When you click on a color, a circle appears on the curve in the Curves dialog box, and values appear in the Input/Output boxes, displaying where you are positioned on the curve.

> You can perform the following operations with shortcuts in the Curves dialog box:
>
> ➤ To set a point on the curve only in the composite channel (RGB or CMYK), select that channel in the Channel option menu, and then press Cmd/Ctrl when you click in the image with the eyedropper. (Actually, this shortcut sets the point on the curve of whichever channel is selected in the Channel option menu.)

> ➤ To set a point on the curve only in the components channels (Red, Green, and Blue), press Shift+Cmd/Shift+Ctrl as you click in the image with the eyedropper. This shortcut works regardless of which channel is selected in the Channel option menu.
>
> ➤ Press the arrow keys to move the activated point one brightness value in that respective direction.
>
> ➤ Activate multiple points by Shift+clicking.
>
> ➤ Pressing Cmd/Ctrl and the Tab key cycles forward (upward) through the points on the curve, and pressing Shift+Cmd+Tab/Shift+Ctrl+Tab cycles in the other direction.
>
> ➤ Deselect all the points on the curve either by pressing Cmd+D/Ctrl+D, or by pressing Cmd/Ctrl and clicking anywhere on the graph.

When the brightness bar displays dark values to the left and light values to the right, dragging the midpoint adjusts the gamma of an image in the same way that sliding the Levels dialog box sliders adjusts the gamma. Dragging the midpoint up or left darkens the gamma, and dragging the midpoint down or right lightens the midpoint. (These instructions would be just the opposite if you reverse the display of the curve.)

The Color Balance Command

Choose Image|Adjust|Color Balance (Cmd+B/Ctrl+B) to open the Color Balance dialog box. Select one of the three general tones in the Tone Balance area; then drag the sliders toward a color to increase it or away from it to decrease it. You can also enter numerical values for the amount of change of a color, from -100 to +100.

The Preserve Luminosity option is for RGB and CMYK images. It allows you to change the colors of an image without changing their brightness.

The Hue/Saturation Command

Choose Image|Adjust|Hue/Saturation (Cmd+U/Ctrl+U) to open the Hue/Saturation dialog box. This command allows you to alter the color (Hue) of a range of colors, the intensity (Saturation) of a range of colors, and/or the lightness (Lightness) of a range of colors. You can make these adjustments individually, and you can adjust only one or all of them. In the Edit option menu, you can select the Master option, which is all the colors in an image, or you can select one of the six additive and subtractive primary color components (Red, Yellow, Green, Cyan, Blue, or Magenta).

Adjust colors by either sliding the triangles under each adjustment type or by entering numerical values in the values boxes. These three adjustments change colors in three distinct ways:

➤ **Hue** Sliding this triangle moves a color around the color wheel. You can move up to 180 degrees in either direction. Enter values of -180 to +180.

➤ **Saturation** Sliding this triangle increases or decreases the intensity of a color. Decrease the intensity by sliding the triangle to the left, and increase the intensity by sliding the triangle right. Enter values of -100 to +100.

➤ **Lightness** Sliding this triangle darkens or lightens the colors in an image. Enter values of -100 to +100.

The color bars at the bottom of the dialog box represent the before and after values of the colors, top to bottom, respectively.

The Cancel/Reset button works as it does in other dialog boxes, as do the Load and Save buttons and the Preview option. The remainder of the options and features of the Hue/Saturation dialog box are as follows:

➤ **Edit** Select either the Master group or one of the individual color groups. If you select one of the individual color components, an adjustment slider is inserted between the color bars at the bottom of the box. (Using the adjustment slider is explained later in this section.)

➤ **Colorize** Use this option to colorize grayscale images. After you convert the image from grayscale to RGB (by choosing Image|Mode|RGB), select a foreground color. Open the Hue/Saturation dialog box (see Figure 6.8) and choose Colorize. The image is then colorized with the hue of the foreground color. You can then vary the color using the three adjustment types.

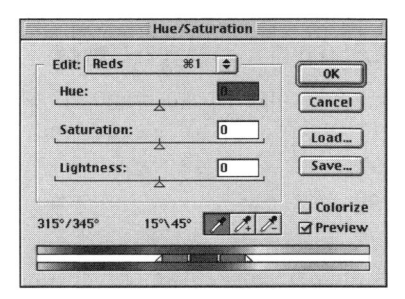

Figure 6.8 The Hue/Saturation dialog box with the adjustment slider active.

If you select one of the individual color components in the Edit option menu of the Hue/Saturation dialog box, the adjustment slider is inserted between the color bars at the bottom of the dialog box, the values of the four individual sliders of the adjustment slider are displayed next to the eyedropper icons, and the eyedropper icons become available. The darker area in the middle of the adjustment slider displays the range of colors contained in the selected component. The lighter areas adjacent to the central area display the range of colors that will be decreasingly adjusted—the fall-off. Narrower fall-off ranges may result in dithering.

Here's how the adjustment slider works:

- Move the entire slider by dragging the dark-gray center bar. This operation changes the hue of the color component without altering the width of its range. As you slide into the ranges of the other components, the Edit menu changes to reflect the position of the slider.

- Move the adjustment slider to a specific color by clicking in the image with the Eyedropper tool.

- Widen the range of colors in the component, without altering the width of the fall-off range, by dragging the fall-off range area.

- Alter the range of the color component by clicking with the Eyedropper + tool in the image to add a color to the range or by clicking with the Eyedropper - tool to subtract a color from the range. (Select one of these Eyedropper tools by clicking on its respective icon or by clicking Shift for the + tool or Option/Alt for the - tool when the Eyedropper tool is selected.)

- Decrease or increase the comparative amounts of color range and fall-off by dragging the white bars.

- Widen the fall-off range by dragging the white triangles.

- Move the color bars left or right by dragging while holding Cmd/Ctrl.

The Replace Color Command

You can select specific color ranges in an image to adjust with the Replace Color command. With the Replace Color command, you create a mask, or selection, of specific colors, and then you can adjust the hue, saturation, and lightness of only those colors.

Choose Image|Adjust|Replace Color to open the Replace Color dialog box. This dialog box has many of the same features of other color correction features. Use the Cancel/Reset button, the Load/Save button, and the Preview checkbox as described in earlier sections.

When the Replace Color dialog box is open, you can select whether to view the actual image with the Image radio button or to view the mask that you are creating by selecting the Selection Image radio button.

Click with the Eyedropper tool to select a color. Use the Eyedropper + tool and the Eyedropper - tool to add or subtract colors to or from the selection. Each click of the Eyedropper tools changes the Sample swatch to the color you have selected.

Slide the Fuzziness control to the right to increase the range of related colors to be included in the selection.

After you select the range of colors to adjust, slide the color adjustment sliders left or right to increase or decrease a specific color component. You can also enter values from -180 to +180 in the Hue values box or values from -100 to +100 in the Saturation and Lightness values boxes.

The Selective Color Command

Primarily used for adjusting the amounts of the four process color inks, the Selective Color command allows you to adjust the individual ink levels for the process colors independently.

Choose Image|Adjust|Selective Color to open the Selective Color dialog box. This dialog box has many of the same features of other color correction features. Use the Cancel/Reset button, the Load/Save button, and the Preview checkbox as described in earlier sections.

Select a color range to adjust from the Colors option menu. Slide the adjustment sliders left or right to increase or decrease the amount of ink to be applied for the selected color range. You can enter values from -100 to +100 in the respective values boxes.

The Relative method adjusts the colors relative to their current value. The percentage of adjustment that you enter or slide to will be the percentage of that color's current value.

The Absolute method adjusts the color amounts by the exact percentage selected or entered.

The Variations Command

The Variations command allows you to view previews of potential color adjustments before you make the adjustments. Choose Image|Adjust|Variations to open the Variations dialog box (shown in Figure 6.9).

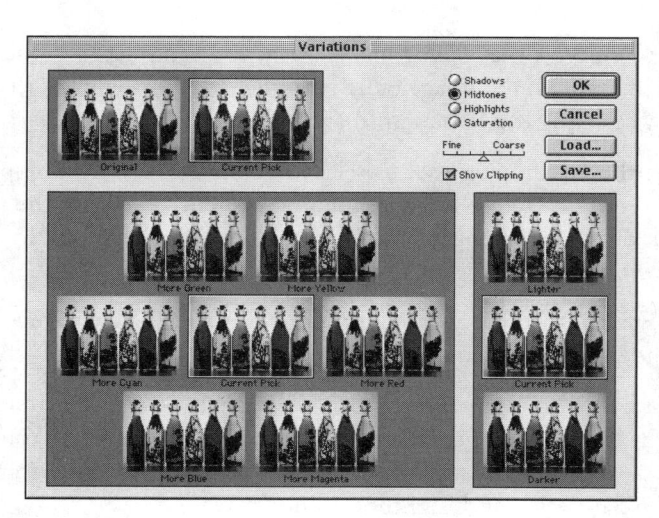

Figure 6.9 The Variations dialog box.

Use the Cancel/Reset button and the Load and Save buttons as you would with other dialog boxes.

The Original and Current Pick thumbnails at the top of the box show the state of the image when the dialog box was opened (Original) and the state based on any corrections you have made in the dialog box (Current Pick).

You can choose to adjust the Shadows, Midtones, or the Highlights.

The large square display area shows the current state of the image (Current Pick) and the various adjustments you can make. Opposite colors are opposite each other across the current pick. So, if you want less yellow, for example, you select the More Blue thumbnail. The Current Pick thumbnails change to reflect any corrections you make.

The three thumbnails displayed on the right give you the option of adjusting the brightness of the three general tones. Select Shadows, Midtones, or Highlights, and then click on either the Lighter or Darker thumbnail.

Adjust the amount of correction to make by sliding the Fine to Coarse slider toward Fine for less correction and toward Coarse for more correction.

The Show Clipping option displays a neon preview of pixels (as shown in Figure 6.10) that will be clipped either to pure white or pure black (which is the same as what happens to pixels when you set the white point or black point with the Levels or Curves commands). This display appears only when you adjust the Shadows or Highlights or when you adjust the Saturation.

Selecting the Saturation radio button changes the dialog box (as shown in Figure 6.11) to display only the two saturation adjustment thumbnails.

Adjusting Images **175**

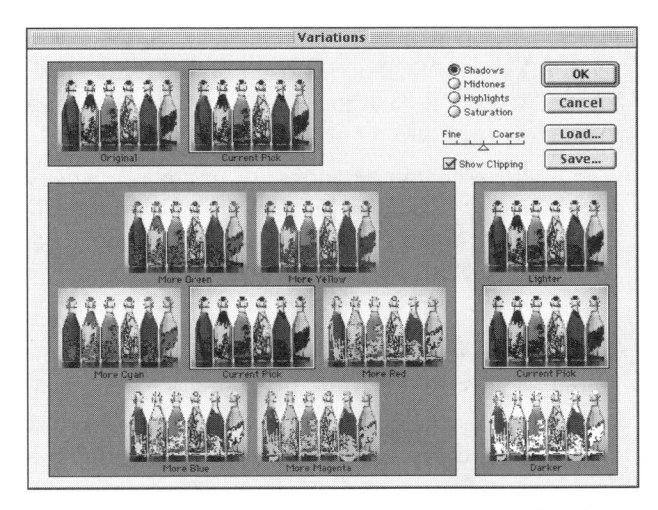

Figure 6.10 Clipping displayed in the Variations dialog box.

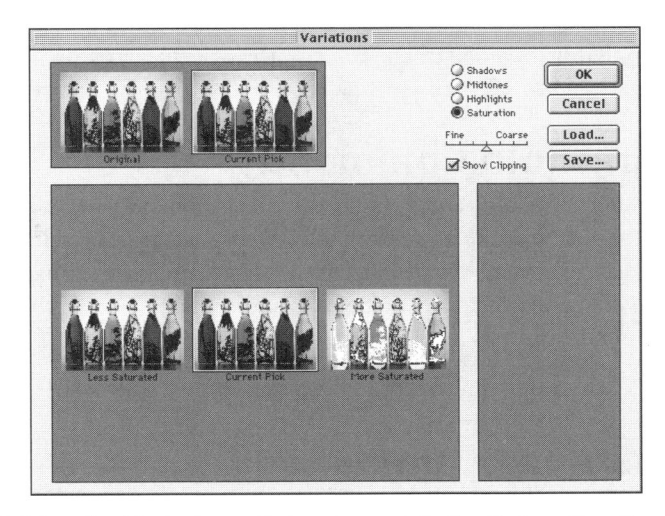

Figure 6.11 The Variations dialog box with the Saturation thumbnails.

Click on Less Saturated to decrease the intensity, of the colors in the image, or click on More Saturated to increase the intensity of the colors in the image. Increasing the saturation to more than the maximum for a color results in the neon Show Clipping display.

The Invert Command
The Invert Command inverts an image from positive to negative. Choose Image|Adjust|Invert (Cmd+I/Ctrl+I) to convert the image.

> **STUDY ALERT**
>
> Don't confuse the Invert command with the Inverse command (under Select|Inverse) or the Invert option (under Image|Apply Image). Remember that the Invert command creates a positive image from a negative image and vice versa.
>
> Also, the Invert command does not create a negative image that could serve as a negative for photographic printing. The plastic base of photographic films has a distinct color of its own that is not compensated for with this command.

The Equalize Command

The Equalize command works similarly to the Auto Levels command, mapping the lightest pixel range to white and the darkest pixel range to black and then spreading out the pixels in the image across the 256-value brightness range.

If you have nothing selected in the image, choosing Image|Adjust|Equalize performs the operation on the entire image. If you have selected an area in the image, choosing Image|Adjust|Equalize opens a dialog box that gives you the choice of applying the adjustment to only the selected area or to the entire area, but based on the selected area.

The Threshold Command

The Threshold command converts all the pixels above a specific brightness level (a Threshold) to white and below that level to black, converting color and grayscale images to bitmap-type, high-contrast black-and-white images. Choose Image|Adjust|Threshold to open the Threshold dialog box. Either drag the slider or enter a brightness level value (from 1 to 255) to set the Threshold.

You can make this adjustment to an entire image or to a selected area only.

The Posterize Command

Whereas the Threshold command converts all the colors in an image to only two colors (either black or white), the Posterize command allows you to convert the colors to a specific number of other colors, from 2 to 255. You don't, however, have the option of setting a threshold or defining the color ranges. Choose Image|Adjust|Posterize, and then enter a number of Levels of color to use.

The Desaturate Command

The Desaturate command allows you to convert an image to grayscale by discarding the color information from an image without converting it from its current color mode. Choose Image|Adjust|Desaturate.

Fixing Color Casts

If the images that you are importing from a particular scanner all seem to have the same undesirable color cast, that scanner may be incorrectly calibrated. If so, you can use the Load/Save buttons in the Levels or Curves dialog boxes to correct that color cast for every file imported from that scanner.

First, create an 11-step grayscale ladder by creating a new file, and then use the Gradient tool to create a gradient from pure black to pure white. Use the Posterize command to delineate the 11 separate steps, and then output the file. Scan the file output with the problem scanner, and open the new scan in Photoshop. Correct the color cast with the Levels or Curves dialog boxes; then save the new settings from the dialog box and load them for each file imported from that particular scanner.

Adjusting Sharpness

Sharpening images is often necessary to adjust image quality. In Photoshop, sharpening involves increasing the contrast between pixels, particularly those pixels that are adjacent to pixels of different colors.

Working With The Sharpen Filters

The effects of each of Photoshop's four default sharpening filters are applied to the entire image or to whatever area, if any, is selected. Access the following Photoshop Sharpen filters by choosing Filter|Sharpen:

- **Sharpen** Applies minimal sharpening effects to the entire image, with no variables.

- **Sharpen Edges** Applies minimal sharpening effects to the "edges" of an image by sharpening only those pixels adjacent to pixels that are vastly different in brightness.

- **Sharpen More** Applies a greater level of sharpening effects to the entire image, with no variables.

- **Unsharp Mask** Applies sharpening to an image based on several variables, providing greater control over the sharpening operation.

Using The Unsharp Mask Filter

Adobe recommends using the Unsharp Mask filter after you reduce an image's size. It is also useful for improving the apparent sharpness of any image that may be slightly blurry looking. Choose Filter|Sharpen|Unsharp

Mask to access the Unsharp Mask dialog box. The Cancel/Reset button and Preview checkbox work as they do in other dialog boxes.

The Unsharp Mask filter's options are as follows:

- **Amount** Specify the amount of contrast (sharpening) to apply to affected pixels. Drag the slider to a specific amount or enter a value between 1 and 500. Lower values apply less sharpening.

- **Radius** Specify the size of the area of pixels in which Photoshop will compare pixel levels. This size is often referred to as *edge thickness*. Drag the slider or enter a value between 0.1 and 250.0. Adobe recommends a radius of 1 to 2 for high-resolution images and advises that the effects of sharpening will be less noticeable in printed images than on-screen images.

- **Threshold** Specify the number of difference in brightness levels between one pixel and its surrounding pixels required for that pixel to be considered an edge pixel and sharpened. This difference is specified by a value between 0 and 255. A lower value results in more sharpening throughout the image, and a higher value results in sharpening of only higher-contrast areas.

Adjusting Image Size And Resolution

You can alter an image's size, either by cropping part of it or by reducing or enlarging the entire image. (Resolution is discussed in greater detail in Chapter 2.)

The Crop Command And The Crop Tool

You can crop an image using either the Crop command or the Crop tool.

The Crop command simply crops an image down to any rectangular area you have selected. First, select a rectangular area, and then choose Image|Crop. The Feathering option must be set to 0 pixels.

The Crop tool (the far-right tool shown in Figure 6.12) allows you to select the crop area and rotate and resize the image if you wish. Choose the Crop tool

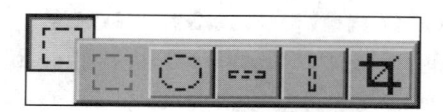

Figure 6.12 The Marquee tool and its hidden tool menu.

Adjusting Images

from the Toolbox by holding down the cursor over the Marquee tool to activate its menu of hidden tools and sliding over to the Crop tool.

Select the area you want to keep by dragging the Crop tool as if it were a Marquee tool. This operation creates a marquee with handles that you can move by dragging inside the marquee or resize by dragging a handle. Constrain the proportions as you resize by holding down Shift as you drag.

You can rotate the crop marquee simply by moving the cursor outside the marquee and dragging in the direction you want. You can drag the circle at the center of the marquee to adjust the rotation point. The crop marquee doesn't rotate in Bitmap mode.

Complete the crop by pressing Return/Enter or by double-clicking in the crop marquee. Cancel the crop by pressing Esc or Cmd+period/Ctrl+period.

The Image Size Command

Use the Image Size command to reduce or enlarge an image. You can choose from two methods for changing an image's size. You can *resample* an image, which increases or decreases the number of pixels in the image (its pixel dimensions), or you can simply change the image resolution, which displays or prints the image at a different size without altering its pixel dimensions.

> Resampling is the increasing or decreasing of the number of pixels in an image that occurs when an image's pixel dimensions are altered. You need to understand how resampling affects image quality. When you resample up to a higher resolution, Photoshop must create new pixels using an *interpolation* method. What this boils down to is that Photoshop guesses what colors to make the new pixels, which results in a loss of image quality.
>
> Interpolation is the guessing (or approximating) that Photoshop does when adding pixels to an image. Various interpolation methods result in varying levels of image quality loss. In Photoshop, you have three choices for an interpolation method:
>
> ➤ **Nearest Neighbor** The fastest method, resulting in a potentially greater loss of image quality
>
> ➤ **Bilinear** An intermediate method, which is a bit slower but results in less image quality loss
>
> ➤ **Bicubic** The slowest method, resulting in the least loss of image quality

> Resampling up, or increasing an image's resolution or size, is not recommended. You should rescan images at a larger size or higher scanning resolution if you want them larger.
>
> Downsampling, or reducing an image's resolution or size, usually results only in a loss of sharpness, which is the reason that the Unsharp Mask filter is recommended for downsampled images.

Choose Image|Image Size to access the Image Size dialog box (shown in Figure 6.13). The Image Size dialog box displays the pixel dimensions, the file size, the print size, and the resolution of the image. You can choose the measurement unit to use for the resizing in the option menus.

The chain icons appear in the dialog box when the Constrain Proportions checkbox is selected. This selection locks the aspect ratio of the image, and its dimensions change in unison. If the Constrain Proportions checkbox is deselected, you can distort the image by changing its dimensions separately.

If you choose to resample the image, changing its pixel dimensions, you work from the Image Size dialog box as it appears in Figure 6.13. If you intend to alter only the image resolution, deselect the Resample Image checkbox.

As you see in Figure 6.14, the Image Size dialog box changes to reflect the limited options you have when altering only the image resolution. Notice that the chain link icon now connects all three options in the Print Size area and that the Pixel Dimensions area is no longer available.

Select the interpolation method in the Resample Image option menu, and choose a measurement unit. Change the width, height, or resolution values and click on OK.

Use the Auto button to let Photoshop automatically select the optimum resolution of an image. Clicking the Auto button opens the Auto Resolution dialog

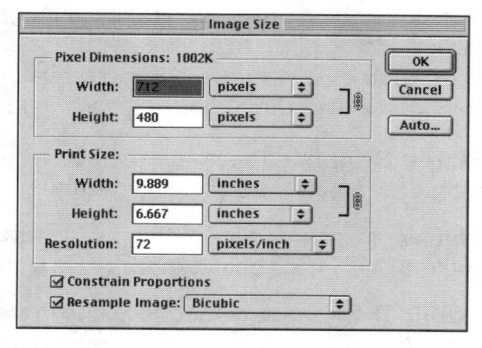

Figure 6.13 The Image Size dialog box.

Adjusting Images **181**

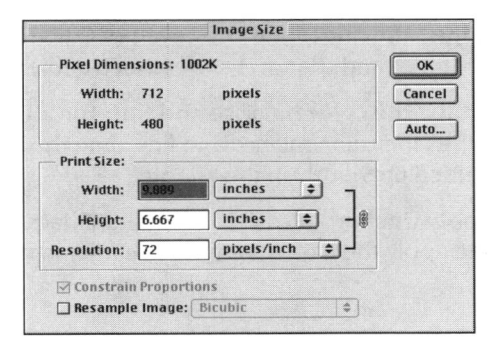

Figure 6.14 The Image Size dialog box with Resample Image deselected.

box, where you enter the halftone screen frequency of the output device and select Draft, Good, or Best, for a resolution that is 1, 1.5, or 2 times the screen frequency. After you click on OK, the file size displayed next to Pixel Dimensions changes and shows both the before and after file sizes. If the new file size is larger than the original file size, a loss of image quality is probable, and you should rescan the image at a higher scanning resolution. (See Chapter 5 for more details on how to determine the optimum scanning resolution.)

Adjusting The Canvas Size

If you need to create a larger canvas on which to edit an image, use the Canvas Size command. (The Canvas Size command is explained in Chapter 3.)

Optimizing The Color And Tone Of Scans

After you scan and import an image into Photoshop, you might need to make several adjustments before it is ready to be edited.

Adobe specifies the following workflow for optimizing the color and tone of scans:

➤ **Calibrate** Use Adobe Gamma to calibrate the monitor as described in Chapter 4.

➤ **Check the scan quality** Open a histogram of the image to check its quality and tonal range.

➤ **Set the highlights and shadows** Use Levels, Curves, or the Auto Levels command to set the highlights and shadows as described earlier in this chapter.

➤ **Adjust the midtones** Use Levels or Curves to set the midtones and shadows as described earlier in this chapter.

➤ **Adjust the color balance and fine-tune** Use Curves to adjust the color balance and fine-tune the image as described previously in this chapter.

➤ **Apply Unsharp Mask** Choose Filter|Sharpen|Unsharp Mask, and apply the filter as described earlier in this chapter.

Practice Questions

Question 1

> Which checkbox in the Display & Cursors dialog box affects color table animation?
>
> ○ a. Color Table Animation
> ○ b. Color LUT Animation
> ○ c. Video LUT Animation
> ○ d. Video Table Animation

Answer c is correct. The Video LUT Animation checkbox toggles color table animation on and off.

Question 2

> How many brightness values are displayed across the bottom of a histogram?
>
> ○ a. However many are in the selected image area
> ○ b. 255
> ○ c. 256
> ○ d. 3 in RGB and 4 in CMYK

Answer c is correct. The histogram is a graph showing the number of pixels in the brightness levels from 0 to 255.

Question 3

> What is the maximum number of downsamplings Photoshop will save?
>
> ○ a. 4
> ○ b. 16
> ○ c. 1 through 100
> ○ d. 8

Answer d is correct. You can specify a number from 1 through 8 in the Image Cache dialog box.

Question 4

Which adjustment commands utilize a histogram?
- ❏ a. Levels
- ❏ b. Curves
- ❏ c. Color Balance
- ❏ d. Threshold
- ❏ e. Variations

Answers a and d are correct.

Question 5

After you open the Levels dialog box, how do you edit more than one color channel at a time?
- ○ a. Hold down Shift, and select the channels you want from the Channel option menu.
- ○ b. Hold down Shift, and select the channels you want from the Channels palette.
- ○ c. Press Option/Alt, and click on the curve of the channels you want to edit.
- ○ d. None of the above.

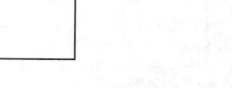

Trick question

Answer d is correct. You must hold down Shift and select the channels you want to edit from the Channels palette *before* you open the Levels dialog box.

Question 6

If you are editing an image's color, and you want to change the brightness value of one particular pixel level, which command should you use?
- ○ a. Levels
- ○ b. Curves
- ○ c. Replace Color
- ○ d. Selective Color

Answer b is correct. You can select a point on the brightness curve of an image and change that particular brightness level.

Question 7

> How do you set a point in the Curves dialog box on only the component channels?
>
> ❍ a. Hold Cmd/Ctrl and click on the curve.
>
> ❍ b. Hold Shift and click on the curve.
>
> ❍ c. Hold Shift+Cmd/Shift+Ctrl and click on the curve.
>
> ❍ d. Hold Option/Alt and click on the curve.

Answer c is correct. Pressing Shift+Cmd/Shift+Ctrl while clicking on the curve sets points in the components channels but not the composite channel. Pressing Cmd/Ctrl and clicking on the curve sets a point on the channel selected in the Channel option menu.

Question 8

> Which color adjustment creates a mask to allow you to adjust only specific colors?
>
> ❍ a. Selective Color
>
> ❍ b. Replace Color
>
> ❍ c. Masked Color
>
> ❍ d. Threshold

Answer b is correct. In the Replace Color dialog box, you can select a specific color to adjust, and you can add or subtract colors to that selection.

Question 9

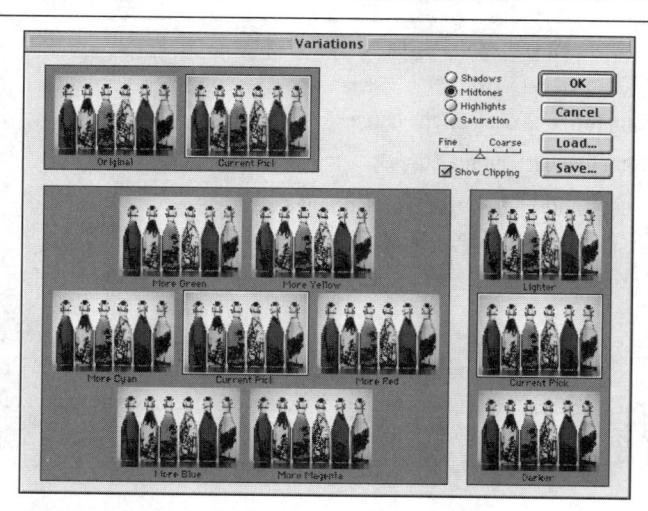

Figure 6.15 The Variations dialog box.

If you want less magenta in the midtones of the image displayed in the Variations dialog box shown in Figure 6.15, which thumbnail do you choose?

- ❍ a. More Green
- ❍ b. More Yellow
- ❍ c. More Red
- ❍ d. More Magenta
- ❍ e. More Blue
- ❍ f. More Cyan

Answer a is correct. The thumbnails in the Variations dialog box are arranged so that the theoretical opposite of that color is directly across the "circle" formed by the thumbnails. Clicking on the More thumbnail for one color decreases the color across the circle.

Question 10

If you want to convert an image from positive to negative, which of the following do you use?

- ❍ a. Image|Adjust|Inverse
- ❍ b. Image|Adjust|Invert
- ❍ c. Select|Inverse
- ❍ d. The Invert option in the Apply Image dialog box

Answer b is correct. The Invert command inverts the colors in an image to their counterparts on the other side of the color wheel.

Question 11

> Which of the following commands create a high-contrast black-and-white image from a grayscale or color image? (Select all that apply.)
>
> ❏ a. Invert
>
> ❏ b. Equalize
>
> ❏ c. Threshold
>
> ❏ d. Posterize

Trick! question

Only answer c is correct. The Threshold command converts all the colors above a specific level—a threshold—to white and below that level to black. You set this threshold on a histogram of the image.

Question 12

> Which of the following sharpening filters can provide the most sharpening?
>
> ○ a. Sharpen
>
> ○ b. Sharpen Edges
>
> ○ c. Sharpen More
>
> ○ d. Unsharp Mask

Answer d is correct. Unsharp Mask is the only sharpening filter that allows you to set the amount of sharpening, up to 500 percent.

Question 13

> Which of these statements are true about the Crop tool and the Crop command? (Select all that apply.)
> - a. The Crop tool doesn't let you resample the image as you crop.
> - b. The Crop command doesn't let you resample the image as you crop.
> - c. The Crop command crops only rectangular selections.
> - d. The Crop tool allows you to rotate the image as you crop.

Answers b, c, and d are correct. Choosing Image|Crop crops an image down to the rectangular area selected, as does the Crop tool. However, the Crop tool also allows you to rotate and resample the image as you crop.

Question 14

> Which of the following resampling methods results in the greatest loss of image quality?
> - a. Nearest Neighbor
> - b. Bilinear
> - c. Bicubic
> - d. None of the above

Trick question

Answer d is correct. These answers are actually interpolation methods, not resampling methods. Interpolation occurs only when you're resampling up. Of these three interpolation methods, Nearest Neighbor is more likely to result in greater loss of image quality.

Question 15

> What is the first step in optimizing the color and tone of scans?
> - a. Calibrate
> - b. Set highlights and shadows
> - c. Adjust midtones
> - d. Apply Unsharp Mask

Answer a is correct. Adobe emphasizes that calibration is the first and maybe most important step in optimizing color.

Need To Know More?

London, Sherry and David Xenakis: *Photoshop 5 In Depth*. The Coriolis Group. ISBN 1-57610-293-9. Contains detailed explanations of all the topics covered in this chapter.

McClelland, Deke: *Photoshop 5 for Macs for Dummies*. IDG Books Worldwide, Inc. ISBN 0-7645-0391-X.

McClelland, Deke: *Macworld Photoshop 5 Bible*. IDG Books Worldwide, Inc. ISBN 0-7645-3231-6.

Selecting Image Areas

Terms and concepts you'll need to understand:

- Selection
- Marquee/selection border
- Lasso
- Polygon
- Feather
- Intersect
- Path
- Work path
- Subpath
- Anchor point
- Direction lines
- Direction points
- Direct-Selection tool
- Fill
- Stroke
- Clipping path

Techniques you'll need to master:

- Selecting image areas with the Marquee tools
- Selecting image areas with the Lasso tools
- Selecting image areas with the Magic Wand tool
- Selecting image areas with the Color Range command
- Altering selections
- Converting selections to paths
- Drawing paths
- Altering paths
- Adjusting anchor points and direction points

The first step in editing an area in an image is to select that area. You select an area by drawing a *marquee*, or *selection border*, that is the shape and size that you want. This marquee is shown as a black-and-white dashed line that appears to move like the lights on an old-fashioned theater marquee and is sometimes referred to as "the marching ants."

You can create rectangular, elliptical, or polygonal selection borders. After you create a selection border, you can add to or subtract from that selection, modify it in a number of ways, use it in another image, and convert it to one of Photoshop's vector-based paths for saving.

You can also create and modify original paths. With paths, you can create much more precise selection borders, and you can export an image that is "masked" when used in or printed from another application.

Using Photoshop's Selection Tools

Use the Photoshop tools described in the following sections to create and move selection borders.

Selection Commands

You can use several commands to affect selections:

- ➤ Choose Select|All (Cmd+A/Ctrl+A) to select an entire image.
- ➤ Choose Select|Deselect (Cmd+D/Ctrl+D) to release a selection.
- ➤ Choose Select|Reselect (Shift+Cmd+D/Shift+Ctrl+D) to reselect the last deselected selection.

Marquee Tools

Use the Marquee tools to draw simple rectangular or elliptical selection borders. The Marquee tools (shown in Figure 7.1) are located in the top-left corner of the Toolbox. Select the visible Marquee tool, or hold down the mouse button while the mouse pointer is over the icon to display the hidden tool menu.

> The shortcut to access the Marquee tool selected in the Toolbox is the M key. You can cycle through the hidden tools (except for the Crop tool) by pressing Option/Alt as you click on the visible tool's icon in the Toolbox. You can toggle between the rectangular and elliptical marquees by holding down Shift and pressing M.

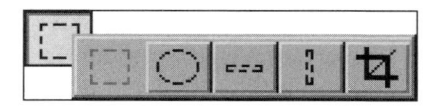

Figure 7.1 The Marquee tools.

The tools and their uses are as follows:

➤ **Rectangular marquee** The tool marked by the square icon, draws rectangular or square selection borders.

➤ **Elliptical marquee** The tool marked by the elliptical icon, draws elliptical or circular selection borders.

➤ **Single Row marquee** The tool marked by the horizontal rectangle, draws a selection border that is one pixel wide and the width of the image.

➤ **Single Column marquee** The tool marked by the vertical rectangle draws a selection border that is one pixel wide and the height of the image.

(The final tool displayed in the hidden tool menu shown in Figure 7.1 is the Crop tool, which is described in Chapter 6.)

The Marquee tools draw from a corner, in the direction you drag. To draw from the center of the selection, press Option/Alt as you drag. Constrain the selection border to a square or a circle by holding down Shift as you drag.

When either the single row or the single column marquee is selected, a vertical or horizontal dashed line appears on the image. Drag the line to the area you want to select, and let go. Because these selections are only one pixel wide, you may need to increase the magnification of the image to see the selection.

Double-click on the selected tool to open its Options palette. You can set these options:

➤ **Feather** If you want to "fade," or feather, the edges of a selection, set a feathering width here.

➤ **Anti-aliased** If you want the edges of a selection to be less jagged, check this option. You must choose this option before you draw a selection. Anti-aliased is available in the Marquee tool Options palette only for the Elliptical marquee tool.

➤ **Normal** If you want to draw a selection normally, leave the Style option menu set to Normal.

194   Chapter 7

> **Constrained Aspect Ratio** If you want to draw a selection of a specific aspect ratio, select Constrained Aspect Ratio from the Style option menu, and then set values for the height and width ratios.

> **Fixed Size** If you want to draw a selection of an absolute pixel size, select Fixed Size from the Style option menu, and set the values for the height and width.

The Style options are not available for the single row and single column marquees.

Lasso Tools

Use the Lasso tools (shown in Figure 7.2) to draw custom selection shapes. By default, the Lasso tool draws free-form selections, and the Polygon Lasso tool draws straight-edged selections. You can toggle between the two with keyboard shortcuts to draw selections that have both free-form edges and straight edges. The new Magnetic Lasso tool draws a selection border that snaps to edge pixels as you drag.

> The keyboard shortcut to access the Lasso tool selected in the Toolbox is L. You can cycle through the hidden tools by pressing Option/Alt as you click on the visible tool's icon in the Toolbox or by pressing Shift+L.
>
> To switch between the Lasso tool and the Polygon Lasso tool as you draw a selection, press Option/Alt.
>
> To switch to the Lasso tool as you draw with the Magnetic Lasso tool, press and hold Option/Alt and begin dragging.
>
> To switch to the Polygon Lasso tool as you draw with the Magnetic Lasso tool, press Option/Alt and click on the next point.
>
> To narrow the lasso width of the Magnetic Lasso tool as you draw, press] or [to increase or decrease the width, respectively, by one pixel.

The Lasso tool is the icon on the left in the hidden tool menu, the Polygon Lasso tool is the middle icon, and the Magnetic Lasso tool is the far right icon. Here's how to draw selection borders with the Lasso tools:

> **Lasso tool** Draw freehand selections with the Lasso tool by dragging around in the image. As long as you hold down the mouse button, you

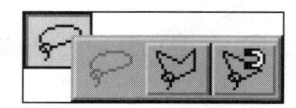

Figure 7.2 The Lasso tools.

continue to draw a selection. When you release the mouse button, a straight-line segment is drawn from that point to the initial point to close the selection. If you want to delete a line you have drawn (only before the selection is closed), hold down the Delete key and wait as the selection border slowly deletes backward from that point.

The Feathering and Anti-aliasing options are available for the Lasso tool in the Options palette.

➤ **Polygon Lasso tool** Draw straight-line selections with the Polygon Lasso tool by clicking on an initial point and then moving the cursor to another point and clicking again. A straight-line segment is drawn between the points. Close the selection border by moving the cursor back over the initial point, where a closed circle will appear next to the cursor, and then releasing the mouse button. If the mouse cursor is away from the initial point, you can close the selection by double-clicking. Delete segments of the polygon one at a time by pressing Delete.

The Feathering and Anti-aliasing options are available for the Polygon Lasso tool in the Options palette.

➤ **Magnetic Lasso tool** Draw selection borders that snap to similar colors with the Magnetic Lasso tool. Click on an initial point, and then drag or draw along an area in an image. The Magnetic Lasso draws a selection border as you move the mouse cursor around in the image, periodically inserting fastening points and snapping to colors according to specifications you enter in the Options palette. You can enter fastening points manually by clicking. Close the selection with a magnetic segment by double-clicking or pressing Return/Enter. Close the selection with a straight-line segment by holding down Option/Alt as you double-click. Delete segments and fastening points one at a time by pressing Delete.

The Feathering and Anti-aliasing options are available for the Magnetic Lasso tool in the Options palette. The additional options/specifications for the Magnetic Lasso tool are as follows:

➤ **Lasso Width** Sets the width of the area within which the Magnetic Lasso tool will compare colors. Enter a pixel value from 1 to 40.

➤ **Frequency** Specifies how frequently the Magnetic Lasso tool will set fastening points. Enter a value from 0 to 100, where 0 is less frequent and 100 is more frequent.

➤ **Edge Contrast** Specifies the amount of color contrast that the Magnetic Lasso tool will consider an edge. Enter a percentage value from 1 to 100, where 1 is low contrast and 100 is high contrast.

➤ **Stylus: Pressure** Turns on and off the Stylus: Pressure option (when using a tablet), which narrows the lasso detection width as you increase stylus pressure.

Magic Wand Tool

Using the Magic Wand tool, you can select adjacent areas of similar color. The Magic Wand tool (shown in Figure 7.3) is not available in Bitmap mode.

You specify the Magic Wand tool's range of color, or Tolerance, in its Options palette. This tolerance can be any value from 0 through 255. If you enter 0, the Magic Wand selects only those adjacent pixels that are of that same value. If you enter 255, the Magic Wand selects all the colors in an image. Anti-aliasing also is available for the Magic Wand tool.

If you select the Use All Layers checkbox, the Magic Wand creates a selection based on adjacent pixels in all visible layers. If this selection is unchecked, the Magic Wand selects pixels in only the active layer. Press the Shift key, and use the Magic Wand again to add pixels of similar color from other areas that are not adjacent.

> **STUDY ALERT**
> If you are selecting areas of similar color that are spread out in an image and not adjacent, you can save time by using the Magic Wand tool and the Similar command (described later in this chapter). Instead of Shift+clicking all over the image, you can use the Magic Wand tool to specify a color and range you want to select. Then, you can use the Similar command to select similar colors from areas in the image that are not adjacent.

Color Range Command

Using the Color Range command, you can make a selection based on a specific color. Choose Select|Color Range to access the Color Range dialog box. You can make the color selection from the entire image or from a selected area in the image.

The display area of the Color Range dialog box (shown in Figure 7.4) presents either a full-color thumbnail of the composite image (Image) or a grayscale thumbnail of the area you have selected (Selection). In the Selection thumbnail, the selected areas are the lighter areas. You can switch between the two

Figure 7.3 The Magic Wand tool.

Selecting Image Areas

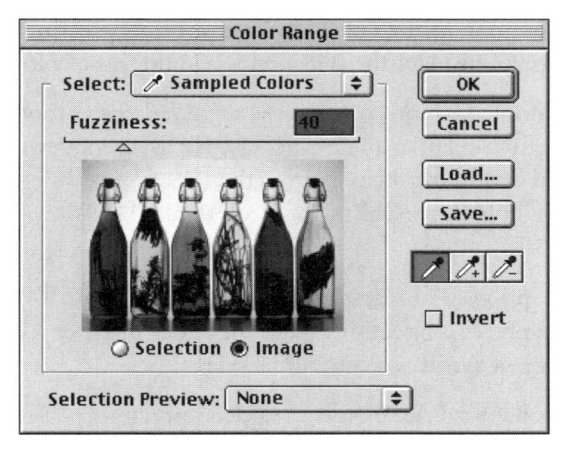

Figure 7.4 The Color Range dialog box.

thumbnails by clicking on the respective radio button. From either thumbnail, pressing Cmd/Ctrl toggles the display temporarily to the other thumbnail.

Use the Cancel/Reset button and the Load/Save buttons as you would in other dialog boxes.

Specify how you want to select colors by first choosing an option from the Select option menu (shown in Figure 7.5). The Sampled Colors option allows you to use the Eyedropper tools to select colors from the Image thumbnail or from the image. The other options select those specific color ranges. In RGB and Lab mode images, you can view any out-of-gamut colors by choosing the Out Of Gamut option.

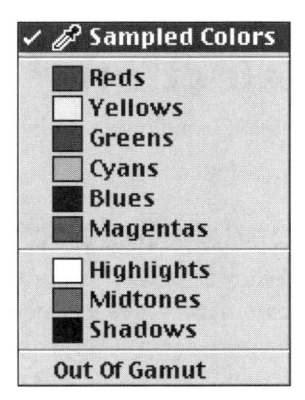

Figure 7.5 The Select option menu in the Color Range dialog box.

When you choose one of the color ranges from the Select option menu, the Selection thumbnail displays the selection based on those colors.

If you choose Sampled Colors, you can use the Eyedropper tool to select colors from the Image thumbnail or the image. Use the Eyedropper + and Eyedropper - tools to add and subtract colors from the selection. While you're using the Eyedropper tool, hold down Shift to add colors, and hold down Option/Alt to subtract colors.

The Fuzziness option is similar to the Magic Wand tool's Tolerance setting, described in the preceding section. Drag the slider or enter a value to specify how wide a range of similar colors will be selected.

The Invert option, of course, inverts the selection.

By default, you do not see the selection previewed in the image window. However, you can choose one of the following preview modes from the Selection Preview option menu:

➤ Grayscale

➤ Black Matte

➤ White Matte

➤ Quick Mask

If you have already made a selection, with either the Color Range command or any other selection tool, you can use the Color Range command to further refine that selection. While the original selection is still active, open the Color Range dialog box again and make a selection. Any areas of specified color in the original selection are then selected.

Adjusting Selections

After you create a selection, you can alter and adjust it by using various tools and commands.

Hiding And Showing Selections

The method for hiding and showing selection borders can be hard to remember because the necessary command refers to the selection borders as edges. Choose View|Hide/Show Edges to hide or show any existing selection border. If you hide a selection border and then create a new selection border, the new selection border is shown automatically.

Moving The Marquee

You can move a selection border, but not with the Move tool. If you use the Move tool, you actually move the selected pixels. To move the selection border, or marquee, remain in a selection tool and drag from inside the selection border. You can drag selection borders to other image windows, and you can position selection borders partially off the canvas and then move them back intact.

Press Shift after you begin dragging to constrain the move to multiples of 45 degrees. You can also move the selection 1 pixel at a time by pressing the arrow keys and 10 pixels at a time by holding Shift as you press the arrow keys.

You can also move the selection as you are drawing it. Hold down the spacebar as you drag, and the selection border that you have already drawn moves as you drag.

Adding To A Selection

Add new areas to any existing selection by holding down Shift and selecting again. A plus sign then appears next to the cursor.

Subtracting From A Selection

Subtract areas from any existing selection by holding down Option/Alt and selecting again. A minus sign then appears next to the cursor.

Intersecting Selections

Intersecting selections creates a selection of the common area of the two selections. First, create a selection; then press Shift+Option/Shift+Alt (an X appears next to the cursor) and drag a new selection that includes part of the original selection. When you release the mouse, a new selection is created containing only the area that the two selections shared.

Modifying Selections

You can also these commands to alter or modify existing selections:

- **Inverse** Choose Select|Inverse (Shift+Cmd+I/Shift+Ctrl+I) to select the unselected areas.
- **Border** Choose Select|Modify|Border to create a "frame," or border, of 1 to 64 pixels around the selection.
- **Smooth** Choose Select|Modify|Smooth to smooth out the raggedy edges of a selection. The Sample Radius value determines the amount that Photoshop rounds off corners. Enter a pixel radius from 1 to 16. A Sample Radius of 1 results in less round corners.

> ➤ **Expand** Choose Select|Modify|Expand and specify a pixel amount from 1 to 16 by which to expand a selection border.
>
> ➤ **Contract** Choose Select|Modify|Contract and specify a pixel amount from 1 to 16 by which to contract a selection border.
>
> ➤ **Grow** Choose Select|Grow to add adjacent areas of similar color. This command is like using the Magic Wand tool and actually uses the Tolerance value specified in the Magic Wand's Options palette. (This command is not available in Bitmap mode.)
>
> ➤ **Similar** Choose Select|Similar to add to a selection those areas of similar color that are not adjacent. This command also uses the Tolerance value from the Magic Wand's Options palette. (This command is not available in Bitmap mode.)
>
> ➤ **Feather** Choose Select|Feather (Cmd+Option+D/Ctrl+Alt+D) to feather an existing selection. Enter a Feather Radius value from 0.2 to 250.0, which is the radius outward from the selection border you want feathered.

Each time you choose the Grow or Similar commands, the specified tolerance value is added to the values of the pixels already selected. Using the Grow or Similar commands repeatedly, therefore, increases the color range of added pixels in small increments, so you can use the commands to increase the size of a selection a little bit at a time by choosing the commands again and again.

Using And Understanding Paths

Paths are the lines that you draw with the different Pen tools. These lines can remain open or can be closed to form precise selection borders. Paths can be moved, adjusted, swapped between image files, swapped between applications, and filled and stroked with color. You can also convert paths to selection borders, add paths to selection borders, and intersect paths and selection borders. You can create and export a clipping path, which "masks" an image when it is used in or it prints from another application.

Navigating The Paths Palette

You manage paths by using the Paths palette (shown in Figure 7.6). From the Paths palette, you can create, duplicate, name and rename, select and deselect, and fill and stroke paths. From the Paths palette, you can also convert a path to a selection border and convert a selection border to a path. Open the Paths palette by clicking on its tab in its palette group or by choosing Window|Show Paths.

Selecting Image Areas

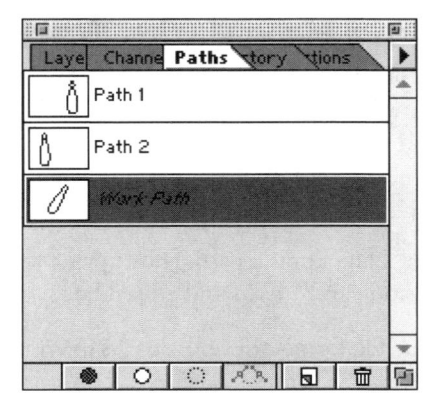

Figure 7.6 The Paths palette.

Selecting And Deselecting Paths
Click on the name of a path or on the open area of the Paths palette to select and deselect a path.

Naming And Renaming Paths
If you create a new path from the Paths palette menu, the New Path dialog box opens, in which you can give the path a name. Unless you specify a path name, paths are named Path 1, Path 2, and so on. To rename a path, double-click on the path's name to open the Rename Path dialog box. Enter a name and click on OK.

Choosing The Palette Options
Change the size of the thumbnails displayed in the Paths palette by choosing Palette Options from the Paths palette menu and selecting a different thumbnail size.

Moving A Path In The Paths Palette
If you need to move a path up or down in the Paths palette, simply drag it above or below another path. A solid line appears to indicate where the path will be inserted.

Hiding And Showing Paths
Choose View|Hide/Show Path to hide or show a path. You can also Shift+click on the path's name in the Paths palette to toggle between hide and show.

Understanding How Paths Work

Paths are vector-based objects and do not print. (The differences between bitmap graphics and vector graphics are discussed in Chapter 2.) Paths can be simple lines or closed shapes. Paths can consist of both straight and curved lines, or of segments. These segments have anchor points at each end. You change the shape of a path by adjusting these anchor points.

Although paths (other than clipping paths) don't print with an image, they are saved with the image and can be used and edited later.

> **STUDY ALERT**
>
> Only these file formats support paths in Windows:
> - Photoshop (PSD)
> - JPEG
> - DCS
> - EPS
> - PDF
> - TIFF
>
> On the Mac, all file formats except GIF89a support paths.

Working With Anchor Points

Anchor points are the control points for the Bézier curves that define the radii and shapes of the curved segments of paths. As you draw paths with the Pen tool, you insert anchor points manually. As you draw paths with the Freeform Pen or Magnetic Pen tool, anchor points are inserted automatically (as are fastening points when you use the Magnetic Lasso), according to the specifications you enter in the tool's options menu.

When an anchor point of a curved segment is selected, direction lines and direction points extend from the anchor point. These direction lines and direction points are the control features of the anchor point. By dragging the direction points, you can alter the shape of the curve extending from that particular anchor point.

Depending on the type of line or curve that extends from them, anchor points can be of the following types:

- **Smooth point** The curve defined by a smooth point forms a smooth arc; that is, curves that extend from it in each direction. The direction lines of a smooth point are coordinated, changing both curves at the same time.

➤ **Corner point** The points defined by a corner point are sharp. Both straight lines and curves can extend from a corner point. If a straight line extends in one direction from a corner point and a curve extends in the other direction, the corner point has only one direction line for the curve. If two curves extend from a corner point, the two direction lines of that point move individually, changing only one of the curves at a time.

For maximum efficiency and to prevent printing problems with clipping paths, you should use as few anchor points as possible in paths.

Creating Paths

You can create a path by choosing New Path from the Paths palette options menu or by clicking on the New Path button at the bottom of the Paths palette (shown in Figure 7.7). Alternatively, you can create a new path by selecting a Pen tool and drawing. If you create a new path by drawing or by converting a selection border to a path, it remains a *work path* until you save it. If you deselect a work path before saving it, it is replaced by any new path you create. If you create a path using New Path, the path is saved as you draw.

Hold down Option/Alt when you click on the New Path button to open the New Path dialog box immediately and name the path.

Saving Paths

To save a work path, either drag the work path name to the New Path button, or select Save Path from the Paths palette menu. The Save Path command opens the Save Path dialog box, and there you can name the path.

Deleting Paths

You can delete paths in several ways. You can drag the path name to the Trash button in the Paths palette. You can click on the Trash button (you have to approve deletions in a dialog box). You can Option+click/Alt+click on the Trash button (deleting the selected path without approval). Finally, you can choose Delete Path from the Paths palette menu.

Converting Selection Borders To Paths

Convert any selection border to a path either by choosing Make Work Path from the Paths palette menu, by clicking on the Make Work Path button in

Figure 7.7 The New Path button.

Figure 7.8 The Make Work Path button.

the Paths palette (shown in Figure 7.8), or by pressing Option/Alt and clicking on the Make Work Path button.

If you select the Make Work Path command from the Paths palette menu or press Option/Alt and click on the Make Work Path button, the Make Work Path dialog box opens. In the Tolerance value box, you specify how precisely Photoshop will trace the selection border as it is converted to a path. Enter a tolerance value from 0.5 to 10 pixels. Lower tolerance values result in more anchor points being used to define the path, which increases the complexity of the path, perhaps causing printing problems for clipping paths.

Converting Paths To Selection Borders

Convert a path to a selection border by selecting the path in the Paths palette and then choosing Make Selection for the Paths palette menu. Alternatively, click on the Make Selection button (shown in Figure 7.9) in the Paths palette. You can also convert a path to a selection by clicking on a path with any Pen tool and pressing the Enter key on the keypad.

By choosing the Make Selection command from the Paths palette menu or by pressing Option/Alt as you click on the Make Selection button, you open the Make Selection dialog box, where you set these options for the selection:

➤ **Rendering** Set a Feathering Radius for the new selection by entering a value from 0.0 to 250.0. You can also select or deselect Anti-aliasing for the selection. (Feathering and anti-aliasing were discussed previously in this chapter.)

➤ **Operation** Select how to add the selection to the image. If no other selection is active, you will have only the New Selection option. If you have already made a selection in the image, you can add, subtract, or intersect this new selection with the existing selection in the image. (Selections were described in detail previously in this chapter.)

Figure 7.9 The Make Selection button.

Here are the keyboard shortcuts for converting a path to a selection border:

➤ Press the Enter key on the keypad while you click on a path with any Pen tool.

➤ Cmd+click/Ctrl+click on the path's thumbnail in the Paths palette to convert the path to a new selection, applying the settings last entered in the Make Selection dialog box.

➤ Cmd+Shift+click/Ctrl+Shift+click on the path's thumbnail to add the path to an existing selection.

➤ Cmd+Option+click/Ctrl+Alt+click on the path's thumbnail to subtract the path from an existing selection.

➤ Shift+Cmd+Option+click/Shift+Ctrl+Alt+click on the path's thumbnail to intersect the path with an existing selection.

Drawing With The Pen Tools

Besides the Pen tool and the Freeform Pen tool, which works like the Lasso tool, Photoshop 5 includes the new Magnetic Pen tool, which works like the Magnetic Lasso (the Lasso and Magnetic Lasso were described previously in this chapter).

Note that, although the Freeform Pen tool and the Magnetic Pen tool allow you to create paths by drawing in the image window and are easier to use than the Pen tool, the Pen tool provides far greater precision and control over the creation of paths.

The Rubber Band option in the Pen tools' Options palette displays a path segment as you draw it. Otherwise, you see a path segment only after you place its second anchor.

The Toolbox contains seven different tools. Click and hold the selected Pen tool to display the hidden tools (as shown in Figure 7.10). The first tool is the Pen tool, followed from left to right by the Magnetic Pen tool, the Freeform Pen tool, the Add-Anchor-Point tool, the Delete-Anchor-Point tool, the Direct-Selection tool, and the Convert-Anchor-Point tool.

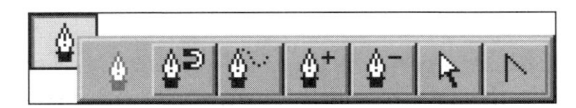

Figure 7.10 The Pen tools.

Chapter 7

Table 7.1 The Photoshop Pen tool activation and switching shortcuts.

Key or Key Combo	Performs This Function
Shift+P	Cycles through the Pen tool, Freeform Pen tool, and Magnetic Pen tool
P	Activates the selected Pen tool
A	Activates the Direct-Selection tool
+	Activates the Add-Anchor-Point tool
-	Activates the Delete-Anchor-Point tool
Cmd/Ctrl	Switches from any Pen tool to the Direct-Selection tool
Option/Alt	Switches from the Pen tool to the Convert-Anchor-Point tool
Cmd+Option/Ctrl+Alt	Switches from the Direct-Selection tool to the Convert-Anchor-Point tool
Option/Alt	Switches between the Add-Anchor-Point tool and the Delete-Anchor-Point tool
Option+drag/Alt+drag	Switches from the Magnetic Pen tool to the Freeform tool
Option+click/Alt+click	Switches from the Magnetic Pen tool to the Pen tool

> **STUDY ALERT** You should learn the keyboard shortcuts for activating and switching between the pen tools, displayed in Table 7.1.

Using The Pen Tool

You can draw either straight-line segments or curved segments with the Pen tool. Look at the following procedures for the two methods:

▶ **To draw straight-line segments** Click where you want the line to begin; then click where you want the line to end. Anchor points are added at each click. Subsequent clicks create additional lines and anchor points. You can constrain the lines to multiples of 45 degrees by pressing Shift as you click.

▶ **To draw curved segments** Click and hold where you want the curve to begin. Drag in the direction of the curve, which activates a direction line. You are now pulling the direction point, which you drag to form the curve. Move to the place where you want the next anchor point, and repeat the procedure to complete the curved segment. To create a sharp angle or reverse the direction of the next curve, press Option/Alt to activate the Direct-Selection tool, drag a direction point in the new direction you want for the next curve, and then release the mouse button and move to where you want the next anchor point. Drag again to create the next curve.

To stop drawing if the path is to remain a line or series of lines, click on the Pen tool icon in the Toolbox or press Cmd/Ctrl and click away from the path.

To close a path, return to the initial anchor point, and click when the closed circle appears next to the cursor.

Using The Freeform Pen Tool

The Freeform Pen tool allows you to create a path much as you would create a selection with the Lasso tool (which is described previously in this chapter), with the exception that you can leave open a free-form path.

To draw a path with the Freeform Pen tool, click and drag from the point where you want the path to begin. If you release the mouse button, you can continue with the same path by clicking and dragging from an endpoint of the path.

The Freeform Pen tool automatically inserts anchor points as you drag, according to the Curve Fit value you enter in the tool's Options palette. Curve Fit values range from 0.5 to 10.0, and they determine how closely the drawn path will approximate the path of the cursor. Lower values result in more complex paths with more anchor points.

Using The Magnetic Pen Tool

Just as the Freeform Pen works like the Lasso tool, the Magnetic Pen tool draws paths much the same way that the Magnetic Lasso (also described previously in this chapter) draws selections. Like the Magnetic Lasso, the Magnetic Pen tool snaps to edges defined by a level of contrast that you specify. Again, however, the main difference between the two tools is that you can create open-ended paths.

To draw a path with the Magnetic Pen tool, drag or draw along an edge in the image. The path is created as you drag or draw, and anchor points are inserted according to the specifications you set in the tool's Options palette. You can manually insert a fastening (anchor) point by clicking.

Entered in the Magnetic Pen tool's Options palette, the following are the tool's variable specifications:

> ➤ **Curve Fit** Ranges from 0.5 to 10.0 and determines how closely the drawn path will approximate the path of the cursor. Lower values result in more complex paths with more anchor points.

- **Pen Width** Sets the width of the area within which the Magnetic Pen tool will compare colors. Enter a pixel value from 1 to 40.
- **Frequency** Specifies how frequently the Magnetic Pen tool will set fastening points. Enter a value from 0 to 100, where 0 is less frequent and 100 is more frequent.
- **Edge Contrast** Specifies the amount of color contrast that the Magnetic Pen tool will consider an edge. Enter a percentage value from 1 to 100, where 1 is low contrast and 100 is high contrast.
- **Stylus: Pressure** Turns on and off the Stylus: Pressure option (when using a tablet), which narrows the pen's detection width as you increase stylus pressure.

Many of the Magnetic Pen tool's operations can be controlled, changed, and accessed through keyboard shortcuts, shown in Table 7.2.

Creating Additional Subpaths

A *subpath* is any group of connected path segments. These subpaths can be open or closed, and more than one subpath can appear in a saved path. Subpaths do not have to be connected to any other subpaths.

To create or add additional subpaths, simply complete a path by one of the methods described previously in this chapter, and then draw another path.

Table 7.2 The Photoshop Magnetic Pen tool operation shortcuts.

Key or Key Combo	Performs This Function
Delete	Deletes the last point created
Double-click	Closes a path with a magnetic segment
Option+Double-click/Alt+Double-click	Closes a path with a straight-line segment
Enter/Return	Ends an open path
Esc or Cmd/Ctrl+.	Cancels an operation of the Magnetic Pen tool
Option+drag/Alt+drag	Switches from the Magnetic Pen tool to the Freeform tool
Option+click/Alt+click	Switches from the Magnetic Pen tool to the Pen tool
[	Decreases pen width by one pixel
]	Increases pen width by one pixel

Altering Paths

After you draw a path, you may need to edit it for more precision. To alter a path, you must first select that segment or point to alter. You can then move the points or segments, delete segments, change the arcs and radii of curves, add and subtract points, and convert points.

Selecting The Parts Of A Path

To select part of a path, first make sure that the path's name is selected in the Paths palette. Then, use the Direct-Selection tool to select path segments. Click directly on an anchor point or draw a marquee with the Direct-Selection tool to select a group of points and lines. Select an entire subpath by pressing Option/Alt as you select.

Appearing as hollow squares when unselected, anchor points turn to filled black squares when selected. The direction lines and direction points for a curve, which together look like lollipops, appear when the associated anchor point is selected. You can add additional points and lines by holding down Shift as you select. Add additional subpaths by holding down Shift+Option/Shift+Alt while selecting.

Remember that you can toggle to the Direct-Selection tool from any other Pen tool by placing the cursor over an anchor point and pressing Cmd/Ctrl.

Managing Path Segments

After you create subpaths and paths, you can modify them by moving and reshaping them, and you can delete them. Use the Direct-Selection tool and follow these instructions for modifying path segments:

- ➤ **Move a path segment** by first selecting all of the associated anchor points by using a method described in the preceding section. Drag the segment. Constrain the movement of the segment to multiples of 45 degrees by pressing Shift as you drag.

- ➤ **Reshape a curved path segment** by selecting the segment and dragging between the anchor points. Alternatively, select an anchor point, and drag the anchor point or one of its direction points. Constrain the movement of the points to multiples of 45 degrees by pressing Shift as you drag.

- ➤ **Erase any path segment** by selecting the segment and pressing Delete/Backspace. The lines extending from both directions of each selected anchor point are then erased. Pressing Delete/Backspace again erases any remaining subpath.

Managing Path Anchor Points

You can add, delete, and convert the anchor points on a path or subpath. Follow these procedures to add and delete anchor points:

- **Add an anchor point** by selecting the Add-Anchor-Point tool (+) and clicking on a path. Reshape the path segment as you add the point by clicking and dragging on the path.

- **Delete an anchor point** by selecting the Delete-Anchor-Point tool (-) and clicking on the anchor point. The path is automatically reshaped to conform to the attributes of the remaining anchor points. To manually reshape the segment as you delete the point, click and drag.

Use the Convert-Anchor-Point tool to change the nature of anchor points. Remember that you can toggle to the Convert-Anchor-Point by pressing Cmd+Option/Ctrl+Alt when the Direct-Selection tool is over an anchor point. Use these procedures for converting anchor points.

- **Convert a smooth point to a corner point without direction lines** by clicking on the smooth point with the Convert-Anchor-Point tool.

- **Convert a smooth point to a corner point with direction lines** by selecting the anchor point with the Direct-Selection tool and then dragging one of the anchor point's direction points with the Convert-Anchor-Point tool.

- **Convert a corner point to a smooth point** by dragging away from the anchor point with the Convert-Anchor-Point tool, creating new direction lines and direction points.

Transforming Paths And Points

You can apply two-dimensional transformations to paths and subpaths by using the Transform and Free Transform commands, discussed in Chapter 8.

Adding Colors To Paths

You can add colors to paths or subpaths either by stroking the path with color or by filling the path with color. Because paths are not really a part of the bitmap image in Photoshop, you are really adding color to the active layer in the image in the shape of the selected path.

Filling A Path

Use the Fill Path button (shown in Figure 7.11) in the Paths palette or the Fill Path command in the Paths palette menu to fill a path with color. The path

Figure 7.11 The Fill Path button.

need not be completely closed. However, if it is not a closed path, Photoshop fills the path and "closes" it with a straight line of color between the open path segments.

Clicking on the Fill Path button fills the path with the current values and settings in the Fill Path dialog box. To specify different values and settings as you fill the path, press Option/Alt when you click on the Fill Path button to open the Fill Path dialog box, or select Fill Path from the palette menu.

The Fill Path dialog box offers the same options as the Edit|Fill dialog box (described in Chapter 8), with the addition of the Rendering options of feathering and anti-aliasing (which are described throughout this chapter).

Stroking A Path

You can stroke a layer with a color value. This operation essentially paints the foreground color along the shape of the path, on the active layer, using one of the painting tools. Use the Stroke Path button in the Paths palette (shown in Figure 7.12) or the Stroke Path command in the Paths palette menu.

Clicking on the Stroke Path button strokes the path by using the painting or editing tool currently selected in the Toolbox at the size currently selected for that tool in the Brushes palette (which is described in Chapter 3), applying the stroke according to the specifications and values entered in the tool's Options palette. To select a different painting tool, press Option/Alt when you click on the Stroke Path button to open the Stroke Path dialog box, or select Stroke Path from the palette menu. Again, the path is stroked according to the specifications and values and brush size entered and selected for that tool.

Moving, Copying, And Exporting Paths

Use the following procedures if you need to move a path around in an image or into another image, or if you need to export the path into another application:

➤ **Moving paths within an image** Make sure that the path is selected in the Paths palette, and then drag the path with the Direct-Selection tool.

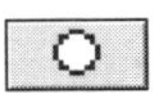

Figure 7.12 The Stroke Path button.

- **Moving paths between Photoshop images** Drag the path with the Direct-Selection tool from the original image window into the destination window. Alternatively, drag the path's name from its Paths palette into the destination window. You can also choose Edit|Copy (Cmd+C/Ctrl+C) and Edit|Paste (Cmd+V/Ctrl+V) to copy and paste the path from one image file to another.

- **Copying paths** Make sure that the path is selected in the Paths palette, and then press Option/Alt as you drag with the Direct-Selection tool. Alternatively, drag the name of the path in the Paths palette to the New Path button. This operation creates a new path with "copy" added to the name of the original path. To rename a path as you copy it, hold Option/Alt as you drag the path name to the New Path button, or select Duplicate Path from the Paths palette menu.

- **Exporting paths** Choose File|Export|Paths To Illustrator. This command saves the path as a file that you can open and edit in Adobe Illustrator.

Clipping Paths

Clipping paths allow you to create a boundary around part of an image that "masks" or hides part of the image when the image is used in or printed from another application. Creating and exporting clipping paths is described in Chapter 5.

Practice Questions

Question 1

> Which of the following commands can you use to select image areas? (Select all that apply.)
>
> ❏ a. Select|All (Cmd+A/Ctrl+A)
> ❏ b. Select|Deselect (Cmd+D/Ctrl+D)
> ❏ c. Select|Reselect (Shift+Cmd+D/Shift+Ctrl+D)
> ❏ d. Select|Invert (Shift+Cmd+I/Shift+Ctrl+I)

Trick! question

Answers a and c are correct. Select|All and Select|Reselect select image areas. Select|Deselect releases the selection of image areas. Although Select|Inverse selects image areas, it is not Select|Invert as it is written in this question.

Question 2

> To draw a marquee from its center rather than from a corner, which key do you press?
>
> ○ a. M
> ○ b. Option/Alt
> ○ c. Shift+Cmd/Shift+Ctrl
> ○ d. C

Answer b is correct. Holding down Option/Alt as you drag draws the marquee from the center.

Question 3

> Which Lasso tool allows you to draw freehand and straight-line selection borders?
>
> ○ a. Lasso tool
> ○ b. Polygon Lasso tool
> ○ c. Magnetic Lasso tool
> ○ d. All the above

Answer d is correct. While drawing with either the Lasso tool or the Polygon Lasso tool, you can switch to the other by pressing Option/Alt. While drawing with the Magnetic Lasso tool, you can switch to the Lasso tool by holding down Option/Alt and dragging, and you can switch to the Polygon Lasso tool by pressing Option/Alt and clicking on the next point.

Question 4

> When you're selecting areas of adjacent color with the Magic Wand tool, which of these Tolerance values selects the most colors?
>
> ○ a. 0
> ○ b. 1
> ○ c. 255
> ○ d. 256

Answer c is correct. The range of Tolerance values for the Magic Wand tool is 0 through 255.

Question 5

> If you want to move a marquee (selection border), which of these operations can you use? (Select all that apply.)
>
> ❑ a. Press M to select the Move tool; then move the selection border.
> ❑ b. Press Shift and drag with the Marquee tool.
> ❑ c. Press an arrow key.
> ❑ d. Hold down the spacebar as you draw the marquee.

Answers b, c, and d are correct. The actual keyboard shortcut for the Move tool is V, and the Move tool moves the selection, not the marquee (selection border).

Question 6

> If you want to enlarge a selection border by a specific amount, which of these commands do you choose?
>
> ○ a. Grow
>
> ○ b. Expand
>
> ○ c. Similar
>
> ○ d. Enlarge

Answer b is correct. Although Image|Modify|Grow does enlarge a selection border, it does so by seeking adjacent areas of similar color. You have no control over exactly how much the selection border will enlarge. Expand allows you to enlarge the selection border by a pixel value from 1 to 16.

Question 7

> If you want to keep a selection border, but you don't want to see it, which command should you use to hide it?
>
> ○ a. View|Hide|Selection
>
> ○ b. View|Hide|Path
>
> ○ c. View|Hide|Edges
>
> ○ d. View|Hide|Border

Answer c is correct. Photoshop refers to selection borders as edges for the sake of this command.

Question 8

> Which of these file formats support paths on the Mac? (Select all that apply.)
>
> ❏ a. TIFF
>
> ❏ b. PSD
>
> ❏ c. DCS
>
> ❏ d. GIF

All the answers are correct. On the Mac, the only file format that does not support paths is GIF89a.

Question 9

Which of the Pen tools allows you the greatest control over drawing precise paths?

○ a. Pen

○ b. Freeform Pen

○ c. Magnetic Pen

Answer a is correct.

Question 10

How do you save a work path? (Select all that apply.)

❏ a. Click on the Save Path button in the Paths palette

❏ b. Drag the work path's name to the New Path button in the Paths palette

❏ c. Select Save Path from the Paths palette menu

❏ d. Press Option/Alt and click on the work path's thumbnail

Answers b and c are correct.

Question 11

How do you save a selection border as a path? (Select all that apply.)

❏ a. Make a selection; then click on the New Path button in the Paths palette

❏ b. Make a selection; then select Make New Path from the Paths palette menu

❏ c. Make a selection; then click on the Make Work Path button in the Paths palette

❏ d. Make a selection; then select Make Work Path in the Selections palette

Only c is correct. Although you are using the Make Work Path commands, no Make Work Path command appears in the Selections palette (in fact, there is no Selections palette).

Question 12

> Which of the following keyboard shortcuts convert a path to a selection border? (Select all that apply.)
>
> ❏ a. Cmd+click/Ctrl+click on the path's thumbnail in the Paths palette
> ❏ b. Cmd+Shift+click/Ctrl+Shift+click on the path's thumbnail in the Paths palette
> ❏ c. Cmd+Option+click/Ctrl+Alt+click on the path's thumbnail in the Paths palette
> ❏ d. Shift+Cmd+Option+click/Shift+Ctrl+Alt+click on the path's thumbnail in the Paths palette

All these answers are correct.

Question 13

> If you want to see a preview of the path you are drawing, which of these options do you select?
>
> ○ a. View|Preview|Paths
> ○ b. Rubber Band in the Pen tools' Options palette
> ○ c. Preview Paths in the Paths palette menu
> ○ d. Path Animation in the Display & Cursors dialog box, which you open by choosing File|Preferences|Display & Cursors

Answer b is correct. The Rubber Band option displays an animated preview of the path you are drawing, as you draw.

Question 14

> Which of the following Pen tools cannot be accessed by pressing Shift+P? (Select all that apply.)
>
> ❏ a. Pen tool
> ❏ b. Direct-Selection tool
> ❏ c. Magnetic Pen tool
> ❏ d. Add-Anchor-Point tool

Answers b and d are correct. Shift+P cycles through the Pen, Freeform Pen, and Magnetic Pen tools.

Question 15

> Which of these shortcuts narrows the pen width of the Magnetic Pen tool as you draw?
>
> ○ a. [
> ○ b.]
> ○ c. +
> ○ d. -

Answer a is correct.

Question 16

> When a Pen tool is activated, and the cursor is over an anchor point, which of these shortcuts activate the Direct-Selection tool? (Select all that apply.)
>
> ❏ a. Option/Alt
> ❏ b. A
> ❏ c. Cmd/Ctrl
> ❏ d. D

Answers b and c are correct. Pressing A switches to the Direct-Selection tool, and Cmd/Ctrl temporarily activates the Direct-Selection tool.

Question 17

> Which of these operations applies color to a path according to the brush size selected?
>
> ○ a. Fill Path
>
> ○ b. Stroke Path
>
> ○ c. Paint Path
>
> ○ d. Brush Path

Answer b is correct. The Stroke Path operation uses the brush size and the other specifications and values entered for the selected tool.

Need To Know More?

McClelland, Deke: *Photoshop 5 for Macs for Dummies*. IDG Books Worldwide, Inc. ISBN 0-7645-0391-X.

McClelland, Deke: *Macworld Photoshop 5 Bible*. IDG Books Worldwide, Inc. ISBN 0-7645-3231-6.

Painting And Editing

8

Terms and concepts you'll need to understand:

- √ Blending mode
- √ Opacity
- √ Base color
- √ Blend color
- √ Result color
- √ Preserve Transparency
- √ Gradient
- √ Rubber Stamp
- √ Pattern Stamp
- √ Pattern
- √ Transform
- √ Scale
- √ Skew
- √ Distort
- √ Perspective
- √ Bounding corder
- √ 3D Transform
- √ Filters
- √ Fade

Techniques you'll need to master:

- √ Selecting painting tools and hidden tools
- √ Using the Paintbrush, Airbrush, and Pencil tools
- √ Setting the options for the painting tools
- √ Using the Eraser tool
- √ Understanding the different Blending modes
- √ Using the Paint Bucket tools
- √ Applying and editing gradient fills
- √ Filling and stroking elements
- √ Using the Rubber Stamp tool and the Pattern Stamp tool
- √ Transforming images, selections and selection borders, layers, and paths
- √ Applying filters

Photoshop's powerful painting and retouching tools and features offer tremendous creative possibilities and tremendous challenges at the same time. Many of the basic editing operations, such as choosing commands and operations, navigating the palettes and palette groups, cutting, copying, pasting, measuring, and using the History palette, are covered in Chapter 3. This chapter discusses the specific procedures and options for using the painting and retouching tools and features.

"Painting" And Retouching Images

Photoshop allows you to digitally alter images much more easily and comprehensively than was ever possible with conventional mechanical retouching methods. For instance, you can easily apply color changes to an image by "painting" or drawing with several tools.

Painting Tools

Photoshop provides several tools that simulate the application of color using actual painting and drawing tools, including the following:

- **Paintbrush tool** The Paintbrush tool (shown in Figure 8.1) simulates the variable strokes of a paintbrush, allowing you to apply color in short or long strokes of various widths. The Paintbrush tool also has a Wet Edges option that simulates the appearance of water colors applied by a paintbrush.

- **Airbrush tool** The Airbrush tool (shown in Figure 8.2) applies color like an actual airbrush, applying a soft, diffused "spray" of color in various widths. Like an actual airbrush, the longer you hold the airbrush over an area, the more color is sprayed onto the image.

- **Pencil tool** The Pencil tool (see Figure 8.3) draws dots of varying sizes that can be applied individually or as freehand lines. You can also Auto Erase from the foreground color to the background color with the Pencil tool.

- **Eraser tool** The Eraser tool (see Figure 8.4) is included in this group of painting tools because it also applies color to an image. However, unlike a real eraser, it can paint with a selected color or even a previous state of the image. (Using the Eraser tool is described later in this chapter.)

With the exception of a few options specific to an individual tool, using the Paintbrush tool, the Airbrush tool, and the Pencil tool is very much the same.

Figure 8.1 The Paintbrush tool.    **Figure 8.2** The Airbrush tool.

Figure 8.3 The Pencil tool.    **Figure 8.4** The Eraser tool.

To paint with the Paintbrush, Airbrush, or Pencil tool, you first select a color to apply (described in Chapter 4), you select a brush size (discussed later in this chapter), you set the application options such as the Blending mode (discussed later in this chapter) and opacity in the tool's Options palette, and then you click or click and drag in the image to apply color. You can paint or draw true straight lines by clicking in the image, pressing Shift, and then clicking at another point in the image.

Double-click on the tool's icon, or click on the Options tab in its palette group to access the Options palette and specify these tool options:

- **Blending Mode** This option determines how the color is applied to the image. (Blending modes are described in detail later in this chapter.)

- **Opacity** This option specifies how transparent or opaque the applied color is in relationship to the layers beneath it. The opacity values range from 1 percent through 100 percent opacity. Lower opacity values allow more of the underlying layers to show through the color you are applying.

- **Paint Fadeout Rate** This combination of options allows you to further simulate real painting by applying strokes that fade, or diffuse, as you drag the tool. The heaviest buildup of color is at the point where you begin dragging, and the color fades automatically as you stroke with the tool. In the Fade values box, you specify the number of "steps" for this option. A step is one application of the tip of the selected brush, and you can enter the number of steps from 1 to 9,999, providing a gradual fade from the initial point to the entered number of brush widths. In the Fade To option, you select whether the color fades to the underlying image (Transparent) or the background color (Background).

- **Stylus Pressure** This option specifies the behavior of pressure-sensitive digitizing tablets. As you increase the stylus pressure on the tablet, the brush widens if you select the Size option, the color is more opaque if you select the Opacity option, and the color makes the transition from the background color to the foreground color if you select the Color option.

Line Tool

The Line tool (shown in Figure 8.5) draws simple straight lines. Access the Line tool by holding down the cursor on the Pencil tool icon in the Toolbox to open the tool's hidden tool menu. Simply drag in the image with the Line tool to draw straight lines. Holding the Shift key constrains the line to multiples of 45 degrees.

Double-click on the Line tool or click on the Options tab in its palette group to access and set these Line tool options:

- **Blending Mode** Specify a blending mode. (Blending modes are described in detail later in this chapter.)
- **Opacity** Specify an opacity. (Opacity is described in the preceding section on the painting tools.)
- **Weight** Specify the width, in pixels, of the line you want to draw.
- **Anti-aliased** Select whether to anti-alias the line. (Anti-aliasing is described in Chapter 5.)
- **Arrowheads** Specify whether you want to draw arrowheads automatically at either end of the line you draw. You can choose to draw arrowheads automatically at the start of the line or at the end of the line, or both. If you select an arrowhead option, the Shape button activates and you can open the Arrowhead Shape dialog box and set the width, length, and concavity of the arrowhead to be drawn.

Eraser Tool

As I mentioned previously in this chapter, the Eraser tool performs the same types of operations as the other tools that are considered "painting" tools. The Eraser tool paints over an image area, either with transparency or with the background color.

You can even choose to apply the effects of the Eraser tool with the characteristics of the Paintbrush, Airbrush, and Pencil tools, or you can erase with the simple block eraser.

To use the Eraser tool, specify the same options as described earlier in this chapter for the other painting tools, and select a brush size.

Figure 8.5   The Line tool.

Erasing To A Previous State

The Eraser tool also utilizes the History palette, one of the great new features of Photoshop, allowing you to paint one state of the image onto another state. To use this feature, first select the Eraser tool and the layer on which you want to paint. Choose Erase To History in the Eraser tool's Options palette, and then select a state in the History palette by clicking on the box next to the state's name, which places the History Paintbrush tool icon in the little box. When you drag the Eraser tool over the image, the pixels in the area you "erase" on the layer you selected are replaced by the pixels in the same respective position from the previous state you selected.

Auto Erasing With The Pencil Tool

While you're using the Pencil tool, use the Auto Erase option by selecting Auto Erase from the Pencil tool's Options palette. Auto Erase automatically erases, or paints, pixels of the foreground color to the background color, or, if you drag across pixels that don't contain the foreground color, erases pixels of other colors to the foreground color.

Additional Retouching Tools

The Smudge tool (shown in Figure 8.6) simulates the results of a finger drawn through wet paint. The Focus tools (the Blur and Sharpen tools shown in Figure 8.6) either reduce detail or sharpen edges. The Burn and Dodge tools (shown in Figure 8.7) simulate traditional darkroom techniques of allowing more or less light to strike the photographic print paper in particular areas to darken or lighten those areas of the final print. The Sponge tool (also shown in Figure 8.7) increases or decreases color saturation.

Apply the effects of this group of tools by dragging or clicking with the tool. The following are the options for using these additional tools:

➤ **Smudge** Specify a blending mode, brush size, and stylus pressure in the tool's Options palette and Brush palette as you would for the tools described earlier in this chapter. Enter a Pressure value from 1% through 100% that will provide the amount of "smudging" that you prefer. A

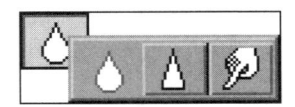

Figure 8.6 From left to right, the Blur tool, Sharpen tool, and Smudge tool.

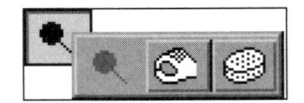

Figure 8.7 From left to right, the Dodge tool, Burn tool, and Sponge tool.

lower Pressure value produces a less noticeable smudge than a higher Pressure value. The Finger Painting option determines whether the Smudge tool smudges with the color of the image under the cursor (deselected) or with the foreground color (selected). You can toggle on and off the Finger Painting option by pressing Option/Alt. The Use All Layers option determines whether to smudge only the colors in the active layer (deselected) or to smudge the colors of all visible layers (selected).

▶ **Focus (Blur or Sharpen)** Specify a blending mode, brush size, and stylus pressure in the tool's Options palette and Brushes palette as you would for the tools described earlier in this chapter. Enter a Pressure value from 1% to 100% that will provide the amount of focusing that you prefer. A lower Pressure value produces a less noticeable smudge than a higher Pressure value. The Use All Layers option determines whether to apply the blurring or sharpening effects using only pixel data from the active layer (deselected) or the pixel data of all visible layers (selected).

▶ **Toning (Dodge and Burn)** Select a brush size from the tool's Brushes palette as you would for the tools described earlier in this chapter. Specify an Exposure value from 1% to 100% that will provide the amount of lightening or darkening that you prefer. A lower Exposure value produces a less noticeable change of brightness than a higher Exposure value. Select either Shadows, Midtones, or Highlights to choose the individual range of brightness values to affect.

▶ **Sponge** Select a brush size from the tool's Brushes palette as you would for the tools described earlier in this chapter. Enter a Pressure value from 1% to 100% that will provide the amount of color change that you prefer. A lower Pressure value produces a less noticeable adjustment than a higher Pressure value. Select either Saturate or Desaturate to increase or decrease, respectively, the intensity of the colors under the tool.

Specifying Blending Modes

Blending modes affect how colors are "mixed" when painting. The visual effects of blending modes are determined by the mathematical calculations of the different color values performed for a specific blending mode. Understanding how these Blending mode calculations actually work is not as important as understanding what each specific blending mode does to the colors in an image. You must also know the difference between these color terms:

▶ **Base color** The original color of the pixels to be altered

▶ **Blend color** The new color to be applied

▶ **Result color** The final color

> Learn the differences between the Blending modes, particularly how each Blending mode calculates the values of the base and blend colors. A good way to remember what each one does is to study its position in the menu (shown in Figure 8.8). Note how the Blending modes are grouped, and remember that many of the Blending modes complement each other or are opposites of each other.
>
> The Color Dodge, Color Burn, Lighten, Darken, Difference, and Exclusion Blending modes are not available in Lab mode.

The following are Photoshop 5's Blending modes, in their menu order:

- **Normal** Simply replaces the base color with the blend color. This mode's name changes to Threshold when in Bitmap or Indexed Color modes.

- **Dissolve** Replaces color depending on the opacity of the layer, on the amount of feathering of a selection, or on the opacity of a painting tool. Fully opaque (100-percent opacity) layers, selections, or painted colors are not affected. When a layer, selection, or painted color is less than 100-percent opacity, Dissolve replaces a percentage of pixels that have opacity values less than 100 percent with a random pattern of blend-colored pixels based on the reciprocal of the opacity percentage. This means if you paint with a tool's opacity set at 50 percent, only 50 percent

Figure 8.8 The Blending mode's menu.

of the pixels you drag across will wind up with the blend color. If the tool's opacity is 70 percent, then 30 percent of the pixels will have the blend color.

- **Behind** Paints only to transparent areas of layers and only when the Preserve Transparency option in the Layers palette is deselected.
- **Clear** Actually paints transparency with the Line tool, the Paint Bucket tool, the Fill command, and the Stroke command, when the Preserve Transparency option is deselected.
- **Multiply** Darkens colors by multiplying the base color by the blend color.
- **Screen** Lightens colors by multiplying the *inverse* of the blend color and the base color.
- **Overlay** Mixes colors depending on the lightness or darkness of the base colors. If the base colors are lighter, Overlay actually works like the Screen Blending mode. If the base colors are darker, Overlay works like the Multiply Blending mode. Consequently, less blend color is applied to the lighter base-color areas on a layer and more blend color is applied to the darker base-color areas of a layer.
- **Soft Light** Darkens or lightens base colors, depending on the lightness or darkness of the blend colors. Blend colors that are lighter than 50-percent gray lighten the underlying base colors, whereas blend colors that are darker than 50-percent gray darken the underlying base colors. The effects of this mode have been compared to using the Dodge tool to lighten light areas and the Burn tool to darken dark areas.
- **Hard Light** Mixes colors like the Overlay mode, except that the blend colors, rather than the base colors, determine the effect. If the blend colors are lighter than 50-percent gray, Hard Light works like the Screen Blending mode. If the blend colors are darker than 50-percent gray, Hard Light works like the Multiply blending mode.
- **Color Dodge** Lightens base colors to a varying degree, depending on the brightness of the blend colors. The lighter the blend colors are, the more they lighten the base colors, whereas darker blend colors produce less lightening of the base colors.
- **Color Burn** Darkens base colors to a varying degree, depending on the brightness of the blend colors. The darker the blend colors are, the more they darken the base colors, whereas lighter blend colors produce less darkening of the base colors.

Painting And Editing   229

- **Darken** Applies the blend color only to pixels that contain a base color darker than the blend color and leaves untouched pixels that contain a base color lighter than the blend color. This Blending mode produces easily predictable changes to grayscale images, but its effects are less easily predicted on color images because it applies its calculations separately to each color channel.

- **Lighten** Applies the blend color only to pixels that contain a base color lighter than the blend color and leaves untouched pixels that contain a base color darker than the blend color. This Blending mode produces easily predictable changes to grayscale images, but its effects are less easily predicted on color images because it applies its calculations separately to each color channel.

- **Difference** Subtracts the base color and blend color values to determine the result color. If the resulting number is a negative, the number is simply converted to a positive.

- **Exclusion** Subtracts the base color and blend color values as does the Difference Blending mode, but uses a complicated midtone calculation that results in less contrast between the base color and blend color.

- **Hue** Changes the base color to a result color that has the base color's original luminance and saturation and the hue of the blend color. The Hue Blending mode is available only in RGB, CMYK, and Lab color modes.

- **Saturation** Changes the base color to a result color that has the base color's original luminance and hue and the saturation of the blend color. This blending mode does not affect gray pixels because they have no saturation. The Saturation Blending mode is available only in RGB, CMYK, and Lab color modes.

- **Color** Changes the base color to a result color that has the base color's original luminance and the hue and saturation of the blend color. This blending mode does not affect the brightness levels of an image, so the grayscale levels remain untouched. The Color Blending mode is available only in RGB, CMYK, and Lab color modes.

- **Luminosity** Changes the base color to a result color that has the base color's original hue and saturation and the luminance of the blend color, the opposite of the Color blending mode. The Luminosity Blending mode is available only in RGB, CMYK, and Lab color modes.

Editing Color Across Large Image Areas

You can apply sweeping color changes to image areas by using these painting tools.

The Paint Bucket Tool

As the Paint Bucket tool's name might suggest, you can "pour" color into an area by using the Paint Bucket tool (see Figure 8.9). You could call it the "Magic Fill tool" because it combines the selection capabilities of the Magic Wand tool with the color filling capabilities of the Fill command. When you click on an area in an image, the Paint Bucket tool pours the foreground color into adjacent areas of similar color, depending on a tolerance level you specify.

> **STUDY ALERT:** The Paint Bucket tool also works like the Replace Color command, which allows you to select specific colors from an image and alter them. However, with the Replace Color command, you can select all pixels of similar colors in an image, not just adjacent pixels.

You select a blending mode and specify the opacity for the Paint Bucket tool as you would with the other painting tools described in this chapter.

Just as you would with the Magic Wand tool (which is described in Chapter 7), you specify the Paint Bucket tool's range of color, or Tolerance, in its Options palette. This value specifies how much difference the Paint Bucket tool will tolerate as it seeks similar colors. This tolerance can be any value from 0 to 255. If you enter 0, the Paint Bucket tool pours the foreground color into only those adjacent pixels that are of the exact same value. If you enter 255, the Paint Bucket tool pours the foreground color into all the colors in an image.

You can also pour a pattern into an area by defining a pattern and selecting Pattern from the Contents option menu in the Options palette.

The Anti-aliasing option in the Options palette smoothes the edges of the area into which the color is applied.

If you select the Use All Layers checkbox in the Options palette, the Paint Bucket paints according to the color values of all visible layers, as if the layers

Figure 8.9 The Paint Bucket tool.

were merged. If this selection is unchecked, the Paint Bucket uses the color data from only the active layer.

Select Preserve Transparency in the Layers palette to avoid pouring color into any transparent areas of the active layer.

If you are editing an image in an image window that is larger than the image, Photoshop fills that area with medium gray. If you want to change that color, use the Paint Bucket tool. Select a foreground color for the new window color. Select the Paint Bucket tool, and Shift+click in the empty window area to fill with the foreground color. (It doesn't matter whether you have selected Foreground or Pattern from the Content option menu for the Paint Bucket tool. The foreground color is used either way.)

The Paint Bucket tool is not available in Bitmap mode.

The Gradient Tools

You use the Gradient tools to fill an area with a gradual blend of colors in five different patterns. The Gradient tools blend from the foreground color to the background color. You can select from a variety of supplied blends, or you can create a custom blend. To create a gradient fill, drag the cursor from the place where you want to start the gradient to where you want the gradient to end. If you want a gradient to fill only part of an image, you must select that part of the image to protect the other areas of the image. You can also use a Transparency Mask to create gradients that blend the gradient fill colors with the underlying colors.

The following are the different Gradient tools and how to use them:

➤ **Linear Gradient** Creates a gradient blend along a line from one point to another (see the tool's icon in Figure 8.10). Click in a spot, and then drag the line to the ending spot. The gradient fills the color at the left of the color bar (the starting color) in the Options palette from the initial point and gradually makes a transition to the color at the other end of the bar (the ending color), finishing at the ending spot. The length of the gradient is determined by the length of the line you draw. Outward from the starting and ending points, the respective colors are solid.

➤ **Radial Gradient** Creates a gradient blend in a circular pattern (see the tool's icon in Figure 8.11). When you click and drag a line, you specify

Figure 8.10 The Linear Gradient icon.

Figure 8.11 The Radial Gradient icon.

the radius of the gradient fill. The color on the left side of the color bar appears at the center of the circular gradient and makes the transition in concentric circles to the other color. Any areas outside the radius of the gradient fill are filled with solid ending color.

▶ **Angular Gradient** Creates a gradient blend that appears to conform to an angular shape that may appear conical (see the tool's icon in Figure 8.12). The direction you drag determines the direction of the starting/ ending line. The length of the line you drag is not consequential. The gradient fans out in a complete circle around the starting point from a line drawn in the direction you drag.

▶ **Reflected Gradient** Creates a gradient blend that appears to be a reflection of itself (see the tool's icon in Figure 8.13). Dragging a line determines the length and direction of the gradient. The gradient fills to the ending point and is "reflected" with an exact copy that runs from the starting point in the opposite direction of the ending point. Areas beyond the ending point are filled with the solid ending color.

▶ **Diamond Gradient** Creates a gradient blend in a diamond shape (see the tool's icon in Figure 8.14). Dragging a line determines both the radius of the "diamond" and the orientation of its points. Areas beyond the ending point are filled with the solid ending color.

In the Gradient tools' Options palette (shown in Figure 8.15), you select a blending mode and set the opacity of the fill as described for other tools in this chapter. Here, you also select the gradient to use from the Gradient option menu. The Gradient option menu lists all available gradients, including any custom gradients you create in the Gradient Editor dialog box, which you access with the Edit button. The color bar at the bottom of the Options palette shows the gradient fill that is selected. You can flip this bar and reverse the direction of the colors in the gradient by clicking on the Reverse checkbox. Select Transparency to activate any Transparency Mask a gradient may have. Selecting Dither smoothes the transitions from color to color (dithering is discussed in Chapter 4).

Figure 8.12 The Angular Gradient icon.

Figure 8.13 The Reflected Gradient icon.

Figure 8.14 The Diamond Gradient icon.

Figure 8.15 The Gradient Tools' Options palette.

Open the Gradient Editor dialog box (shown in Figure 8.16) by clicking on the Edit button. Here, you can edit the supplied gradient fills and create custom gradient fills. The bottom color bar is a preview of the gradient fill.

Edit a gradient by first creating a new gradient (New), copying an existing gradient (Duplicate), loading a gradient or gradients (Load), or selecting an existing gradient from the list of gradients. You can create a copy of any gradient by using the Duplicate button. You can rename any of the existing gradients by using the Rename button. And you can save one or more gradients by clicking and Shift+clicking the name or names in the list and clicking on the Save button.

Edit the colors of a gradient by first selecting the Adjust: Color radio button. Then, click on the left color stop slider under the upper color bar to edit the starting color, or click on the right color stop slider to edit the ending color.

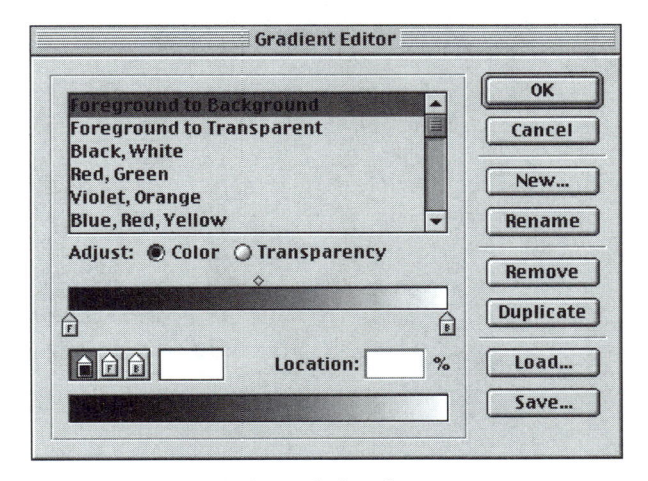

Figure 8.16 The Gradient Editor dialog box.

The "roof" of the active color stop slider turns black to indicate it is active. Any color editing now affects that active color stop slider. Double-clicking on either color stop slider or the color swatch between the color bars opens the Color Picker. Clicking in the upper color bar selects a sample from the bar. Clicking on the F color stop slider icon selects the foreground color, and clicking on the B color stop slider icon selects the background color.

Dragging a color stop slider or entering a value between 0% and 100% moves the starting or ending point of the gradient fill, changing the starting and/or ending colors to be used. Dragging the midpoint diamond above the color bar moves the point at which the colors are mixed.

Add new, or intermediate, colors to the gradient by clicking just beneath the color bar. A new color stop slider and a new midpoint diamond then appear. Edit and adjust these intermediate colors as you would the original color stop sliders.

Edit the Transparency Mask of a gradient by clicking on the Adjust: Transparency radio button. The upper color bar in the Gradient Editor dialog box changes to grayscale (see Figure 8.17), indicating the opacity of the Transparency Mask (black is opaque, grays are partially transparent, and white is transparent). The Opacity and Location values boxes appear between the color bars. Edit the gradient's Transparency Mask by clicking on either of the transparency stops to activate that stop. Move this stop by dragging or by entering a location value from 0% to 100% in the Location values box. Enter an opacity value from 0% (white/transparent) to 100% (black/opaque) in the Opacity values box to set the opacity at that location. The bottom color bar previews the effect of any changes to the gradient, and the transparency checkerboard shows through any transparency or semi-opaque areas of the gradient

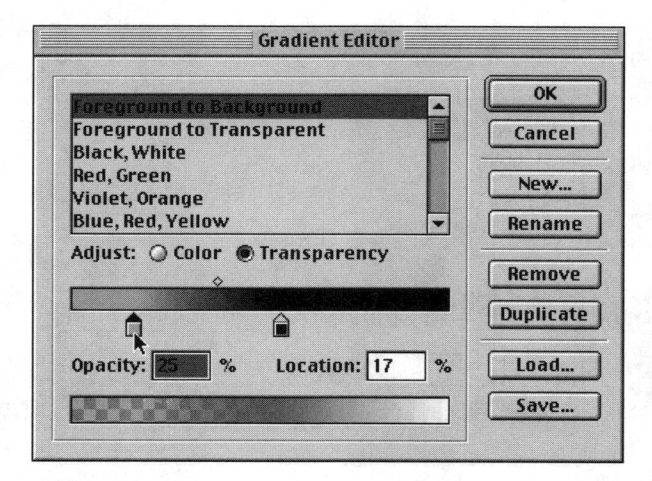

Figure 8.17 The Adjust Transparency appearance of the Gradient Editor dialog box.

fill. Dragging the midpoint diamond moves the point at which the opacity values make a transition. You can add intermediate opacities, just as you would add intermediate colors.

The Gradient tools are not available in Bitmap or Indexed Color modes.

The Fill And Stroke Commands

You can also fill an image area with color, other images, or patterns by using the Fill command. You can apply color to a selection border by using the Stroke command.

Using The Fill Command

Use the Fill command to fill selected areas. Choose Edit|Fill to open the Fill dialog box. Specify a blending mode and opacity, and select Preserve Transparency as described earlier in this chapter. For Contents, you can choose to fill the selection with the foreground or background colors, with a pattern or a previous History state, or with black, white, or 50% gray.

To fill a selection with a pattern, first select a rectangular area of an image with the Marquee tool. Choose Edit|Define Pattern to save that selected area as a pattern. Select the image area into which you want to place that pattern, choose Edit|Fill, and select Pattern from the Use option menu of the Fill dialog box. The saved pattern then fills the selected area and tiles if the selected area is larger than the pattern. A set of patterns is supplied with the Photoshop application, and each is stored as an EPS file in the Adobe Photoshop 5.0\Goodies\Patterns\PostScript Patterns folder. You can open each file to edit it and/or define it as a pattern.

To fill a selection with a previous History state, open the History palette, and choose a state to use as the fill contents by clicking in the box to the right of the state's name. Then, select the layer into which you want to place this state, and make a selection in the image. Choose Edit|Fill and select History from the Use option menu. The area you select on the layer you select is filled with the area of the selected History state that is within that same selection border. (The History state you choose must also have the same layer that you intend to fill.)

> Be sure to review carefully the keyboard shortcuts for the Fill command, which are listed in Table 8.1.

Using The Stroke Command

To use the Stroke Command, define a selection border and select a foreground color; then choose Edit|Stroke to open the Stroke dialog box. In the Stroke Width

Table 8.1 The keyboard shortcuts for the Fill command.

Key or Key Combo	Performs This Function
Shift+Delete/Shift+Backspace	Opens the Fill dialog box
Option+Delete/Alt+Backspace	Fills with the foreground color
Shift+Option+Delete/Shift+Alt+Backspace	Fills with the foreground color and preserves transparency
Cmd+Delete/Ctrl+Backspace	Fills with the background color
Shift+Cmd+Delete/Shift+Ctrl+Backspace	Fills with the background color and preserves transparency
Cmd+Option+Delete/Ctrl+Alt+Backspace	Fills with the selected History state

values box, specify the pixel width of the stroke, from 1 to 16. In the Location area of the dialog box, select the respective radio button to have the color stroked completely inside the selection border (Inside), to have the color stroke straddle the selection border (Center), or to have the color stroked completely outside the selection border (Outside). Specify and select opacity, a Blending mode, and Preserve Transparency as described previously in this chapter.

Selecting And Using Brushes

When using any of the painting tools, you can select from a number of predefined "brushes," or you can define custom brushes in the Brushes palette. The Brushes palette is coordinated with whatever tool you have selected, and the last brush you specified for that tool remains specified even if you have specified another brush for another tool. To select a brush for the selected tool, open the Brushes palette by clicking on its tab in its palette group or by choosing Window|Show Brushes; then click on a brush's icon.

Using the Brushes palette is described in detail in Chapter 3.

"Stamping" Color, Patterns, And Image Selections

Photoshop also allows you to "clone" areas of an image and "stamp" the clones onto other areas of the image with the Rubber Stamp tool and the Pattern Stamp tool (shown in Figure 8.18). Both of these tools allow you to pick up pixels from one area of an image and then put down those pixels in another area of that image or even another open image in the same color mode. The main difference between these two tools is that the Pattern Stamp tool stamps

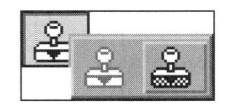

Figure 8.18 The Rubber Stamp tool and the Pattern Stamp tool.

only rectangular pieces, or patterns, of an image, whereas the Rubber Stamp samples and stamps whatever brush size and/or shape is selected.

The Options palette for either of these tools includes the familiar opacity and blending mode features. As with other painting tools, the Rubber Stamp tool samples pixels from all visible layers when the Use All Layers option is selected. While using a digitizing tablet, you can also select between increasing the brush size (Size) or increasing the opacity (Opacity) as you increase the pressure on the tip of the stylus.

You can use the Brushes palette to specify the brush size and type for each tool. The Rubber Stamp tool both samples and stamps according to the brush specifications, but the Pattern Stamp tool either stamps that part of the defined pattern that will fit into a brush size that is smaller than the defined pattern, or it stamps a tiled pattern of patterns into a brush size that is larger than the defined pattern.

To use the Rubber Stamp tool, you must first sample an area by Option+clicking/Alt+clicking on the area you want to sample. The inverted black triangle on the tool changes to a white triangle (as shown in Figure 8.19). After you begin to stamp, the position of the sampled area is marked by a crosshair.

To use the Pattern Stamp tool, you must first define a pattern by selecting a rectangular area and choosing Edit|Define Pattern.

Before stamping with either of these tools, you must choose between aligning the tool or not aligning the tool by either selecting or deselecting the Align checkbox in the Options palette.

Align affects the stamping operation for the Rubber Stamp tool and the Pattern Stamp tool as follows:

➤ **Rubber Stamp** When Align is selected, the sample area moves in alignment with the Rubber Stamp tool, according to the vertical and horizontal distance away from the sample you first stamp. Each time you move the tool after that first stamp, the sample area moves the same distance both vertically and horizontally to sample whatever pixels are beneath it.

Figure 8.19 The Rubber Stamp tool when sampling.

When Align is deselected, the sample remains fixed, and no matter where you go on the image, you stamp the same sample you first collected.

➤ **Pattern Stamp** When Align is selected, the defined pattern locks to a tiled grid of itself—as if you had created a layer filled with the tiled pattern—centered on the place where you first stamp. As you move the Pattern Stamp tool and stamp again, that tiled pattern is revealed according to the brush specifications of the tool. The best way to see this effect is to select Align and stamp with the Pattern Stamp tool and then "paint" away the active layer by dragging the tool around the image. You'll see that the tiled pattern remains fixed and you are simply revealing it.

When Align is deselected, the pattern is centered on the tool each time you stamp, regardless of where you are in relationship to the first stamp.

Transforming Images, Selections And Selection Borders, Layers, And Paths

In addition to the 2D transformations such as skew, rotate, scale, and distort that you can apply to selections and images, Photoshop 5 includes the new 3D Transform filter. The 3D Transform filter enables you to transform images in ways that make them appear three-dimensional.

Follow these procedures to select a layer, a path, points, or a selection for transformation:

➤ To transform an entire layer, select that layer in the Layers palette, and make sure no part of the image is selected. (Using layers is discussed in Chapter 9.)

➤ To transform an entire path, select that path in the Paths palette, and select the path in the image window with the Direct-Selection tool. (Paths are discussed in Chapter 7.)

➤ To transform only select anchor points of a path, select the path in the Paths palette, and then select the desired anchor points with the Direct-Selection tool. (Paths are discussed in Chapter 7.)

➤ To transform a selection or selection border, make a selection. (Selecting image areas is discussed in Chapter 7.)

You choose a 2D transformation command based on what you want to transform and how you want to work with the transformation options. Here are the transformation commands and their uses:

Painting And Editing   239

➤ To rotate or flip an entire image, choose Image|Rotate Canvas.

➤ To transform a selection border only and not the contents of the selection, choose Select|Transform Selection.

➤ The Edit|Free Transform command (Cmd+T/Ctrl+T) places a bounding border on the selected item, allowing you to manipulate one or more of the transformation options right on the image. To duplicate while using Free Transform, press Cmd+Option+T/Ctrl+Alt+T.

➤ The Edit|Transform commands allow you to select individual transformations or to transform selections by entering values for individual transformation options. To duplicate while using the Transform commands, press Option/Alt while choosing Edit|Transform.

➤ If you are editing an entire path, the Edit|Free Transform command changes to Edit|Free Transform Path, and the Edit|Transform command changes to Edit|Transform Path. (Paths are discussed in Chapter 7.)

➤ If you are editing only selected anchor points on a path, the Edit|Free Transform command and the Edit|Transform command change to Edit|Free Transform Points and Edit|Transform Points, respectively. (Paths are discussed in Chapter 7.)

> Particular limitations and capabilities apply to transformations. You should know these transformation guidelines:
>
> ➤ Applying transformations to a linked layer applies those transformations to all the layers in that linked group. (Using layers is discussed in Chapter 9.)
>
> ➤ You cannot transform the entire background layer, but you can transform selections on the background layer.
>
> ➤ A 16-bit-per-channel image does not support transformations.
>
> ➤ You can transform a selected alpha channel. (Using channels is discussed in Chapter 10.)
>
> ➤ You can transform an active layer mask. (Using layers is discussed in Chapter 9.)
>
> ➤ The interpolation method specified in the General dialog box (which you open by choosing File|Preferences) applies to the transformation calculations that are necessary with all transformations. (Interpolation is discussed in Chapter 6.)

Figure 8.20 A transformation bounding border.

When you're using the Free Transform command or the Scale, Rotate, Skew, Distort, or Perspective commands, a bounding border (as shown in Figure 8.20) appears around the layer, image, or selection you are transforming. The crosshair/target in the center of the bounding border is the center point for transformations. You can drag the center point of the transformation bounding border anywhere inside or outside the bounding border.

You transform the layer, image, path, points, or selection by manipulating this bounding border. To apply the transformations, press Return/Enter or double-click inside the bounding border. Repeat transformations by pressing Cmd+T/Ctrl+T after transforming, or choose Edit|Transform|Again. To cancel transformation, press Esc or Cmd+period/Ctrl+period. You can undo the last transformation before applying the transformations by choosing Edit|Undo.

The following are the various procedures for transforming with the bounding border:

➤ **Scale** Drag any handle to resize the layer, image, path, points, or selection. To avoid distortion and constrain the proportions during scaling, hold down the Shift key as you drag.

Painting And Editing   241

- **Rotate** Place the cursor anywhere outside the bounding border to activate the Rotate cursor. Drag to the desired rotation. Constrain the rotation to 15-degree increments by pressing Shift as you drag.

   Note: When transforming an entire layer, you may need to resize the image and the image window so that the image window is larger than the image to see the Rotate cursor.

- **Skew** Press Shift+Cmd/Shift+Ctrl and drag any side handle.

- **Distort** Press Cmd/Ctrl and drag any handle. Pressing Option/Alt while dragging constrains the distortion symmetrically around the center point. (Distort is not available when you're transforming individual points or path segments.)

- **Perspective** Press Shift+Cmd+Option/Shift+Ctrl+Alt and drag a corner handle. (Distort is not available when you're transforming points.)

You can enter numeric values to apply transformations by choosing Edit|Transform|Numeric. Select the individual transformation checkbox or checkboxes you want and enter the appropriate values. You can set these Numeric Transform dialog box options:

- **Position** Move the item by choosing a measurement unit and entering values for X and Y. Selecting Relative moves the item the specified amount in relation to its current position. Deselecting Relative moves the item relative to the X and Y zero point at the top left of the image.

- **Scale** Resize the item by choosing a measurement unit and entering values for the width and height. Scale proportionally by selecting Constrain Proportions.

- **Skew** Skew the item by entering horizontal and/or vertical angle values in degrees.

- **Rotate** Rotate the item by entering an angle value from -360.00 to 360.00 (or -180 to 180) or by dragging the radius line in the circle.

Also included in the Edit|Transform submenu are the rotate and flip options for layers, paths, points, or selections. The rotate and flip options are as follows:

- **Rotate 180°** Rotates the item 180 degrees

- **Rotate 90° CW** Rotates the item 90 degrees clockwise

- **Rotate 90° CCW** Rotates the item 90 degrees counterclockwise

242 Chapter 8

> **Flip Horizontal** Flips the left side of the item over to the right side
> **Flip Vertical** Flips the top down to the bottom

Image|Rotate Canvas

You can also rotate or flip an entire image by choosing Image|Rotate Canvas and selecting from the same rotation options as described for the Edit|Transform submenu. Plus, you can select the Arbitrary option, which opens the Rotate Canvas dialog box. Here, you can enter a rotation value from -359.99 to +359.99 degrees.

Filter|Render|3D Transform

One of Photoshop 5's powerful new features is the 3D Transform filter. This feature enables you to draw a primitive wire frame, apply a selection to it, and then manipulate the selection as though it were a 3D object. You can use cube, sphere, and cylinder wire frames.

To use the 3D Transform filter, choose Filter|Render|3D Transform to open the 3D Transform dialog box (shown in Figure 8.21). You should be familiar with the procedures for creating and editing paths, as presented in Chapter 7.

Choose either the Cube, Sphere, or Cylinder icon, and drag it in the preview window to create the wire frame. Then, edit the wire frame using the Pen tools included in the 3D Transform dialog box, or manipulate the wire frame in three dimensions using the Pan Camera tool or the Trackball tool (as shown in

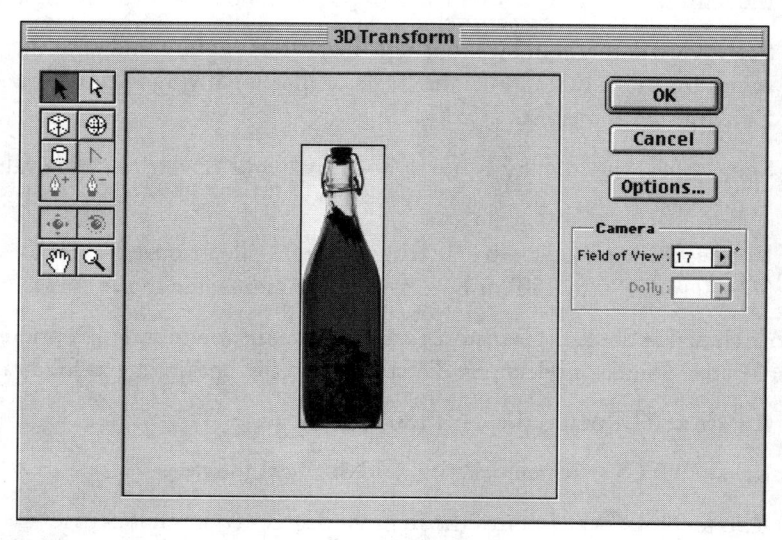

Figure 8.21 The 3D Transform dialog box.

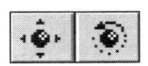

Figure 8.22 The Pan Camera tool (left) and the Trackball tool.

Figure 8.22). Set the Field Oof View value to approximate the angle of the camera when the object was originally photographed.

The Options button accesses these rendering options:

➤ **Resolution** Choose Low, Medium, or High resolutions.

➤ **Anti-Aliasing** Choose None, Low, Medium, or High anti-aliasing.

➤ **Display Background** Choose to leave the background visible when the object is rendered or to delete the area behind the object when it is rendered.

Using Filters

Photoshop filters are plug-ins that change the appearance of an image in ways that range from the simple to the extraordinary. You may never find a use for many of these filters, but for the purposes of becoming an Adobe Certified Expert, you must at least know the basics of what they are, what they generally do, and how to use them.

Use a filter by choosing it from its Filter submenu. The filters are grouped according to how they affect an image. Some filters are applied simply by choosing them, whereas others require additional input.

> Note that filters are not supported in Bitmap, Indexed Color, or 16-bit-per-channel images and that at least a few of them support only RGB images.

Filter effects can be applied to complete layers by not selecting any areas or can be limited to selected areas by selecting those areas.

Table 8.2 lists the keyboard shortcuts used for filters.

Chapter 8

Table 8.2 The keyboard shortcuts for using filters.

Key Or Key Combo	Performs This Function
Esc or Cmd+period (Mac only)	Cancels a filter as it is being applied
Cmd+F/Ctrl+F	Reapplies the last filter applied
Cmd+Option+F/Ctrl+Alt+F	Opens the dialog box for the last filter applied
Shift+Cmd+F/Shift+Ctrl+F	Accesses the Fade dialog box

Previewing Filter Effects

If a filter's dialog box includes a Preview checkbox, you can preview the filter's effects in the full image window. Many filters have preview windows in their dialog boxes. The preview in these preview windows can be moved around and enlarged or reduced. The size of the preview is displayed as a percentage under the preview window. A flashing line under the preview size percentage indicates that the preview is still being rendered.

Follow these preview window navigation guidelines:

➤ To zoom the preview in or out, click on either the + or - buttons, respectively.

➤ To move the image around in the preview window, click in the preview window and drag.

➤ To move the preview image to a particular area of an image, some filters allow you to click in the image window.

Applying A Filter

Apply filters by selecting the desired filter from the Filter menu and submenus. If a filter requires additional input after choosing it from its Filter submenu, enter any required or desired values, and then click on OK.

Using The Fade Command

After you apply a filter, use the Fade command to adjust the effects of the filter. You can select a blending mode and specify an opacity different from those that may have been originally applied.

> *Note: The Fade command is also available immediately after you use any painting tool or color adjustments.*

Understanding Special Filter Procedures

You may need to perform various special procedures for some filters to define or limit their effects.

To use the Conté Crayon, Displace, Shear, Wave, Offset, Glass, Lighting Effects, Rough Pastels, Texture Fill, Texturizer, Underpainting, and Custom filters, you may need or want to load an image or texture from their dialog boxes.

When using Displace, Shear, Wave, and Offset filters, you can select from the following options for handling the areas left undefined by the filter:

- Set to Background (Offset filter only)
- Repeat Edge Pixels
- Wrap Around

You can control the textures and glass surfaces applied by the Conté Crayon, Glass, Rough Pastels, Texturizer, and Underpainting filters. The following are the texture and glass surface controls:

- **Texture** Select a texture from the option menu.
- **Scaling** Drag the slider, or enter a value from 50% to 200% to reduce or enlarge the filter's effect across the image.
- **Relief** Drag the slider, or enter a value from 0 to 50 to specify the height of any simulated relief on the image.
- **Light Direction** Select a direction from the option menu for shadowing of the filter's simulated relief.
- **Invert** Select this option to swap the light and dark colors of the surface.

Working Efficiently With Filters

Some of the memory-gobbling filters may slow your computer or even refuse to work if adequate RAM isn't available. If you have this problem, you can allocate more RAM to Photoshop, you can use the Purge command to empty memory, you can try different settings and values with different filters, you can test a filter's effects on a lower-resolution copy of your image, you can test the filter's effects on a small area of the image, or you can even apply the filter to one color channel at a time (be careful, however, because some filters produce different effects when applied one channel at a time).

Exploring The Filter Categories

The various native Photoshop filters are grouped according to the type of effect they produce. The categories and filters are presented in this section.

Artistic

As you can tell by many of their names, the Artistic filters are designed to simulate the visual effects applied by artists with more traditional tools. The Artistic submenu includes these filters:

- Colored Pencil
- Cutout
- Dry Brush
- Film Grain
- Fresco
- Neon Glow
- Paint Daubs
- Palette Knife
- Plastic Wrap
- Poster Edges
- Rough Pastels
- Smudge Stick
- Sponge
- Underpainting
- Watercolor

Blur

The Blur filters do just that: blur an image. This blurring can be subtle or intense, depending on the filter and the settings and values specified. They work in the opposite way from the Sharpen filters, by softening the differences between edge pixels. The Blur submenu includes these filters:

- Blur
- Blur More
- Gaussian Blur

Painting And Editing   **247**

- Motion Blur
- Radial Blur
- Smart Blur

> **STUDY ALERT:** The Blur filters can be applied to the outer edges of a layer as long as Preserve Transparency is deselected for that layer in the Layers palette.

Brush Strokes

The Brush Strokes filters also simulate "artistic" effects, concentrated on the effects of conventional paint brushes and inking tools. The Brush Strokes submenu includes these filters:

- Accented Edges
- Angled Strokes
- Crosshatch
- Dark Strokes
- Ink Outlines
- Spatter
- Sprayed Strokes
- Sumi-e

Distort

Like the Blur filters, the Distort filters do just what their name says: distort an image. And, as with the Blur filters, this distortion can be subtle or extreme. The Distort submenu includes these filters:

- Diffuse Glow
- Displace
- Glass
- Ocean Ripple
- Pinch
- Polar Coordinates
- Ripple

- Shear
- Spherize
- Twirl
- Wave
- ZigZag

Noise

To understand Photoshop's Noise filter, you can equate the term *noise* with more familiar electronic noise, such as static on a radio, or "snow" on a TV. The Noise filters can add or remove this electronic noise either to create special effects or to improve the appearance of an image. Common uses for the Noise filters include creating textures, reducing dust and scratches, reducing color banding, and smoothing retouched areas of an image. The Noise submenu includes these filters:

- Add Noise
- Despeckle
- Dust & Scratches
- Median

Pixelate

The Pixelate filters producing interesting effects that may appear "tiled" or "mosaic" by creating cells of similar color from the colors in an image. The Mosaic and Pointillize filters produce effects that are similar to the fine art techniques of mosaic tiling and pointillist painting. The Pixelate submenu includes these filters:

- Color Halftone
- Crystallize
- Facet
- Fragment
- Mezzotint
- Mosaic
- Pointillize

Render

As opposed to the Blur and Sharpen filters, among others, the name of the Render group of filters doesn't help you figure out what the filters in its submenu might do to an image. In fact, the filters in this submenu don't all do the same things. (I guess we must figure that at the programming level, they must have something in common, eh?) This submenu is home to the 3D Transform filter discussed previously, as well as the supposed cloud-producing and the lighting effects filters. The Render submenu includes these filters:

- 3D Transform
- Clouds
- Difference Clouds
- Lens Flare
- Lighting Effects
- Texture Fill

Sharpen

Yes, the Sharpen filters sharpen images. They increase the contrast of edge pixels to enhance the appearance of focus. The Unsharp Mask filter, described in detail in Chapter 6, is often used to improve the sharpness of resampled images. The Sharpen submenu includes these filters:

- Sharpen
- Sharpen Edges
- Sharpen More
- Unsharp Mask

Sketch

The Sketch filters are yet another group of filters that simulate various traditional fine art techniques. The Sketch submenu includes these filters:

- Bas Relief
- Chalk & Charcoal
- Charcoal
- Chrome
- Conté Crayon

- Graphic Pen
- Halftone Pattern
- Note Paper
- Photocopy
- Plaster
- Reticulation
- Stamp
- Torn Edges
- Water Paper

Stylize

The Adobe Photoshop 5 manual describes the effects of the Stylize filters as producing "a painted or impressionistic effect on a selection by displacing pixels and by finding and heightening contrast in an image." Okay, whatever. Probably the most popular filter in this group is the Emboss filter, which produces effects that appear stamped or quilted on an image. The Stylize submenu includes these filters:

- Diffuse
- Emboss
- Extrude
- Find Edges
- Glowing Edges
- Solarize
- Tiles
- Trace Contour
- Wind

Texture

As you might expect, the Texture filters produce a variety of simulated relief, or textures, to a selection. The Texture submenu includes these filters:

- Craquelure
- Grain

- Mosaic Tiles
- Patchwork
- Stained Glass
- Texturizer

Video

The Video filters can be used both to enhance an image intended for display on television (NTSC Colors) and to enhance an image captured from television (De-Interlace). The Video submenu includes these filters:

- NTSC Colors
- De-Interlace

Other

I guess after Adobe arranged all the previous filters into groups, a few didn't seem to fit anywhere else, so they plopped them in an "Other" group. You can create custom filters with the Custom dialog box. The Other submenu includes these filters:

- Custom
- High Pass
- Maximum
- Minimum
- Offset

Digimarc

The Digimarc filter is a third-party filter that you can use to protect copyrighted images by embedding a supposedly invisible "watermark" of digital information about the image or by reading any watermark saved with an image. You must pay Digimarc to register any images you want to watermark. The Digimarc submenu includes these filters:

- Embed Watermark
- Read Watermark

Practice Questions

Question 1

> Which of the following tools has the Wet Edges feature? (Select all that apply.)
>
> ❏ a. Paintbrush tool
> ❏ b. Airbrush tool
> ❏ c. Pencil tool
> ❏ d. Pen tool

Answer a is correct. The Wet Edges feature simulates painting with water colors.

Question 2

> Which of the following tools can you use to apply color directly to an image? (Select all that apply.)
>
> ❏ a. Paintbrush tool
> ❏ b. Airbrush tool
> ❏ c. Pencil tool
> ❏ d. Pen tool
> ❏ e. Eraser tool

Answers a, b, c, and e are correct. The Pen tool is for creating and editing paths. The Eraser tool also applies color to an image.

Question 3

> If you want to paint with a color that is semi-transparent, for which options do you need to specify values? (Select all that apply.)
> - a. Preserve Transparency
> - b. Opacity
> - c. Paint Fadeout Rate
> - d. Stylus Pressure

Answers b, c, and d are correct. Setting any Opacity value less than 100% allows some of the colors underneath the applied color to show through. The Paint Fadeout Rate specifies the rate at which colors applied by a painting tool fade, or become transparent. Selecting the Stylus: Opacity checkbox decreases the opacity of an applied color as less pressure is applied with the stylus. Preserve Transparency protects only "already transparent" areas of a layer.

Question 4

> Which of these operations can you **not** perform with the Eraser tool? (Select all that apply.)
> - a. Paint with the foreground color
> - b. Paint with transparency
> - c. Paint with a previous state of the image
> - d. Auto Erase from the foreground color to the background color

Answers a and d are correct. The Eraser tool paints with either transparency, the background color, or a previous state of the image. The Auto Erase feature is an option of the Pencil tool.

Question 5

> Which of the following tools lightens specific areas of an image?
>
> ○ a. Burn
>
> ○ b. Dodge
>
> ○ c. Sponge

Answer b is correct. The Dodge tool simulates the traditional darkroom technique of shading an area of a print as it is exposed, lightening that area.

Question 6

> Which of these colors combine to produce a final color after using a Blending mode? (Select two.)
>
> ❑ a. Base Color
>
> ❑ b. Blend Color
>
> ❑ c. Result Color

Answers a and b are correct. The Base color is the original color of pixels, and the Blend color is the color of new pixels being applied. The calculation performed by a blending mode produces the Result color from the Base Color and the Blend color.

Question 7

> Which of these blending modes results in the opposite effect of the Multiply Blending mode?
>
> ○ a. Normal
>
> ○ b. Divide
>
> ○ c. Screen
>
> ○ d. Overlay

Answer c is correct. Whereas the Multiply Blending mode multiplies the base color by the blend color, the Screen Blending mode multiplies the inverse of the base color and the blend color.

Question 8

> If you want to select only immediately adjacent image areas of similar color and then replace that color, which of these procedures work? (Select all that apply.)
>
> ❏ a. Choose Select|Color Range and then choose Edit|Fill.
> ❏ b. Select the Magic Wand tool, click in an area in the image, and then choose Edit|Fill.
> ❏ c. Select the Paintbrush tool and click in an area.
> ❏ d. Select the Paint Bucket tool and click in an area.

Answers b and d are correct. Although you can use Select|Color Range to select areas of similar color, those areas are not all necessarily adjacent. The Paint Bucket tool performs an operation that is similar to using the Magic Wand tool and then choosing Edit|Fill.

Question 9

> Which of the following is **not** a Gradient pattern available in Photoshop 5?
>
> ○ a. Linear Gradient
> ○ b. Radial Gradient
> ○ c. Angular Gradient
> ○ d. Geometric Gradient
> ○ e. Reflected Gradient
> ○ f. Diamond Gradient

Answer d is correct.

Question 10

> Which of the following color modes does not support the Gradient tools? (Select all that apply.)
>
> ❏ a. Bitmap
> ❏ b. RGB
> ❏ c. CMYK
> ❏ d. Lab

Answer a is correct. Neither the Bitmap nor the Indexed Color mode supports the Gradient tools.

Question 11

> Which of the following operations can you perform with the Fill command? (Select all that apply.)
>
> ❏ a. Fill a selection with the foreground color
> ❏ b. Fill a selection with the background color
> ❏ c. Fill a selection with a pattern
> ❏ d. Fill a selection with a previous state of the image

All these answers are correct.

Question 12

> What is the keyboard shortcut to open the Fill dialog box?
>
> ○ a. Option+Delete/Alt+Backspace
> ○ b. Cmd+Delete/Ctrl+Backspace
> ○ c. Shift+Delete/Shift+Backspace
> ○ d. Cmd+Option+Delete/Ctrl+Alt+Backspace

Answer c is correct.

Painting And Editing   257

Question 13

> If the Align checkbox is off in the Rubber Stamp's Options palette, which of these operations can you perform?
>
> ○ a. Apply a sample of the image to another area of the image; then move to a different area, and apply a different sample to that different area
>
> ○ b. Apply an aligned pattern to an area of the image
>
> ○ c. Apply the same sample of the image to different areas of the image
>
> ○ d. Apply an aligned sample to different areas of the image

Answer c is correct.

Question 14

> If you want to rotate an entire image, which of these should you choose? (Select all that apply.)
>
> ❏ a. Image|Rotate Canvas
>
> ❏ b. Image|Free Transform
>
> ❏ c. Image|Transform
>
> ❏ d. Image|Transform|Rotate

Trick question

Answer a is correct. Although the Transform|Rotate command rotates an entire image if that entire image is selected, that command is located under the Edit menu, not the Image menu.

Question 15

> Which key combination do you press to skew a bounding border?
>
> ○ a. Cmd/Ctrl
>
> ○ b. Shift+Cmd+Option/Shift+Ctrl+Alt
>
> ○ c. Shift+Cmd/Shift+Ctrl
>
> ○ d. Cmd+Option/Ctrl+Alt

Answer c is correct.

Question 16

Which keyboard shortcut accesses the Fade dialog box after applying a color adjustment or filter?

○ a. Esc

○ b. Cmd+F/Ctrl+F

○ c. Cmd+Option+F/Ctrl+Alt+F

○ d. Shift+Cmd+F/Shift+Ctrl+F

Answer d is correct. Pressing Cmd+F/Ctrl+F reapplies the last-used filter but bypasses the dialog box. Pressing Shift+Cmd+F/Shift+Ctrl+F opens the Fade dialog box and allows you to make changes.

Question 17

Which Filter group contains the new 3D Transform filter?

○ a. Distort

○ b. Transform

○ c. Render

○ d. Stylize

Answer b is correct.

Need To Know More?

London, Sherry and David Xenakis: *Photoshop 5 In Depth*. The Coriolis Group. ISBN 1-57610-293-9. Contains detailed explanations of all the topics covered in this chapter.

McClelland, Deke: *Photoshop 5 for Macs for Dummies*. IDG Books Worldwide, Inc. ISBN 0-7645-0391-X. This book contains great explanations of the uses of all the painting tools, transform commands, and filters.

Working With Layers

Terms and concepts you'll need to understand:

- ✓ Layers
- ✓ Linked layers
- ✓ Align
- ✓ Distribute
- ✓ Merge
- ✓ Flatten
- ✓ Blend If
- ✓ Adjustment layer
- ✓ Layer mask
- ✓ Transparency mask
- ✓ Clipping group
- ✓ Base layer
- ✓ Layer effects
- ✓ Drop shadow
- ✓ Inner shadow
- ✓ Outer glow
- ✓ Inner glow
- ✓ Bevel
- ✓ Emboss
- ✓ Type layer
- ✓ Type mask

Techniques you'll need to master:

- ✓ Navigating the Layers palette
- ✓ Creating layers
- ✓ Copying and duplicating layers
- ✓ Hiding and revealing layers
- ✓ Rearranging layers in the Layers palette
- ✓ Linking layers
- ✓ Aligning layer content
- ✓ Distributing layer content
- ✓ Merging layers
- ✓ Flattening images
- ✓ Deleting layers
- ✓ Using the Blend If options
- ✓ Creating adjustment layers
- ✓ Creating layer masks
- ✓ Editing layer masks
- ✓ Loading transparency masks
- ✓ Creating clipping groups
- ✓ Using layer effects
- ✓ Applying type to an image
- ✓ Using the new type layer

Photoshop's layers make the creation of more complex images faster, safer, and more convenient. If you understand how layers work, you can quickly raise your level of Photoshop creative ability.

Understanding Photoshop's Layers

Photoshop's layers are just what they sound like—layers. They enable you to create more complex digital images with a high degree of "editability." By using layers, you experience less danger that you'll be permanently stuck with something now that you'll change your mind about later. In short, layers can prevent you from having to re-create a slightly different image from scratch, Photoshop saves the layers, allowing you to go back and make changes and improvements.

In Photoshop, when you open a photo for the first time, the image becomes the "background" layer. Each time you paste something onto the canvas, Photoshop creates a new "layer." This layer can have a hole—or "mask"—in it. It can be transparent or translucent. It can change the appearance of all the layers under it.

Layers are "stacked" in the Layers palette, with the background at the bottom of the stack and the bottom of the list of layers in the palette. An opaque layer obscures any layer or layers under it, any transparent areas of layers reveal the layers beneath, and translucent layers reveal underlying layers depending on the translucent layer's opacity.

You can also create a new layer with nothing on it and then draw or color new images. You can "test" a change to your image by turning layers on and off. You can change the order, or position, of layers. You can also delete layers, merge layers, name layers, rename layers, and rename them again and again.

> **STUDY ALERT:** The Photoshop (PSD) file format is the only file format in which you can save layers.
>
> Depending on how much memory you have in your system, you can create up to 100 layers in an image.

Managing Layers In The Layers Palette

To use layers, you must understand how to navigate and tweak the Layers palette. Access the Layers palette (shown in Figure 9.1) by clicking on its tab in its palette group or by choosing Window|Show Layers.

Working With Layers   **263**

Figure 9.1   The Layers palette.

The Layers palette displays all the layers of a document, the names of the layers, whether the layers are visible, which layer is active for editing, the Blending mode and opacity of a layer, which layers might be linked, which layers are in a clipping group, and whether the layer has a layer mask.

Anatomy Of The Layers Palette

Each existing layer in a document is displayed as one of the horizontal bars in the Layers palette. (The image represented by the Layers palette in Figure 9.1 has only one layer.) The thumbnail displays the contents of that layer, and the layer's name is to the right of the thumbnail. The presence of the eyeball icon in the box to the far left of the layer's name and thumbnail indicates that the layer is visible. The paintbrush icon next to that shows the active layer, which is the layer on which you write, draw, paint, adjust, or do whatever you want to do. The active layer's name is also highlighted.

The Blending mode option menu, the Opacity values box and slider, and the Preserve Transparency checkbox at the top of the Layers palette access their respective features. (Blending modes, opacity, and Preserve Transparency are also used with the painting tools and are discussed in Chapter 8.) The buttons at the bottom of the Layers palette are, from left to right in Figure 9.1, the New Layer Mask button, the New Layer button, and the Trash button.

Figure 9.2 shows a palette with two layers. The eyeball icon, the paintbrush icon, and the fact that the layer's bar is highlighted indicate that Layer 1 is active and is visible. Layer 1 has areas of transparency, so the transparency grid is visible in the layer's thumbnail.

> *Note: Remember that you can change the appearance of the transparency grid by choosing File|Preferences|Transparency & Gamut.*

The bottom layer is the Background.

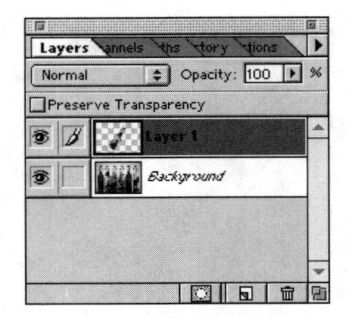

Figure 9.2 A Layers palette with two layers.

The Background layer differs from other layers. Several special conditions apply when you're working with the Background layer, including the following:

➤ You can move the Background layer up in the stacking order of layers only after you convert it to a layer by double-clicking on its name in the Layers palette and giving it a new name. This operation leaves the image file with no Background layer.

➤ Neither the Blending modes nor Opacity options are available for the Background layer.

➤ No Background layer is included with newly created transparent images.

➤ You can create a Background layer in a transparent image or any other image that doesn't have a Background layer by choosing Layer|New|Background. The new Background layer is filled with the selected background color.

➤ Flattening a transparent image that has no Background layer fills the transparent areas with white.

The palette menu options for the Layers palette are as follows:

➤ New Layer

➤ New Adjustment Layer

➤ Duplicate Layer

➤ Delete Layer

➤ Layer Options

➤ Merge Layers

➤ Merge Visible

➤ Flatten Image

➤ Palette Options

Layers Palette Basic Operations

From the Layers palette, you can perform a variety of layers management operations, including the following:

➤ **Selecting Different Thumbnail Sizes** Four thumbnail options are available from Palette Options in the palette menu. You can choose not to display a thumbnail or select one of three thumbnail sizes.

➤ **Making Layers Visible And Invisible** Simply click on the eyeball icon next to a layer's name to make that layer visible or invisible. Pressing Option/Alt while clicking on the eyeball icon makes all layers invisible but that one layer. Repeating that operation displays all the layers. You can drag your cursor up or down through the eyeball icons to hide or display layers quickly.

Note: Even when an active layer is invisible, any editing or adjustments affect that layer.

➤ **Rearranging Layers In The Layers Palette** You can move the layers up or down in the Layers palette to change their order by dragging their names up or down in the Layers palette. As you drag, a bold rule appears to indicate the new placement of the layer. Alternatively, you can move a layer by activating it, choosing Layer|Arrange, and selecting from the following options:

➤ **Bring to Front** Moves the active layer to the top of the list

➤ **Bring Forward** Moves the active layer up one place on the list

➤ **Send Backward** Moves the active layer down one place on the list

➤ **Send To Back** Moves the layer to the bottom of the list, just above the background (if a background is available)

➤ **Linking Two Or More Layers** You can activate a layer and then click in the empty box to the left of the thumbnail of any other layers you want to link to the active layer. The chain icon appears (as shown in Figure 9.3) to indicate the linked layer. When you select a layer, any layers linked to that layer have the chain icon. You can click on this icon to unlink the layers.

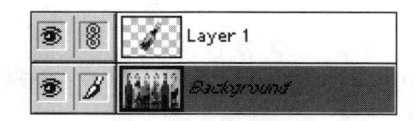

Figure 9.3 Two linked layers as displayed in the Layers palette.

The following guidelines apply to linked layers:

➤ Any 2D transformations (as described in Chapter 8) that you apply to a layer are also applied to any layers linked to that layer.

➤ You can align the contents of linked layers by using Layer|Align Linked. (See the "Coordinating Layers And Layer Contents" section, later in this chapter, for more information on aligning layers.)

➤ You can merge linked layers (by using Layer|Merge Linked), even if they are not adjacent in the stacking order.

➤ You can use one layer to mask the contents of layers above it by creating a clipping group of linked layers. (See the "Masking Image Areas With Layers" section, later in this chapter, for more information about clipping groups.)

Working With Layers

This section presents the procedures and options for creating and working with layers.

Creating And Managing Layers

You can create, copy, and delete layers from the Layers palette by using key combinations and/or by using several available commands. New layers are created automatically when you paste a selection into an image and when you use one of the Type tools. (Using type layers is discussed later in this chapter.)

Creating And Duplicating Layers

You can create new layers from scratch by pasting selections cut or copied from existing layers, by duplicating existing layers, and even by copying layers from other images. New layers are inserted directly above the selected, or active, layer in the stacking order. New layers contain any pixel data copied, duplicated, or pasted to them, but they are otherwise transparent.

Create a new layer or duplicate an existing layer by using one of these commands or procedures:

Figure 9.4 The New Layer button.

- **Clicking On The New Layer Button** Clicking On the New Layer button (shown in Figure 9.4) in the Layers palette adds a new layer above the selected layer. The name of this new layer is "Layer 1" or "Layer 2," and so on, based on the order of its creation. The new layer uses the Normal Blending mode and has 100% opacity.

- **Opening The New Layer Dialog Box** Open the New Layer dialog box by choosing New Layer from the Layers palette menu, by choosing Layer|New|Layer (Shift+Cmd+N/Shift+Ctrl+N), or by pressing Option/Alt as you click on the New Layer button in the Layers palette. In the New Layer dialog box, you can specify a name, Blending mode, and opacity for the new layer. You can also choose to include the new layer in a clipping group by selecting Group With Previous Layer. (See the "Masking Image Areas With Layers" section later in this chapter for more information about clipping groups.)

- **Choosing Layer|New|Layer Via Copy** By activating a layer, making a selection, and then choosing Layer|New|Layer Via Copy (Cmd+J/Ctrl+J), you can create a new layer that contains a copy of the selected image area, surrounded by transparency, leaving intact the layer from which the selection was copied. The position of the content of the new layer matches its position in the layer from which it was copied.

- **Choosing Layer|New|Layer Via Cut** By activating a layer, making a selection, and then choosing Layer|New|Layer Via Cut (Shift+Cmd+J/Shift+Ctrl+J), you can create a new layer that contains a copy of the selected image area, surrounded by transparency. When creating a new layer from any layer but the background with Layer Via Cut, you can select the Preserve Transparency option, which would leave a transparent hole in the layer from which the selection was cut. Otherwise, Layer Via Cut leaves a hole filled with the background color in the layer from which the selection was cut. The position of the content of the new layer matches its position in the layer from which it was cut.

- **Choosing Edit|Paste** By activating a layer, making a selection, copying the selection to the clipboard with either Edit|Copy (Cmd+C/Ctrl+C) or Edit|Cut (Cmd+X/Ctrl+X), and then choosing Edit|Paste (Cmd+V/Ctrl+V), you can create a new layer that contains a copy of the image from the clipboard, surrounded by transparency. If the original copied or cut selection is still active, the position of the content of the new layer matches its position in the layer from which it was copied or cut, otherwise, the pasted image will be positioned in the center of the image window.

- **Converting The Background Layer** By double-clicking on the Background layer and specifying a name, Blending mode, and opacity, you can create a new layer. The new layer is at the bottom of the stacking order and, by default, is named Layer 0.

- **Creating A New Background Layer** Choosing Layer|New|Background creates a new Background layer that is filled with the selected background color.

- **Dragging A Layer From Another Image** Dragging a layer from its image window with the Move tool or dragging a layer's name from its Layers palette onto the image window of another image creates a new layer above the layer currently selected in the destination image. The position of the new layer in the destination image depends on where you release the cursor, unless you hold down Shift as you drag, which places the dragged layer in the same relative position in a destination image with the same pixel dimensions and in the center of a destination image with different pixel dimensions. Any area of the layer that is not visible in the window is still available.

- **Pasting A Layer From Another Image** Pasting a layer copied or cut from one image into another image creates a new layer above the layer currently selected in the destination image. The contents of the new layer are centered in the destination image window. Any area of the layer that is not visible in the window is still available.

- **Dragging Linked Layers From Another Image** Dragging the contents of linked layers with the Move tool from one image window to another creates a new layer above the currently selected layer in the destination image. (Unlike layers that are not linked, you cannot drag linked layers from their Layers palette to another image.) The position of the new layer in the destination image depends on where you release the cursor, unless you hold down Shift as you drag, which places the dragged layers in the same relative position in a destination image with the same pixel dimensions and in the center of a destination image with different pixel dimensions. Any area of the layer that is not visible in the window is still available.

- **Duplicating A Layer** By selecting a layer and then selecting Duplicate Layer from the Layers palette menu or by choosing Layer|Duplicate Layer, you open the Duplicate Layer dialog box, where you specify the options for creating an exact copy of the selected layer in the same image or in another open image, immediately above the selected layer of the destination image. The default name of the duplicate layer is the name of the selected layer, plus "copy" (and a number if more than one copy of that selected layer exists).

Deleting Layers
You can delete layers by using one of the following procedures:

➤ Clicking on the Trash button in the Layers palette, which opens a dialog box requesting approval of the delete operation

➤ Pressing Option/Alt and clicking on the Trash button in the Layers palette, which deletes the layer without approval

➤ Choosing Layer|Delete Layer

➤ Choosing Delete Layer in the Layers palette menu

➤ Dragging the layer's name to the Trash button in the Layers palette

Coordinating Layers And Layer Contents
As I described previously in this chapter, you can change the position of a layer in the stacking order of the Layers palette. You can also move the contents of the layer around in the image to new positions. In addition, the contents of layers can be aligned relative to a selection or to the contents of other layers. The contents of a layer or layers can be combined with the contents of another layer or layers.

Moving The Contents Of Layers And Linked Layers
When nothing is selected in an image, you can drag the entire contents of a layer or the entire contents of linked layers with the Move tool to reposition them in the image. Pressing Shift as you drag constrains the movement of the contents to multiples of 45 degrees. You can also move the contents with the arrow keys by selecting the Move tool and pressing an arrow key to move the contents one pixel at a time. By holding the Shift key as you press an arrow key, you can move the contents 10 pixels at a time. (If you are editing a Filmstrip file, pressing Shift and an arrow key advances or moves the file back by one frame.)

Aligning The Contents Of Layers And Linked Layers
You can align layer content to the contents of other layers, or you can align layer content to a selection. You can align only layers that contain pixels that are at least 50 percent or higher opacity.

If you want to align layer content to a selection, make the selection and then select a layer or multiple linked layers. Choose Layer|Align To Selection and one of the alignment options.

If you want to align the contents of a layer with the content of other layers, select all the layers you want to align and link them. Make sure the layer to which you want the other layers to align is the active, or selected, layer. Choose Layer|Align Linked and one of the alignment options.

Choosing Layer|Align Linked reveals the alignment options. As you can see in Figure 9.5, visual references to the options appear next to the names of the options. The alignment options are as follows:

- **Top** Aligns the tops of layer content with the top of the content of the active layer or with the top of the selection
- **Vertical Center** Aligns the vertical centers of the layer content to the vertical center of the content of the active layer or with the vertical center of the selection
- **Bottom** Aligns the bottoms of the layer content to the bottom of the content of the active layer or with the bottom of the selection
- **Left** Aligns the left sides of the layer content to the left side of the content of the active layer or with the left side of the selection
- **Horizontal Center** Aligns the horizontal center of the layer content to the horizontal center of the content of the active layer or with the horizontal center of the selection
- **Right** Aligns the right sides of the layer content to the right side of the content of the active layer or with the right side of the selection

Distributing The Contents Of Layers And Linked Layers

You can distribute—spread out evenly—the contents of three or more linked layers between the positions of the content of two of those linked layers. You can distribute only layers that contain pixels that are at least 50 percent or higher opacity.

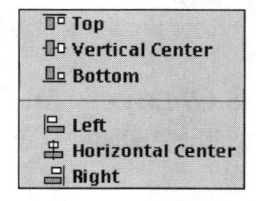

Figure 9.5 The Layer|Align Linked options.

Working With Layers

To distribute the contents of layers, follow these steps:

1. Determine which two layers you want to use as the "extreme" layers for purposes of positioning. If you are distributing layer content vertically, select a layer that is in the uppermost position you want and a layer that is in the lowermost position you want. If you are distributing layer content horizontally, select a layer that is in the leftmost position you want and a layer that is in the rightmost position you want. Photoshop distributes the remaining layer or layers evenly between the positions of these two layers, according to the distribution option you select.

2. Determine the remaining layer or layers you want to distribute between the "extreme" layers.

3. Link the first two layers with all the layers you want to distribute.

4. Choose Layer|Distribute Linked and select a distribution option.

Choosing Layer|Distribute Linked reveals the distribution options. As you can see in Figure 9.6, visual references to the options appear next to the names of the options. The distribution options are as follows:

➤ **Top** Distributes the tops of the layers' contents evenly between the tops of the contents of the "extreme" layers.

➤ **Vertical Center** Distributes the vertical center of the layers' contents evenly between the vertical centers of the contents of the "extreme" layers.

➤ **Bottom** Distributes the bottoms of the layers' contents evenly between the bottom of the contents of the "extreme" layers.

➤ **Left** Distributes the left sides of the layers' contents evenly between the left sides of the contents of the "extreme" layers.

➤ **Horizontal Center** Distributes the horizontal centers of the layers' contents evenly between the horizontal centers of the contents of the "extreme" layers.

➤ **Right** Distributes the right sides of the layers' contents evenly between the right sides of the contents of the "extreme" layers.

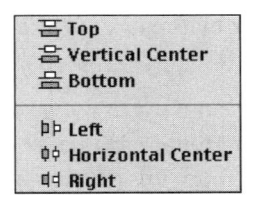

Figure 9.6 The Layer|Distribute Linked options.

Merging And Flattening Layers

As I mentioned earlier in this chapter, Photoshop allows up to 100 layers in an image. Each layer's pixel data contributes to the size of the image file and to how much RAM is needed to process the image during operations. If you have layers that you are sure you will no longer need, you can delete them as described earlier in this chapter. To retain layer data and still reduce file size, however, you might need to *merge* one or more layers or completely *flatten* all the layers in an image to reduce the file's size.

> *Note:* You can undo merging and flattening using Edit\Undo or the History palette (as long as the layered states remain in memory), but after you merge layers and/or flatten a file and then save and close that file, the merging and/or flattening is permanent, and those merged and/or flattened layers cannot be "relayered." Either save a copy of an image file with layers intact, or don't merge or flatten the layers until you are convinced you have a file in a finished state.

When you're merging layers, the pixel data of upper layers is added to the pixel data of lower layers. Also, the degree of opacity of layers is preserved when the layers are merged. Consequently, if the image area of an upper layer is completely opaque and is larger than the image area of a lower layer, the lower layer is covered by the image area of the upper layer.

All layers to be merged must be visible, and one of them must be selected.

The commands for merging two or more layers are as follows:

➤ **Layer|Merge Down** If you want to merge only two layers, make sure the two layers are positioned together in the stacking order in the order you want for the effect you want. Choose Layer|Merge Down to merge the two layers. This command is also available in the Layers palette menu. To copy and leave intact the active layer as you merge it down, press Option/Alt as you choose Layer|Merge Down.

➤ **Layer|Merge Linked** If you want to merge three or more layers while keeping other layers visible, position and link the layers you want to merge, and then choose Layer|Merge Linked. Merge the linked layers to the active layer by pressing Option/Alt as you choose Layer|Merge Linked.

➤ **Layer|Merge Group** If you want to merge a clipping group, select the base layer of the clipping group, and then choose Layer|Merge Group. (See the next section for more information about clipping groups.)

> **Layer|Merge Visible** If you want to merge all the visible layers, make sure only the layers you want to merge are visible and not linked, and then choose Layer|Merge Visible. This command is not available if any of the visible layers are linked. This command is also available in the Layers palette menu. Merge the visible layers to the active layer by pressing Option/Alt as you choose Layer|Merge Visible.

> You can merge the visible layers into an empty layer, while keeping the original merged layers intact, by selecting the empty layer and then pressing Option/Alt as you choose Layer|Merge Visible.

Flattening a file merges all visible layers and discards all hidden layers, leaving a file with only one layer. All remaining transparent areas of the file are filled with white. Files must be flattened to be saved as any file format other than Photoshop, and converting a file between certain color modes flattens the file (Photoshop asks your permission first).

Editing A Layer's Contents

After you create a layer, you can edit that layer just as you would any image. You can paint and retouch the layer and filter it. In addition, you can apply special layer effects, and you can use an adjustment layer to preview changes to a layer and those beneath it before actually rendering those changes to the layer. You can also use the contents of one layer to mask other layers by creating a clipping group.

Editing Options For Layers

As with the painting and retouching tools, you can select various options for layers. These options affect how the layers appear and blend with other layers.

> *Note: Any specified layer options affect the appearance of a layer in combination with any options set for the painting and retouching tools. In other words, if you have a layer with 50% opacity, and you paint with the Paintbrush tool set at 50% opacity, you will be painting with 50 percent of 50% opacity.*

Preserve Transparency

Preserve Transparency is like having a mask or protective cover over any transparent areas of a layer. As you edit or paint the layer with Preserve Transparency selected, none of the effects of the editing or painting are applied to the existing transparent areas.

Use All Layers

Selecting Use All Layers enables the Magic Wand, Smudge, Blur, Sharpen, Rubber Stamp, and Pattern Stamp tools to affect or sample pixel data from all visible layers rather than just the active layer.

Fill With Neutral Color

Layers must have pixel data to be affected by some editing effects and filters. When you create a new layer with the New Layer button or the New Layer dialog box, it is transparent by default. However, if you create a layer that has a selected Blending mode other than Normal, Dissolve, Hue, Saturation, Color, or Luminosity, you can select the Fill With Neutral Color option to add pixel data to the layer. Photoshop supplies a specific neutral color for each supported Blending mode.

Opacity

The opacity of a layer determines how much the content of any underlying layers is visible through the layer. A setting of 100% opacity renders the layer completely opaque, and a setting of 1% opacity renders the layer completely transparent.

Blending Modes And The Blend If Options

The same Blending modes are available for layers as the Blending modes for the painting and retouching tools, as described in Chapter 8, with the exception of the Clear and Behind modes. Also, the Lab mode does not support the Color Dodge, Color Burn, Darken, Lighten, Difference, and Exclusion Blending modes.

Using the Blend If sliders in the Layer Options dialog box (as shown in Figure 9.7), you can specify how the pixel data of a layer is combined with the visible underlying layers. Double-click on a layer's name in the Layers palette to open the Layer Options dialog box.

From the Blend If option menu, you select the color channel for which you want to specify Blend If effects. Gray is the composite channel.

Drag the triangular black and white sliders of the two color bars to specify brightness values. Any pixels with brightness values to the left of the black slider or to the right of the white slider are not applied or are protected, according to which of these two color bars you adjust:

> **This Layer** Sets the range of brightness values for pixels in the selected layer to be applied to underlying layers

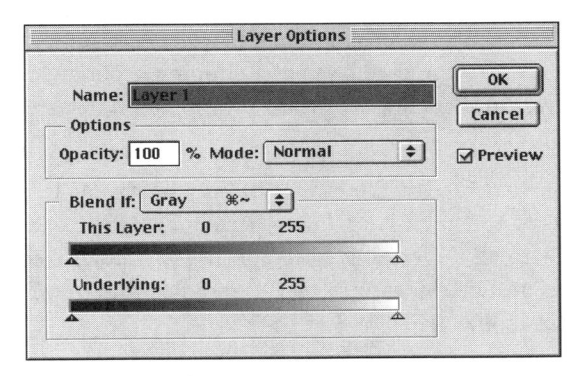

Figure 9.7 The Layer Options dialog box.

➤ **Underlying** Sets the range of brightness values for pixels in the underlying layers to be "protected" from being covered by the pixel data of the selected layer

To prevent harsh or abrupt color transitions in the blended layers, you can also specify a range of brightness values across which to gradually apply this blending or protecting of underlying layers. Press Option/Alt as you drag a slider to split the slider and specify the width of the range.

Special Blending Procedures For Layers And Channels

Using the features described in this section, you can preview color and tonal adjustments with adjustment layers, before actually applying them to an image. You also can combine the layers and/or channels of two individual images with Calculations and Apply Image.

Adjustment Layers

Like "normal" layers, adjustment layers are displayed in the Layers palette, can be managed like other layers, and share many common features of other layers, such as Blending modes, opacity, and the capability of being used as a mask. However, unlike other layers, adjustment layers are used primarily to apply color and tonal adjustments on a "trial" basis for previewing and/or removal before being rendered permanently to an image. By default, the name of an adjustment layer is the name of the color or tonal adjustment you make with that adjustment layer (as shown in Figure 9.8), but you can name the adjustment layer as you create it.

An adjustment layer affects all visible layers beneath that adjustment layer, unless you link the adjustment layer to a layer or layers, which restricts the effects of the layer to the underlying linked layers. Alternately, you can create an adjustment layer for the base layer of a clipping group, which restricts the effects to the layers in that clipping group. (Clipping groups are discussed later in this section.)

When you are satisfied with the effects of an adjustment layer and want to apply the effects to the underlying layers permanently, you can merge the adjustment layer with all underlying layers, or just with its linked layers, or just with its clipping group. You cannot merge an adjustment layer with only another adjustment layer.

If any area of the image is selected, the new adjustment layer masks all other areas of the image, allowing you to apply the effects of the adjustment layer to just the selected area in the visible layers beneath it. If no area is selected, the adjustment layer's effects apply to the entire image in all the visible layers beneath it.

Create an adjustment layer by using one of the following procedures:

➤ Click on the New Layer button in the Layers palette while holding Cmd/Ctrl.

➤ Choose Layer|New|Adjustment Layer.

➤ Select New Adjustment Layer from the Layers palette menu.

Each of these three procedures opens the New Adjustment Layer dialog box, where you name the adjustment layer if you want, select an adjustment from the Type option menu, and specify any layer options you want.

After an adjustment layer is created, you can adjust its effects by double-clicking on its name in the Layers palette or by choosing Layer|Adjustment Options, which opens the dialog box for that adjustment layer's specific adjustment.

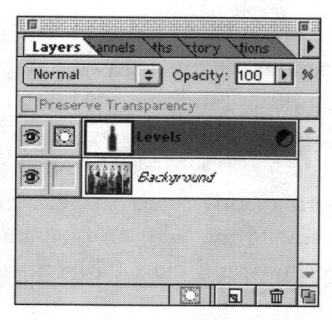

Figure 9.8 The Layers palette with an adjustment layer.

Figure 9.9 The Image represented by the Layers palette in Figure 9.8.

As you can see in Figure 9.9, the adjustment layer, named Levels in the Levels palette in Figure 9.8, affects the layer beneath it, but only where the layer's transparency mask is less than full black. To view the grayscale transparency mask in the image window, press Option/Alt and click on the adjustment layer's thumbnail. To view the transparency mask as the masking color specified for the Quick Mask (see Chapter 10 for more information on the Quick Mask feature), press Shift+Option/Shift+Alt when you click on the adjustment layer's thumbnail. You can edit this transparency mask by selecting the mask name in the Layers palette and painting with black to reveal unaffected areas beneath the adjustment layer, with gray to partially adjust areas, or with white to apply the adjustment to areas beneath the adjustment layer. You can turn on and off the masking effects of the transparency mask by pressing Shift and clicking on the adjustment layer's thumbnail.

Apply Image And Calculations

The Apply Image command allows you to blend the color channel of one layer of an open image with another color channel of a layer of its own or of another open image that has the exact same pixel dimensions, and to specify a Blending mode and opacity for the operation. The Calculations command works like Apply Image, but it allows you to blend only two individual color channels, and it enables you to create an entirely new image file, a new channel, or a selection with the blended information.

The steps for using the Apply Image command or the Calculations command are the much the same, as you can see here:

1. Open the image or images you want to use.

2. For Apply Image, select an image and a layer and channel into which you want to blend the data in that image. This image will be your *destination image*.

3. Choose Image|Apply Image to open the Apply Image dialog box, or choose Image|Calculations to open the Calculations dialog box.

4. Select Preview if you want to see the results of the calculations before you accept them.

5. Select an image from the Source option menu in the Apply Image dialog box or the Source 1 option menu in the Calculations dialog box. All open images that have the exact same pixel dimensions of the destination image are available in these option menus—including the destination image itself.

6. Select a layer from the Layer option menu. Each layer in the source image is listed in this menu. The Merged option selects all the layers in the source image.

7. Select a channel from the Channel option menu. Selecting the Invert option inverts the channel to its negative. The Gray option in the Calculations dialog box uses brightness values that would exist if the image were converted to a grayscale image.

8. For the Calculations command, repeat Steps 5 through 7 for the Source 2 options.

9. Select a Blending mode.

10. Specify the opacity.

11. In the Apply Image dialog box, you can select Preserve Transparency to protect the transparent areas of the layer in the destination image.

12. Select Mask to apply the effects of the command through a mask. Selecting this option expands the Apply Image dialog box to enable you to select a channel to use as a mask from a layer in one of the available source images. The Invert command reverses the mask.

13. For the Calculations command, select New Document, New Channel, or Selection from the Result option menu.

The Add and Subtract Blending modes also are available for the Apply Image command and the Calculations command. They, respectively, add the pixel values from two channels or subtract the pixel values of the source channel from the pixel values of the target channel.

Masking Image Areas With Layers

Besides the simple mask represented by the Preserve Transparency option available in many dialog boxes and in the Layers palette, you can create custom masks for individual layers with layer masks, you can load those masked areas as selections with transparency masks, and you can mask a group of layers so that they blend only into the opaque content of a selected layer with clipping groups.

Working With Layer Masks

A *layer mask* is a mask that is specific to an individual layer. This layer mask remains separate from the content of the layer until you decide to apply the mask permanently to the layer. You can edit this mask by painting with black, white, and grays. All the layer masks are saved with their layers when you save a file with layers in the Photoshop file format.

Creating Layer Masks

You can create a layer mask that is the full size of the image or a layer mask that is based on a selection. As it is created, either of these layer mask types can be filled with white or with black, to reveal or hide, respectively, the layer or selection. The content of a layer mask is displayed as a second thumbnail next to the layer's name in the Layers palette. When you select the layer mask for editing, the Layer Mask icon appears in the little box to the left of the thumbnails, as opposed to the Paintbrush icon when the layer is selected.

Depending on whether you have made a selection, these procedures create layer masks:

➤ To create a layer mask that reveals the entire layer or just the selected area of the layer, click on the New Layer Mask button in the Layers palette (see Figure 9.10). Optionally, you can choose Layer|Add Layer Mask|Reveal All when no selection exists or Layer|Add Layer Mask|Reveal Selection when a selection does exist.

➤ To create a layer mask that hides the entire layer or just the selected area of the layer, press Option/Alt and click on the New Layer Mask button

Figure 9.10 The New Layer Mask button from the Layers palette.

in the Layers palette (see Figure 9.10). you also can choose Layer|Add Layer Mask|Hide All when no selection exists or Layer|Add Layer Mask|Hide Selection when a selection does exist.

Editing Layer Masks

Layer masks are essentially grayscale alpha channels—and even appear temporarily in the Channels palette when their layer is selected—masking black areas, partially revealing gray areas, and fully revealing white areas. Consequently, you can edit layer masks just like you edit the alpha channels located in the Channels palette (see Chapter 10 for more information about alpha channels)—by painting or editing them with grayscale colors.

> Remember that the black areas of a mask are opaque, hiding the underlying layer content; gray areas are partially transparent; and white areas are transparent, revealing the underlying layer content.

After you create a layer mask, you can view the grayscale layer mask in the image window for editing by pressing Option/Alt and clicking on the layer mask's thumbnail. You return to the image display by either repeating this procedure or clicking on any of the eyeball icons. You can display the layer mask in the masking color specified in the Quick Mask Options dialog box by pressing Shift+Option/Shift+Alt while clicking on the layer mask's thumbnail. (See Chapter 10 for more information on the Quick Mask feature.) You can return to the image display by repeating this procedure.

Edit a layer mask by first clicking on the little box left of the layer's thumbnail in the Layers palette. The Layer Mask icon then appears in the box, indicating that the mask is active. The foreground and background colors in the Toolbox revert to black and white (and to return to the previous color selections when you deactivate the layer mask).

You can edit the mask by painting with black, white, or gray, using any of the painting and retouching tools. You can also add to the area of the mask by pasting a selection from the clipboard with Edit|Paste (Cmd+V/Ctrl+V). After it is pasted onto the layer, the selection can be moved and/or filled to create the mask you want.

When the link icon is visible between the layer thumbnail and the layer mask thumbnail, any repositioning of the layer content also moves the layer mask, and any repositioning of the layer mask moves the layer content. To move the layer content or layer mask independently, click on this link icon.

Disabling And Discarding Layer Masks

If you want to display a layer temporarily without the effects of its layer mask, press Shift and click on the layer mask's thumbnail in the Layers palette, or choose Layer|Disable Layer Mask. A red "X" appears over the thumbnail to indicate that you have a layer mask, but that it is disabled. Repeat this procedure to redisplay the layer mask.

To apply the effects of a layer mask to its layer permanently, or if you no longer want a layer mask, you can drag its thumbnail to the Trash icon in the Layers palette, select the layer mask thumbnail and click on the Trash icon, or choose Layer|Remove Layer Mask. This operation opens a warning box that asks if you want to discard the layer mask or apply the layer mask before discarding it (or cancel the operation). Selecting Discard deletes the layer mask without applying its effects to the layer. Selecting Apply applies the effects of the layer mask to the layer permanently and then discards the layer mask.

Working With Transparency Masks

A *transparency mask* is simply a selection based on the opaque areas of a layer. If a layer's contents contain areas of transparency, these areas are excluded from the transparency mask. The transparency mask can be based on the content of a layer or a layer mask.

You can use these procedures to load transparency masks from the Layers palette:

➤ **Load** the opaque areas of a layer as a selection by pressing Cmd/Ctrl and clicking on the thumbnail of the layer or the layer mask you want.

➤ **Add** the opaque areas of a layer to an existing selection by pressing Shift+Cmd/Shift+Ctrl while clicking on the thumbnail of the layer or the layer mask you want.

➤ **Subtract** the opaque areas of a layer from an existing selection by pressing Cmd+Option/Ctrl+Alt while clicking on the thumbnail of the layer or the layer mask you want.

➤ **Intersect** the opaque areas of a layer with an existing selection by pressing Shift+Cmd+Option/Shift+Ctrl+Alt while clicking on the thumbnail of the layer or the layer mask you want.

Working With Clipping Groups

Clipping groups allow you to use the contents of a layer as a mask and apply that mask to the content of other layers.

The image in Figure 9.11 has three separate layers. In their current stacking order, the top layer (Layer 2) obscures much of the Background layer and all of Layer 1, which is a black circle the size and shape of the porthole window. However, when you create a clipping group of Layers 1 and 2, that black circle in Layer 1 becomes a mask, hiding all but that shape of Layer 2 (see Figure 9.12). The bottom layer of a clipping group is the *base* layer, and the shape of its contents acts as a mask for the layers above it in the clipping group. Layers beneath the clipping group are not affected and are visible through any transparent areas of the clipping group's base layer.

Figure 9.11   The image represented by the Layers palette in Figure 9.13.

Figure 9.12   The image represented by the Layers palette in Figure 9.14.

Working With Layers **283**

Create a clipping group by positioning two or more layers as you want them to appear and choosing Layer|Group With Previous (Cmd+G/Ctrl+G). You also can do so by linking the layers you want and choosing Layer|Group Linked (Cmd+G/Ctrl+G). Alternately, press Option/Alt and place the cursor on the dividing line between two of the layers in the Layers palette and click on that border when the cursor turns into the Clipping Group icon (see Figure 9.13). After you create the clipping group, notice that the name of the base layer is underlined, and the thumbnails for the layers above it are indented (see Figure 9.14).

You can add additional overlying layers by positioning them above the topmost grouped layer and clicking between that topmost layer and the new layer with the Clipping Group icon. Alternatively, you can choose Layer|Group With Previous (Cmd+G/Ctrl+G), or link the new layer with the layers in the clipping group and choose Layer|Group Linked (Cmd+G/Ctrl+G).

The Blending mode and opacity of the base layer are applied to all the layers in the clipping group.

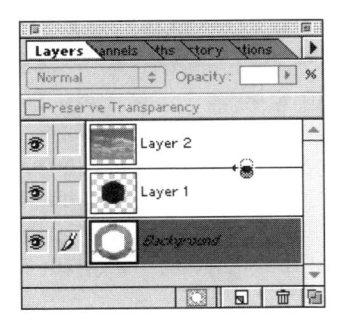

Figure 9.13 The Layers palette and the Clipping Group icon between two layers.

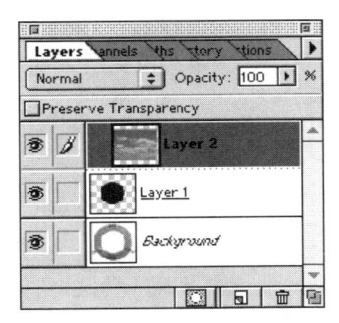

Figure 9.14 The Layers palette with a clipping group.

You remove a layer from the clipping group by again pressing Option/Alt and clicking with the Clipping Group icon between the layer you want to remove and the layer below it in the group. Or, you can select a layer and choose Layer|Ungroup (Shift+Cmd+G/Shift+Ctrl+G). These actions remove from the group all layers above the Clipping Group icon or the selected layer. You can ungroup the entire clipping group by selecting the base layer and choosing Layer|Ungroup (Shift+Cmd+G/Shift+Ctrl+G).

Applying Special Effects To Layers

Photoshop 5's new Layer Effects allow you to apply visual effects to the contents of a layer, separately from the rest of the image. Now, you can more easily apply drop shadows, inner shadows, inner and outer glows, beveling, and embossing, which automatically change as layer contents are changed and can themselves be changed or edited. You can copy and paste effects from one layer to another, and you can convert individual effects to a layer.

Working In The Effects Dialog Box

To apply layer effects to a layer, select the layer you want and choose Layer|Effects; then select an effect from the submenu. The Effects dialog box opens (see Figure 9.15). From this dialog box, you can access all the individual layer effects, you can apply and remove individual layer effects, you can edit individual layer effects, and you can specify a "global" lighting angle. Figure 9.16 shows the effects and their keyboard shortcuts.

To apply a specific layer effect, either select that effect from the menu at the top of the dialog box, click on the Prev or Next buttons to cycle through the

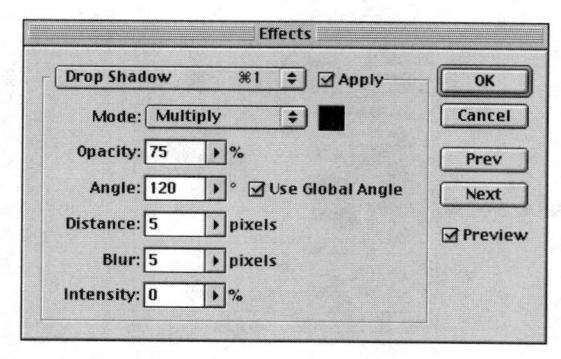

Figure 9.15 The Effects dialog box.

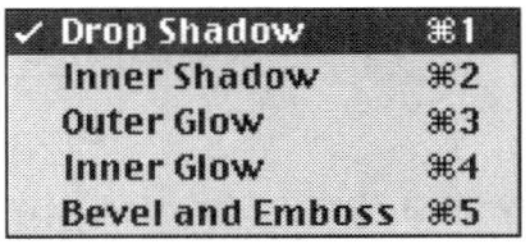

Figure 9.16 The Effects option menu.

effects, or press one of the dialog box-specific keyboard shortcuts. Then, click on the Apply checkbox to apply or remove that effect.

For each of the layer effects, you can specify a Blending mode and opacity. Adobe advises that the default mode for each layer will probably produce the best results.

You can also specify a color for each individual effect by clicking on the color swatch to the right of the Mode option menu to open the Color Picker.

Select Preview to view the effects of the layer effect in the image window.

The Use Global Angle option tells Photoshop to apply to individual effects the lighting angle that has been specified as the "global" lighting angle, for visual consistency. You can set the global lighting angle in the Effects dialog box or by choosing Layer|Effects|Global Angle. Set the global lighting angle by entering a value in the Angle value box or by dragging the radius bar in the circle accessed by clicking on the arrowhead to the right of the value box. By choosing Use Global Angle for a specific effect and then changing the angle for that effect, you can change the global angle.

Applying Specific Layer Effects To A Layer

This section details the layer effects and their options and specifications. You can apply one of these effects or any number of these effects to a layer.

The Drop Shadow And Inner Shadow Effects

Drop shadows produce a 3D effect by simulating a shadow cast by one item onto another. Inner shadows do the same, but they cast their shadows inside a shape, giving the appearance of a 3D cutout.

To apply drop shadow or inner shadow effects, select a layer on which to apply the effects and then access the Effects dialog box as described in the preceding section. If you want, you can make changes to the Blending mode, opacity, color, and lighting angle.

Additionally, you can alter the appearance of these shadows by altering these options:

- **Blur** Specify how fuzzy you want the shadows.
- **Intensity** Specify how bright you want the simulated light to appear, thereby intensifying the shadow.
- **Distance** Specify the distance from the shape to cast the shadow.

You can also drag the shadow in the image window to position it, which changes the Distance and Lighting Angle values.

The Outer Glow And Inner Glow Effects

A shape to which the outer glow effect is applied appears to glow like a light bulb or neon light. The inner glow produces the same effect, but toward the inside of the shape.

To apply outer glow or inner glow effects, select a layer on which to apply the effects and then access the Effects dialog box as described previously. For these effects, you can make changes to the Blending mode, opacity, color, blur, and intensity.

For the inner glow effect, you also need to choose between Center, which produces a glow from the center of the layer's shapes, or Edge, which produces a glow from the inside edges of the layer's shapes.

The Bevel And Emboss Effects

Outer beveling makes a shape appear to "rise" from the surface of an underlying layer, as if that underlying layer had been carved away around the beveled shape. Inner beveling, however, produces an effect that makes the shape appear to have been "carved" from the underlying layer. Embossing a shape makes it look as though it was stamped onto an underlying layer, much like the numbers on a plastic credit card. Pillow embossing resembles quilting. You can apply only one of these effects at a time.

To apply a bevel or emboss effect, select a layer on which to apply the effect and then access the Effects dialog box as described previously. For these effects, you can make changes to the Blending mode, opacity, color, blur, and lighting angle for both a highlight and a shadow. You also specify a simulated depth for the effect, which affects the apparent 3D relief of the effect.

Working With The Effects Applied To A Layer

After you apply any layer effect to a layer, the Layer Effects icon appears to the right of the layer's name in the Layers palette (as shown in Figure 9.17).

Editing, Copying, And Removing Layer Effects

To edit the layer effects, double-click on the Layer Effects icon. You can select and edit any applied option by selecting it from the Effects option menu, and you can apply or remove an effect by clicking on its Apply checkbox. You can also remove an effect applied to a layer by selecting the layer and then pressing Option/Alt and choosing the effect from the Layer|Effects submenu. You can remove all effects applied to a layer by first selecting the layer and then choosing Layer|Effects|Clear Effects. To undo the most recent effect you applied, press Option/Alt as you double-click on the Layer Effects icon.

You can copy layer effects from one layer to another by selecting the layer that has the desired effects, choosing Layer|Effects|Copy Effects, selecting the layer into which you want to paste the effects, and then choosing Layer|Effects|Paste Effects. You can also paste effects to linked layers by selecting one of the linked layers, which enables the command Layer|Effects|Paste to Linked. Pasting effects to a layer or layers that already have effects replaces those effects on that layer or layers.

Converting A Layer's Effects To A New Layer

You can convert the effects applied to a layer to layers of their own by selecting a desired layer and choosing Layer|Effects|Create Layer. The effects are detached from the original layer and can no longer be edited.

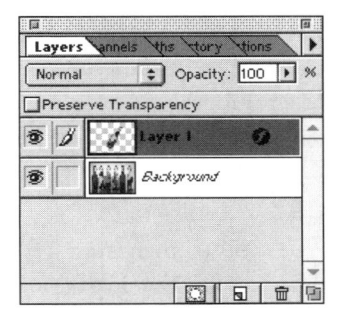

Figure 9.17 The Layers palette when layer effects have been applied to a layer.

Working With Photoshop's New Type Layer

If you have used Photoshop previously, you may have long hoped for the development of a feature similar to the New Type Layer included with Photoshop 5. You can now edit type even after you've saved, closed, and reopened an image file (as long as it's in Photoshop file format, of course). You can apply layer effects to the type, and the layer effects will conform to any new type or edited type on that layer. Type layers appear in the Layers palette, and you manage them just as you would any other layer. When you are satisfied with the type layer, or you want to export the image to another file format, you must *render* the type layer, converting it to a regular layer, by choosing Layer| Type|Render Layer.

> You can edit and adjust the type only as long as the type layer remains a type layer. After you render the layer, you can no longer edit the type, but you can still edit the layer effects.
>
> Also, the type layer supports limited editing features. You cannot apply filters to the type layer until it has been rendered, and only these features are supported:
>
> ➤ The Edit|Transform features (except Perspective and Distort), when applied to the entire type layer.
>
> ➤ All the Layer effects.
>
> ➤ The Edit|Fill keyboard shortcuts (as listed in Chapter 8). The Edit|Fill command itself is not available.
>
> The type layer is not available in Bitmap, Indexed Color, or Multichannel Color modes.

Remember that Photoshop is a bitmap graphics application and edits the pixels making up an image. Consequently, the type that Photoshop uses is also bitmapped, or rasterized. As a result, the type of a lower-resolution image may become ragged if the file is scaled up or resampled up.

Type Tool Basics

Photoshop now has four Type tools (shown from left to right in Figure 9.18): the Type tool, the Vertical Type tool, the Type Mask tool, and the Vertical Type Mask tool. The Type tool and the Vertical Type tool employ the new type layer, but the Type Mask tool and the Vertical Type Mask tool produce selection borders on the active layer—in the shape of type—that share the same characteristics of other selection borders. (Selections are discussed in Chapter 7.) The selections created by the Type Mask tools cannot be edited as type.

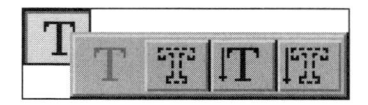

Figure 9.18 The Type tools.

As the names suggest, the vertically named type tools create type that is either stacked or aligned vertically. (Note that, by default, the type characters themselves are horizontal and stacked, not aligned sideways on a vertical baseline, an effect that you can select by checking the Rotate checkbox in the Type Tool dialog box.) After you create type with any of the four Type tools, you can change it from horizontal to vertical type by choosing Layer|Type|Vertical or from vertical to horizontal type by choosing Layer|Type|Horizontal.

You should also note that Photoshop is still not a word processor or page layout program. Type set in long lines does not break automatically. You must enter returns for the line breaks you want.

To enter type onto a new type layer or onto the active layer as a selection border, select the tool you want and click in the image, in the approximate position where you want the type to be placed. The Type Tool dialog box opens, and you can enter the type and specify its font, size, and other attributes.

The Type Tool Dialog Box

The Type Tool dialog box (shown in Figure 9.19) is the control center for specifying and editing type before you place it and—except for type created with the Type Mask tools—after it is placed on a type layer. You apply type to an image by first typing in this dialog box in the white area beneath the options.

Figure 9.19 The Type Tool dialog box.

You can size the Type Tool dialog box to fit your monitor to see more of the type in the typing area, and you can click on the Fit In Window checkbox to scale the type to fit the dialog box's current size. You can deselect this option and then scale the type's display by clicking on the plus and minus buttons in the area to the left of the Fit In Window checkbox. If you selected the Fit In Window option and want to return the type display to 100 percent size, you can click on the percentage number in the area to the left of the Fit In Window checkbox. As I mentioned previously, the type lines do not break automatically—not even in the Type Tool dialog box—so you may need to use these display options to see all the type in the typing area.

To see the type on the image while you are still in the Type Tool dialog box, select the Preview option. You can actually drag the preview type around in the image to reposition it. The Preview option is not available when you're using the Type Mask tools.

Before you type any text in the text area, or after you type text in the text area, you can specify the various attributes. If you already typed within the text area, you edit the text by selecting it as you would in word processors. You have several options: drag with the cursor, click on one character and then Shift+click on another character, double-click to select a word, or press Cmd+A/Ctrl+A to select all the text in the text area.

When you are satisfied with the type you enter in the text area, you can click on OK to apply the type to the type layer or the type-shaped selection border to the active layer. Type layers appear in the Layers palette, and you double-click on their names to reopen the Type Tool dialog box and edit the type layer.

The Type Attributes And Options

Specifying any of the type attributes before typing text applies the attributes to the text as you type. If you are editing type, the changed attributes affect only selected text. As a result, you can create type that has a variety of attributes by selecting different characters or words and specifying attributes for those characters or words—with the exception of anti-aliasing, the alignment of lines, and the color of the characters, each of which applies to all text on a particular type layer.

You can set the following specifications for type in the Type Tool dialog box:

➤ **Font** Select a typeface from the Font option menu. All fonts in the System Folder's Fonts folder and in the Photoshop 5 application's Fonts folder appear in this option menu; however, any fonts in the Photoshop Fonts folder appear only in Photoshop.

Working With Layers

- **Font Style** Select a type style from the option menu immediately to the right of the Font option menu. Type styles are Regular (Plain), Bold, Italic, and so on.

- **Size** Enter a size for the type in the Size value box.

- **Measurement Unit** Specify the measurement unit to apply to the size value entered in the Size value box. Choose from pixels or points.

- **Kerning** Specify an amount for kerning of the type in the Kerning value box. *Kerning* refers to the amount of space between two individual characters. This option is available only when the Auto Kern option is deselected for any characters you want to kern manually. Click to place the cursor between two characters that you want to kern and deselect the Auto Kern option. Then enter negative numbers to tighten the kerning or positive numbers to loosen the kerning. Kerning and tracking units are 1/1000 of the old printer's em space, which is based on the size of the *m* character of type. (See Tracking and Auto Kern later in this list.)

- **Color** Set a color for the type in the Color swatch by clicking on the swatch to open the Color Picker.

- **Leading** Specify the amount of vertical space between the baselines of horizontal lines of text or the horizontal space between the baselines of vertical lines of text in the Leading value box.

- **Tracking** Specify an amount for tracking of the type in the Tracking value box. *Tracking* refers to the amount of space between a group of characters, as opposed to kerning, which refers to the amount of space between two individual characters. Select the group of characters, such as a word or a line of text, and specify an amount of tracking to apply equally between each of the characters in the group or line. Enter negative numbers to tighten the tracking or positive numbers to loosen the tracking. Kerning and tracking units are 1/1000 of the old printer's em space, which is based on the size of the *m* character of type. (See Kerning earlier in this list and Auto Kern later in this list.)

- **Baseline** Specify any amount by which to raise or lower a character over or under its baseline. The *baseline* is the line on which rest the bodies of the text. Raise the type over its baseline by entering positive numbers, and lower the type under its baseline by entering negative numbers.

- **Alignment** Select one of the three alignment buttons to specify the alignment of the type. *Alignment* refers to the behavior of lines of type. If you want the lines to be aligned on the left and not aligned on the right, select the button on the far left in Figure 9.20. For centered lines

Figure 9.20 The Alignment buttons in the Type Tool dialog box.

of type, select the middle button in Figure 9.20. To align the right sides of lines of type and not the left sides, select the button on the far right in Figure 9.20. For vertical type, the alignment options are top, center, and bottom.

➤ **Auto Kern** Select the Auto Kern option to let Photoshop decide how much space to use between individual characters. If you want to kern two letters manually, click the cursor between them, and deselect Auto Kern to activate the Kerning option for those two characters. (See Kerning and Tracking earlier in this list.)

➤ **Anti-Aliased** Select Anti-Aliased to smooth the edges of the type.

➤ **Rotate (Vertical Tools Only)** Select Rotate to change type created with the Vertical Type tool or the Vertical Type Mask tool from stacked letters to vertical lines.

The keyboard shortcuts for editing text are listed in Table 9.1.

Table 9.1 The keyboard shortcuts for editing type.

Key or Key Combo	Performs This Function
Shift+Cmd+;/Shift+Ctrl+;	Decreases type size by 2 units
Shift+Cmd+./Shift+Ctrl+.	Increases type size by 2 units
Shift+Cmd+Option+;/Shift+Ctrl+Alt+;	Decreases type size by 10 units
Shift+Cmd+./Shift+Ctrl+.	Increases type size by 10 units
Option+Up arrow/Alt+Up arrow	Increases leading by 2 units
Cmd+Option+Up arrow/Ctrl+Alt+Up arrow	Increases leading by 10 units
Option+Down arrow/Alt+Down arrow	Decreases leading by 2 units
Cmd+Option+Down arrow/Ctrl+Alt+Down arrow	Decreases leading by 10 units
Shift+Option+Up arrow/Shift+Alt+Up arrow	Increases baseline shift by 2 units
Shift+Cmd+Option+Up arrow/Shift+Ctrl+Alt+Up arrow	Increases baseline shift by 10 units
Shift+Option+Down arrow/Shift+Alt+Down arrow	Decreases baseline shift by 2 units
Shift+Cmd+Option+Down arrow/Shift+Ctrl+Alt+Down arrow	Decreases baseline shift by 10 units
Option+Left arrow/Alt+Left arrow	Decreases leading by 20/1000 ems
Cmd+Option+Left arrow/Ctrl+Alt+Left arrow	Decreases leading by 100/1000 ems
Option+Right arrow/Alt+Right arrow	Increases leading by 20/1000 ems
Cmd+Option+Right arrow/Ctrl+Alt+Right arrow	Increases leading by 100/1000 ems
Type Tool+Shift+Cmd+L	Selects left alignment
Type Tool+Shift+Cmd+C	Selects center alignment
Type Tool+Shift+Cmd+R	Selects right alignment
Vertical Type Tool+Shift+Cmd+L	Selects top alignment
Vertical Type Tool+Shift+Cmd+C	Selects center alignment
Vertical Type Tool+Shift+Cmd+R	Selects bottom alignment

Practice Questions

Question 1

> Which of the following file formats supports the saving of layers? (Select all that apply.)
>
> ❑ a. Photoshop (PSD)
>
> ❑ b. TIFF
>
> ❑ c. PICT
>
> ❑ d. GIF

Answer a is correct. The Photoshop (PSD) format is the only format in which you can save an image file's layers.

Question 2

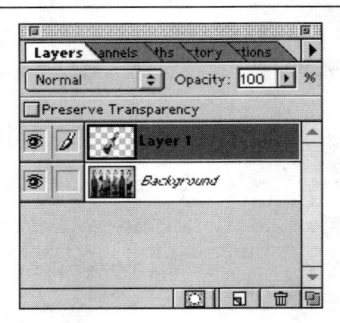

Figure 9.21 Exhibit 1.

> You just started to paint on the background of the image represented by the Layers palette in Exhibit 1, but the effect doesn't appear on the Background layer. Why not?
>
> ○ a. You weren't using the Paintbrush tool.
>
> ○ b. The Background layer was not visible.
>
> ○ c. Layer 1 was the active layer.
>
> ○ d. The Background layer was locked.

Answer c is correct. The Paintbrush icon in the box to the left of the thumbnail for Layer 1 indicates that Layer 1 is the active layer. All editing effects apply only to the active layer.

Question 3

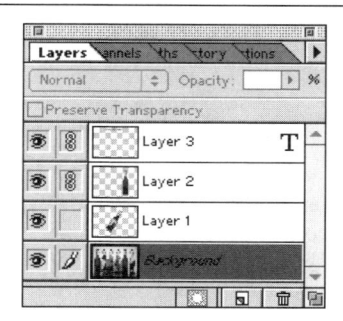

Figure 9.22 Exhibit 2.

Which of the following answers list all the linked layers in Exhibit 2?

○ a. Layer 2 and Layer 3

○ b. Layer 1, Layer 2, and Layer 3

○ c. Background, Layer 1, Layer 2, and Layer 3

○ d. Background, Layer 2, and Layer 3

Answer d is correct. Activating a layer displays the linked layer icon in any layers linked to that active layer.

Question 4

Which of the following is true about the linked layers in Exhibit 2? (Select all that apply.)

❏ a. You can merge the layers by choosing Layer|Merge Linked without rearranging them in the stacking order.

❏ b. You can merge the layers by choosing Layer|Merge Linked, but you must first rearrange them in the stacking order so that they are adjacent.

❏ c. You can apply a 2D transformation to Layer 2 without affecting the other linked layers.

❏ d. You must reposition the linked layers so that they are adjacent in the stacking order to align them.

Answer a is the only correct answer. You can merge linked layers even if they are not adjacent in the stacking order. Any 2D transformations applied to one linked layer apply to all layers linked to that layer. You can align the content of linked layers even if they are not adjacent in the stacking order.

Question 5

If you want to create a new layer composed of a selection from an existing layer while leaving the existing layer intact, which procedure or command do you use?

- ○ a. Make a selection in the existing layer, and click the New Layer button while pressing Option/Alt.
- ○ b. Make a selection in the existing layer, and choose Layer|New|Layer Via Copy.
- ○ c. Make a selection in the existing layer, and choose Layer|New|Layer Via Cut.
- ○ d. Make a selection in the existing layer, and choose Layer|New|Layer Via Copy while pressing Shift.

Answer b is correct. Layer|New|Layer Via Copy copies the selection from the existing layer and creates a new layer with that selection, leaving the existing layer intact. Layer|New|Layer Via Cut cuts the selection from the existing layer and creates a new layer with that selection.

Question 6

> Which statements are true about the Background layer? (Select all that apply.)
>
> ❏ a. You can select a Blending mode and specify opacity just like other layers.
>
> ❏ b. Newly created transparent images have a transparent Background layer.
>
> ❏ c. You can create an additional Background layer for an image by choosing Layer|New|Background.
>
> ❏ d. You can move the Background layer up in the stacking order at any time.
>
> ❏ e. Flattening a transparent image fills its background with white.

Trick! question

Answer e is the only correct answer. Even though you do use Layer|New| Background to create new backgrounds, you cannot create an *additional* Background layer. The new Background layer can be created only for an image that has no Background layer. Blending modes and opacity are not available options for the Background layer. You can move the Background layer up in the stacking order of layers only after you convert it to a layer by double-clicking on its name in the Layers palette and giving it a new name, which leaves the image file with no Background layer.

Question 7

> Which of these operations can you perform for copying layers between images?
>
> ○ a. Drag a layer from one image to the other
>
> ○ b. Copy and paste a layer from one image to another
>
> ○ c. Drag linked layers from one image to the other
>
> ○ d. Duplicate a layer from one image to the other

All the answers are correct.

Question 8

> If you have three layers and you want to spread out the contents evenly between two positions, which of these commands/operations can you use? (Select all that apply.)
>
> ❑ a. Layer|Align
>
> ❑ b. Layer|Align Linked
>
> ❑ c. Layer|Distribute
>
> ❑ d. Layer|Distribute Linked

Answer d is correct.

Question 9

> If you want to combine the contents of two of four layers in an image while leaving the other layers intact, which of these operations/commands can you use? (Select all that apply.)
>
> ❑ a. Layer|Merge Down
>
> ❑ b. Layer|Merge Linked
>
> ❑ c. Layer|Merge Visible
>
> ❑ d. Layer|Flatten Image

Answers a, b, and c are correct. Flattening an image combines the contents of all visible layers and discards the hidden layers.

Question 10

> If you are splitting a slider on the Underlying color bar to prevent a harsh or abrupt color transition between the contents of two layers, which option do you adjust?
>
> ○ a. Color Range
>
> ○ b. Opacity
>
> ○ c. Blend If
>
> ○ d. Preserve Transparency

Answer c is correct.

Question 11

If you want to apply a color or tonal adjustment to an image without permanently affecting the image, which of these features do you use?

- ○ a. Adjustment Preview
- ○ b. Adjustment Layer
- ○ c. Layer Preview
- ○ d. Temporary Layer

Answer b is correct.

Question 12

If you are creating a new layer mask wherein the entire layer or the selection is filled with black, which of these commands do you use? (Select all that apply.)

- ❏ a. Layer|Add Layer Mask|Reveal All
- ❏ b. Layer|Add Layer Mask|Reveal Selection
- ❏ c. Layer|Add Layer Mask|Hide All
- ❏ d. Layer|Add Layer Mask|Hide Selection

Answers c and d are correct.

Chapter 9

Question 13

If you create a selection on one layer and then want to intersect that selection with the opaque areas of a second layer, which of these operations works?

○ a. Intersect the second layer's transparency mask with the selection on the first layer by pressing Shift+Cmd+Option/Shift+Ctrl+Alt while clicking on the second layer's thumbnail or layer mask thumbnail in the Layers palette.

○ b. Intersect the second layer's transparency mask with the selection on the first layer by pressing Cmd/Ctrl while clicking on the second layer's thumbnail or layer mask thumbnail in the Layers palette.

○ c. Intersect the second layer's transparency mask with the selection on the first layer by pressing Option/Alt while clicking on the second layer's thumbnail or layer mask thumbnail in the Layers palette.

○ d. Intersect the second layer's transparency mask with the selection on the first layer by pressing Cmd+Option/Ctrl+Alt while clicking on the second layer's thumbnail or layer mask thumbnail in the Layers palette.

Answer a is correct.

Question 14

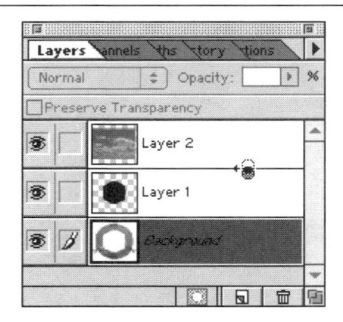

> Figure 9.23 Exhibit 3.
>
> What operation is about to be performed in Exhibit 3?
>
> ○ a. Creating a clipping path
> ○ b. Linking layers
> ○ c. Creating a clipping group
> ○ d. Deleting a layer

Answer c is correct. You can create a clipping group by choosing either Layer|Group with Previous (Cmd+G/Ctrl+G) or Layer|Group Linked (Cmd+G/Ctrl+G). Or, you can press Option/Alt to change the cursor to the Clipping Group icon and click on the line between two layers, which is the operation depicted in Exhibit 3.

Question 15

> What do you do to edit the Layer Effects applied to a layer?
>
> ○ a. Double-click on the layer in the Layers palette
> ○ b. Double-click on the layer's thumbnail in the Layers palette
> ○ c. Double-click on the Layer Effects icon to the right of the layer's name in the Layers palette
> ○ d. Choose Layer|Layer Effects|Edit

Answer c is correct.

Question 16

For which layer effect is Center an option?

- ○ a. Drop Shadow
- ○ b. Bevel
- ○ c. Inner Glow
- ○ d. Inner Shadow
- ○ e. Emboss
- ○ f. Outer Glow

Answer c is correct.

Question 17

Which of the following features can be applied to a type layer *before* it has been rendered? (Select all that apply.)

- ❑ a. Edit|Transform|Distort
- ❑ b. Edit|Transform|Scale
- ❑ c. Layer|Layer Effects|Drop Shadow
- ❑ d. Option+Delete/Alt+Delete
- ❑ e. Filter|Sharpen|Sharpen More

Answers b, c, and d are correct.

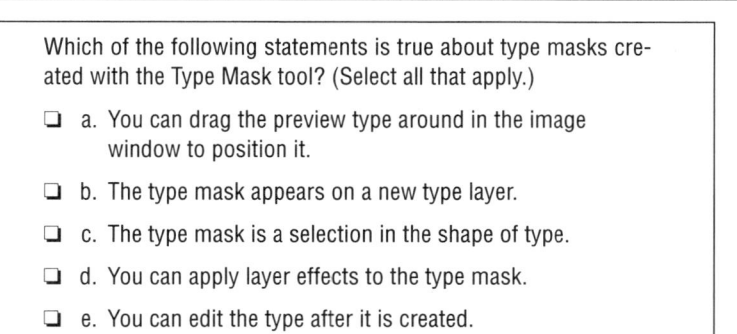

Question 18

> Which of the following statements is true about type masks created with the Type Mask tool? (Select all that apply.)
>
> ❏ a. You can drag the preview type around in the image window to position it.
>
> ❏ b. The type mask appears on a new type layer.
>
> ❏ c. The type mask is a selection in the shape of type.
>
> ❏ d. You can apply layer effects to the type mask.
>
> ❏ e. You can edit the type after it is created.

Only answer c is correct. Type masks are applied to the active layer; they cannot be edited as type layers can. The preview option is not available as they are created, and you cannot apply layer effects to the type mask.

Need To Know More?

London, Sherry and David Xenakis: *Photoshop 5 In Depth*. The Coriolis Group. ISBN 1-57610-293-9. Layers are explained in detail in Chapter 6, which starts on page 357, and using type is described starting on page 190.

Lourekas, Peter and Elaine Weinmann: *Visual Quickstart Guide, Photoshop 5 for Windows and Macintosh*. Peachpit Press. ISBN 0-201-35352-0. Chapters 7 and 13 discuss layers and start on pages 103 and 183, respectively. Type is presented in Chapter 16, which starts on page 227.

McClelland, Deke: *Photoshop 5 for Macs for Dummies*. IDG Books Worldwide, Inc. ISBN 0-7645-0391-X. This description of layers and text starts on page 475.

Working With Channels And Masks

10

Terms and concepts you'll need to understand:

- √ Mask
- √ Rubylith
- √ Channel
- √ Color channel
- √ Alpha channel
- √ Spot color channel
- √ Channel Mixer
- √ Quick Mask mode

Techniques you'll need to master:

- √ Navigating the Channels palette
- √ Creating channels
- √ Saving selections as channels
- √ Adding selections to channels and layer masks
- √ Loading selections from channels
- √ Editing channels
- √ Swapping channels between images
- √ Using the Channel Mixer
- √ Splitting and merging channels
- √ Adding spot color channels
- √ Converting alpha channels to spot color channels
- √ Working in the Quick Mask mode

This chapter presents the masking features represented by the Channels features, as well as the Quick Mask mode.

Learning Mask Basics

The term *mask* comes from the old printers' process of actually cutting pieces of colored acetate to cover areas of a plate negative that were to be protected from one or another ink. The pieces of colored acetate were actually two pieces of acetate, a clear layer and a translucent reddish layer referred to as *rubylith*. This translucent layer was opaque to the photographic process that was used, but it allowed you to see what was covered. You cut away the rubylith from areaa that you wanted to expose and left the rubylith over the areas that were to be masked.

Knowing this information can help you remember what is represented by a mask in Photoshop, especially when you view the mask as a rubylith overlay or in the rubylith-colored Quick Mask mode. The rubylith-colored areas (the black areas of the grayscale mask display) are masked—covered—and the transparent areas (the white areas of the grayscale mask display) are clear for printing.

Masks, then, are areas of an image that you want to protect from an editing operation, a color adjustment, an ink overlay, and so on.

You can edit masks just like you edit layers, images, and channels, using the painting and editing tools—except that you paint with either various opacities of rubylith or with black, white, and gray. When you're editing a mask while other channels are visible, you see the mask represented by its rubylith overlay, and you edit with the rubylith color. You can specify whatever color you want to use for the rubylith overlay by double-clicking on the Quick Mask Mode icons in the Toolbox and selecting a color in the Quick Mask Options dialog box. When you're editing a mask while no other channels are visible, you see the mask represented by its grayscale image, and you edit with black, white, and gray.

The fully selected areas of a mask are full rubylith or full black, and they are protected from whatever you do to the clear areas in the rubylith display or the white and gray areas in the grayscale display.

I have already discussed one type of mask in Chapter 9, when I talked about layer masks. This chapter presents, along with color channels, the other two types of masks—alpha channels and Quick Masks.

Understanding Channels

Channels are the various 8-bit grayscale images in which you store the masks you have defined.

Although you might look at the Channels palette and see what resembles the stacking order of layers in the Layers palette, channels are not like layers. And, as if you didn't have enough to remember about channels, you also need to remember some more about color channels and alpha channels and spot color channels.

A Photoshop image can contain up to 24 channels, including all its color channels, alpha channels, and spot color channels. However, channels affect a file's size, depending on how much pixel information a channel may have. The color channels of an RGB image with no alpha channels, for example, each contain approximately one-third of the file's pixel data, so duplicating one of those channels increases the file size by about 30 percent. Consequently, you can choose File|Save A Copy and select the Exclude Alpha Channels and Exclude Non-Image Data options in the Save As dialog box as one way to reduce dramatically the size of a file that has many alpha channels.

> Channels are supported in every color mode except Bitmap.
>
> Although your color channels are retained if you save your image in a file format that is compatible with the image's color mode, you can save your alpha channels only in these file formats:
>
> ➤ Photoshop (PSD)
>
> ➤ Photoshop 2 (Mac only)
>
> ➤ DCS 2.0
>
> ➤ PICT
>
> ➤ TIFF
>
> ➤ Raw

Color Channels

Color channels contain the pixel brightness information or the ink intensity information for a particular color, depending, for example, on whether the image is RGB or CMYK. When the color channels for an image are combined on screen or for printing, the color channel information combines to create the colors you see and print. If you are working in an RGB file, you have the composite channel and three channels of separate color information. CMYK files have five channels: one each for the four process colors and the composite. As you edit an image, another channel is displayed: the combination—or composite—of the separate color channels.

Color channels are always displayed in their respective colors when more than one is visible, but when they are viewed individually, color channels appear as a grayscale image by default. You see this grayscale image, again, because the color channels contain only pixel brightness or ink intensity information, which can be expressed as black, white, and shades of gray. (You can display individual color channels in their respective colors by selecting Color Channels in Color in the Display & Cursors dialog box, under File|Preferences.)

Alpha Channels

Alpha channels are any channels other than the basic color component channels that are added to an image; they are basically warehouses of images that can be used again and again to mask areas of an image or select areas of an image. Unlike paths, which store vector-based lines, alpha channels are 8-bit grayscale (256-color) images that store shapes that can be used to apply editing and retouching operations selectively to an image. You also can use alpha channels to "fade" an image or effect through various levels of opacity. You can save regular selections as alpha channels and load alpha channels as selections. You can edit channels just as you can images and layers, using the painting and retouching tools, except that you are editing with only black, white, and gray—as with layer masks.

> Remember that the black areas of an alpha channel are masked, the white areas are unmasked, and the gray areas are partially masked. The nonblack areas become the selected areas if the channel is loaded as a selection.

You manage alpha channels from the Channels palette like color channels. You can rename alpha channels, change their place in the stacking order, specify a color for their display, specify the opacity of their display, and convert them to spot color channels. If you are working with image files of the exact same pixel dimensions (such as two copies of an image, one of which you use as the storage site for disk-space-gobbling layers and channels), you can store alpha channels in one file and copy them to the other file as needed.

Spot Color Channels

Spot color channels are channels that are used to apply one specific color of ink to a printed image. For example, look at the cover of this book. Notice how the Exam Cram logo and other areas seem to be "shinier" than the rest of the cover? The shiny areas have an extra ink color—actually a varnish in this case—that was applied through shapes defined in a spot color channel. In other cases, spot colors can be applied to a printed image as a replacement for one or all of the process colors to produce a duotone-type image. (Duotones are discussed in Chapter 12.)

Navigating The Channels Palette

The Channels palette (shown in Figure 10.1) displays an image's composite channel and all of the image's color channels, alpha channels, and spot color channels. The color channels are always displayed at the top of the Channels palette, but the alpha channels and spot color channels can be rearranged beneath them by dragging the channel names until a heavy line appears beneath or above another channel. Access the Channels palette by clicking on its tab in its palette group or by choosing Windows|Show Channels.

As with layers in the Layers palette, a channel is active and is affected by any editing when its name is highlighted. Unlike Layers, however, you can activate multiple channels by pressing Shift and clicking on their names.

Also like the layers in the Layers palette, the little eyeball icons to the left of the channels' names indicate whether channels are visible in the image window. Clicking on the eyeball icon of one of the color channels hides the composite channel but not the other color channels. Clicking on the eyeball icon of the composite channel or pressing Shift+~ reveals all the color channels. You can drag your cursor up and down the column of eyeball icons to hide or reveal channels.

Double-clicking on a channel's name opens the Channel Options dialog box, where you can change the mask display to show the overlay over the selected areas, rather than the masked areas, and select a new color and color opacity for the channel's overlay display.

You can view alpha channels as grayscale images when you view them individually, with all the color channels hidden. However, when the composite channel is visible or when one or any combination of the color channels is

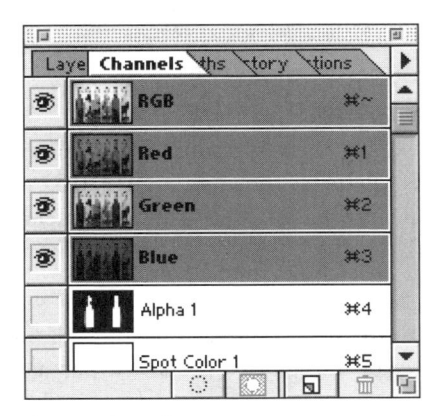

Figure 10.1 The Channels palette.

Figure 10.2 The Quick Mask icons in the Toolbox.

visible, alpha channels appear as the rubylith overlay. You can select the color of the rubylith overlay by double-clicking on the Quick Mask icons in the Toolbox (as shown in Figure 10.2).

You can select different sizes for the channel icons—or turn them off completely—in the Channels palette by choosing Palette Options from the Channels palette menu.

Working With Channels

After you create a channel or Photoshop creates channels for you, you can work with them much as you work with layers or full images. You can edit, duplicate, and swap channels between images. You can also use the Channel Mixer to blend channels for color correction and color-to-grayscale image conversion. You can separate an image's channels into separate freestanding images, and you can combine separate freestanding images into one image.

Creating Channels, Saving Selections As Channels, And Adding Selections To Channels And Layer Masks

When you open an image file, Photoshop automatically separates the image into its component color channels, depending on the file type. If you want to add additional alpha channels, you can create a raw, blank channel, or you can convert a selection to a channel or add a selection to an existing channel or layer mask.

Creating New Channels

To create a new, raw channel, press Option/Alt and click on the New Channel button in the Channels palette (as shown in Figure 10.3), or choose New Channel in the Channels palette menu. The New Channel dialog box opens (as shown in Figure 10.4).

In the New Channel dialog box, you can name the new channel or leave it at the default name. You can choose between having the rubylith or black areas define the masked areas or the selected areas. You can also define the color to

Figure 10.3 The New Channel button in the Channels palette.

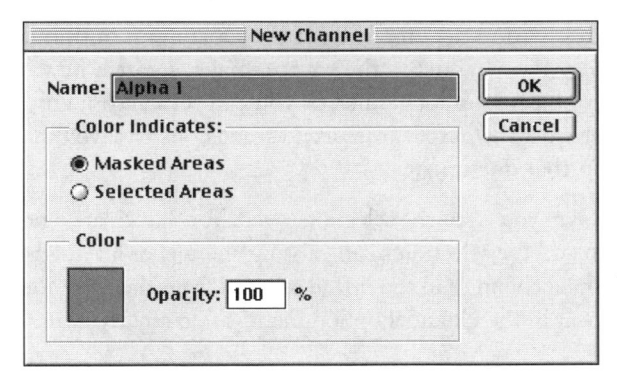

Figure 10.4 The New Channel dialog box.

be used for the overlay and its opacity, which affects only how the mask is displayed. When you click on OK, the new channel is created, filling the image window with its grayscale display.

You can also create a new channel using the most recent settings of the New Channel dialog box—without opening the New Channel dialog box—by clicking on the New Channel button in the Channels palette.

Saving Selections, Adding Selections To Channels And Layer Masks, And Loading Selections From Channels

To create a new channel based on a selection, or to add a selection to an existing channel or layer mask, follow these steps:

1. Make a selection in the image.

2. Access the Save Selection dialog box (as shown in Figure 10.5) by choosing Select|Save Selection.

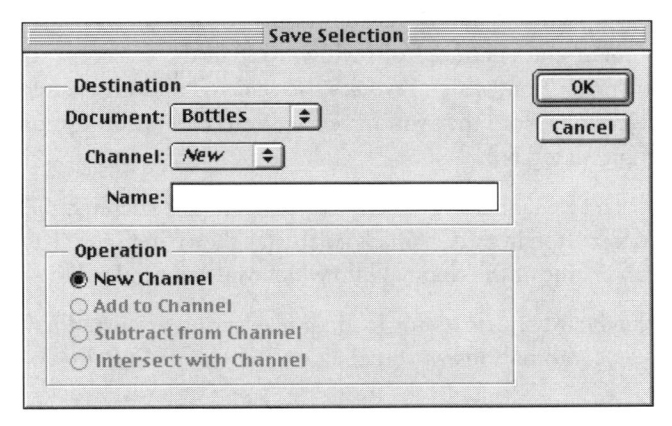

Figure 10.5 The Save Selection dialog box.

3. Select a destination document from the Document option menu. You can create a new channel in the source image, create a new image with this selection saved as a channel, or you can select from any open document with the exact same pixel dimensions to save the selection as a channel in that document.

4. Specify where you want the selection saved. You can create a new channel, or you can add the selection to an existing channel or layer mask. Any existing alpha channels in the image selected from the Document option menu appear in the Channel option menu, as do any layer masks that exist.

5. If you are creating a new channel, enter a name in the Name text area.

6. When saving a selection to an existing channel, you can select from the following Operation options:

   ➤ **Replace Channel** Completely replaces any existing unmasked area of the existing channel

   ➤ **Add To Channel** Adds the selection to the unmasked area of the existing channel

   ➤ **Subtract From Channel** Subtracts the selection from the unmasked area of the existing channel

   ➤ **Intersect With Channel** Intersects the selection from the unmasked area of the existing channel

You can also create new channels from selections using the default New Channel options—without opening the New Channel dialog box—by clicking on the Save Selection button in the Channels palette (as shown in Figure 10.6).

To load a channel's unmasked area as a selection, access the Load Selection dialog box by choosing Select|Load Selection. The Load Selection dialog box offers similar options to the Save Selection dialog box. You can choose the source document and channel from which to load the selection. You can also select the Invert option, which reverses the selected and unselected areas as it loads the selection. Note that you have the same Operation options as in the Save Selection dialog box.

You can also load a channel as a selection by selecting the channel, clicking on the Load Selection button in the Channels palette (as shown in Figure 10.7), and then clicking on the name of the channel into which you want to load the selection.

The other keyboard shortcuts for loading a selection are listed in Table 10.1. Use these key combinations as you click on the channel's name in the Channels palette.

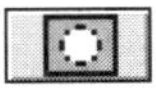

Figure 10.6 The Save Selection button in the Channels palette.

Figure 10.7 The Load Selection button in the Channels palette.

Table 10.1   The keyboard shortcuts for loading selections.

Key or Key Combo	Performs This Function
Cmd/Ctrl	Loads the unmasked areas of a channel as a selection
Shift+Cmd/Shift+Ctrl	Adds the unmasked area of a channel to an existing channel
Cmd+Option/Ctrl+Alt	Subtracts the unmasked area of a channel to an existing channel
Shift+Cmd+Option/Shift+Ctrl+Alt	Intersects the unmasked area of a channel with an existing channel

Editing Channels

To edit a channel, simply activate it and paint it with a painting or editing tool. When you activate a channel, the foreground and background colors automatically change to black and white. If you click on one and select any other color, you see only the grayscale brightness value of that color in the foreground and background color swatches. Again, black is the masking color, white is the color of the unmasked areas, and grays are the partially masked areas.

Duplicating Channels In The Same Image Or To Other Images

Photoshop allows you to duplicate channels both within an image and between images. You can duplicate channels by using the Duplicate Channel command or by dragging.

To duplicate a channel, select the channel in the Channels palette, and then drag its name to the New Channel button in the Channels palette (shown in Figure 10.3). You can also choose the Duplicate Channel command from the Channels palette menu, which opens the Duplicate Channel dialog box. In this dialog box, you can name the new channel and select a destination for it. All open images with the exact same pixel dimensions of the source image appear in the Document option menu. You can rename the channel in the destination image, and you can select the Invert option to reverse the black and white areas as you copy it to the destination. You can also duplicate an alpha channel by dragging its name from the Channels palette into another image's window.

You can't duplicate channels to Bitmap mode images.

Deleting Channels From An Image

You can delete channels from the Channels palette by dragging the channel's name to the Trash button, by choosing Delete Channel from the palette menu, or by pressing Option/Alt and clicking on the Trash button. Simply clicking on the Trash button when a channel is selected opens the warning/approval dialog box.

Deleting a color channel automatically converts an image to Multichannel mode. Consequently, you lose the layers if you make this conversion, and Photoshop asks whether you want to flatten the image if you attempt to delete a color channel from an image with layers.

Using The Channel Mixer

Using Photoshop's Channel Mixer, you can combine the brightness values of two or more channels. You can use the Channel Mixer to convert color images to grayscale images with more control over the quality of the image, to correct or repair individual channels, and to create images that appear to be hand tinted. Open the Channel Mixer dialog box by choosing Image|Adjust|Channel Mixer (as shown in Figure 10.8).

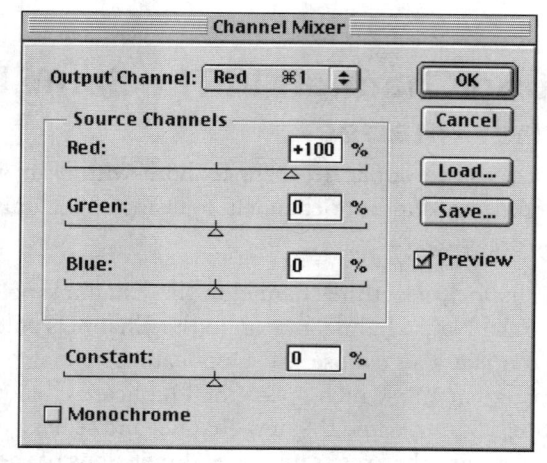

Figure 10.8 The Channel Mixer dialog box.

You can select to adjust the color information of any of the available color channels in the Output Channel option menu. This is the channel into which the other channels' color information can be blended.

Add or subtract color information to or from this output channel by dragging the sliders or entering percentage values from -200% to 200% for any of the listed Source Channels. Negative values invert a color channel before blending.

Using the Constant option is like setting an opacity value for the output channel. Dragging the slider to or entering negative values darkens the image, and dragging the slider to or entering positive values lightens the image.

The Monochrome option automatically matches the brightness values for all channels, which creates a grayscale image. (To understand how this process works, remember that you get black when all the RGB values are at zero, white when they are 255, and shades of gray when they are set equally at other levels. So, setting the channels to the same levels produces shades of gray.)

Also from the Channel Mixer dialog box, you can load previously saved settings and save the current settings. You can select the Preview option to see the effects of your adjustment in the image window.

Creating New Grayscale Images From Individual Channels

You can actually convert individual channels to completely new files using the Split Channels command in the Channels palette menu. This command creates one new file for each existing channel in an image, opens those new files, and closes the original file. The new files can be edited and managed just like any other image files.

If you have edited the original file and want to keep the changes in that file, you should save the original file before using the Split Channels command because that original file is closed without saving. However, even changes that have not been saved are incorporated into the new individual files.

Creating New Color Images From Multiple Grayscale Images

Working just the opposite of the Split Channels command, the Merge Channels command in the Channels palette menu combines multiple grayscale images that are the exact same pixel dimensions into one image. Each image can be assigned to a specific color channel in the new image. This command offers one way to repair Photoshop DCS files that are corrupted and have lost their links to each other, which prevents the files from being automatically recombined as one image. You can open the individual DCS files and merge them back into one image. You can also use the Merge Channels command to recombine the channels of a file that you split with the Split Channels command.

To use the Merge Channels command, open the files you want to merge. Make sure no other files with the exact same pixel dimensions are open; otherwise, Photoshop adds them to the new image, too. Choose Merge Channels from the Channels palette menu. The Merge Channels dialog box opens, allowing you to select an available mode from the Mode option menu. Because Photoshop creates a new channel in the new image for each of the grayscale source images, the number of open source files determines the availability of various modes. You can select the number of channels to create. If you select a number other than the default that Photoshop offers, you automatically create a Multichannel mode image (the Multichannel color mode is discussed in Chapter 4). Click on OK to proceed. Another dialog box opens, allowing you to assign the individual images to the color channels in the new image.

As with the original file used for the Split Channels command, if you have edited one or more of the original grayscale files you use for the Merge Channels command and want to keep the change, you should save the original files before using the Merge Channels command because the original files are closed without saving. Again, even changes that have not been saved are incorporated into the new file.

Working With Spot Color Channels

As described earlier in this chapter, you can use spot color channels to add additional inks to specific areas of a four-color printed publication or to add individual inks to specific areas of any printed publication. Spot color channels are not necessarily the best choice for applying a tint to an entire image, for which you may choose to convert the image to Duotone mode and apply an individual color to the image. (Duotone mode images are discussed in Chapter 12.)

Spot color channels are much like alpha channels. In fact, you can convert alpha channels to spot color channels.

Other guidelines for using spot color channels are as follows:

➤ Spot color channels apply to an entire image, not individual layers.

➤ Spot colors print on top of all the other color channel inks, with multiple spot colors overprinting in the order they appear in the stacking order.

Working With Channels And Masks   **317**

- Spot channels cannot be moved above the color channels in the stacking order—to print under those color channels—unless you convert the file to Multichannel mode.

- Spot color channels print out as individual pages on composite printers.

- Spot color channels can be merged into the color channels of an image, which converts the spot colors to their process color equivalents.

- The name of the specific color to be used for a spot color channel prints on that spot color's separation.

- You may want to use a page-layout or an illustration application to use spot color graphics most efficiently.

Adding Spot Color Channels To An Image

You can create a "raw" spot color channel that you can paint or edit from scratch, you can create a spot color channel that is based on a selection in an image, or you can convert an existing alpha channel to a spot color channel.

Creating New Spot Color Channels

The steps for creating a raw spot color channel or a spot color channel from a selection are as follows:

1. Access the Channels palette by clicking on its tab in its palette group or by choosing Window|Show Channels.

2. Make any desired selection in the image. The respective area in the new spot color channel is filled with the spot color.

3. Access the New Spot Channel dialog box (as shown in Figure 10.9) to create the new spot color channel by choosing New Spot Channel from the Channels palette menu, or by pressing Cmd/Ctrl and clicking on the New Channel button in the Channels palette (as shown in Figure 10.3).

4. Select a color by clicking on the swatch next to the Color option, which opens the Color Picker. Although you can select a color from the Color

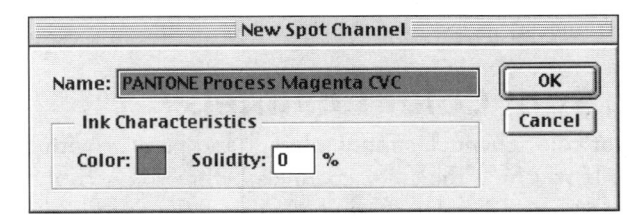

Figure 10.9   The New Spot Channel dialog box.

Picker, you should click on the Custom button to open the Custom Color dialog box, where you can select a color from one of the custom color systems supported by Photoshop. (For more information on selecting colors and descriptions of the specific custom-color systems, see Chapter 4.) Selecting a color from one of the custom color systems will more likely ensure that you wind up with a printed color you want.

5. Specify a display opacity for the spot color in the Solidity text box. This option enables you to set a high solidity for a transparent spot color so that you see where it will be applied or to set a low solidity for an opaque spot color so that it doesn't obscure your view of the underlying colors. This option doesn't affect the printing of the ink; it affects only the display of the image.

6. For the sake of organization and efficient identification of the spot color channels, you should leave the name of the spot color as the name of the spot color channel. However, if you want to name it something else, type the new name in the Name text box.

7. Click on OK.

Converting Alpha Channels To Spot Color Channels

Converting an alpha channel to a spot color channel changes that existing alpha channel. Don't worry; if you need that alpha channel later, you can always load the spot color channel as a selection by pressing Cmd/Ctrl and clicking on the channel's name in the Channels palette, and then creating a new alpha channel with it.

Convert an alpha channel to a spot color channel by double-clicking on the alpha channel's name in the Channels palette. When the Channel Options dialog box opens, you can click on the Spot Color radio button. You can select a color for the spot color channel from this dialog box by clicking on the swatch next to the Color option and/or a solidity percentage by entering a value next to the Solidity option, or you can go ahead and click on OK.

By default, the spot color ink will be applied to all but the white areas of the spot color channel. You can reverse this application of spot color by choosing Image|Adjust|Invert.

Editing Spot Color Channels

To edit a spot color channel, simply select it and paint it with a painting or editing tool. If you hide the color channels before you activate a spot color channel, the foreground and background colors automatically change to black and white. Then, if you click on either the foreground or background color and select any other color, you see only the grayscale brightness value of that color in the foreground and background color swatches. Paint with black to apply the spot color, with white to remove the spot color, and grays to vary the density of the ink.

You can also use the opacity option of whatever tool you use to vary the ink intensity.

If you leave the color channels visible and select a channel to edit, the foreground and background colors do not change to black and white, and you paint with the grayscale values of whatever colors are selected for the foreground and background colors.

Setting Spot Color Options

You can change the name, color, or solidity of an existing spot color channel by double-clicking on its name in the Channels palette, which reopens the Spot Channel Options dialog box.

Merging Spot Color Channels

If, for some reason, you decide to apply the spot color channel directly to the other color channels, choose Merge Spot Channel from the Channels palette menu.

> *Note: Merging spot channels automatically flattens layered images and can potentially distort not only the color of the spot channel, but possibly the colors of the color channels as well. Photoshop attempts to convert the color channels' values to match the CMYK values of the spot color channels, which might result in an unplanned color.*
>
> *Also, the solidity option setting, which usually has no effect on the output of the image, is used as an opacity setting when the spot color channel is merged.*

Exporting Spot Color Channels

You must convert image files with spot color channels to Photoshop DCS to export the spot color channel with the other color separations.

Preparing Spot Color Channels For Printing

As mentioned previously, spot color channels overprint each other and the color channels according to their stacking order. If you have areas of spot color that overprint other spot colors or the process colors, you could wind up with undesirable results. You can "knock out"—or clear—the areas under a spot color by selecting the spot color channel by pressing Cmd/Ctrl, clicking on the channel's name in the Channels palette, and then selecting the channel you want to clear and pressing Delete. You need to repeat this process for each channel that you want cleared.

If you want to "trap" the spot color and other colors so that they slightly overlap to prevent white paper from showing through, choose Select|Modify| Expand/Contract to create the slight overlap. (Trapping is discussed in Chapter 12.)

Working In The Quick Mask Mode

You can create and edit masks without accessing the Channels palette by switching from the Standard display mode over to the Quick Mask mode. Switch to the Quick Mask mode by clicking on the Quick Mask button in the Toolbox (the button on the right in Figure 10.10).

> The Quick Mask mode applies a rubylith overlay to the image. The colored areas of the overlay represent the masked areas, and the areas with no overlay represent the unmasked areas.
>
> If you hide all the other channels in the image, the overlay turns to black and white, with black representing the masked areas and white representing the unmasked areas.

You can start with any selection already made in the image and edit the resulting Quick Mask with any of the painting, editing, or selection tools, or you can start from scratch and create a Quick Mask with the painting, editing, and selection tools. You can also apply filters and other effects to the Quick Mask. When you switch back to Standard mode, the unmasked areas of the Quick Mask are loaded as a selection.

When you enter the Quick Mask mode, a temporary channel appears in the Channels palette. This temporary channel serves only to indicate that you are working in Quick Mask mode. As long as this temporary channel is selected, you edit the Quick Mask. However, if you select any other channel, you edit

Figure 10.10   The Standard Mode button and the Quick Mask Mode button in the Toolbox.

that channel. You can create an alpha channel from the selection you create with the Quick Mask by returning to the Standard mode and then saving the selection to a channel or by dragging the temporary Quick Mask "channel" in the Channels palette to the New Channel button

By default, the rubylith display is a 50 percent opacity of red. You can change this color by double-clicking on either of the Mode buttons to open the Quick Mask Options dialog box. Here, you can change the color and opacity of the overlay and switch between overlaying the rubylith color over the selected or masked areas. You can toggle between the Masked and Selected options by pressing Option/Alt as you click on the Quick Mask Mode button. Remember that the opacity of the overlay affects only the display of the overlay and not the opacity of the painting effect you may be using.

You edit the Quick Mask overlay by painting with black to mask areas, with white to uncover or select areas, and with grays to create partially selected or feathered and anti-aliased areas.

Practice Questions

Question 1

> Which of the following are 8-bit grayscale images? (Select all that apply.)
>
> ☐ a. Color channels
>
> ☐ b. Alpha channels
>
> ☐ c. Spot color channels
>
> ☐ d. Layer masks

All the answers are correct.

Question 2

> If you want to work with channels in an image, which of the following modes can you **not** use?
>
> ○ a. Bitmap
>
> ○ b. Grayscale
>
> ○ c. RGB
>
> ○ d. CMYK
>
> ○ e. Lab

Answer a is correct. Channels are not available in Bitmap mode.

Question 3

What colors represent the masked areas of a channel or mask? (Select all that apply.)

❐ a. Rubylith overlay

❐ b. Transparency

❐ c. Black

❐ d. White

Trick! question

All the answers are correct. Although the default opaque colors for a mask or channel are the rubylith color and black, you can select Selected Areas in the Quick Mask Options dialog box or the Channel Options dialog box to switch to representing the masked areas of the channel or mask with transparency or white.

Question 4

What operation do you use to create a new channel without opening the New Channel dialog box?

○ a. Press Option/Alt and click on the New Channel button.

○ b. Click on the New Channel button.

○ c. Choose New Channel from the Channels palette menu.

○ d. Choose Channel|New|Default.

Answer b is correct.

Question 5

Which keyboard shortcut do you hold while clicking on the Load Selection button to intersect a selection with the selected areas of a channel?

○ a. Cmd/Ctrl

○ b. Shift+Cmd/Shift+Ctrl

○ c. Cmd+Option/Ctrl+Alt

○ d. Shift+Cmd+Option/Shift+Ctrl+Alt

Answer d is correct.

Question 6

> What properties must a file have to be available as a destination for duplicating a channel? (Select all that apply.)
>
> ❑ a. It must be open.
> ❑ b. It must be in the same color mode.
> ❑ c. It must have the exact same pixel dimensions.
> ❑ d. It must have the exact same number of channels.

Answers a and c are correct. For a file to be included in the Destination Document option menu of the Duplicate Channel dialog box, it must be open, and it must have the exact same pixel dimensions as the source file.

Question 7

> If you want to convert a color image to grayscale by selectively blending the color channel information, which operation do you use?
>
> ○ a. Image|Mode|Grayscale
> ○ b. Image|Adjust|Desaturate
> ○ c. Image|Adjust|Channel Mixer
> ○ d. Image|Convert|By Channel

Answer c is correct. Among other possible uses, the Channel Mixer allows you to blend the color channel information to improve the conversion of a color image to a grayscale image.

Question 8

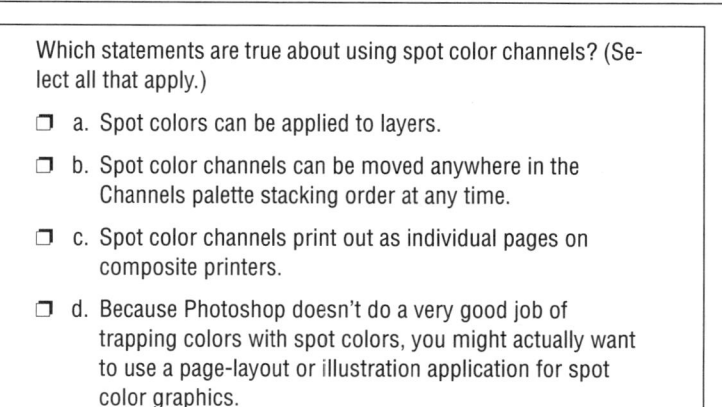

> Which statements are true about using spot color channels? (Select all that apply.)
>
> ❐ a. Spot colors can be applied to layers.
>
> ❐ b. Spot color channels can be moved anywhere in the Channels palette stacking order at any time.
>
> ❐ c. Spot color channels print out as individual pages on composite printers.
>
> ❐ d. Because Photoshop doesn't do a very good job of trapping colors with spot colors, you might actually want to use a page-layout or illustration application for spot color graphics.

Answers c and d are correct. Spot colors can be applied only to an entire image, not to its individual layers; spot color channels can't be moved above the color channels, except in a Multichannel mode file.

Question 9

> Which command loads a Quick Mask as a selection?
>
> ❍ a. Pressing Cmd/Ctrl and clicking on the Load Quick Mask button in the Channels palette
>
> ❍ b. Selecting Load Quick Mask as Selection from the Channels palette menu
>
> ❍ c. Pressing Q
>
> ❍ d. Clicking on the name of the temporary Quick Mask in the Channels palette with the Marquee tool

Answer c is correct. Q is the keyboard shortcut to toggle between the Standard and Quick Mask display modes. Any time you use the Quick Mask mode to create a mask, returning to the Standard mode loads the Quick Mask as a selection.

Need To Know More?

London, Sherry and David Xenakis: *Photoshop 5 In Depth*. The Coriolis Group. ISBN 1-57610-293-9. Channels are presented starting on page 295.

Lourekas, Peter and Elaine Weinmann: *Visual Quickstart Guide, Photoshop 5 for Windows and Macintosh*. Peachpit Press. ISBN 0-201-35352-0. Masking is presented starting on page 203.

McClelland, Deke: *Macworld Photoshop 5 Bible*. IDG Books Worldwide, Inc. ISBN 0-7645-3231-6. Masking is described in detail starting on page 435.

Working With Actions And Automation

11

Terms and concepts you'll need to understand:

- ✓ Actions
- ✓ Sets
- ✓ Modal tool
- ✓ Modal control
- ✓ Button mode
- ✓ Recording
- ✓ Batch processing
- ✓ Automation
- ✓ Assistant
- ✓ Wizard

Techniques you'll need to master:

- ✓ Navigating the Actions palette
- ✓ Recording actions
- ✓ Editing actions
- ✓ Duplicating actions and sets
- ✓ Rearranging actions and sets
- ✓ Saving actions and sets
- ✓ Including and excluding commands and actions during playback
- ✓ Applying an action to a batch of files
- ✓ Selecting and using the automation assistants/wizards

I love actions. They can help you work so much faster in Photoshop. *Actions are scripts that perform certain Photoshop operations for you.* Photoshop includes a set of actions that you can use, and you can create your own actions. This chapter presents the Actions palette and its features, as well as the *automation assistants* (as they're called on the Mac) and *wizards* (as they're called in Windows).

Learning Action Basics

Actions are basically scripts that play back a series of commands, enabling you to apply the same series of commands to multiple files without having to painstakingly apply each command individually.

Capabilities And Limitations Of Actions

The following list includes those things that you can and cannot do with actions:

- ▶ You can apply an action to a whole folder—a batch—of files and then walk away as it processes this whole batch of files.

- ▶ You can insert "stops" in an action so that the action waits for a response from you.

- ▶ You can set the actions in the Actions palette to a Button mode to play them when you click on them.

- ▶ Photoshop can't record some actions, such as using the painting tools. However, you can insert space in an action for the commands in the View and Window menus that can't be recorded.

- ▶ You can set the playback of the action to play without stopping, to stop after each command, or to pause for a specific amount of time between commands.

- ▶ You can even record a command that plays another action.

- ▶ Photoshop 5 can play the actions you created for Photoshop 4, but you can't use Photoshop 5 actions in version 4.

The Actions Palette

Actions are both organized in and operated from the Actions palette (shown in Figure 11.1). Access the Actions palette by clicking on its tab in its palette group or by choosing Window|Show Actions.

Working With Actions And Automation   **329**

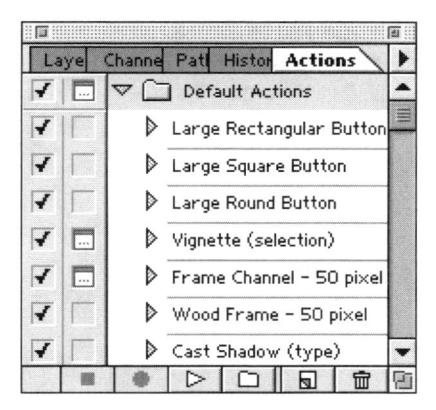

Figure 11.1   The Actions palette.

> Be sure you know how to manage commands, actions, and sets from the Actions palette.

Sets—groups—of actions appear in the Actions palette on a gray bar with a folder icon to the right of their names. Sets can be collapsed or expanded to hide or display all the actions in the set. The actions in each set are indented from the set's position and can be expanded to display all the commands in them. The commands in each action can also be expanded to display all the values and settings recorded in that command.

The checkmark to the far left of an action's name indicates whether the action or command will be executed as the action is played. The little dialog box icon indicates that an action or command includes a dialog box and whether the specifications recorded when the action was recorded will be used when it is played back. (Both of the options relating to these icons are discussed later in this chapter.)

The palette menu for the Actions palette (shown in Figure 11.2) has an extensive list of options and commands that apply to recording, playing, editing, and managing options.

Controlling Action Operations With The Actions Palette Buttons

The buttons at the bottom of the Actions palette (shown in Figure 11.1) allow you to control the recording and management of actions. From left to right, the buttons are the Stop, Record, Play, New Set, New Action, and Trash buttons.

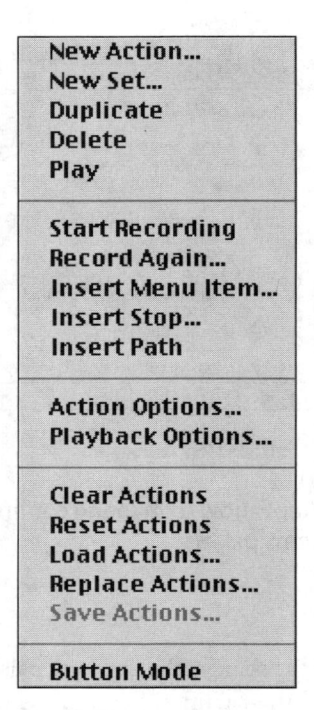

```
New Action...
New Set...
Duplicate
Delete
Play

Start Recording
Record Again...
Insert Menu Item...
Insert Stop...
Insert Path

Action Options...
Playback Options...

Clear Actions
Reset Actions
Load Actions...
Replace Actions...
Save Actions...

Button Mode
```

Figure 11.2 The Actions palette menu.

Stopping Actions To Enter Different Dialog Box Values Or Modal Tool Operations During Playback

When you record and then play back an action, the values you entered into any dialog boxes and the operations you performed with any modal tool are applied as they were recorded. (A *modal tool* is any tool or command that requires you to respond to a dialog box or that requires you to press Enter or Return to apply the effects of that tool or command, such as the Feather command or the Fill commands.) You can stop a command or action at any dialog box or modal tool by clicking on the box to the immediate left of the list of actions in the Actions palette. The Modal Control icon then appears, indicating that the action will stop at any dialog boxes or modal tools in that particular set, action, or command.

Activating the modal control next to a set of actions stops all the actions in that set at their dialog boxes and modal tools. Activating the modal control next to an action stops all the commands in that action at their dialog boxes and modal tools. Activating the modal control next to a command stops the playback of the action at the dialog boxes and modal tools in that command.

Accessing The Options For An Action

Double-click on the name of an action in the Actions palette to open the Action Options dialog box. This dialog box is similar to the New Action dialog box (which is discussed in the "Creating New Actions" section later in this chapter), but without the option to assign the action to a set. Here, you can rename an action, change its button color, and assign or reassign the action to a function key with or without modifiers.

Setting Actions To The Button Mode

Selecting Button mode from the Actions palette menu sets the actions to a list of buttons in the Actions palette (as shown in Figure 11.3). Clicking on any of the buttons launches the action. While you're working in the Button mode, you cannot edit, rearrange, or record actions, but you can clear, reset, load, and replace the actions in the Actions palette. You can specify a color for the button by double-clicking on the action's name (when the Actions palette is not set to Button mode) and selecting a new color.

Grouping And Saving Actions As Sets

You might want to organize your Actions palette into groups of actions that apply to specific operations or types of files. If so, you can create and manage sets of actions. As shown in the Actions palette in Figure 11.1, a set is displayed as a folder on a gray bar. You can move this set around in the Actions palette as described in the preceding section.

To create a new set, choose New Set from the Action palette menu, or click on the New Set button in the Actions palette (shown in Figure 11.4). The New Set dialog box opens, and you can enter a name for the set. After you create and name a set, you can rename it by double-clicking on its name to

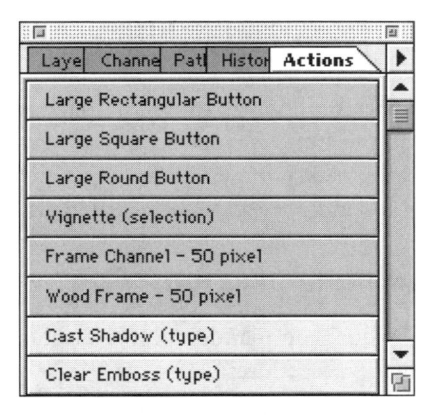

Figure 11.3   The Actions palette set to Button mode.

Figure 11.4 The New Set button in the Actions palette.

open the Action Options dialog box or by choosing Set Options from the Actions palette menu.

Photoshop automatically saves actions as you create them, but only to a temporary file. To save actions permanently, you must include them in a set and then save the set. Choose Save Actions from the Actions palette menu, and specify a name and location for the saved set. By default, actions are saved in the Settings folder inside the Photoshop application folder.

Rearranging Actions And Sets In The Actions Palette

You can move actions and sets around in the Actions palette just as you move layers in the Layers palette and channels in the Channels palette. To move an action, simply drag the name of the action to another position in a set or onto the name of another set. To move a set, just drag the name of the set to another position above or below other sets. The usual heavy line appears between action names to indicate where the action or set will be repositioned.

Loading, Replacing, And Resetting The Actions In The Actions Palette

You can load a previously saved set of actions, which adds the loaded set to the set or sets currently in the Actions palette, or you can replace the sets in the Actions palette.

Load an additional set of actions into the Actions palette by choosing the Load Actions option in the Actions palette menu.

Completely replace all the actions in the Actions palette by choosing the Replace Actions option in the Actions palette menu.

Reset the Actions in the Actions palette to the default set by choosing the Reset Actions option in the Actions palette menu. A warning/alert box opens, allowing you to choose between completely replacing all the actions and sets in the Actions palette or appending—adding—the default set to the current list.

Duplicating Commands, Actions, And Sets

You can duplicate individual commands, complete actions, and complete sets using one of the following procedures:

➤ **Drag commands or actions** to the New Action button in the Actions palette. New copies of commands appear after the selected original

Working With Actions And Automation

command, and new copies of actions appear at the bottom of the Actions palette.

➤ **Drag sets** to the New Set button in the Actions palette. New copies of sets appear after the selected original set.

➤ **Choose the Duplicate command in the Actions palette menu** after selecting any command, action, or set. You can also duplicate multiple items in the Actions palette by pressing Option on the Mac or either Shift or Control in Windows to select multiple items from the list. New copies of commands appear after the selected original command, and new copies of actions and sets appear at the bottom of the Actions palette.

➤ **Press Option/Alt and drag a command or action** to a new spot in the Action palette list. The heavy line indicates where the new copies will appear.

Deleting Commands, Actions, And Sets

You can delete individual commands, complete actions, and complete sets by dragging them to the Trash button in the Actions palette. Alternatively, you can select the command, action, or set you want to delete and choose the Delete option in the Actions palette menu, or click on the Trash button and OK the deletion. You can delete multiple Action palette items by pressing Option on the Mac or either Shift or Control in Windows to select multiple items and then proceed with one of the delete procedures.

Recording Actions

In addition to the many actions that are supplied with the Photoshop application and any other actions you may import from third-party suppliers, you can create your own actions.

> *Note: As you record new actions, you need to pay attention to application specifications such as the measurements units specified in the preferences; the foreground and background colors; a file's format, resolution, and color mode; as well as which layer is selected, because those specifications will be used by the action when it is played back.*

Creating New Actions

To create a new action, open an image to which you want to apply the commands and operations that you will record as an action, and then choose New Action from the Actions palette menu or click on the New Action button (as shown in Figure 11.5).

Figure 11.5 The New Action button in the Actions palette.

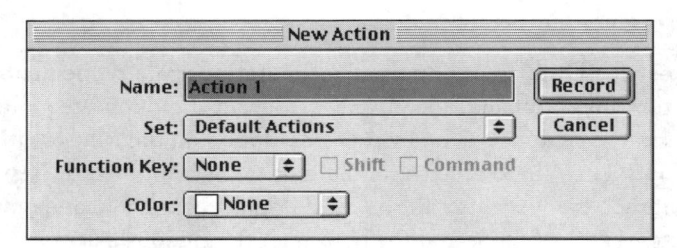

Figure 11.6 The New Action dialog box.

The New Action dialog box (shown in Figure 11.6) is basically the same as the Action Options dialog box, which was described previously in this chapter. Here, you can name the new action or accept the default name, assign the action to an existing set, assign the action to a Function key (with or without the Shift or Cmd/Ctrl modifiers), and specify a color to be used for the action's button in Button mode.

Recording New Actions

Clicking on Record in the New Action dialog box starts the recording process and turns the Record button at the bottom of the Actions palette red. Now, you just go on and choose commands and apply operations to the image. Photoshop "records" what you do, saving each specific command and operation. Photoshop actually performs the operations that you record, so you should rehearse the operations and/or perform them on an expendable file.

While you're recording, if you cancel an operation in a dialog box, that operation is not recorded. You can proceed to another operation.

If you enter a file name in the Save As or Save A Copy dialog boxes, that name is applied to all files to which the action is applied. You should leave the naming text area blank so that Photoshop either uses the same name or adds "copy" to the file's name. You can specify a new path to a different folder without entering a new file name.

Click on the Stop button when you complete the operations.

Inserting Paths In An Action

If you want to include a path in an action, select a path and choose the Insert Path command from the Actions palette menu.

Working With Actions And Automation

Including Nonrecordable Menu Commands In An Action

You can insert a stop for many of the nonrecordable commands in the pull-down menus, including those in the View and Window menus, by using the Insert Menu Item included in the Actions palette menu. When the action is played, it performs the command if it doesn't have a dialog box or stops at that command and waits for you to enter values in a dialog box or okay the command.

You can also use this feature to insert any recordable menu command.

The Insert Menu Item dialog box even includes a search feature. Enter a partial name for the command you want, and click on the Find button. You can also pull down the menus and drag to the command you want.

Inserting Pauses In An Action

Inserting pauses—stops—in an action allows you the stop the playback of an action to view its effect on an image, to display a message to yourself, or maybe to perform some nonrecordable operation, such as painting, and then continue the playback of the action. Strangely enough, though, you can't do anything in Photoshop when the stop stops the action other than clicking on Stop, which stops the action (after which you can restart the action from that point), or clicking on Continue, which continues the action. If you want to paint or perform some other nonrecordable action, you could just as easily create an action that leads up to that point and another action that you start when you're done with that nonrecordable action.

Insert a stop by selecting an action or command after which to insert the stop and choosing Insert Stop from the Actions palette menu.

When the Record Stop dialog box opens, you have the opportunity to enter any message you want to appear when the action reaches that stop. Check the Allow Continue checkbox to add the Continue button to the stop's alert window; otherwise, any stop you record without a message only stops the action cold, and a stop with a message has only a Stop button.

Editing Actions

You don't have to worry about recording an action perfectly the first time. Even after recording, you can record new commands in an action or change the commands previously recorded in an action. Remember, you can also rearrange the commands in an action by dragging their names in the Actions palette.

Adding New Actions To A Previously Recorded Action

You can record new commands in a specific place in an action or at the end of the action.

To record a new command from a specific place, select the name of a command after which you want to add the new command, click on the Record button or choose Start Recording from the Actions palette menu, and then perform the command or operation you want to insert. Click on the Stop button when you are done. The new command is then inserted after the command you selected. To add a new command at the end of an action, select the name of the action from the Actions palette, click on the Record button or choose Start Recording from the Actions palette menu, and then perform the command or operation you want to insert. Click on the Stop button when you are done. The new command is then added at the end of the action you selected.

Rerecording Previously Recorded Actions And Commands

You can change the settings and values of previously recorded actions and commands by using the Record Again command in the Actions palette menu. This command essentially zips through an action or command and seeks out those dialog boxes and modal tools that could be altered. It stops when it reaches them, allowing you to make any changes or to continue on to the next.

Playing Actions

Playing a recorded command, action, or set performs the operations that are included in that command, action, or set. You can choose to play actions as they were recorded, you can start the playback of an action at any of its recorded commands, you can play back entire sets, you can skip any commands in an action, or you can even play just one of the commands in an action. Also, you can apply an action to an entire folder—batch—of files without even opening them.

> *Note: Remember that Photoshop offers only one Undo and the number of states you have specified to be included in the History palette. If an action includes a number of operations, you may want to make a snapshot of the image before you play back the action, just in case you want to return to the pre-action state. (The History palette is discussed in Chapter 3.)*

Playing Actions As They Were Recorded

To play back an action or set, select one and either click on the Play button in the Actions palette or choose Play from the Actions palette menu. To start the playback of an action from a point other than the beginning, click on the name of the command where you want playback to begin, and then either click on the Play button in the Actions palette or choose Play from the Actions palette menu.

To play back only one command, drag the name of the command onto the Play button in the Actions palette. Alternately, you can select that command and then press Cmd/Ctrl as you choose Play from the Actions palette menu, as you double-click on the command's name, or as you click on the Play button in the Actions palette.

Skipping Recorded Commands In An Action

The checkmarks to the left of the commands', actions', and sets' names in the Actions palette indicate whether a specific command, action, or set will be included during playback. The checkmarks to the left of the names of the actions turn red if any command is excluded from the playback of that action, and the checkmarks to the left of the names of the sets turn red if any command or action is to be excluded from the playback of that set.

To prevent the playback of a command or action, click on the checkmark of that command or action to exclude it from playback. To exclude all commands but that one, press Option/Alt as you click on its checkmark, after which you can repeat that procedure to include all the commands. You can also include all commands in an action or set by clicking on the red checkmark.

Setting A Playback Speed

You can choose from three playback "speeds" for your actions. Select a speed by choosing Playback Options from the Actions palette menu.

The following are the playback speeds for actions:

- **Accelerated** Plays back the actions at normal speed.
- **Step By Step** Plays back the actions at normal speed, but shows you the new state in between each command.
- **Pause** Stops the playback for a period of 1 to 60 seconds, according to the value you enter.

Applying Actions To Batches Of Files

You can apply the playback of an action or set to multiple files by choosing File|Automate|Batch. The files must be in the same folder, at the same level. Batch processing can process multiple files and then leave them open, close them, or leave the originals intact and send modified copies to another folder. You can include the Save As or Save A Copy in an action to convert files to different file formats. You can also apply multiple actions to a batch of files by creating an action that includes the File|Automate|Batch command for each of the other actions you want.

Choosing File|Automate|Batch opens the Batch dialog box (as shown in Figure 11.7). The following are the options for Batch processing:

➤ **Play|Set** Select the set that contains the action you want.

➤ **Play|Action** Select the action that you want.

➤ **Source** Select the Folder selection in the Source option menu to specify the location of the folder of files to which the action will be applied.

Click on the Choose button to browse and select the desired folder.

Select the Import selection in the Source option menu when you're using batch processing to import image files from a scanner or digital camera. Your scanner or digital camera must support this option, or you may need a plug-in.

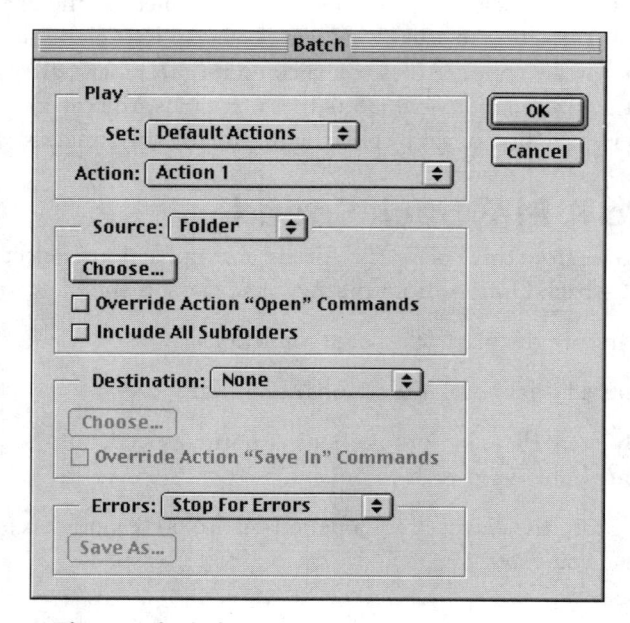

Figure 11.7 The Batch dialog box.

- **Override Action "Open" Commands** Select this option to ignore any Open commands that may have been recorded with the action.

- **Include All Subfolders** Select this option to tell Photoshop to open files even in subfolders located in the selected folder.

- **Destination** Choose an option for the disposition of the adjusted files. None leaves the files open and unsaved, Save And Close saves and closes files, and Folder saves the files to a new location. Click on the Choose button to browse and select the desired folder.

- **Override Action "Save In" Commands** Select this option to ignore any Save As or Save A Copy commands that may have been recorded with the action.

- **Errors** Specify how Photoshop will respond to errors while processing. Stop For Errors stops the batch processing so that you can see and respond to the error message, and Log Errors To File continues processing but saves the errors to a file and alerts you that errors occurred. Selecting Log Errors To File activates the Save As button, and you define a name and location for the errors file.

Using Automation Assistants And Wizards

Photoshop 5 also includes several automation assistants (on the Mac) and automation wizards (in Windows) that perform a series of specific operations—from just one dialog box—to produce different results. You can access these assistants/wizards by choosing File|Automate.

The following automation assistants/wizards are supplied with Photoshop:

- **Conditional Mode Change** Converts image files from one color mode to another based on their original color mode. This assistant/wizard is particularly useful when recorded in actions, where it can convert images on the fly. Choosing File|Automate|Conditional Mode Change opens the Conditional Mode Change dialog box (shown in Figure 11.8), where you can specify what source modes are automatically converted to what target mode. You can select as many source modes as you want.

- **Contact Sheet** Produces a page-layout index of the images in a folder (the images must all be closed). Choosing File|Automate|Contact Sheet opens the Contact Sheet dialog box (shown in Figure 11.9), where you select the source folder (Source); specify the page size, resolution, color mode, and arrangement options for the finished contact sheet (Contact

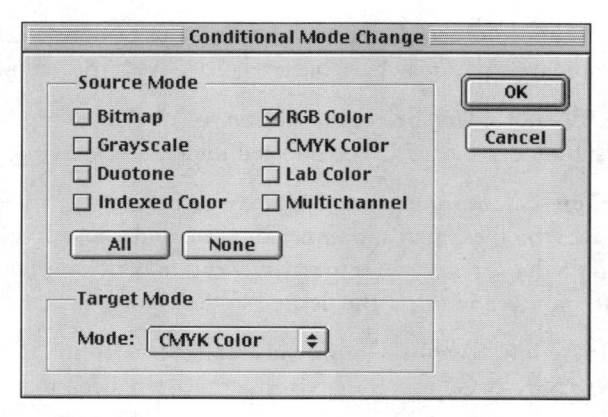

Figure 11.8 The Conditional Mode Change dialog box.

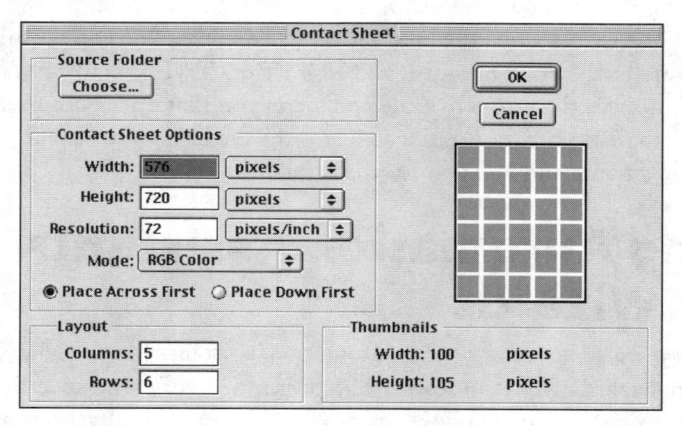

Figure 11.9 The Contact Sheet dialog box.

Sheet Options); and the number of columns and rows of image thumbnails (Layout), which determines the size of the thumbnails (Thumbnails).

➤ **Fit Image** Automatically resamples an image to fit within one or both of the parameters you enter in the Fit Image dialog box (shown in Figure 11.10), without affecting the image's aspect ratio.

Figure 11.10 The Fit Image dialog box.

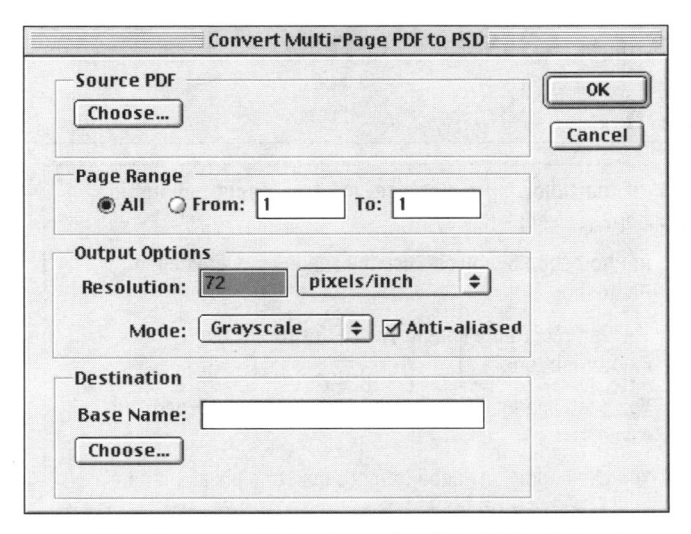

Figure 11.11 The Convert Multi-Page PDF To PSD dialog box.

➤ **Multi-Page PDF To PSD** Automatically opens an individual Photoshop (PSD) file for each page of a PDF-format file with multiple pages, saving you the hassle of having to open each page separately by choosing File|Open. From the Convert Multi-Page PDF To PSD dialog box (shown in Figure 11.11), you select the file you want to open (Source PDF), the pages you want to open (Page Range), the resolution and mode you want with or without anti-aliasing (Output Options), and the base name of the files to be created (Destination). Photoshop opens a new file for each page of the document and names it according to the base name, adding a numerical suffix to that name for each page.

Photoshop also supports some additional external automation through AppleScript on the Mac and OLE Automation in Windows. These features are discussed on the Adobe Web site.

Practice Questions

Question 1

> Which of the following statements are true about actions in Photoshop? (Select all that apply.)
>
> ☐ a. In Photoshop 5, you can use the actions you created in Photoshop 4.
>
> ☐ b. You can record the editing you perform with the Paintbrush tool.
>
> ☐ c. You can't change an action after it has been recorded and saved.
>
> ☐ d. You can't apply an action to more than one file at a time,

Only answer a is correct. Although you can use the Photoshop 4 actions in Photoshop 5, you can't use Photoshop 5 actions in Photoshop 4. You can record any of the painting tools, you can edit an action at any time after you record and save it, and you can use batch processing to apply an action to more than one file at a time.

Question 2

> What does a red checkmark mean if it appears next to an action's name in the Actions palette?
>
> ○ a. A problem occurred when recording that action.
>
> ○ b. The action won't be included in playback.
>
> ○ c. A command in that action won't be included in playback.
>
> ○ d. Nothing; all action checkmarks are red.

Answer c is correct.

Question 3

> If you want to stop an action at one specific command's dialog box to enter new values during playback, what do you do?
>
> ○ a. Click on the checkmark next to the command's name in the Actions palette.
>
> ○ b. Make sure that the checkmark next to the action's name in the Actions palette is red.
>
> ○ c. Click on the little dialog box icon next to the command's name in the Actions palette.
>
> ○ d. Click on the empty box immediately to the left of the command's name in the Actions palette.

Answer d is correct. Modal control stops an action at the dialog box of a particular command. When modal control is activated for a command, you see a little dialog box icon immediately to the left of the command's name in the Actions palette. If the little dialog box is there, and you click on it, you turn off modal control, and the command applies the values entered during recording.

Question 4

> If you want to edit an action while you have the Actions palette set to Button mode, what do you do?
>
> ○ a. Select an action and edit it as you normally would.
>
> ○ b. Select an action and choose Edit Action from the Actions palette menu.
>
> ○ c. Turn off Button mode in the Actions palette menu.
>
> ○ d. Make sure the action you want to edit hasn't been locked.

Answer c is correct. You can't edit, rearrange, or record actions in Button mode.

Question 5

What happens when you press Option/Alt and drag a command to another position in the Actions palette?

- ○ a. The command is moved to that new position, and the Actions Options dialog box opens.
- ○ b. The command is automatically saved to the preferences file.
- ○ c. The command is duplicated.
- ○ d. The command is moved to that new position and automatically set to modal control.

Answer c is correct.

Question 6

Which command allows you to record a space for a nonrecordable operation?

- ○ a. Insert Nonrecordable Item in the Actions palette menu
- ○ b. Insert Menu Item in the Actions palette menu
- ○ c. Insert Stop in the Actions palette menu
- ○ d. Insert Path in the Actions palette menu

Answer b is correct.

Question 7

What do you do when you want to record a new command at the end of an action?

- ○ a. Click on the name of the last command in the action and start recording.
- ○ b. Click on the name of the action and start recording.
- ○ c. Click on the name of the last command in the action, and choose Start Recording from the Actions palette menu.
- ○ d. Click on the name of the action, and choose Start Recording from the Actions palette menu.

All these answers are correct.

Question 8

> Which of the following playback speeds plays back an action at "normal" speed?
>
> ○ a. As Recorded
> ○ b. Accelerated
> ○ c. Step By Step
> ○ d. Pause

Answer b is correct.

Question 9

> In which of the following areas of the Batch dialog box is "Folder" an option? (Select all that apply.)
>
> ❏ a. Play
> ❏ b. Source
> ❏ c. Destination
> ❏ d. Errors

The correct answers are b and c. You can select a folder from which to process all the image files in the Source area, and you can specify a folder to which to copy processed files in the Destination area.

Question 10

> In which of the following areas of the Multi-Page PDF To PSD dialog box do you specify the number of PSD image files you want the PDF file opened into?
>
> ○ a. Source PDF
> ○ b. Page Range
> ○ c. Output Options
> ○ d. Destination

Answer b is correct. The Multi-Page PDF To PSD assistant/wizard automatically opens (as an individual PSD file) each page of the PDF file you specify in the Page Range area. The number of pages you select for opening will determine the total number of PDF files that will be created.

Need To Know More?

London, Sherry and Dave Xenakis: *Photoshop 5 In Depth*. The Coriolis Group. ISBN 1-57610-293-9. Actions are presented starting on page 52.

McClelland, Deke: *Macworld Photoshop 5 Bible*. IDG Books Worldwide, Inc. ISBN 0-7645-3231-6. Deke refers to actions as *scripts* and discusses them starting on page 94.

Printing From Photoshop

Terms and concepts you'll need to understand:

- √ Color separations
- √ Halftones
- √ Trapping
- √ Page setup
- √ Screen
- √ Calibration bars
- √ Registration marks
- √ Crop marks
- √ Emulsion down
- √ Space
- √ Monotones
- √ Duotones
- √ Tritones
- √ Quadtones
- √ Duotone presets

Techniques you'll need to master:

- √ Converting images to CMYK
- √ Accessing the Page Setup dialog box
- √ Specifying halftone screen options
- √ Specifying output options
- √ Converting images to other color spaces when printing
- √ Trapping colors
- √ Creating duotones
- √ Editing duotones
- √ Locating and loading duotone presets
- √ Selecting duotone inks
- √ Editing duotone curves
- √ Printing and exporting duotone images

To print an image from Photoshop onto paper using a printing press, you must first prepare the image for the printing process. This chapter presents the process of preparing Photoshop images for printing and associated production processes. You should know how to determine the optimum scanning resolution and file size for your images and that calibration of your system is the first step in producing image output that appears as you expect. Resolution is discussed in Chapter 5, and calibration and other output preparations are discussed in Chapter 4.

Before any four-color image can be printed on a commercial press, the colors of the image must be separated. These *color separations* produce the individual printing plates that apply the colored inks appropriately to reproduce the images you have created and edited in Photoshop. Remember that the four process colors are cyan (C), magenta (M), yellow (Y), and black (K) and that Photoshop generates four separate positive or negative images, one for each of those colors of ink—and, of course, one each for any spot colors you have applied. (Color theory is discussed in Chapter 4.)

More frequently these days, images are output directly to film as negatives used to make printing plates, whether directly from Photoshop or from a page-layout or other graphics program. You also can output an image as a positive to paper, from which printing plates will be created eventually.

Two of the most important printing concepts that you must understand are halftones and color trapping. Halftones are discussed in detail in the section called "Determining The Appropriate Scanning Resolution" in Chapter 5. You should know the concepts, guidelines, and principles associated with halftones. Trapping is discussed later in this chapter.

Converting Images To CMYK For Printing

After you finish editing and are ready to output an image as color separations to be used for four-color printing, you must convert the image to CMYK. Photoshop can perform this task during printing, as described in the following sections. Because of possible color changes due to the differences in the gamuts of different color spaces, you might want to control much of the conversion process manually.

Managing color for accurate reproduction is discussed in detail in Chapter 4. Remember that the steps and options for previewing CMYK color and possible out-of-gamut colors, described in Chapter 4, include using the following commands and tools:

➤ View|Preview|CMYK

➤ View|Gamut Warning

- Warning Triangles in the Info palette, Color Picker, and Color Palette
- Color Samplers and the Info Palette

Using the preceding tools and commands, you can preview the CMYK colors that will be created from the colors in the other color mode in which you are working. You can then specify color changes rather than accept the colors created by Photoshop.

You should be familiar with the options and settings of the CMYK setup, also described in Chapter 4.

Note these important guidelines for converting files to and from CMYK:

- Always save a copy of the file from which you convert to CMYK in case you aren't satisfied with the conversion results and want to reconfigure the CMYK setup to convert the image again.
- Don't convert images back and forth from RGB to CMYK because you'll lose color integrity as the color values are rounded for calculation each time.
- All images are first converted to the Lab mode and then to CMYK.
- While you're working with CMYK images on an RGB monitor, Photoshop must convert the color information to RGB for display, slowing processing times but not affecting the data in the file.

Printing From Photoshop

Of course, you can print simply from Photoshop to a composite laser or other desktop printer. You can also print Photoshop files to high-end imagesetters as positive or negative film or as paper output. Regardless of where you are sending your files, however, you must tell Photoshop how to handle the file as it is output.

To prepare a file for printing, you first open the Page Setup dialog box by choosing File|Page Setup (Shift+Cmd+P/Shift+Ctrl+P); then you can specify printing options. The printer, printer driver, and/or operating system you are using determines the specific look of the Page Setup and Print dialog boxes, but Photoshop-specific options appear, regardless of the printer driver.

The generic options commonly found in Page Setup dialog boxes include the following:

- **Paper Size** Determines the size of the paper sheet on which the printer will print your image. Commonly includes radio buttons for selecting common paper sizes and a custom-sizing option.

► **Orientation** Determines whether your file will print with the long edge of the sheet oriented vertically (portrait) or horizontally (landscape). This choice is usually pictured with some sort of icon so that you can easily identify the option you want.

► **Scale** Allows you to print the image at other than the default 100-percent size.

► **Properties/Options** Opens another dialog box for other printer-specific settings and/or options.

The options added by Photoshop to Page Setup dialog boxes include the following:

► **Screen** Opens the Halftone Screens dialog box (as shown in Figure 12.1). Here, you specify the settings and options you want an output device to use for your image file. The settings in the Halftone Screens dialog box apply only when you're sending an image directly from Photoshop to an output device. You should consult your printer documentation for more information about the optimum halftone screen settings for that particular device or contact your service bureau or printer for the recommended settings.

The following are the Halftone Screens dialog box options:

► **Use Printer's Default Screens** Click on this option to use the default halftone screen settings of the output device or to toggle on the halftone screen attributes available in this dialog box.

► **Ink** Select one of the separate color channels—plates—available for this particular image for which you want to specify halftone screen attributes. When you're preparing to print a grayscale image, the

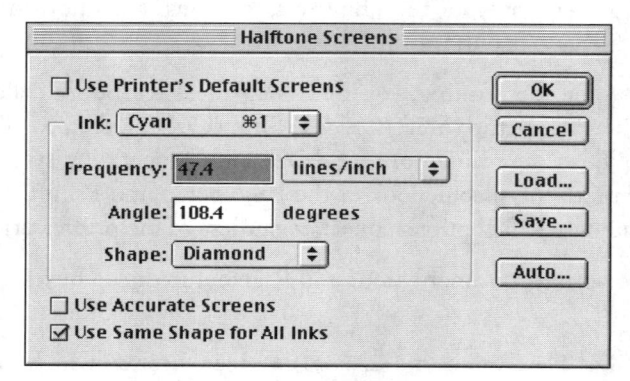

Figure 12.1 The Halftone Screens dialog box.

Halftone Screens dialog box doesn't access this menu, but you can change any of the other options in this dialog box.

> **TIP** Entering different halftone screen attributes for different plates or channels in the same image produces undesirable results.

- **Frequency** Specify a halftone screen frequency for the ink you selected above. Select either lines per inch or lines per centimeter from the option menu. Enter a value from 1 through 999.999.

- **Angle** Specify the position, in degrees, around a circle where the colored dots for that ink will print. Enter a value from -180 through 180.

- **Shape** Select a dot shape from the option menu, or select Custom to specify a custom dot shape.

- **Use Accurate Screens** Click on this option when you're printing to a PostScript Level 2 or higher output device or a device equipped with an Emerald controller and you want Photoshop to use the correct halftone screen attributes from the device automatically.

- **Use Same Shape For All Inks** Click on this option to apply the selected dot shape to all of the inks.

- **Load** Click on this button to load halftone screen attributes saved from this or another file. You can load the current default halftone screen attributes by pressing Option/Alt to change the Load button to the <-Default button.

- **Save** Click on this button to save the halftone screen attributes from this file to disk. You can save the current halftone screen attributes as the new default attributes by pressing Option/Alt to change the Save button to the ->Default button.

- **Auto** Click on this button to have Photoshop automatically determine the most appropriate halftone screen attributes for each ink.

- **Border** Prints a black border the width of which you specify when the Border dialog box opens.

- **Transfer** Opens the Transfer Functions dialog box, where you specify the options for transfer functions. Transfer functions are discussed in Chapter 4.

- **Bleed** Prints the crop marks inside the image area, which would be appropriate for full-bleed printing, where the image is printed outside the final page size so that the image completely covers the visible paper on a particular page.

- **Background** Prints a specific color, which you choose from the Color Picker, for the area outside the image area.

- **Caption** Prints any text entered in the Caption section of the File Info dialog box in 9-point Helvetica. Entering file info is discussed in Chapter 5.

- **Calibration Bars** Prints color calibration bars just outside the image area. Prints a grayscale bar graduated in 11 steps on grayscale images and (when printing color images) prints on the black plate. When you're printing color images, this option prints a progressive color bar on the right of the image and a gradient tint bar on the left of the image.

- **Registration Marks** Prints the registration marks used by print operators to align the different plates.

- **Corner Crop Marks** Prints the marks indicating the final page size, only on the corners.

- **Center Crop Marks** Prints the marks indicating the final page size, only at the centers of the vertical and horizontal limits of the image.

> **TIP** You can print the Corner Crop Marks and the Center Crop Marks individually, both at the same time, or neither.

- **Labels** Prints the name of the image and the name of the color channel with the image.

- **Negative** Prints the image as a negative.

- **Emulsion Down** Prints the image with the image right-reading when the emulsion side of the film or paper is away from you as you read it.

- **Interpolation** Automatically resamples up an image that is smaller than its print size. Resampling and interpolation are discussed in Chapter 6.

After you set the Page Setup dialog box as you want, you are ready to print. Choose File|Print (Cmd+P/Ctrl+P) to access the Print dialog box. Again, the appearance of this dialog box depends on the printer, printer driver, and/or operating system you are using.

Photoshop adds the following options to the Print dialog box:

➤ **Print Selected Area** You can actually print only a portion of an image by first selecting a rectangular area before accessing the Print dialog box. In this case, the Print Selected Area option is available, and you can print only that selected area.

➤ **Space** If your image is already in CMYK or Multichannel mode, you can specify the printing of color separations here. If you are in Indexed Color, RGB, CMYK, or Lab mode, you can convert the color mode of the image for printing only by selecting one of the modes available in the Space option menu. Grayscale images can only be converted to another gamma setting. Multichannel mode images can be printed as separations or converted to RGB.

➤ **Printer Color Management/PostScript Color Management** You can choose to use the printer's specific color space by selecting this option, which either is Printer Color Management or PostScript Color Management, depending on the type of printer to which you are printing. You can print CMYK images to PostScript Level 3 printers with PostScript Color Management, but you must convert a CMYK image to Lab Color to print with PostScript Color Management to a PostScript Level 2 printer.

Trapping Colors

Trapping, or color trapping, is the practice of slightly overlapping printed colors to prevent any white paper from showing through if the respective plates are misaligned. Trapping can actually lower the quality of photographic images, and it is usually necessary only when you add overprints of spot colors or other areas of solid colors to your photographic images. Trapping is another area in which you should consult with your service bureau or printer for specifications.

The trapping option is available only for images in CMYK mode. To specify the amount of overlap you want, choose Image|Trap to open the Trap dialog box, where you enter an amount between 1 and 10 and specify pixels, points, or millimeters for the measurement unit.

Printing Color Separations From Other Applications

As described earlier in this chapter, printing color separations for CMYK and Multichannel images is as simple as selecting the Separations option from the Space option menu in the Print dialog box. However, if you are planning to print an image with spot color channels as separations from another application, you must save the file in the DCS 2.0 format, which retains the spot color channels. (Spot color is discussed in Chapter 10, and file formats are discussed in Chapter 5.)

Creating And Printing Duotones

Duotone is a generic name for a grayscale image that is tinted with one to four colors for special effect. Among other effects, this process can increase the tonal range of grayscale images, simulate the appearance of black-and-white photographs that have been hand-tinted, or produce images that appear to have discolored with age. You also can use duotones to improve the printed appearance of untinted grayscale images by printing the images with more than one black plate.

A grayscale image printed with one color other than black is a *monotone*, whereas *duotones*, *tritones*, and *quadtones* are grayscale images printed with two, three, and four colors, respectively.

You work with duotones in Photoshop's Duotone color mode. To convert an image to Duotone mode, you must first convert it to Grayscale mode. After an image is converted to Duotone mode, you manipulate its separate colors in the Duotone Options dialog box (see Figure 12.2), not in the Channels palette.

If you want to view the separate colors of a Duotone mode image as color channels, you can convert a Duotone mode image to Multichannel mode, which separates the colors into color channels. Remember, however, that you cannot convert a Multichannel mode image to the Duotone mode. So, you should use

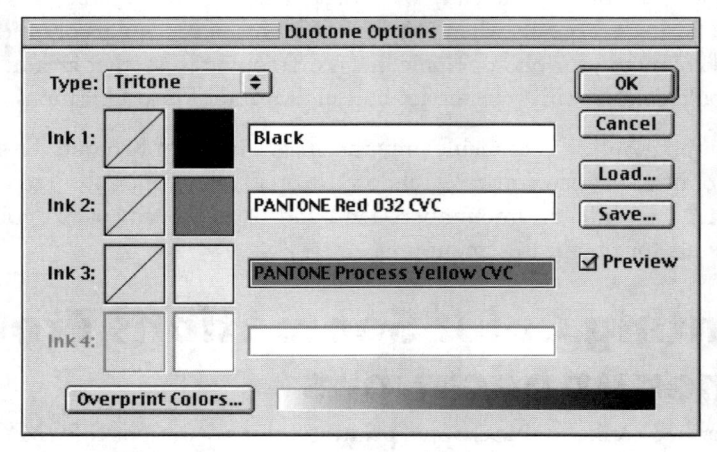

Figure 12.2 The Duotone Options dialog box for a tritone.

the Multichannel mode only to view the color channels, and then revert to the duotone state of the image to adjust the colors in the Duotone Options dialog box.

In one instance, however, you may want to convert a Duotone mode image to Multichannel mode. To apply a duotone effect to only a small part of an image, you could produce the color effect you want in the Duotone mode and then convert the image to Multichannel mode, and finally clear away the image areas where you don't want the duotone effect, in all but the black channel, preserving a smaller area of duotone effect that is surrounded by grayscale. (You can, of course, apply this process by using any combination of the color channels in the Multichannel image.)

Creating Duotones

After you convert an image to grayscale, you can convert it to duotone by choosing Image|Mode|Duotone. The Duotone Options dialog box opens (see Figure 12.2). Selecting the Preview option updates the image window as you make changes to the colors and curves in the Duotone Options dialog box. The color bar at the bottom of the Duotone Options dialog box previews the range of color that will be applied to the image based on the settings you make.

The steps for creating and editing duotones in the Duotone Options dialog box are as follow:

1. Select a duotone type from the Type option menu. The duotone type you select determines how many of the ink-color control areas will be activated in the Duotone Options dialog box.

    Note: Adobe supplies a number of Duotone Presets with the application, and they are located in the Adobe Photoshop 5/Goodies/Duotone Presets folder. You can load them, third-party presets, or your own saved presets by clicking on the Load button.

2. Set the color for each ink by clicking on the color swatch for each ink and then selecting a color from the Custom Colors dialog box. Although you can name each color any name you choose, if you are printing the image via a printing press, leaving the color name after its custom color will help the press operators match the proper ink and plate.

    Note: When you output a Duotone from Photoshop, Photoshop creates printing screens based on the inks you specify in the Duotone Options dialog box and their specific order, from 1 to 4 according to the color controls in the dialog box. Consequently, to best prepare the file for printing optimum colors, you should set the darkest color at 1 and set progressively lighter inks at progressively higher numbers.

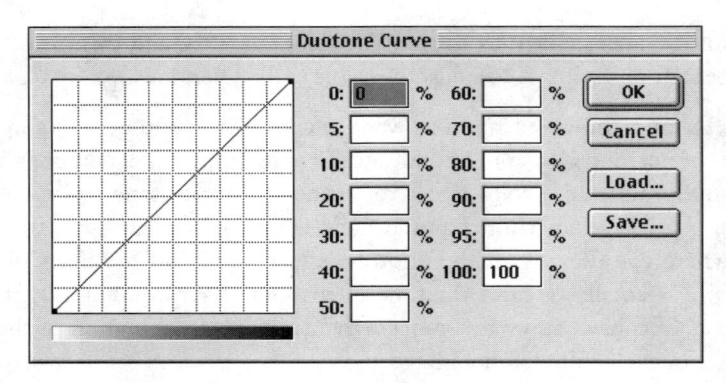

Figure 12.3 The Duotone Curve dialog box.

3. Click on the curve icon to adjust the distribution of each ink color by manipulating its curve in the Duotone Curve dialog box (shown in Figure 12.3). You can specify the ink intensity of 13 different points on the curve either by clicking on the curve and dragging the curve points or by entering percentage values in the respective values boxes. As the grayscale bar at the bottom of the dialog box indicates, highlights are at the bottom of the curve, and shadows are at the top of the curve. Displayed values indicate the percentage of ink that will be printed at specific areas of brightness values. For instance, a 30-percent value entered in the 50% values box prints the midtones of the image with 30-percent ink dots, which would lighten the image. Click on OK when you finish.

Note: Click on the Save button to save the curves you create in the Duotone Curve dialog box to use with another color or in another image. By clicking on the Load button, you can load curves saved from another color or another image—and you can even load curves saved from the Curves command dialog box. (The Curves command is discussed in Chapter 6.)

4. Click on the Overprint Colors button to open the Overprint Colors dialog box (shown in Figure 12.4). The Overprint Colors feature allows you to preview how the colors selected for a duotone will appear in areas where they overprint and then actually change the overprint color. As you can see in Figure 12.4, the Overprint Colors dialog box displays all possible combinations for the colors you have selected. To edit one of these combinations, click on the color swatch to select a new color for the overprint. Click on OK when you finish.

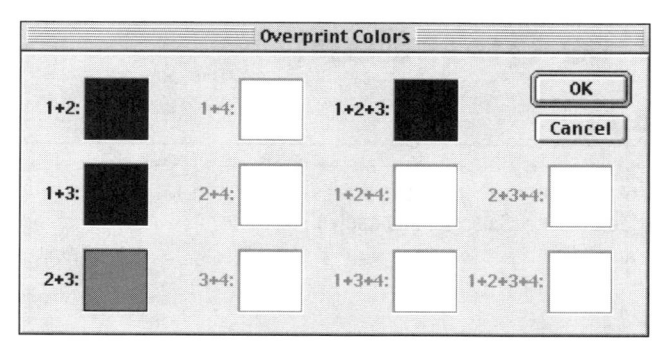

Figure 12.4 The Overprint Colors dialog box.

5. You can save the preset you have just created by clicking on the Save button.

6. Click on OK to create the Duotone.

Printing And Exporting Duotones

As noted previously, to assure optimum color saturation, order the inks in the Duotone Options dialog box with the colors ascending from the darkest color at 1 to the lightest color at the end of the list, whether it is 2, 3, or 4. If you comply with this rule, you can use the Auto option in the Halftone Screens dialog box (described in a previous section of this chapter) to define the screen frequency and screen angles that should produce the best printing results. (Remember, as described earlier in this chapter, you should also select Use Accurate Screens in the Auto Screens dialog box to print to a PostScript Level 2 or higher device or a device equipped with an Emerald controller.)

Although you don't have to convert a Duotone mode image to CMYK to produce the color separations, you must still select Separations from the Space option menu of the Print dialog box after choosing File|Print.

> **TIP** Converting a Duotone mode image to CMYK mode prior to printing converts the colors from any color system-specific inks to their CMYK equivalents, which could result in colors other than those for which you have planned.

Export duotones to other applications as EPS files.

Practice Questions

Question 1

> Which of these letters represents a process color, Cyan, Magenta, Yellow, and Black? (Select all that apply.)
>
> ☐ a. C
> ☐ b. M
> ☐ c. Y
> ☐ d. B

The correct answers are a, b, and c. Black is represented by the letter K.

Question 2

> How many plates will be generated for a CMYK image with two spot color channels?
>
> ○ a. 4
> ○ b. 5
> ○ c. 6

Answer c is correct.

Question 3

> What is a halftone?
>
> ○ a. An image in which the colors have been reduced by 50 percent for better saturation
> ○ b. An image for which only two plates are necessary to print all four colors
> ○ c. An image that has been converted to a grid of varying sized dots for printing on a press
> ○ d. An image that has half the tonal range of a calibration color file

Answer c is correct. Halftone is the generic term for any image that has been converted from continuous tones to a grid of varying sized dots for printing on a press.

Question 4

> Which of these abbreviations refers to the frequency of a halftone screen?
>
> ○ a. ppi
> ○ b. dpi
> ○ c. spi
> ○ d. lpi

Answer d is correct. The frequency of halftone screens is defined by the number of lines of halftone dots that fill every inch—lines per inch or lpi.

Question 5

> Which of the following marks on a plate indicate the final trim size of the printed image? (Select all that apply.)
>
> ❐ a. Calibration Bars
> ❐ b. Registration Marks
> ❐ c. Corner Crop Marks
> ❐ d. Center Crop Marks

Answers c and d are correct.

Question 6

> From which color modes can you create separations in the Print dialog box? (Select all that apply.)
>
> ❐ a. Grayscale
> ❐ b. RGB
> ❐ c. CMYK
> ❐ d. Indexed Color
> ❐ e. Lab
> ❐ f. Multichannel

The correct answers are c and f.

Question 7

In which of the following option menus of the Print dialog box is the Separations option?

○ a. Separation

○ b. Space

○ c. Output

○ d. Options

Answer b is correct.

Question 8

What is the name of a Duotone mode image that has black and two other colors?

○ a. Monotone

○ b. Duotone

○ c. Tritone

○ d. Quadtone

Answer c is correct. Black counts as one of the colors when you're counting up the colors for a Duotone mode image.

Question 9

For how many different spots on a duotone curve can you specify ink intensity?

○ a. 8

○ b. 13

○ c. 20

○ d. However many you set when you choose File|Preferences|Duotone Options

Answer b is correct.

Question 10

> In which file format should you save Duotone mode images that you intend to import into Adobe PageMaker?
>
> ○ a. DCS 2.0
>
> ○ b. Duotone
>
> ○ c. EPS
>
> ○ d. Multichannel

Answer c is correct.

Need To Know More?

London, Sherry and David Xenakis: *Photoshop 5 In Depth*. The Coriolis Group. ISBN 1-57610-293-9. Calibration and color reproduction are covered in Chapter 10, starting on page 653. Preparing files for printing is covered in detail in Chapter 9, starting on page 517. Duotones are discussed starting on page 575.

McClelland, Deke: *Macworld Photoshop 5 Bible*. IDG Books Worldwide, Inc. ISBN 0-7645-3231-6. Color management is the subject of Chapter 6, starting on page 191. Color trapping is discussed starting on page 245. The discussion of duotones follows on page 246.

Sample Test

You're ready to take the sample test. The following sample test is as accurate a representation as I've been able to make in terms of what you'll see in the exam room.

I covered many test-taking strategies in the Introduction and Chapter 1 of this book, and you should feel comfortable about your knowledge before you take this sample test. After you complete the sample test, you can turn to Chapter 14 to check your answers.

You get only one chance to be surprised in a book like this. No matter how much you pretend to be surprised, if you skim the answers and take the test again, it won't be the same. You can read the end of a novel, and then go back and experience some excitement by finding out how the ending was brought about. The experience isn't the same with a sample test. Do yourself a favor and try to re-create the real test-taking conditions as you take this sample test.

Give yourself 90 minutes to complete this sample exam. Sit at a table or desk, and try to make the table as clear of any other items as possible. Lay down a piece of paper and a pencil, and spend 5 minutes writing down the facts that you most want to have handy (from the Cram Sheet and your notes). Try to re-create the atmosphere of any exam rooms you may have been in and remember from your past. The more accurately you create a virtual final environment, the more comfortable you'll feel when your scheduled exam day comes around.

Picking The Right Answer

Go back and refresh your memory with the Introduction and Chapter 1, and think about the types of questions you're about to encounter. Keep in mind that the people creating the test (myself included) take a kind of twisted pleasure in making things difficult. I've been where you are, and I made it through, so you can, too!

Keep your eyes peeled for the following:

➤ **Words such as *best*, *required*, and *most appropriate*** These words are red flags telling you that the question may contain multiple possibilities, based on how an unstated industry standard might apply.

➤ **Long lists of commands** You can easily read these commands in the wrong order if you don't have your eyes focused. Write them on your scratch paper, and put numbers next to them to ensure the proper order.

➤ **Multiple answers** Remember that although the exam contains 67 questions, it has more like 75 to 80 correct answers. Some questions may require you to select more than one answer, and you won't get full credit for answers you miss.

Confusing Questions

By the time this test reaches your hands, many people have read it through, reviewed it, made suggestions, and researched every single word and punctuation mark. This test has been designed with psychology in mind and with a full knowledge of many other tests. If you are confused about a particular question, you can probably bet your next paycheck that the confusion was specifically designed into the question.

I found a number of questions on the exam that really *were* confusing. To that end, I tried to highlight these areas of knowledge in this book, and to give you my thoughts and how I analyzed the questions. In this version of the exam, I tried to cause you some confusion as well, but in a very specific manner.

Part of my preparation methodology is based on the idea that if you've read the book and you're feeling comfortable, you should have a fair amount of intuition going for you. Based on that assumption, I still want to throw a few curve balls at you so that you'll be somewhat familiar with the "Yikes!" feeling when it hits you in the real exam (it will!).

Just remember—trust your instincts. If you get some of my most confusing questions right, then you'll probably do extremely well on the Photoshop 5 exam. If you get them wrong, don't feel bad. The questions are *designed* to be difficult. After you check your answers by using Chapter 14's answer key, the likelihood that you'll remember where you got tripped up is far greater than before, and I've crammed just that much more into your head.

The Exam Framework

The questions you're about to work with have been organized in a general order. I made no attempt to follow the progression of this book, nor to follow any other sort of logical order. This exam is a general test of your overall knowledge of Photoshop 5.

Begin The Exam

From the time you complete your notes on the blank sheet of paper, you have 90 minutes to complete the test. Take your time, and imagine you're shipwrecked on a desert island and have all the time in the world. Read every word carefully, and then read the whole question a second time before you look at the responses.

Read each response on its own, and don't try to fit it in with the question. After you read each response as though it were a random statement of fact, go back and read the question one more time.

A common flaw in the human mind is that it immediately attempts to make sense out of incoming data. This flaw is often used against you on various exams. By reading the question on its own and then reading each response without thinking about the question, you overload the "surprise circuit." After your mind stops trying to puzzle over the question, you're ready to actually read the question as it stands.

Start your timer, and begin the exam now.

Question 1

When the Eyedropper tool is selected, which keyboard shortcut toggles to the Color Sampler tool?

○ a. Cmd/Ctrl

○ b. Option/Alt

○ c. Shift

○ d. Spacebar

Question 2

Which of the following operations can be performed on linked layers or created from linked layers? (Select the two best answers.)

❏ a. 3D Transform

❏ b. Align

❏ c. Merge

❏ d. Clipping Path

Question 3

What operations can be performed on a Type Layer while retaining its editability? (Select the two best answers.)

❏ a. Edit|Transform|Perspective

❏ b. Filter|Artistic|Poster Edges

❏ c. Edit|Transform|Scale

❏ d. Layer|Effects

Question 4

What is the selection loaded from the opaque areas of a layer called?

○ a. Alpha channel

○ b. Transparency mask

○ c. Layer mask

○ d. Opacity channel

Question 5

If you want to import a vector graphic from Adobe Illustrator into an open Photoshop image, which of these menu commands could you use? (Select all that apply.)

- ❑ a. Edit|Paste
- ❑ b. File|Place
- ❑ c. Drag from the Illustrator window to the Photoshop window
- ❑ d. File|Import
- ❑ e. File|Open

Question 6

Which of the following are color models used in Photoshop? (Select all that apply.)

- ❑ a. Lab
- ❑ b. RGB
- ❑ c. CMYK
- ❑ d. Bitmap

Question 7

Which one of the following Photoshop features specifically allows you to create additional plate negatives for more than the four process colors?

- ○ a. Alpha channels
- ○ b. Color channels
- ○ c. Spot color channels
- ○ d. Multi-separation channels

Question 8

What Photoshop command can you use to access a feature that allows you to preview color and tonal adjustments to specific layers of an image?

- ○ a. Image|Preview
- ○ b. Image|Adjust|Preview
- ○ c. Layer|New|Adjustment Layer
- ○ d. Layer|Adjust|Preview

Question 9

What are transfer functions?

- ○ a. Options that affect files that are transferred from Windows to Macintosh and vice versa
- ○ b. Dot gain compensations for files printed to a miscalibrated output device
- ○ c. File preferences that must be set before dragging and dropping between Photoshop and Illustrator
- ○ d. The total printing option settings that must be saved to the file when it is transferred from one computer or storage device to another

Question 10

What is the result if you convert an RGB mode image to Grayscale mode and then back to RGB mode?

- ○ a. The hues of the image's colors rasterize to 180 degrees opposite their original values.
- ○ b. The image's colors become more saturated.
- ○ c. The image looks the same as it did when it was originally in RGB mode.
- ○ d. The image looks the same as it did when it was in Grayscale mode.

Question 11

What are the factors that limit the number of layers allowed in an image?

- ❏ a. Memory
- ❏ b. Photoshop's 100-layer limit
- ❏ c. Processor speed
- ❏ d. Available storage space

Question 12

When you're using the Curves dialog box, which of the following shortcuts sets a point on the curves of all color channels except the composite channel?

- ○ a. Pressing Cmd/Ctrl and clicking on a color in the image window
- ○ b. Pressing Shift+Cmd/Shift+Ctrl and clicking on a color in the image window
- ○ c. Pressing Cmd/Ctrl and clicking on the grid area in the Curves dialog box
- ○ d. Pressing Shift+Cmd+Tab/Shift+Ctrl+Tab

Question 13

If you get an error message that an operation cannot be completed because of insufficient RAM, but you think you might have enough if you empty the buffers, which command do you choose? (Select the one best answer.)

- ○ a. File|Purge|All
- ○ b. Edit|Purge|Undo
- ○ c. File|Purge|Histories
- ○ d. File|Purge|Clipboard

Question 14

How does the mask created in the Quick Mask mode differ from masks created in the Channels palette? (Select all that apply.)

- ❏ a. You don't have to open the Channels palette to create and edit Quick Masks.
- ❏ b. You can use the Paintbrush tool to edit masks created in the Channels palette, but not Quick Masks.
- ❏ c. You can't save Quick Masks in the Channels palette.
- ❏ d. You can't change the color of the Quick Mask overlay.

Question 15

If you want to smooth the jagged edges of a vector-based graphic from an Adobe Illustrator file opened as a new Photoshop file by applying anti-aliasing, in which dialog box do you need to select Anti-Aliasing?

- ○ a. Rasterize Generic EPS Format
- ○ b. File Info
- ○ c. Layer Effects
- ○ d. Layer Options

Question 16

Which Cache Level setting turns off the Image Cache?

- ○ a. 0
- ○ b. 1
- ○ c. 4
- ○ d. 8

Question 17

When you're measuring an area in an image with the Measure tool, where do you see the associated numerical information?

- ○ a. Measure Options palette
- ○ b. Info palette
- ○ c. Toolbox
- ○ d. Next to the Measure tool icon in the image

Question 18

If you want to paint with a past state of an image, which tools can you use? (Select all that apply.)

- ❑ a. History Paintbrush
- ❑ b. Eraser tool
- ❑ c. Paintbrush
- ❑ d. History Stamp

Question 19

What happens when you press Option/Alt and drag an action to a new spot in the list of actions in the Actions palette?

- ○ a. The action is moved to the new spot, along with all its commands.
- ○ b. The action is moved to the new spot, but as a new, empty action.
- ○ c. The commands of that action are moved to the new spot, and you are prompted for a name for the new action.
- ○ d. The action is duplicated.

Question 20

How do you open all the pages of a PDF file at once, as separate Photoshop files? (Select all that apply.)

- ❒ a. Select the Open All Pages option when the Open PDF dialog box opens.
- ❒ b. Opening the file by choosing File|Open always opens all the pages of a PDF.
- ❒ c. You cannot open all the pages of a PDF file as separate Photoshop files.
- ❒ d. Choose File|Automate|Multi-Page PDF To PSD.

Question 21

When is it best **not to** resample an image? (Select the one best answer.)

- ○ a. When the image's dimensions remain the same and its resolution increases
- ○ b. When the image's resolution remains the same and its dimensions decrease
- ○ c. When the image's file size remains the same and its dimensions increase
- ○ d. When the image's file size remains the same and its resolution decreases

Question 22

What are the scanning ratios acceptable for determining optimum scanning resolution?

- ○ a. 1:1 and 1.5:1
- ○ b. 1.5:1 and 2:1
- ○ c. 133 lpi and 266 lpi
- ○ d. 85 lpi and 133 lpi

Question 23

Which of the following commands or options can be used or selected to help minimize file size?

- ❏ a. File|Reduce Size
- ❏ b. Layer|Flatten
- ❏ c. Exclude Non-Image Data
- ❏ d. Exclude Alpha Channels

Question 24

A color lookup table (CLUT) is generated when converting to which color mode?

- ○ a. Lab
- ○ b. Multichannel
- ○ c. Indexed Color
- ○ d. Bitmap

Question 25

Which of the following modes does not support any of the filters? (Select all that apply.)

- ❏ a. Bitmap
- ❏ b. Grayscale
- ❏ c. RGB
- ❏ d. CMYK
- ❏ e. Indexed Color
- ❏ f. Multichannel

Question 26

When you're making a selection with the Magnetic Lasso tool, which shortcut can you use to switch to the Polygon Lasso tool for the next section of the selection?

- ○ a. Releasing the mouse and then dragging to the next point
- ○ b. Releasing the mouse and then clicking on the next point
- ○ c. Pressing Option/Alt and dragging to the next point
- ○ d. Pressing Option/Alt and clicking on the next point

Question 27

Which of these commands allow you to alter the size of a selection by a certain number of pixels? (Select two.)

- ❏ a. Select|Grow
- ❏ b. Select|Modify|Expand
- ❏ c. Select|Similar
- ❏ d. Select|Modify|Contract

Question 28

Which of the following filters allows you to specify an amount of sharpening?

- ❏ a. Sharpen
- ❏ b. Sharpen More
- ❏ c. Sharpen Edges
- ❏ d. Unsharp Mask

Question 29

If you want to use the contents of a layer as a mask for the contents of other layers, but not all the layers in an image, which of the following is the best choice?

- ○ a. Transparency mask
- ○ b. Alpha channel
- ○ c. Clipping group
- ○ d. Clipping path

Question 30

What commands and shortcuts convert a selection border to a path? (Select all that apply.)

- ☐ a. Clicking on the Make Work Path button
- ☐ b. Pressing Option/Alt and clicking anywhere in the selection
- ☐ c. Pressing Cmd+Option/Ctrl+Alt and clicking on the path's thumbnail
- ☐ d. Clicking on the Make Selection button

Question 31

Which Blending mode multiplies or screens colors using a 50-percent gray threshold?

- ○ a. Multiply
- ○ b. Screen
- ○ c. Soft Light
- ○ d. Hard Light

Question 32

Which mode or feature should you use when you want to tint an entire image with a spot color? (Select the one best answer.)

- ○ a. Spot Color channel
- ○ b. Duotone mode
- ○ c. Multichannel mode

Question 33

What is a color called when it cannot be reproduced with the four process color inks of the CMYK printing process?

- ○ a. Custom
- ○ b. Out-of-gamut
- ○ c. Unprintable
- ○ d. Dithered

Question 34

Because the Magic Wand tool selects pixels of similar color only when they are adjacent, which command can you use after the Magic Wand tool to add pixels of similar color that are not adjacent?

- ○ a. Select|Grow
- ○ b. Select|Similar
- ○ c. Select|Inverse
- ○ d. Select|Distant

Question 35

Which of these Photoshop features applies color to adjacent areas of similar color? (Select the one best answer.)

- ○ a. Replace Color command
- ○ b. Color Range command
- ○ c. Paint Bucket tool
- ○ d. Gradient tool

Question 36

How do you create a selection border and then select a "frame" of pixels around that selection? (Select all that apply.)

- ☐ a. Create a selection and then press Shift to create another selection just inside or outside the original selection.
- ☐ b. Create a selection and then choose Select|Modify|Border.
- ☐ c. Create a selection and then choose Select|Modify|Frame.
- ☐ d. Create a selection and then choose Select|Inverse.

Question 37

What kind of application is Photoshop? (Select all that apply.)

- ☐ a. Bitmap image editing
- ☐ b. Painting
- ☐ c. Vector graphics
- ☐ d. Drawing

Question 38

How many file formats support Photoshop's layers?

- ○ a. one
- ○ b. two
- ○ c. four
- ○ d. six

Question 39

In which of the following color modes can you not work with color channels? (Select all that apply.)

- ☐ a. Bitmap
- ☐ b. Grayscale
- ☐ c. RGB
- ☐ d. CMYK
- ☐ e. Indexed Color
- ☐ f. Duotone
- ☐ g. Multichannel

Question 40

Which of the following statements are true about the Edit|Transform commands? (Select all that apply.)

- ☐ a. You must unlink layers to apply transformations.
- ☐ b. You can apply transformations to the background as layers.
- ☐ c. You can apply transformations to layer masks.
- ☐ d. Edit|Transform|3D Transform can be applied to selections.

Question 41

Which option or tool in the Color Range dialog box specifies the range of colors selected?

- ○ a. Selection
- ○ b. Fuzziness
- ○ c. Eyedropper
- ○ d. Invert

Question 42

Which of these features can you use to improve the contrast of an image by adjusting the brightness values of individual pixel-brightness levels? (Select two.)

- ☐ a. Curves
- ☐ b. Levels
- ☐ c. Brightness & Contrast
- ☐ d. Desaturate

Question 43

How many alpha channels and/or spot channels can you have in an RGB image?

- ○ a. 16
- ○ b. 21
- ○ c. 24
- ○ d. 100

Question 44

According to the standard rules of color trapping, which of the following CMYK inks spreads under all three of the other CMYK inks?

- ○ a. Cyan
- ○ b. Magenta
- ○ c. Yellow
- ○ d. Black

Question 45

In which of the following file formats can you save the editable type layer? (Select all that apply.)

- ☐ a. Photoshop (PSD)
- ☐ b. EPS
- ☐ c. Photoshop DCS
- ☐ d. TIFF
- ☐ e. GIF
- ☐ f. PICT

Question 46

What keystrokes toggle between the Standard mode and the Quick Mask mode, and between the Standard screen mode, the Full screen mode with menu bar, and the Full screen mode?

- ○ a. S and M
- ○ b. Q and S
- ○ c. F and Q
- ○ d. F and M

Question 47

Which of the following is **not** an option for specifying the rendering intent method to be used to convert the colors of an image to the color gamut of a printer specified with an ICC profile?

- ○ a. Perceptual (Images)
- ○ b. Saturation
- ○ c. Relative Colorimetric
- ○ d. Gray Component Replacement

Question 48

Where is the data in a scratch disk stored?

- ○ a. RAM
- ○ b. ROM
- ○ c. Hard disk
- ○ d. Scratch RAM

Question 49

Figure 13.1 Exhibit 1.

Based on the History palette pictured in Exhibit 1, what is the name of the state that is used by the Eraser tool when the Erase To History option is selected?

- ○ a. Bottles1
- ○ b. Open
- ○ c. Smudge Tool
- ○ d. Airbrush

Question 50

What feature that you can turn off in the Display & Cursors dialog box changes the entire monitor screen when you're previewing color and tonal adjustments of an image?

○ a. Accurate Screens

○ b. Screen Redraw

○ c. Color Table Animation

○ d. CLUT

Question 51

Which of these lossy compression methods is available when you're saving flattened Photoshop mode files? (Select all that apply.)

❐ a. RLE

❐ b. LZW

❐ c. ZIP

❐ d. JPEG

Question 52

With which file formats can you export an image that has a particular color defined as transparent for background transparency? (Select all that apply.)

❐ a. GIF

❐ b. GIF89a

❐ c. JPEG

❐ d. PNG

Question 53

In which of the following dialog boxes would you **not** see a histogram? (Select all that apply.)

- ❏ a. Histogram
- ❏ b. Levels
- ❏ c. Curves
- ❏ d. Threshold

Question 54

Which path-editing tool can be selected by pressing A?

- ○ a. Add anchor point
- ○ b. Delete anchor point
- ○ c. Convert anchor point
- ○ d. Direct Selection

Question 55

If you are exporting a file with a clipping path defined to protect areas of the image from printing on a non-PostScript printer, in which file format must you save the file? (Select all that apply.)

- ❏ a. Photoshop EPS
- ❏ b. DCS
- ❏ c. PICT
- ❏ d. TIFF

Question 56

With what option in the Layer Options dialog box can you specify how pixels with particular brightness levels will be combined with the visible underlying layers?

- ○ a. Opacity
- ○ b. Options
- ○ c. Mode
- ○ d. Blend If

Question 57

Which of the following mask types is an 8-bit (256-level) grayscale image that you can permanently save in the Channels palette so that you can use the mask again?

○ a. Quick mask

○ b. Layer mask

○ c. Alpha channel

○ d. Permanent mask

Question 58

With which of the following commands/features/operations can you convert an RGB image to grayscale while controlling how the individual colors affect the final appearance of the image? (Select all that apply.)

❏ a. Image|Mode|Grayscale

❏ b. Image|Adjust|Desaturate

❏ c. Image|Adjust|Grayscale Options

❏ d. Image|Adjust|Channel Mixer

Question 59

With which one of the following could you stop the playback of an action at the dialog box of a particular recorded command so that you can enter different values? (Select all that apply.)

❏ a. Modal Control

❏ b. Step By Step

❏ c. Pause

❏ d. Stop button

Question 60

With which one of the following can you apply an action or actions to a group of files at one time?

- ○ a. Batch in the Actions palette menu
- ○ b. File|Automate|Batch
- ○ c. Image|Adjust|Batch
- ○ d. Edit|Batch

Question 61

If your printer advises you to specify a line screen of 85 lpi, for which of these publication types are you most likely printing?

- ○ a. Low-quality jobs on porous paper
- ○ b. Newspaper
- ○ c. Four-color magazine
- ○ d. Fine art publication

Question 62

Which of the following has a bit depth of 1? (Select all that apply.)

- ❐ a. Bitmap image
- ❐ b. L*a*b model image
- ❐ c. Bitmap mode image
- ❐ d. Duotone mode image

Question 63

Select the Preserve Transparency option in the Layers palette if you want to perform which of these operations? (Select all that apply.)

- ❑ a. Replace a selection with transparency
- ❑ b. Use the Eraser tool to erase with transparency
- ❑ c. Apply color to only the opaque areas of a layer
- ❑ d. Blend a source layer to the transparent areas of a destination layer with the Apply Image command

Question 64

From the Space option in the Print dialog box, to which of these can you convert a Multichannel mode image when printing?

- ○ a. CMYK
- ○ b. Indexed Color
- ○ c. RGB
- ○ d. Duotone

Question 65

In which of the following dialog boxes is the Clipping option available? (Select all that apply.)

- ❑ a. Equalize
- ❑ b. Threshold
- ❑ c. Brightness/Contrast
- ❑ d. Variations

Question 66

In which filter submenu is the Despeckle filter located?

❍ a. Brush Strokes

❍ b. Other

❍ c. Pixelate

❍ d. Noise

Question 67

What key(s) do you press to copy a selection as you move it? (Select all that apply.)

❏ a. Cmd/Ctrl

❏ b. Option/Alt

❏ c. Shift+Cmd/Shift+Ctrl

❏ d. Cmd+Option/Ctrl+Alt

Answer Key To The Sample Test

The following are the answers to the questions presented in the sample test in Chapter 13.

Question 1

The correct answer is c. You place color samplers with the Color Sampler tool or by pressing Shift when the Eyedropper tool is selected.

Question 2

The correct answers are b and c. You can apply two-dimensional transformations to linked layers by choosing the Edit|Transform commands, but you cannot apply 3D transformations with the 3D Transform filter. You can create clipping groups with linked layers, but not clipping paths, which are created with paths, in the Paths palette. You can use the Layer|Align Linked options on linked layers, and you can use the Layer|Merge Linked option on linked layers.

Question 3

The correct answers are c and d. Although you can perform most of the Edit|Transform commands to a type layer, you can't apply Perspective or Distort. You can't apply any filters to the type layer without first rendering it as a regular layer, which also renders it uneditable. You can apply Layer Effects to a type layer and continue to edit the text.

Question 4

The correct answer is b. You load a transparency mask, which is a selection based on the nontransparent pixels of a layer, by pressing Cmd/Ctrl and clicking the layer or the thumbnail of the layer in the Layers palette.

Question 5

The correct answers are a and b. You can paste Illustrator artwork that has been cut or copied from the Illustrator file into an open Photoshop image. You choose File|Place to import an entire Illustrator file into an open Photoshop image. You can also drag and drop artwork from Illustrator to Photoshop, but this is not a menu command. The File|Open command opens an Illustrator file as a new Photoshop file.

Question 6

The correct answers are b and c. The RGB and CMYK color models are used in Photoshop, as is the L*a*b color model. Lab and Bitmap are color modes.

Question 7

The correct answer is c. Spot color channels are color channels created for additional colors to be applied during the printing process. You can create four-color images that have additional spot colors that are applied according to a spot color channel, or you can create Multichannel images that apply spot colors according to spot color channels.

Question 8

The correct answer is c. Adjustment layers allow you to make color and tonal adjustments, which affect all the visible layers underneath the adjustment layers. You can turn the adjustment layers on and off to preview the effects until you are satisfied with the adjustments, and then you can apply the adjustments by merging the layers or flattening the image.

Question 9

The correct answer is b. You can use the Transfer Functions settings in the Page Setup dialog box to compensate for otherwise uncorrectable dot gain problems when printing to a miscalibrated printer with ICC profiles.

Question 10

The correct answer is d. Converting an RGB image to Grayscale mode discards all the image's color information. Converting a Grayscale image to RGB mode creates three color channels with pixels that have values based on the brightness values in the grayscale image—grays. So, the image still looks like a grayscale image when it is converted back to RGB from Grayscale.

Question 11

The correct answers are a and b. Photoshop allows up to 100 layers in an image, but the actual number can be affected by the amount of RAM in your computer.

Question 12

The correct answer is b. Pressing Cmd/Ctrl and clicking on a color in the image window sets a point on the curve for the composite channel but not the other channels. Pressing Shift+Cmd/Shift+Ctrl while clicking on a color in the image window, however, sets a point on the curves of each of the color channels except the composite channel. Pressing Cmd/Ctrl and clicking on the grid area in the Curves dialog box deselects all the points on the curve, and pressing Shift+Cmd+Tab/Shift+Ctrl+Tab cycles backward through the points on the curve.

Question 13

The correct answer is b. You can purge the Undo buffer, the clipboard, the defined Pattern, the Histories, or all of them at once by using the Purge commands that are under the Edit menu—not the File menu. Because b is the only correctly listed command, it is the best answer.

Question 14

The correct answers are a and c. You create Quick Masks simply by clicking on the Quick Mask Mode button in the Toolbox, with or without an area selected. The areas covered by the colored overlay are protected from any effects you apply to the image, and the areas not covered by the colored overlay are a selection. You can then edit the Quick Mask as you would edit masks created in the Channels palette, with the painting and retouching tools—including the Paintbrush. You can change the color of the Quick Mask overlay by double-clicking on the Quick Mask Mode button or Standard Mode button in the Toolbox and selecting a color in the Quick Mask Options dialog box. You cannot save the temporary Quick Mask that appears in the Channels palette, but you can return to the Standard Mode, which turns the transparent areas of the Quick Mask into a selection, and then create a mask in the Channels palette from that selection.

Question 15

The correct answer is a. When you open an Adobe Illustrator file as a new Photoshop file, the Rasterize Generic EPS Format dialog box opens. Here, you can specify the size, resolution, and color mode to apply to the new file, as well as whether to apply anti-aliasing.

Question 16

The correct answer is b. By choosing File|Preferences|Image Cache (Mac) or File|Preferences|Memory & Image Cache (Windows), you can set the Cache Levels to any number from 1 through 8, where a setting of 1 essentially turns off the Image Cache.

Question 17

The correct answer is b. The numerical information gathered with the Measure tool is displayed in the Info palette.

Question 18

The correct answers are a and b. The History Paintbrush allows you to paint with a previous state of the image, as does selecting the Erase To History option in the Options palette of the Eraser tool.

Question 19

The correct answer is d. You can duplicate actions in the Actions palette by dragging them to the New Action button, selecting an action and choosing Duplicate from the Actions palette menu, or pressing Option/Alt and dragging an action to a new spot in the list of actions in the Actions palette.

Question 20

The correct answer is d. The Multi-Page PDF To PSD automation assistant/wizard opens all the pages of a PDF file as separate Photoshop (PSD) files.

Question 21

The correct answer is a. When you're using the Edit|File Size command, resampling an image rebuilds the image's file, either increasing or decreasing the amount of data used to represent the image. If you resample an image up to increase its resolution or dimensions, you force Photoshop to interpolate, during which it creates new pixels based on assumptions about the image, potentially decreasing the sharpness and image quality of the image. Resampling occurs only when the Resample Image option is selected. When Resample Image is not selected, you cannot change the resolution and dimensions independently. Consequently, resampling occurs only when Resample Image is selected and you increase either the resolution or the dimensions of the image independently of each other. Also, any time the file's size remains the same, no resampling occurred.

Question 22

The correct answer is b. To determine optimum scanning resolution, you should first determine the percentage of enlargement or reduction of the image from its original size to publication size. Multiply that percentage by the halftone screen frequency of the target publication, and then multiply that number by either 1.5 or 2.

Question 23

The correct answers are b, c, and d. The amount of data in both layers and alpha channels can contribute significantly to the size of a file, so flattening an image by choosing Layer|Flatten Image or the Flatten Image option of the Save A Copy dialog box or by selecting the Exclude Alpha Channels option in the Save A Copy dialog box can reduce the file's size. You can also select the Exclude Non-Image Data option in the Save A Copy dialog box to exclude everything except the actual pixel data.

Question 24

The correct answer is c. The color lookup table contains all the colors—up to 256—that are needed to render the image in Indexed Color mode.

Question 25

The correct answer is a. You cannot apply any of Photoshop's filters to images in the Bitmap mode.

Question 26

The correct answer is d. The shortcuts for switching from the Magnetic Lasso tool to the Polygon Lasso tool or the Freehand Lasso tool both begin by pressing Option/Alt, but then depend on how you proceed to select. When you select with the Polygon Lasso tool, you click one spot and then another spot, and when you select with the Freehand Lasso tool, you drag from one spot to another. So, when you're making a selection with the Magnetic Lasso tool, you switch to the Polygon Lasso tool by pressing Option/Alt and clicking the next point, and you switch to the Freehand Lasso tool by pressing Option/Alt and dragging to the next point.

Question 27

The correct answers are b and d. Select|Modify|Expand and Select|Modify|Contract either expand or contract the selection by a specific number of pixels that you enter immediately after choosing one of them. Select|Grow and Select|Similar both expand a selection by color, according to the Tolerance setting you have entered in the Options palette for the Magic Wand—not by a specified number of pixels.

Question 28

The correct answer is d. The Unsharp Mask filter, which Adobe recommends you use after resampling images, allows you to specify the amount of sharpening (Amount), as well as the distance around a pixel to seek edge pixels (Radius), and the amount of difference between the color values of pixels within that radius that will determine them as edge pixels (Threshold).

Question 29

The correct answer is c. By creating a clipping group, you can use the contents of the base layer of the clipping group as a mask, allowing the contents of the upper layers in the clipping group to appear only where they are directly above the contents of the base layer.

Question 30

The only correct answer is a. You convert a selection border to a path that is precisely the same as the selection border by clicking the Make Work Path button in the Paths palette. You can also convert a selection border to a path that approximates the original selection border by pressing Option/Alt as you click the Make Work Path button and then entering a Tolerance value that determines how closely the path will resemble the original selection border.

Question 31

The correct answer is d. The Multiply Blending mode darkens colors by multiplying the base color by the blend color, but the Screen Blending mode lightens colors by multiplying the *inverse* of the blend color and the base color. And, although the Soft Light Blending mode does use a 50-percent gray threshold in determining its effects, it darkens or lightens base colors depending on the lightness or darkness of the blend colors. The Hard Light Blending mode uses the 50-percent gray threshold, and if the blend colors are lighter than 50-percent gray, it screens. If the blend colors are darker than 50-percent gray, it multiplies.

Question 32

The correct answer is b. Use Spot Color Channels to apply spot colors to specific areas of an image, and use Multichannel mode to apply a duotone-type tint to a specific area of an image, but use Duotone mode to apply a spot color as a tint to an entire image.

Question 33

The correct answer is b. Out-of-gamut colors are those colors that can't be reproduced in the CMYK printing process. Out-of-gamut colors are indicated in the Info palette by an exclamation point next to their values, in the Color Picker by an alert triangle, and in the image when you choose View|Gamut Warning.

Question 34

The correct answer is b. The Select|Similar command adds to the selection colors that are within the tolerance range specified in the Magic Wand's Options palette, from anywhere in the image.

Question 35

The correct answer is c. The Paint Bucket tool applies color to adjacent areas of similar color. The Replace Color command (Image|Adjust|Replace Color) applies color to areas of similar color throughout the image. The Color Range command (Select|Color Range) selects areas of similar color throughout the image. The Gradient tool applies a gradual blend from one color to another, according to specifications you provide.

Question 36

The correct answers are a, b, and d. With the Border command, you can specify a pixel-width for a border—or frame—around an existing selection. You can make a selection and then press Shift to add another selection inside or outside the original selection. You can also use the Inverse command to create a border made up of the unselected areas from around an original selection to the edges of the image.

Question 37

The correct answers are a and b. Photoshop is an image-editing and painting program that you use to edit the pixel data of bitmap images.

Question 38

The correct answer is a. The Photoshop (PSD) file format is the only file format in which you can save layers you have created in Photoshop.

Question 39

The correct answer is a. The Bitmap color mode is the only mode in Photoshop that does not support channels.

Question 40

The correct answer is c. You can apply transformations to a linked layer, and the transformations apply to all the layers in that linked group. You can apply transformations only to selections on the background layer. You can apply transformations to layer masks. The 3D Transform command is a filter and is located in the Filter|Render submenu.

Question 41

The correct answer is b. Use the Color Range tool to select areas of similar color throughout the image. In the Color Range dialog box, the Fuzziness option specifies a tolerance range for selecting similar colors. Selection is a display option, along with Image. You use the eyedropper in the preview window or the image window to select colors. The Invert option changes the selection to the unselected colors.

Question 42

The correct answers are a and b. You use both the Curves and Levels commands to adjust the brightness values of individual pixel brightness levels. The Curves command allows you to specify output brightness levels for up to 13 points on the brightness curve of an image. The Brightness & Contrast command adjusts brightness and contrast across the entire image, without allowing you to adjust individual pixels. Desaturate removes the color saturation from an image.

Question 43

The correct answer is b. Photoshop supports up to 24 channels per image—including all color channels, alpha channels, and spot color channels. By default, RGB and CMYK images have 3 and 4 color channels, so you can add up to 21 additional alpha channels and/or spot color channels to an RGB image and 20 additional alpha channels and/or spot color channels to a CMYK image.

Question 44

The correct answer is c. In general, lighter inks spread under darker inks. So, cyan, magenta, and yellow spread under black—the darkest ink—and yellow—the lightest ink—spreads under cyan, magenta, and black.

Question 45

The only correct answer is a. Only the Photoshop (PSD) file format saves layers of any kind.

Question 46

The correct answer is b. Pressing Q toggles between the Standard mode and the Quick Mask mode, and pressing S toggles between the Standard screen mode, the Full screen mode with menu bar, and the Full screen mode.

Question 47

The correct answer is d. The rendering intent options available in the CMYK Setup dialog box (File|Color Settings|CMYK Setup) are Perceptual (Images), Saturation, Relative Colorimetric, and Absolute Colorimetric. Gray Component Replacement (GCR) is one of the separation options also available in the CMYK Setup dialog box.

Question 48

The correct answer is c. Photoshop's scratch disks feature is a virtual memory feature that uses disk storage space—not RAM—as temporary memory for processing Photoshop operations. As long as you have enough disk storage space, you can specify up to four individual storage devices to use for scratch disks.

Question 49

The correct answer is c. The History Paintbrush icon in the History Palette indicates the state with which you will paint when using the History Paintbrush and the Erase To History option of the Eraser tool.

Question 50

The correct answer is c. When Video LUT Animation is selected in File|Preferences|Display & Cursors and the Preview option is selected in a color or tonal adjustment dialog box, the Color Table Animation or Video Table Lookup feature bypasses the computer's video card when displaying the preview. This preview is a faster but not completely accurate rendering of the image. Deselecting Video LUT Animation causes previews to be displayed only in the Photoshop image window, to an entire image, or to any selected area.

Question 51

The correct answer is d. JPEG is the only lossy compression method listed among these answers.

Question 52

The correct answer is b. This question highlights the important distinctions between "regular" GIF files (those saved in the CompuServe GIF file format) and those exported as GIF89a files. Only the GIF89a files support background transparency. You choose File|Save As or File|Save A Copy to save files from the Bitmap, Grayscale, and Indexed Color modes as GIF files, but you choose File|Export|GIF89a Export to export GIF89a files and define a color to be used for background transparency.

Question 53

The correct answer is c. A histogram is a bar chart that shows the distribution of the brightness levels of the pixels in an image. The brightness values are spread across the histogram, from 0 at the left to 255 at the right. The height of the bars indicates how many pixels in an image have brightness values in the range where the bar is located. Histograms are displayed in the Histogram, Levels, and Threshold dialog boxes.

Question 54

The correct answer is d. You can access the Direct Selection tool from the hidden tools menu of the Pen tool in the Toolbox or by pressing A.

Question 55

The correct answer is d. When printing an image with a clipping path on a non-PostScript printer, you must save the image as a TIFF file and print it from Adobe PageMaker 5 or higher. When printing an image with a clipping path on a PostScript printer, however, you must save the file in either the Photoshop EPS or DCS file formats.

Question 56

The correct answer is d. Using the Blend If sliders in the Layer Options dialog box, you can specify how pixels with particular brightness levels will be combined with the visible underlying layers.

Question 57

The correct answer is c. Even though all masks are 8-bit (256-level) grayscale images, and even though you can permanently save a layer mask, alpha channels are the only mask types here that are saved in the Channels palette. (Photoshop does not contain a type called a Permanent mask.)

Question 58

The correct answer is d. Whereas you can convert an RGB image to grayscale by using the Image|Mode|Grayscale command or the Image|Adjust| Desaturate command, neither of them allows you to determine how the individual color channels will be combined to produce the grayscale image. However, the Channel Mixer does allow you to adjust the mix of the color channels that produce a higher-quality grayscale image.

Question 59

The correct answer is a. You can stop a command or action at any dialog box or modal tool by clicking on the box to the immediate left of the list of actions in the Actions palette. The Modal Control icon then appears, indicating that the action will stop at any dialog boxes or modal tools in that particular set, action, or command. Step By Step and Pause are playback speed options but do not allow you to enter new values. The Stop button stops the recording or playing of an action, but you have less control over when the action actually stops. You could set the playback to Step By Step or Pause and then stop the playback with the Stop button, but the question asks "with which *one*" you could stop at a dialog box.

Question 60

The correct answer is b. The batch processing assistant/wizard is under File|Automate|Batch.

Question 61

The correct answer is b. The common screen frequency for newspapers, according to Adobe, is 85 lpi. For low-quality jobs on porous paper, it is 65 lpi; 133 lpi, for four-color magazines; and 177 lpi, for high-quality print jobs, such as fine art publications, annual reports, and so on.

Question 62

The correct answer is c. This question highlights the important difference between bitmap images and the Bitmap mode. Remember that Photoshop is a bitmap-image editing program and that all images in Photoshop are bitmap images. Bitmap images are made up of a grid of colored pixels that contain varying amounts of color information that combine to create the bitmap image. The number of possible color values of a pixel depends on the image's bit depth—that is, how many bits of information each pixel contains. However, a bitmap image in Photoshop can have a bit depth of up to 16 bits in each channel. The pixels of images in the Bitmap color mode, however, are either black or white, which means they have a bit depth of one.

Question 63

The correct answer is c. Each of these operations is affected by the Preserve Transparency option, but you must remember that the Preserve Transparency option not only acts as a mask over any areas that are already transparent but also preserves the current state of transparency of a pixel. So, in the case of answer a, replacing a selection when Preserve Transparency is selected replaces the selection with the background color because the selection itself—and the areas it occupied—are opaque, and Preserve Transparency protects that state. Erasing with the Eraser tool while Preserve Transparency is selected preserves the transparency—or lack of transparency—of a layer, so you erase with the background color or with a previous state, but not with transparency. And, by selecting Preserve Transparency when using the Apply Image command, you apply the source image only to the opaque areas of the destination image because Photoshop protects those areas that are already transparent. That leaves answer c, which describes how Preserve Transparency works; you apply color to only the opaque areas of a layer.

Question 64

The correct answer is c. You can convert images to other color spaces when you print from Photoshop, but within limitations. The Space option in the Print dialog box is mode-specific and offers only the available conversions for an image in a particular mode. For example, Grayscale images can be converted only to another gamma setting, and Multichannel images can be separated or converted only to RGB.

Question 65

The correct answer is d. When you're using the Variations command to adjust images, selecting the Clipping option in the Variations dialog box produces a "neon" preview of those shadow and highlight areas of the image that will be converted either to full black or full white, which is called clipping.

Question 66

The correct answer is d. Despeckle is one of the Noise filters.

Question 67

The correct answers are b and d. By pressing Option/Alt and dragging, you create a copy that is placed where you release the mouse button. By pressing Option/Alt and an arrow key, you copy the selection and move it one pixel, and by pressing Shift+Option/Shift+Alt and an arrow key, you copy the selection and move it 10 pixels. When a tool other than the Move tool is selected, you can add the Cmd/Ctrl key to the previous shortcuts to select the Move tool and copy the selection as you move it.

Appendix

Photoshop 5's New Features

This appendix presents a summary of many of the important new features and changes included in Photoshop 5 that are discussed in more detail in earlier chapters. If you are familiar with Photoshop 4, you may find this appendix useful in catching up with Photoshop 5.

Brand-New Features, Options, Tools, And Commands

This section covers features new to Photoshop 5. If you are upgrading to Photoshop 5 from an earlier version, you will want to learn the ins and outs of these important new features.

History Palette

Essentially adding multiple undos, the powerful History palette allows you to save previous steps of your work on an image file, keeps a list of previous steps that you can skip to and from, and provides states in which you can use to paint or erase.

The History palette is discussed in Chapter 3.

Reselect Command

Reselect simply reselects the most recent unselected selection. (You could perform this action in the previous versions by using the Undo command, but only if you did so immediately, before you performed any other operation.)

The Reselect command is discussed in Chapters 3 and 7.

Layer Effects

Using Photoshop 5's new Layer Effects, you can apply visual effects to the contents of a layer, separately from the rest of the image. Now, you can more easily apply drop shadows, inner shadows, inner and outer glows, beveling, and embossing, which automatically change as layer contents are changed and can themselves be changed or edited. You can copy and paste effects from one layer to another, and you can convert individual effects to a layer.

Layer effects are discussed in Chapter 9.

Type Layer

If you have used Photoshop previously, you may have long hoped for the development of a feature such as the New Type Layer included with Photoshop 5. You can now edit type even after you save, close, and reopen an image file (as long as it's in Photoshop file format, of course). You can apply layer effects to the type, and the layer effects conform to any new type or edited type on that layer. Type layers appear in the Layers palette, and you manage them just as you would any other layer. When you are satisfied with the type layer or you want to export the image to another file format, you must *render* the type layer, converting it to a regular layer, after which you lose the editability of the type.

The type layer is discussed in Chapter 9.

Layer Alignment And Distribution

As you can align and distribute items in some page-layout programs, now you can align and distribute the content of linked layers, arranging it according to its position relative to a selection or to the content of the other layers in the linked group.

The processes of linking, aligning, and distributing layers are discussed in Chapter 9.

16-Bit Color Support

In version 5, Photoshop includes support for images with up to 16-bits-per-channel. These 16-bit-per-channel images contain much more pixel data, so their potential color reproduction is much higher than 8-bit-per-channel images. However, the downsides are that the 16-bit-per-channel file sizes are much larger, and Photoshop supports limited editing with 16-bit-per-channel images.

Image resolution and bit depth are discussed in Chapter 5.

Color Samplers

Photoshop's new Color Samplers provide a means of sampling the color of pixels in four areas of an image. These samplers don't print, but they are saved with the image. They can be moved and their sample area adjusted. The Color Samplers act like fixed Eyedropper tools: You place them where you want, and there they stay until you delete or move them.

Color Samplers are discussed in Chapter 4.

Channel Mixer

Photoshop's Channel Mixer allows you to combine the brightness values of two or more channels. You can use the Channel Mixer to convert color images to grayscale images with more control over the quality of the image, to correct or repair individual channels, and to create images that appear to be hand-tinted.

The Channel Mixer is discussed in Chapter 10.

Spot Color Channels

Photoshop 5 allows you to create and output spot color channels to add additional inks to specific areas of a four-color printed publication or to add individual inks to specific areas of any printed publication.

Spot color channels are discussed in Chapter 10.

Measure Tool

Photoshop finally provides a tool for measuring both distances and angles right in the image window: the Measure tool.

The Measure tool is discussed in Chapter 3.

Magnetic Lasso Tool

Creating selection borders around areas of high contrast is easier than ever with the new Magnetic Lasso tool, with which you draw selection borders that snap to similar colors. As you draw the selection border by dragging, the Magnetic Lasso tool periodically inserts fastening points and snaps to colors according to specifications you enter in its Options palette.

The Magnetic Lasso tool is discussed in Chapter 7.

Freeform Pen Tool

The Freeform Pen tool allows you to create a path much as you would create a selection with the Lasso tool, except that you are working from the Paths palette to create a path, which can remain open-ended.

The Freeform Pen tool is discussed in Chapter 7.

Magnetic Pen Tool

The Magnetic Pen tool draws paths much the same way that the Magnetic Lasso tool draws selections. Like the Magnetic Lasso, the Magnetic Pen tool snaps to edges defined by a level of contrast that you specify. Again, however, the main difference between the two tools is that you are creating paths rather than selection borders.

The Magnetic Pen tool is discussed in Chapter 7.

Automation

Photoshop 5 also includes several automation assistants (on the Mac) and automation wizards (in Windows) that perform a series of specific operations—from just one dialog box—to produce different results. You can access these assistants/wizards by choosing File|Automate.

The following are the automation assistants/wizards supplied with Photoshop:

- **Conditional Mode Change** Converts image files from one color mode to another based on their original color mode. This assistant/wizard is particularly useful when recorded in actions, where it can convert images on the fly.

- **Contact Sheet** Produces a page layout index of the images in a folder (which must all be closed).

- **Fit Image** Automatically resamples an image to fit within one or both of the parameters you enter in the Fit Image dialog box, without affecting the image's aspect ratio.

- **Multi-Page PDF To PSD** Automatically opens an individual Photoshop (PSD) file for each page of a PDF-format file with multiple pages, saving you the hassle of having to open each page separately by choosing File|Open. Photoshop opens a new file for each page of the document and names it according to the base name, adding a numerical suffix to that name for each page.

- **Export Transparent Image** Prepares and exports Photoshop image files as GIF or PNG files for use online or as an EPS file for use in page-layout applications, such as Adobe PageMaker, with transparency.

> **Resize Image** Depending on your specification of whether you intend to use the image in print or online, resizes the pixel dimensions to new dimensions you specify and/or changes the resolution of the image.

Photoshop also supports some additional external automation through AppleScript on the Mac and OLE Automation in Windows. These features are discussed on the Adobe Web site.

Automation is discussed in Chapter 11.

3D Transform Filter

The 3D Transform filter enables you to draw a primitive wire frame, apply a selection to it, and then manipulate that selection as if it were a 3D object. You can use cube, sphere, and cylinder wire frames.

The 3D Transform filter is discussed in Chapter 8.

Features, Options, Tools, Commands, And Palettes That Have Changed

This section covers features in Photoshop 5 that, although not new, have changed from previous versions. If you are just learning Photoshop 5 after using an earlier version, you will want to study the ins and outs of these revised features.

Changes To The Rubber Stamp Tool

In addition to sampled areas of an image and user-defined patterns, you can now stamp with previous states of an image. As always, the Rubber Stamp tool stamps with sampled areas of an image. However, patterns are now stamped with the new Pattern Stamp tool. The History Paintbrush has also been added to the Toolbox, allowing you to stamp with a previous state of the image.

Tool basics are discussed in Chapter 3. Painting and editing with the Rubber Stamp and Pattern Stamp tools and the History Paintbrush are discussed in Chapter 8.

Changes To The Curves Dialog Box

The Curves dialog box has been upgraded for more efficient color adjustment.

The Curves dialog box is discussed in Chapter 6.

Transformation Of Paths And Selections

Until Photoshop 5, you could apply the Transform command only to images. Now, you can apply transformations to paths and selection borders.

Transforming images, paths, and selections is discussed in Chapter 8.

Upgraded Color Management

Photoshop 5 now supports the use of ICC Profiles for controlling output quality. Adobe also has improved much of the color management interface, updating the color settings dialog boxes and providing an automation assistant/wizard for calibrating monitors.

Color management is discussed in Chapter 4.

Upgraded Hue/Saturation Command

Adobe has upgraded the Hue/Saturation dialog box, providing more control than ever over adjustments made with the Hue/Saturation command.

The Hue/Saturation command is discussed in Chapter 6.

Upgraded Action Palette

The Actions palette was upgraded and now is capable of recording almost everything you can do in Photoshop, except operations that require cursor movement, such as painting and drawing. You can insert stops for nonrecordable actions, and you can insert paths. Actions can now be grouped into sets that can be saved individually. Actions are now saved in a folder called Photoshop Settings in the application folder rather than in the system preferences folder. The Batch processing command has been moved to the File|Automate submenu.

The Actions palette is discussed in Chapter 11.

More Scratch Disks

You can now specify up to four scratch disks of up to 200GB.

Specifying scratch disks is discussed in Chapter 2.

More Previews In Dialog Boxes

Photoshop 5 includes preview options in the Color Settings, Duotone, and Indexed Color dialog boxes for live preview.

Color adjustments are discussed in Chapter 6, creating and editing duotone images are discussed in Chapter 12, and converting images to Indexed Color mode is discussed in Chapter 4.

Importing PDF Files

Photoshop 5 can open all PDF files, but you must specify an individual page to open or use the Multi-Page PDF To PSD automation assistant/wizard to open all the pages of a multiple-page PDF file to individual PSD files.

The processes of opening and placing PDF files are discussed in Chapter 5.

File-Size Reducing Options In The Save As Dialog Box

You can minimize file sizes from the Save As dialog box by using the Flatten Image, Exclude Alpha Channels, and Exclude Non-Image Data options.

The Save As dialog box is discussed in Chapter 5.

DCS 2.0 Support

Photoshop 5 supports the export of DCS 2.0 files, which allows you to output more than four-color separations (which enables you to produce spot color plates) for individual image files.

File formats are discussed in Chapter 5, and creating color separations is discussed in Chapters 4 and 12.

PostScript Level 3 Support

You can now print from Photoshop to PostScript Level 3 printers.

PostScript Level 3 is included in the discussion of color management in Chapter 4, and printing from Photoshop is discussed in Chapter 12.

Glossary

3D Transform—The Photoshop 5 filter that enables you to transform images in ways that make them appear three-dimensional. Accessed by choosing Filter|Render.

Actions—Scripts that play back a series of commands, enabling you to apply the same series of commands to a file without having to painstakingly apply each command individually.

Additive Colors—The colors that, when added together as colored light, create white. The additive colors are red, green, and blue.

Adjustment Layer—A layer, defined by the name of a color or tonal adjustment, that allows you to preview color or tonal adjustments to an image without actually applying the adjustment to the image until you are satisfied.

Alpha Channels—Any channels other than the basic color component channels or spot color channels that are added to an image; they are basically warehouses of images that can be used repeatedly to mask areas of an image or select areas of an image.

Anchor Point—The point that indicates one end of a line in a path or subpath. Path and subpath lines have an endpoint at each end. The direction lines and direction points of curved lines project from these anchor points.

Anti-Alias—To smooth jagged edges of graphics by introducing pixels of varying grayscale levels, which can also cause the graphics to become fuzzier.

Assistant—An automation tool that performs a series of specific operations—from just one dialog box—to produce different results.

Auto Levels—Feature that automatically maps the lightest pixels in an image as white and the darkest pixels as black and then spreads out the midtones between them.

Base Color—The color of the pixels that will be affected by a Blending mode.

Base Layer—The bottom layer of a clipping group.

Batch Processing—Applying a set of actions, an action, or a command to a group of files in a particular folder.

Bevel—An effect that can be applied automatically to a layer with Layer Effects. Outer beveling makes a shape appear to rise from the surface of an underlying layer, as if that underlying layer had been carved away around the beveled shape, whereas inner beveling produces an effect that makes the shape appear to have been carved from the underlying layer.

Bit—The individual digit of binary code, either a zero or a one.

Bit Depth (or Color Depth)—The number of bits of color information stored for a particular image.

Bitmap Images—Also known as *raster images,* they are made up of a grid of small squares called *pixels*. Pixels shine or project or illuminate (however you want to think of them) in various color values or shades—such as a light green, dark blue, or dark red—the variety of which depends on how many bits of information your file provides for each pixel. Adobe Photoshop is a bitmap-image editing program.

Bitmap Mode—Color mode in which images are made up of only two colors: black and white. Bitmap is best used for high-contrast images or line art.

Blend Color—The color that will be applied to base color pixels by a blending mode.

Blend If—The feature through which you define how two layers will be blended, according to their individual color and brightness characteristics.

Blending Mode—Mode that affects how colors are "mixed" when painting. The visual effects of Blending modes are determined by the mathematical calculations of the different color values performed for a specific Blending mode.

BMP—The default format for image files used by many Microsoft/Windows applications. Photoshop supports BMP files up to 24-bit depth; 4- and 8-bit BMP files can use RLE compression.

Bounding Border—A control box that appears around a selection or layer when it is being transformed.

Calibration—The process of "aligning" or "synchronizing" different color reproduction devices, such as monitors and printers, so that they reproduce colors that appear to the eye as consistently as possible.

Calibration Bars—The printer's aids that print along the edges of a page, showing color and grayscale information.

Canvas—The total work area in a Photoshop image.

Channel—Generic term for the various 8-bit grayscale images that define the separate color information for an image and those as which you store the masks you have defined.

Channel Mixer—Photoshop's tool for combining the brightness values of two or more channels.

Clipping Group—A group of layers, wherein the base layer acts as a mask for the overlying layers in the group, allowing the overlying layers to appear only where they overlap the contents of the base layer.

Clipping Path—A feature that allows you to mask areas of an image to create background transparency when printing an image from another application. Created and edited from the Paths palette.

CLUT (Color Lookup Table)—Index of colors generated to define the colors of an Indexed Color mode image.

CMYK—Color model based on the three subtractive primary colors (cyan, magenta, and yellow), used by commercial printers to create colors with ink on paper.

Color Channel—An 8-bit grayscale image that contains the pixel brightness information or the ink intensity information for a particular color, depending, for example, on whether the image is RGB or CMYK.

Color Mode—A numeric system used by Photoshop for reproducing a specific color model. Includes RGB, CMYK, Lab, Bitmap, Grayscale, Duotone, Indexed Color, and Multichannel. You don't have to use the color model with the same name as the color mode you are using (in fact, no HSB mode even exists). For example, when you open an image in RGB mode, you can still use the CMYK model to define colors.

Color Model—A method of describing color objectively so that it can be generally reproduced on a monitor or on paper. Color models include HSB, RGB, CMYK, and L*a*b.

Color Picker—Photoshop's tool for specifying foreground and background colors for editing.

Color Sampler—A tool used to measure the color values of a defined area in an image and display that information in the Info palette.

Color Separation—The output of a color image as its separate color components, usually used for printing four-color publications by the CMYK four-color printing process.

Color Space—The range of color reproducable by a particular device, such as a monitor or printer.

Color Table Animation (VLUT or Video Lookup Table)—The feature that displays throughout the entire computer monitor screen any color or tonal adjustments made to an image, rather than just in the image window. Can result in a less-than-accurate preview and can be turned off by choosing File|Preferences| Display & Cursors and then deselecting Video LUT Animation.

Command—An operation that is accessed through menus, palettes, or keyboard shortcuts.

Compression—The process of reducing a file's size by discarding some digital information. Some methods of compression, such as LZW and RLE, don't affect the quality of an image and are referred to as *lossless*, whereas other methods of compression, such as JPEG, that do negatively affect image quality are referred to as *lossy*.

Contextual Menu—A shortcut of sorts to the options and commands for a specific tool or operation, accessed on the Mac by pressing Ctrl and holding down the mouse button, or in Windows by clicking the right mouse button.

Crop—To cut away unwanted areas of an image.

Crop Marks—The marks that show where a page should be cut to size.

Curves—Color and tone adjustment option that allows you to adjust specific pixel levels at up to 16 points.

Digimarc—Proprietary plug-in that inserts and scans for image copyright information.

Direction Lines—The lines that project from the anchor point of a curved path line, indicating the amount of curve and the direction of the curve of the line.

Direction Points—The points at the ends of direction lines that you drag to alter the shape and curve characteristics of a curved path line.

Direct-Selection Tool—The tool that you use to edit paths and subpaths.

Distort—The Transform command that allows you to distort the appearance of a layer or selection by changing the angle and length of any or all of the edges of the layer or selection.

Dither—To apply an approximate gradation from one color to another when a file contains more bits per pixel than a monitor can display

Dot Gain—An effect that occurs when the printed dots of a halftone image spread out when printed on paper.

dpi (dots per inch)—The number of dots contained in each linear inch of a graphic file, computer display, or printed by a printer. (See also *Resolution*.)

Drop Shadow—A visual effect that simulates the three-dimensional appearance of a shadow cast by an object raised slightly above another surface. Can be applied automatically to a layer with Layer Effects.

Duotone—Generic name for a grayscale image that is tinted with one to four colors for special effect. A grayscale image printed with one color other than black is a *monotone*, whereas *duotones*, *tritones*, and *quadtones* are grayscale images printed with two, three, and four colors, respectively.

Duotone Mode—Color mode in which you can create special "colorized" images. You can create monotone, duotone, tritone, and quadtone images.

Emboss—A visual effect that makes a shape look like it has been stamped onto an underlying layer, much like the numbers on a plastic credit card. Pillow embossing looks like quilting. Can be applied automatically to a layer with Layer Effects or by choosing Filter|Stylize|Emboss.

EPS (Encapsulated PostScript)—File format, based on Adobe's PostScript printing language, most commonly used in vector-oriented drawing programs. They are used primarily for transferring graphics files to output devices and between applications. EPS files can contain (or encapsulate) either vector graphics or bitmap image data—or both. Photoshop rasterizes the vector graphic data when it opens the file.

Fade—The command, accessed under the Filter menu, that lessens the effects of a filter.

Feather—To soften a selection by creating a transitional edge that appears to "fade" or "blend."

File Format—The arrangement of digital information in a specific format, according to a particular encoding scheme. Image files must be saved in a selected file format, and formats affect what information is saved with the file and where and how the image can later be used.

Fill—To apply color to a shape.

Filters—Plug-ins that change the appearance of an image. Filters apply effects that simulate traditional art techniques, simulate lighting effects, blur pixels, sharpen pixels, distort, and so on.

Flatten—To blend all layers in an image into one single layer.

Gamma—The midtone of an image. Adobe Gamma is a utility for calibrating the midpoint between white and black on color monitors.

Gamut—The total range of colors available in or on any color reproduction system.

GCR (Gray Component Replacement)—Separation option that replaces the subtractive primaries with black in areas where the three are to be applied in equal amounts, regardless of the color of the image area, used to improve the printed reproduction of darker colors, and to help the press hold the gray values.

GIF (CompuServe GIF)—File format developed by Unisys specifically for image files prepared for display on the Web. The format uses LZW compression and limits files to 256 colors. (See also *GIF89a*.)

GIF89a—Type of GIF file that supports pixel transparency.

Gradient—A gradual blend of colors, available in Photoshop in five different topologies, or patterns.

Grayscale Mode—Color mode that uses only shades of black (gray) rather than colors. Grayscale mode images are 8-bit (256-color).

Grid—The fixed, underlying cross-hatching of positioning lines that is universal to all open images at one time in Photoshop. You can alter the grid preferences by choosing File|Preferences|Guides & Grid.

Guides—Positioning lines that you add to an image as needed. You can lock guides, move them around, or delete them, and they are specific to the image in which you create them.

Halftones—The continuous-tone images (photographs) for printing on paper, in which images are converted to grids of big and small dots. Areas with many small dots appear lighter; areas with many big dots appear darker. (See also *Screen* and *Screen Frequency*.)

Histogram—A bar chart that shows the distribution of the brightness levels of the pixels in an image. The brightness values are spread across the histogram, from 1 at the left to 255 at the right. The height of the bars indicates how many pixels in an image have brightness values in the range where the bar is located. Histograms appear in the Histogram, Levels, and Threshold dialog boxes.

HSB Model—The color model that is closest to the way humans see and describe colors, based on hue, saturation, and brightness.

ICC Profile—Data that describes the color space of a particular device, such as a monitor or output device.

Image Cache—The location where image previews are saved in memory to speed display. You can set the Cache Levels option by choosing File|Preferences|Image Cache (Mac) or File|Preferences|Memory & Image Cache (Windows) to save from one to eight previews, with four as a default.

Image Resolution—The number of pixels that are available to display the image at its intended size. This resolution, which is related to printer resolution, is usually described in pixels per inch (ppi).

Image Size—The command that changes the size and/or resolution of an image file.

Indexed Color Mode—A color mode effective for reducing file sizes, used primarily for multimedia and Web images. Photoshop allows you to set the bit depth from 3 bits per pixel to 8 bits per pixel for a maximum of 256 colors. A *color lookup table* (*CLUT*), which serves as the index of colors available to display the image, is generated.

Inner Glow—A visual effect that simulates a radiant light emanating from within an object. Can be applied automatically to a layer with Layer Effects.

Inner Shadow—A visual effect that simulates the three-dimensional appearance of a shadow cast by a cutout raised slightly above another surface. Can be applied automatically to a layer with Layer Effects.

Interpolation—The process of guessing, or approximating, that Photoshop does when adding pixels to an image.

Intersect—To create a selection or selection border based on the area or areas where two selections or selection borders overlap.

JPEG—A file format developed by the Joint Photographic Experts Group. Primarily used for preparing photo files for display over the Internet. JPEG compresses files as it saves them, allowing various levels of compression, from zero to 10. JPEG is a *lossy* method of compression.

Lab Mode—Color mode based on the L*a*b color model. Photoshop's internal color mode.

L*a*b Model—Color model that is an international standard for creating consistent color across all device platforms and that contains every color visible to the human eye. Defined by a luminance (L) value and two color values: *a*, which defines its green-to-red color component, and *b*, which is its blue-to-yellow color component.

Lasso—The tool that creates selections by drawing as if with a pen or pencil.

Layer Effects—A set of special effects, such as drop shadows and embossing effects, that you can apply automatically to a particular layer. These effects can be edited and adjusted even after you apply them.

Layer Mask—A grayscale mask for an individual layer.

Layers—The Photoshop feature that simulates individual overlays of image elements.

Levels—An adjustment option that allows you to view a histogram of an image's colors and make adjustments to the image's highlights, midtones, and/or shadows.

Linked Layers—Layers that have been associated for purposes of editing, indicated by a chain link icon that appears in the Layers palette for the layers that are linked to a selected layer.

lpi (lines per inch)—The measurement unit of a halftone screen. (See also *Halftone*, *Screen*, and *Screen Frequency*.)

LZW (Lempel-Ziv-Welch)—Lossless method of compression supported by the TIFF file format.

Marquee (Selection Border)—The shape, indicated by a dotted, blinking line referred to as "marching ants," that defines a rectangular or elliptical *selection*.

Mask—An area of an image that you want to protect from an editing operation, a color adjustment, an ink overlay, and so on.

Menu—The list of commands you pull down from the top of the computer screen.

Merge—To blend two or more layers into one layer.

Modal Control—The option in the Actions palette for stopping the playback of an action at the dialog box of a modal tool so that you can enter different options, text, and so on.

Modal Tool—Any tool or command that requires you to respond to a dialog box or that requires you to press Enter or Return to apply the effects of that tool or command, such as the Feather command or the Fill commands.

Monitor Resolution—The number of pixels (or dots) per inch that are displayed on a computer monitor. The most common resolutions of monitors are 96 dpi for many PC monitors and 72 for Mac monitors.

Multichannel Mode—Color mode in which the color channels contain independent color information. These channels are essentially spot color channels, made up of grayscale channels of 256 colors. Unlike the colors in RGB or CMYK channels, the colors in these channels can be edited without affecting the other channels. As a result, Multichannel mode is excellent for creating duotones and duotone effects.

Multiply—To darken colors by multiplying the base color by the blend color.

Opacity—The degree of apparent transparency or lack of transparency of a specific color, layer, or selection.

Options—The various settings for tools, commands, and so on.

Outer Glow—A visual effect that simulates a radiant light emanating from an object. Can be applied automatically to a layer with Layer Effects.

Out-of-Gamut Colors—Colors that cannot be reproduced within a particular color gamut.

Page Setup—The dialog box, accessed from the File menu, in which you specify printing options, such as paper size, printing size, the halftone screen frequency, and so on.

Palette—A window of lists, options, and thumbnails through which you control the behavior of tools, layers, channels, history states, paths, and so on.

Palette Menu—A list of commands and options that you access by clicking and holding on the triangle at the upper right of a palette or by accessing a contextual menu.

Path—A line drawn with the Pen tools that can be used to create precise selection borders or to create open lines to which color can be applied.

Path Segment—An individual line or a group of connected lines in a path.

Pattern—A portion of an image that has been defined as a brush with which to paint or as a pattern to be applied with the Pattern Stamp tool.

Pattern Stamp—The tool that "stamps," or applies, a defined pattern to an image.

PDF (Portable Document Format)—The file format used by Adobe Acrobat and other applications that create this type of cross-platform document file. Usually, the appropriate "reader" application (Acrobat Reader) is necessary to view these files, but Photoshop can now import them as image files.

Perspective—The Transform command that allows you to distort the appearance of a layer or selection by shortening or lengthening one side of the layer or selection in respect to the opposite, parallel side of the layer or selection.

Photoshop (PSD)—The proprietary Photoshop file format. Photoshop (PSD) is the only file format that supports the saving of all nonimage information such as layers, channels, and effects that you can accumulate while editing in Photoshop.

Photoshop DCS 1.0/2.0—DCS, which is a type of EPS (Encapsulated PostScript) format, stands for desktop color separations. CMYK files saved in these formats automatically separate an appropriate number of color plates. DCS 1.0 saves CMYK files with only four channels, but 2.0 saves multichannel files, CMYK files with spot channels, and one alpha channel. Photoshop clipping paths are compatible with both 1.0 and 2.0.

PICT—A file format developed by Apple for use with the Macintosh operating system. Although this format is widely used on the Mac, you might have trouble using PICT files in Windows applications if the files have been compressed with the QuickTime JPEG compression supported by the PICT format.

Pixel—The small squares of color information that make up a bitmap image.

Pixel Dimensions—The number of pixels that an image has along its two dimensions.

Place Command—The command that allows you to import a vector-based graphic and position it within an open Photoshop image file. Supports Adobe Illustrator, PDF, and EPS files.

PNG (Portable Network Graphics)—A file format developed for Web images as a 24-bit and 48-bit freeware alternative to the patented 8-bit GIF format. PNG is not yet widely used and might not be compatible with some Web browser applications.

Polygon—For Photoshop's purposes, a closed selection or shape made up of three or more lines of any length or angle, created with the Polygon Lasso tool.

ppi (pixels per inch)—The number of pixels contained in each linear inch of a graphic file, computer display, or printed by a printer. (See also *Resolution*.)

Preserve Transparency—An option that acts as a mask over any areas that are already transparent and also preserves the current state of transparency of a pixel.

Printer Resolution—The number of dots per inch an imagesetter or printer can produce.

Profile To Profile—The command, accessed under Image|Mode, used to convert an open image to another color space.

PSD—See *Photoshop (PSD)*.

Quick Mask Mode—A display mode that allows you to create and edit masks without accessing the Channels palette. Accessed from the Toolbox or by pressing Q.

Raster—A grid of pixels that make up a bitmap image.

Rasterize—To convert vector-based graphic data to the raster-based data necessary for a bitmap image.

Registration Marks—"Targets," or marks, from each color plate that overprint each other, showing printing press operators whether the plates are properly registered, or aligned.

Resampling—The process of increasing or decreasing the number of pixels in an image that occurs when an image's pixel dimensions are altered, which can result in a uncorrectable loss of image quality when resampling up.

Resolution—The number of dots per inch (dpi) or sometimes pixels per inch (ppi) that determine how large or small an image can be displayed or printed while maintaining image quality.

Result Color—The new color produced after the application of a blending mode.

RGB—Color model and color mode based on the three additive primary colors (red, green, and blue). The RGB color model is universal to color computer monitors and television screens.

Rubber Stamp—The tool that samples an area of an image and "stamps," or applies, that sample to another area of an image.

Rubylith—The cut pieces of colored acetate used to cover areas of a plate negative that were to be protected from one or another ink (from an old printers' masking process). The pieces of colored acetate were actually two pieces of acetate, a clear layer and a translucent reddish layer referred to as *rubylith*. This translucent layer was opaque to the photographic process that was used, but allowed you to see what was covered. You cut away the rubylith from areas that you wanted to expose and left the rubylith over the areas that were to be masked. Photoshop's translucent red mask overlays are based on this process.

Scale—The Transform command that allows you to alter the size of a layer or selection.

Scanning Resolution—The number of pixels that are captured and stored by a particular scanning device.

Scratch Disk—Virtual memory on your hard disk being used by Photoshop for image processing. You can specify up to four volumes for use as scratch disks.

Screen—Short for *halftone screen*, which refers to the screen, or grid, that is made up of dots of various sizes; this screen is used to print photos on paper. (See also *Halftone*, *lpi*, and *Screen Frequency*.)

Screen—To lighten colors by multiplying the inverse of the blend color and the base color.

Screen Frequency—The density of a *halftone screen*, measured by the number of rows and columns of halftone dots per inch on a specific halftone screen, measured as lines per inch (lpi).

Selection—The area, defined by a selection border or marquee, to which Photoshop editing, painting, and other operations will be confined.

Selection Border (Marquee)—The shape, indicated by a dotted, blinking line referred to as "marching ants," that defines a selection of any shape.

Sets—Groups of actions.

Sharpening—Producing enhanced sharpness in an image by comparing pixels and increasing contrast between pixels with color differences over a particular range. The Sharpen filters include Sharpen, Sharpen Edges, Sharpen More, and Unsharp Mask.

Skew—The Transform command that allows you to distort the appearance of a layer or selection by sliding one side of the layer or selection parallel to the opposite side.

Spot Color Channel—A channel that is used to apply one specific color of ink to a printed image.

State—The appearance of an image file at a point during editing, used by the History palette.

Stroke—To apply color to a line.

Subpath—Any group of connected line segments that can be open, can stand alone, or can be connected to another path.

Subtractive Colors—The colors that, when mixed together as colored pigments, create black (theoretically). The subtractive colors are cyan, magenta, and yellow.

Threshold—The command that converts all the pixels above a specific brightness level (a threshold) to white and below that level to black, converting color and grayscale images to bitmap-type, high-contrast black-and-white images.

TIFF (Tag Image File Format)—One of the most popular and widely compatible file formats. TIFF images can be used on nearly all graphics programs.

Toolbox—The palette of Photoshop tools, located by default along the left side of the screen.

Transfer Functions—Last-resort options for dot gain problems, such as those produced by a miscalibrated imagesetter, that have no other apparent solution. Transfer Functions are a set of instructions to the miscalibrated output device to alter the input values of a file in order to produce a more accurate output.

Transform—To alter the geometry of a selection or layer through the Transform commands or the 3D Transform filter.

Transparency Mask—An opaque area of a layer, loaded as a selection.

Trapping—Slightly overlapping printed colors to prevent any white paper from showing through if the respective plates are misaligned.

Type Layer—Photoshop's powerful new feature that allows you to create a layer of type that can be edited and to which you can apply special effects that can be edited and that update when the type itself is edited.

Type Mask—A selection border created in the shape of entered text.

UCA (Undercolor Addition) Amount—A separation option, available only in GCR separations, that adds some of the three subtractive primary colored inks to the black ink in areas of neutral color to enhance the shadow areas and to prevent posterization in these areas.

UCR (Undercolor Removal)—A separation option that replaces the subtractive primaries with black only in neutral-colored areas where the three are to be applied in equal amounts to produce better blacks and grays and better definition in shadow areas and to produce less ink coverage. Use of this option is recommended for more porous paper stocks, such as newsprint and uncoated papers.

Unsharp Mask—The only sharpening option that allows you to specify the sharpening options of Amount, Radius, and Threshold.

Vector Graphics—Images defined by assigning numbers—or vectors—to the various elements that make up a vector image. Created by applications such as Adobe Illustrator. You can import vector graphics from other applications by dragging and dropping and by opening a vector graphic file. Photoshop's paths are vector graphics and can be exported to vector-based applications.

Virtual Memory—Hard disk space being used by a computer as simulated RAM. Photoshop uses a virtual memory scheme for its scratch disks.

Wizard—An automation tool that performs a series of specific operations—from just one dialog box—to produce different results.

Work Path—A temporary path created in the Paths palette as you begin to draw with a Pen tool or when you convert a selection border to a path. The work path must be saved, or it will be discarded when the file is closed.

Index

A

ACE home page, 8-9
Actions
    Actions palette, 328-330
    batch processing, 338-339
    button mode, 331
    capabilities/limitations, 328
    creating new, 333-334
    defined, 328
    deleting, 333
    duplicating, 332-333
    editing, 335-336
    loading, 332
    modal control, 330
    moving, 332
    nonrecordable commands, 335
    options, 331
    paths, 334
    pauses, 335
    playback speed, 337
    playing, 336-337
    recording, 333-334
    replacing, 332
    rerecording, 336
    resetting, 332
    sets, 329, 331-332
    skipping/excluding commands, 337
    stopping, 330
Actions palette, 44-45, 328-330
Add-Anchor-Point tool, 205, 210
Additive colors, 81-82
Adjusting colors/tones
    Auto Levels command, 166
    Color Balance command, 170
    color table animation, 161
    Curves dialog box, 166-170
    Desaturate command, 176
    Equalize command, 176
    histograms, 161-163
    Hue/Saturation command, 170-172
    image cache, 163
    Invert command, 175-176
    Levels dialog box, 164-166
    Posterize command, 176
    preview, 160-161
    Replace Color command, 172-173
    Selective Color command, 173
    Threshold command, 176
    Variations command, 173-175
Adjusting images, 159-189
    canvas size, 53-56
    color casts, 177
    colors/tones, 160-176
    image size/resolution, 178-181
    optimizing color/tone of scans, 181-182
    sharpness, 177-178
Adjustment layers, 275-277
Adobe, 12
Adobe Certified Expert Program site, 8-9
Adobe Gamma utility, 105-108
Adobe Illustrator
    exporting paths, 149
    pasting artwork, 141-142
    place command, 141
Adobe Online, 69, 71-72
Airbrush tool, 222-223
Alignment, 269-270, 291
Alpha channels, 308
Amiga IFF, 127
Anchor points, 202-203, 210
Angular gradient, 232
ANPA-COLOR, 99
ANPA file information, 142
Anti-aliasing, 139
Apple RGB, 108
Apply Image command, 277-279
Artistic filters, 246

A

Assistants/wizards, 339-341
Auto Levels command, 166
Automation assistants, 339-341

B

Background colors, 50-51, 95-97
Background layer, 264
Base color, 226
Base layer, 282
Baseline, 291
Batch dialog box, 338
Batch processing, 338-339
Behind Blending mode, 228
Bevel, 286
Bit depth, 16-18
Bitmap images, 14-15
Bitmap mode, 15, 84-85
Black, 81
Black Generation, 111
Black Ink Limit/Total Ink Limit, 111
Bleed, 352
Blend color, 226
Blend If, 274
Blending modes, 226-229, 274
Blur filters, 246-247
Blur tool, 225-226
BMP, 127
Border command, 199
Bounding border, 240
Brightness, 81
Brush Strokes filters, 247
Brushes, 236
Brushes palette, 40-41
Built-in color space, 109
Burn tool, 225-226
Button mode, 331

C

Calculations command, 277-279
Calibration, 104-105, 112
Calibration bars, 352
Canvas Size command, 53-56
Canvas Size dialog box, 54
CCITT, 143
Certification exam. *See* Test environment/tips.
Channel Mixer, 314-315
Channel Mixer dialog box, 314
Channels, 17
  alpha, 308
  Channel Mixer, 314-315
  Channels palette, 309-310
  color, 307-308
  creating new, 310-311
  deleting, 314
  duplicating, 313-314
  editing, 313
  Merge Channel command, 315-316
  selections, and, 311-313
  Split Channel command, 315
  spot color. *See* Spot color channels.
  what are they, 306-307
Channels palette, 42-44, 309-310
CIE RGB, 108
Clear Blending mode, 228
Clipping groups, 149, 282-284
Clipping paths, 149, 212
CLUT, 86
CMM, 105
CMYK, converting files to, 348-349
CMYK mode, 83-84
CMYK model, 81-82
CMYK Setup, 109-110
Color Balance command, 170
Color Blending mode, 229
Color Burn Blending mode, 228
Color casts, 177
Color channels, 88, 307-308
Color depth, 16
Color Dodge Blending mode, 228
Color gamuts, 87-88
Color lookup table (CLUT), 86
Color management module (CMM), 105
Color models, 80-82
Color modes, 82-87
  Bitmap, 84-85
  CMYK, 83-84
  duotone, 86
  grayscale, 85
  indexed color, 86
  Lab, 84
  multichannel, 87
  RGB, 83
Color palette, 39, 88, 99-100
Color Picker, 88, 97-99

Delete 427

Color proof, 111-112
Color Range command, 196-198
Color Range dialog box, 197
Color Samplers, 102-104
Color selection area (toolbox), 96
Color separation, 110-111
Color separations, 348, 353-354
Color space, 88
Color system, 79-123
    Adobe Gamma utility, 105-108
    calibration, 104-105, 112
    CMYK setup, 109-110
    color channels, 88
    color gamuts, 87-88
    color management module (CMM), 105
    color models, 80-82
    color modes, 82-87
    Color palette, 99-100
    Color Picker, 97-99
    color proofs, 111-112
    Color Samplers, 102-104
    converting images, 89-95
    converting open images to color space, 115
    custom ink colors, 114
    dithering, 89
    dot gain, 112-113
    Eyedropper tool, 101-102
    foreground/background colors, 95-97
    ICC profiles, 105, 114
    RGB setup, 108-109
    separation options, 110-111
    Swatches palette, 100-101
    transfer functions, 113
Color table animation, 161
Color trapping, 353
ColorMatch RGB, 108
Commands, 30-31
Compression, 143
CompuServe GIF (87a), 127, 147
Conditional Mode Change, 339-340
Conditional Mode Change dialog box, 340
Configuration, 19-21
Contact Sheet, 339-340
Contact Sheet dialog box, 340
Contextual menus, 53
Contract command, 200
Convert-Anchor-Point tool, 205, 210

Convert Multi-Page PDF to PSD dialog box, 141, 341
Converting files to CMYK, 348-349
Converting images, 89-95
    between bit depths, 90-91
    between modes, 91
    grayscale to bitmap, 91-92
    indexed color, 93-95
Converting open images to color space, 115
Copy
    image files, 60-61
    paths, 212
    selections, 63
Copyright and file information, 142-143
Corner point, 203
Correcting mistakes
    History palette, 66-68
    reverting, 69
    stopping an operation, 69
    undo/redo, 65-66
Create
    actions, 333-334
    alpha channels, 317-318
    channels, 310-311
    duotones, 355-357
    files, 59-60, 136-137
    Kodak Photo CD image file, 138
    layers, 266-269
    paths, 203
Crop command, 178
Crop marks, 352
Crop tool, 178-179
Curves dialog box, 166-170
Custom Colors dialog box, 98
Custom ink colors, 114
Cutting selections, 64
Cyan, 81

D

Darken Blending mode, 229
DCS 1.0/2.0, 127-128, 146
Defringe, 65
Delete
    actions, 333
    channels, 314
    layers, 269
    paths, 203
    selections, 65

Delete-Anchor-Point tool, 205, 210
Desaturate command, 176
Destination image, 278
Diamond gradient, 232
DIC Color Guide, 99
Difference Blending mode, 229
Diffusion dithering, 89, 93
Digimarc, 143
Digimarc filter, 251
Digital imaging basics
    bit depth, 16-18
    bitmap images vs. vector graphics, 14-16
    resolution, 18-19
Direct-Selection tool, 205, 210
Direction lines, 202
Direction points, 202
Dissolve Blending mode, 227
Distort, 241
Distort filters, 247-248
Dithering, 89
Dodge tool, 225-226
Dot gain, 112-113
Downsampling, 180
dpi (dots per inch), 18
Drop shadow, 285
Duotone Curve dialog box, 356
Duotone mode, 86
Duotone Options dialog box, 354
Duotone presets, 355
Duotones, 354-357
Duplicate
    actions, 332-333
    channels, 313-314
    image files, 61
    layers, 266-269

E

Edge thickness, 178
Edit graphic object (EGO), 150
Edit menu, 31
Effects dialog box, 284-285
EGO, 150
Ellipsis (...), 31
Elliptical marquee, 193
Emboss, 286
Emulsion down, 352
EPS files, 128, 140, 146

EPS Options dialog box, 146
EPS PICT Preview/EPS TIFF Preview, 128
Equalize command, 176
Eraser tool, 68, 222-225
Exclusion Blending mode, 229
Expand command, 200
Export, 147-150
Exporting paths, 212
Eyedropper tool, 101-102

F

Fade command, 244
Feather command, 200
File formats
    Amiga IFF, 127
    BMP, 127
    CompuServe GIF, 127
    DCS 1.0/2.0, 127-128
    EPS, 128
    EPS PICT Preview/EPS TIFF Preview, 128
    Filmstrip, 129
    FlashPix, 129
    JPEG, 129-130
    Kodak ICC Photo CD, 130
    PCX, 130
    PDF, 130
    Photoshop 2, 126
    PICT File, 130
    PICT Resource, 131
    PIXAR, 131
    PNG, 131
    PSD, 126
    Raw, 131
    Scitex CT, 131
    Targa, 131
    TIFF, 131
File Info dialog box, 142
File menu, 31
File sizes, 144
Files
    creating, 59-60
    opening, 60
Fill command, 235
Fill Path button, 210-211
Fill With Neutral Color, 274
Filmstrip, 129

Filter menu, 32-33
Filters, 243-251
    artistic, 246
    blur, 246-247
    brush strokes, 247
    digimarc, 251
    distort, 247-248
    efficient operation of, 245
    Fade command, 244
    noise, 248
    other, 251
    pixelate, 248
    preview, 244
    render, 249
    sharpen, 249
    sketch, 249-250
    special procedures, 245
    stylize, 250
    texture, 250-251
    video, 251
Fit Image, 340
Fit Image dialog box, 340
FlashPix, 129
Flatness, 149
Flattening a file, 273
FOCOLTONE, 99
Focus tools, 225-226
Foreground colors, 50-51, 95-97
Four-color process printing, 81
Free transform command, 239-240
Freeform Pen tool, 207
Full screen mode, 51
Full screen mode with menu bar, 51
Full-view image, 14
Function keys, 35

G

Gamma, 105-108
Gamut Warning, 87
Gamuts, 87-88
GCR (gray component replacement), 111
GIF 87a files, 127, 147
GIF 89a files, 127, 147-148
GIF89a dialog box, 148
Gradient editor dialog box, 233
Gradient tools, 231-235
Grayscale mode, 85

Grayscale to bitmap, 91-92
Grid, 58
Grow command, 200
Guessing, 6-7
Guides, 58-59

H

Halftone, 134, 348
Halftone screen frequencies, 135
Halftone screening, 14
Halftone Screens dialog box, 350-351
Hard Light Blending mode, 228
Help menu, 33
Help options, 69-71
Hide Color Samplers command, 38
Histogram dialog box, 162
Histograms, 161-163
History palette, 44
    create new file, 61
    Eraser tool, 68
    navigating, 66-67
    Paintbrush tool, 68
    using, 67-68
HSB model, 80-81
Hue, 80
Hue Blending mode, 229
Hue/Saturation command, 170-172
Hue/Saturation dialog box, 171

I

ICC color space, 110
ICC profiles, 105, 114
Illustrator. *See* Adobe Illustrator.
Image cache, 163
Image menu, 32
Image resolution, 133
Image size, 178-181
Image Size command, 53, 179-181
Image Size dialog box, 180-181
Images
    adjusting. *See* Adjusting images.
    import, 138-142
    save/export, 143-150
Import
    images, 138-142
    scans, 60
Indexed Color images, 93-95

Indexed Color mode, 86
Info palette, 36-37, 88
Inner beveling, 286
Inner glow, 286
Inner shadow, 285
Installation, 19-21
Internet search requests, 10
Interpolation, 179
Intersecting selections, 199
Inverse command, 32, 199
Invert command, 32, 175-176
Invert option, 32

J

JPEG, 129-130, 143

K

Kerning, 291
Keyboard operations
    convert path to selection border, 205
    editing type, 293
    Fill command, 236
    filters, 244
    loading selections, 313
    Magnetic Pen tool operations, 108
    moving selections, 63
    Pen tool shortcuts, 206
    shortcuts, 50
    viewing modes, 51
Kodak ICC Photo CD, 130

L

Lab mode, 84
L*a*b color model, 82
Lasso tools, 194-196
Layer Effects, 284-287
Layer mask, 279-281
Layer menu, 32
Layer Options dialog box, 275
Layers, 261-304
    adjustment, 275-277
    alignment, 269-270
    Apply Image command, 277-279
    background layer, 264

Blending modes, 274
Calculations command, 277-279
clipping groups, 282-284
creating, 266-269
deleting, 269
distributing contents of, 270-271
duplicating, 266-269
editing options, 273-275
effects, 284-287
Fill With Neutral Color, 274
flattening, 273
Layers palette, 262-265
linking, 265-266
masking, 279-281
merging, 272-273
moving contents of, 269
opacity, 274
Preserve Transparency, 273
rearranging, 265
thumbnail sizes, 265
transparency mask, 281
Type, 288-293
Use All Layers, 274
visible/invisible, 265
Layers palette, 41-42, 262-265
Levels dialog box, 164-166
Lighten Blending mode, 229
Line tool, 224
Linear gradient, 231
Linked layers, 265-266
Lossless compression, 143
Lossy compression, 143
lpi (lines per inch), 18
Luminosity Blending mode, 229
LZW, 143

M

Mac Open dialog box, 137-138
Mac Photoshop Info dialog box, 20
Mac work area, 30
Macworld Photoshop 5 Bible, 78
Magenta, 81
Magnetic Lasso tool, 195-196
Magnetic Pen tool, 207-208
Make Selection button, 204
Make Work Path button, 204

Marching ants, 192
Marquee, 192
Marquee tools, 192-194
Masks, 306
    alpha channels, 308
    layer, 279-281
    Quick, 320-321
    transparency, 281
Matting, 65
Measure tool, 56-58
Menus
    contextual, 53
    pull-down. *See* Pull-down menus.
Merge Channels command, 315-316
Merge Spot Channel, 319
Minimize/maximize button, 35
Mistakes. *See* Correcting mistakes.
Modal control, 330
Modal tool, 330
Monitor resolution, 133
Monotone, 354
Move
    actions, 332
    layers, contents of, 269
    paths, 211-212
    selections, 61-63
Move tool, 61-63
Moving the marquee, 199
Multi-Page PDF To PSD, 341
Multichannel mode, 87
Multiply Blending mode, 228

N

Navigator palette, 36-37
New Action dialog box, 334
New Channel dialog box, 311
New dialog box, 59, 136
New Path button, 203
New Spot Channel dialog box, 317
New View, 61
Noise filters, 248
Nonrecordable commands, 335
Normal Blending mode, 227
NTSC (1953), 108
Numeric Transform, 63
Numeric Transform dialog box options, 241

O

Object linking and embedding (OLE), 150
Online help, 69-71
Open
    Adobe Illustrator/PDF/EPS files,
        139-140
    existing images, 137-138
    files, 60
Optimizing color/tone of scans, 181-182
Options palette, 39
Orientation, 350
Other group of filters, 251
Out-of-gamut colors, 87-88
Outer beveling, 286
Outer glow, 286
Overlay Blending mode, 228
Overprint Colors dialog box, 357

P

Page Setup dialog box, 349-351
Paint Bucket Options palette, 38
Paint Bucket tool, 230-231
Paintbrush tool, 222-223
Painting tools, 222-225
PAL/SECAM, 108
Palettes, 33-45
    Actions, 44-45
    Brushes, 40-41
    Channels, 42-44
    Color, 39
    History. *See* History palette.
    Info, 37-38
    Layers, 41-42
    Navigator, 36-37
    Options, 39
    Paths, 44
    Placement, 36
    Swatches, 40
Pan Camera tool, 242-243
PANTONE CMYK, 98
Paste As Paths, 65
Paste As Pixels, 64
Paste Into, 64
Pasting Adobe Illustrator artwork, 141-142
Pasting selections, 64-65
Path segments, 209

Paths

Paths
- actions, and, 334
- anchor points, 202-203, 210
- color, and, 210-211
- converting selection borders to, 203-204
- converting, to selection borders, 204-205
- copying, 212
- creating, 203
- deleting, 203
- exporting, 212
- filling a path, 210-211
- hiding/showing, 201
- moving, 211-212
- naming/renaming, 201
- parts of a path, 209
- path segments, 209
- Paths palette, 200-201
- saving, 203
- selecting/deselecting, 201
- stroking a path, 211
- subpaths, 208
- transforming, 238-242
- what are they, 200, 202

Paths palette, 44, 200-201
Pattern dithering, 89, 92
Pattern Stamp tool, 236-238
Pauses, 335
PCX, 130
PDF files, 130, 140
Pen tools, 205-208
Pencil tool, 222-223
Perspective, 241
Photographer's Digital Studio, The, 27
Photoshop
- new features, 13
- what is it, 12-13

Photoshop (PSD), 126
Photoshop DCS 1.0/2.0, 127-128, 146
Photoshop 2, 126
Photoshop 4 WOW! Book, The, 27
Photoshop 5 for Macs for Dummies, 78
Photoshop 5 In Depth, 189
PICT File, 130
PICT Resource, 60, 131
PIXAR, 131
Pixel depth, 16

Pixel dimensions, 133
Pixelate filters, 248
Pixels, 14
Place command, 60, 141
Placement palette, 36
Playback speed, 337
Playing actions, 336-337
Plug-ins, 22-23
PNG, 131
Polygon Lasso tool, 195
Posterize command, 176
ppi (levels per inch), 18
Practice exam, 363-401. *See also* Test environment/tips.
Preferences, 21-23
Preferences dialog boxes, 23
Preferences for saving, 144-145
Preserve Transparency, 273
Preview
- colors, 160-161
- filters, 244
- Type tools, 290

Print dialog box, 352-353
Printer resolution, 134
Printing, 347-362
- color separations, 348, 353-354
- converting files to CMYK, 348-349
- duotones, 354-357
- options, 349-353
- spot color channels, 319-320
- trapping colors, 353

Profile To Profile command, 115
Profiles dialog box, 114
Protractor feature, 57-58
PSD, 126
Pull-down menus, 30-33
- Edit, 31
- File, 31
- Filter, 32-33
- Help, 33
- Image, 32
- Layer, 32
- Select, 32
- View, 33
- Window, 33

Purge command, 32

Q

Quadtones, 354
Quick Mask button, 51
Quick Mask mode, 320-321

R

Radial gradient, 231-232
Raster images, 14
Rasterize Generic EPS Format dialog box, 140
Rasterizing, 140
Raw, 131
Real World Scanning and Halftones, 157
Recording actions, 333-334
Rectangular marquee, 193
Redo, 66
Reflected gradient, 232
Registration marks, 352
Render filters, 249
Replace Color command, 172-173
Resampling, 179
Resampling up, 180
Resolution, 18-19
Result color, 226
Retouching tools, 222-226
Reverting, 69
RGB mode, 83
RGB model, 81
RGB Setup, 108-109
RLE, 143
Rotate, 241
Rotate Canvas dialog box, 242
Rubber Stamp tool, 236-237
Rubylith, 306
Rulers, 56

S

Sample exam, 363-401. *See also* Test environment/tips.
Saturation, 81
Saturation Blending mode, 229
Save A Copy, 61, 145
Save As, 60, 145
Save Selection dialog box, 311
Saving and exporting images
    compression, 143-144
    export, 147-150
    flattening layers, 144
    preferences for saving, 144-145
    reducing file sizes, 144
    save, 145
    save a copy, 145
    save as, 145
    saving files as EPS/DCS files, 146
Saving paths, 203
Scale, 240
Scanning resolution, 132-136
Scitex CT, 131
Scratch disk, 22
Screen, 350
Screen Blending mode, 228
Screen frequency, 134-135
Select menu, 32
Selection border, 192
Selection commands, 192
Selections
    adding new areas, 199
    channels, and, 311-313
    copying, 63
    cutting, 64
    deleting, 65
    hiding/showing, 198
    intersecting, 199
    matting, 65
    modifying, 199-200
    moving, 61-63
    moving the marquee, 199
    pasting, 64-65
    subtracting areas, 199
Selective Color command, 173
Separation Options, 110-111
Sets, 329, 331-332
Sharpen filters, 177, 249
Sharpen tool, 225-226
Sharpness, 177-178
Shortcuts. *See also* Keyboard operations.
    function keys, 35
    keyboard, 50-51
Similar command, 200
Single Column marquee, 193

Single Row marquee, 193
16-bit images, 17-18
Sketch filters, 249-250
Skew, 241
Smooth command, 199
Smooth point, 202
SMPTE-C, 108
SMPTE-240M, 108
Smudge tool, 225-226
Soft Light Blending mode, 228
Space, 353
Split Channels command, 315
Sponge tool, 225-226
Spot color channels
    converting alpha channels to, 318
    creating new, 317-318
    defined, 308
    editing, 318-319
    exporting, 319
    merging, 319
    options, 319
    printing, 319-320
    using, 316-317
sRGB, 108
Standard screen mode, 51
Status bar, 46-47
Stopping an operation, 69
Stroke command, 235-236
Stroke Path button, 211
Stylize filters, 250
Subpaths, 208
Subtractive colors, 82
Swatches palette, 40, 100-101

T

Tables color space, 110
Targa, 132
Test environment/tips, 1-10
    additional resources, 8-9
    budget your time, 7
    checkbox (marking questions), 5
    confusing questions, 364
    Cram Sheet, 2
    guessing, 6-7
    long list of commands, 364
    measuring progress, 5
    multiple answers, 364
    multiple-choice format, 3
    practice exam, 363-401
    question-bundling strategies, 7
    read exam completely, 5
    read questions carefully, 5, 365
    sample questions, 3-4
    words (*best, required, most appropriate*), 364
Texture filters, 250-251
3D Transform dialog box, 242
3D Transform filter, 242
Threshold command, 176
TIFF, 132
Tool pointers, 51-52
Toolbox
    changing tool pointers, 51-52
    foreground/background colors, 50-51
    keyboard shortcuts, 49-50
    tips, 48-49
    viewing modes, 51
TOYO Color Finder 1050, 99
Trackball tool, 242-243
Tracking, 291
Transfer functions, 113
Transform commands, 238-242
Transform Path command, 31
Transform Points command, 31
Transparency mask, 281
Trapping, 353
Tritones, 354
TRUMATCH CMYK, 99
Type layers, 288-293
Type Mask tool, 288-289
Type Tool dialog box, 289-290
Type tools, 288-289

U

UCA (undercolor addition amount), 111
UCR (undercolor removal), 111
Undo, 65
Unsharp Mask filter, 177-178

V

Variations command, 173-175
Variations dialog box, 174-175
Vector graphics, 15-16

Vector image, 15
Vertical Type Mask tool, 288-289
Vertical Type tool, 288-289
Video filters, 251
View menu, 33
Virtual memory, 21-22
Visual Quickstart Guide, Photoshop 5 for Windows and Macintosh, 304

W

Web-based search requests, 10
Wide-Gamut RGB, 108
Window menu, 33

Windows Memory & Image Cache Preferences dialog box, 21
Windows Open dialog box, 138
Windows work area, 31
Wizards, 339-341
Work path, 203

Y

Yellow, 81

Z

ZIP, 143

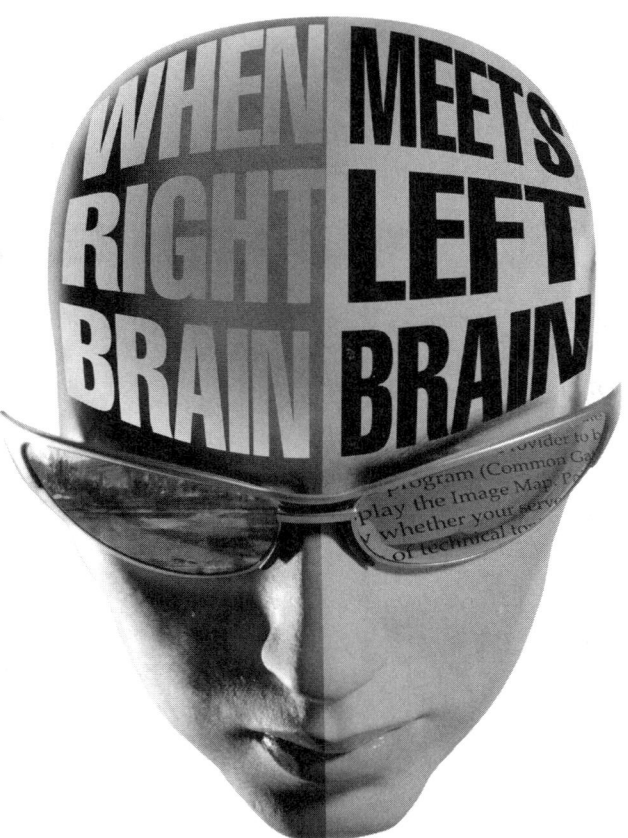

PHOTOSHOP 5 3D TEXTURES
ISBN: 1-57610-274-2 • Available Now
Price: $49.99 U.S. • $69.99 Canada

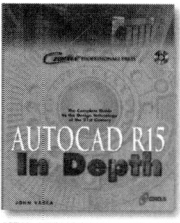

AUTOCAD R15 In Depth
ISBN: 1-57610-316-1 • Avail: Mar. '99
Price: $59.99 U.S. • $84.99 Canada

PHOTOSHOP 5 FILTERS
ISBN: 1-57610-300-5 • Avail: Nov. '98
Price: $49.99 U.S. • $69.99 Canada

PHOTOSHOP 5 In Depth
ISBN: 1-57610-293-9 • Available Now
Price: $59.99 U.S. • $84.99 Canada

LOOKING GOOD IN PRESENTATIONS THIRD EDITION
ISBN: 1-56604-854-0 • Avail: Dec. '98
Price: $29.99 U.S. • $41.99 Canada

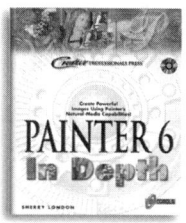

PAINTER 6 In Depth
ISBN: 1-57610-381-1 • Avail: Jan. '99
Price: $49.99 U.S. • $69.99 Canada

FLASH 3 f/x and design
ISBN: 1-57610-382-X • Avail: Jan. '99
Price: $49.99 U.S. • $69.99 Canada

CHARACTER ANIMATION In Depth
ISBN: 1-56604-771-4 • Available Now
Price: $59.99 U.S. • $84.99 Canada

CREATIVITY MEETS TECHNOLOGY!

What you see in your mind's eye, Creative Professionals Press books help you create. Let our books guide you to the cutting edge of today's graphics and tomorrow's unpredictable visual explorations.

Thorough, carefully structured direction along with real-world applications, interactive activities, extensive full-color illustrations, and hands-on projects take you to places you've only imagined. When right brain meets left brain, creativity meets technology. And when creativity meets technology, anything is possible.

CORIOLIS
Creative Professionals Press™

f/x and design Series • In Depth Series • Looking Good Series
800.410.0192 • **International Callers: 602.483.0192**
www.coriolis.com

CORIOLIS™

Prices and availability dates are subject to change.
©1998 The Coriolis Group, Inc. All rights reserved. BM1098

"Taking an exam without an Exam Cram book is worse than going to work without my trousers!"
— Christian, U.K.

ISBN: 1-57610-251-3
$29.99 U.S.
Available Now

ISBN: 1-57610-241-6
$59.99 U.S.
Available Now

"Thank you for writing and making available the valuable Exam Cram series of books. I not only passed the NT Server 4 in the Enterprise exam but also scored very high. I give credit to the very readable and understandable Exam Cram books."
—**Richard Peppel**

"I just wanted to thank you for writing the Exam Cram series of books. I have used them solely for studying for my tests (five in all.) I find that Exam Cram makes for a passing grade."
—**Jack R. Watson**

"The Exam Crams are by far the best studying companions! Since discovering your study guides, I have been able to cut my study time in half. Thank you!"
—**Michael Dominguez, MCSE**

Certification Insider™ Press

CORIOLIS

For more information:
Telephone: 800-410-0192 • Fax: 602-483-0193
International Callers: 602-483-0192 *(8:00 AM to 4:00 PM MST)*
In Canada: 800-268-2222

www.certificationinsider.com

Prices are subject to change without notice.
©1998 The Coriolis Group, Inc.
All rights reserved. BM9/98